The History of Black Studies

"Abdul Alkalimat is one of the most rigorous and committed Black radical thinkers of our time."

—Barbara Ransby, award-winning author of *Ella Baker and the Black Freedom Movement*

"Magisterial [...] The most comprehensive history of the field of Black Studies. This landmark book will become a standard in the history of our field."

—Professor Molefi Kete Asante, Department of Africology, Temple University

"Abdul Alkalimat, one of the pioneers of Black Studies, has done a great service by providing a powerful, expansive, and compelling history of the field."

—Keisha N. Blain, award-winning author and co-editor of the #1 *New York Times* Bestseller *Four Hundred Souls: A Community History of African America 1619–2019*

"This is Alkalimat's magnum opus [...] a focal point for scholarship on the history of Africana thought in the academy. It is required reading for Black Studies scholars and intellectual historians."

—Fabio Rojas, Virginia L. Roberts Professor of Sociology, Indiana University

"A visionary and a documentarian, Alkalimat has been a major figure in the Black Studies movement since its modern inception. This landmark book is indispensable."

—Martha Biondi, author of *The Black Revolution on Campus*

The History of Black Studies

Abdul Alkalimat

First published 2021 by Pluto Press
New Wing, Somerset House, Strand, London WC2R 1LA

www.plutobooks.com

British Library Cataloguing in Publication Data
A catalogue record for this book is available from the British Library

ISBN 978 0 7453 4423 2 Hardback
ISBN 978 0 7453 4422 5 Paperback
ISBN 978 0 7453 4426 3 PDF
ISBN 978 0 7453 4424 9 EPUB

This book is printed on paper suitable for recycling and made from fully managed and sustained forest sources. Logging, pulping and manufacturing processes are expected to conform to the environmental standards of the country of origin.

Typeset by Stanford DTP Services, Northampton, England

Simultaneously printed in the United Kingdom and United States of America

To my comrades in People's College
and the Black student activists of today

Contents

Figures

Tables

Introduction

This book tells the history of Black Studies, familiar to many as the campus units that teach college-level courses about African-American history and culture. This book will present a comprehensive survey of all such programs, but Black Studies has been more than that.

The term "Black Studies" emerged in the 1960s but, as this book will demonstrate, Black Studies developed over the entire course of the twentieth century and into the twenty-first century. This book defines Black Studies as those activities:

(1) that study and teach about African Americans and often Africans and other African-descended people;
(2) where Black people themselves are the main agents, or protagonists, of the study and learning;
(3) that counter racism and contribute to human liberation;
(4) that celebrate the Black experience; and
(5) that see it as one precious case among many in the universality of the human condition.

Each of these five points will be considered further along in this introduction.

Now is an appropriate time to write and read a history of Black Studies because colleges and universities across the USA have been celebrating the fiftieth anniversaries of the founding of their Black Studies programs. Campuses are bringing together the alumni, faculty, and community activists who helped found their respective programs. Each has its own particularity but, to draw larger conclusions, we need to consider frameworks that can be used to compare and talk about all these local histories.

This is also a moment when the generation who founded Black Studies at mainstream colleges and universities is moving into retirement and facing health challenges and mortality. This brings with it a crisis of both individual and institutional memory loss, a crisis that calls for activities to capture local accounts of the founding and development of Black Studies on each campus.

Finally, Black Studies faces threats. The economic downturns of 2008 and 2020, the latter due to the coronavirus pandemic, have put pressure on higher education. Before then, endowments and public funding kept higher education relatively insulated from economic pressure. But for more than a decade, tuition increases and limits to financial support have impacted Black enrollment as well as support for Black programs.

The resurgence of racism contributes to this daunting atmosphere, both as a broad social reaction and at the highest levels of political leadership. All in all, the most fundamental negative obstacle facing Black people all over the world at this moment hinges on the concept of race.

Science has discredited race as a concept (American Anthropological Association 1998; important studies include Gould 1996; Lewontin, Rose, and Kamin 1984; Prewitt 2013). It is a term that posits a biological and hierarchical classification of humans, *Homo sapiens*. On this concept rests the practice of racism: large and small prejudicial beliefs, words, and actions that are systematized, institutionalized, persistent, and more or less violent. A liberal justification for the use of the concept of race argues that race is socially constructed. But this falls woefully short. Race is nothing less than a socially constructed lie.

Race serves as a good example of Alfred North Whitehead's fallacy of misplaced concreteness: an abstract idea that does not fit reality (Whitehead 1985 [1925]). Racism exists, but races do not. But as the sociologist W.I. Thomas observes, "If men define situations as real, they are real in their consequences" ("Thomas Theorem" 2018). Racism infects virtually all areas of scholarship and public policy. Black people are systematically lied about as a justification for their continued exploitation and marginalization in American society.

Racism can be understood as some combination of three false ideas: deficit, difference, and dependency. The deficit idea centers on denying that Black people can reason and think just as well as anyone else. The concept of human reason itself has even been claimed by Eurocentric thinkers as originating in Greece and Rome (see Blaut 1993). Of course, this is self-serving. It also contradicts what we know about the mind and the brain. Any human brain has the same structures or centers that mobilize both thinking and feeling.

The idea of deficit has long taken the form of attacking the capacity of Black people's brains. One early effort involved classifying head size and shape. It defined the cephalic index as "the ratio of the maximum width of the head of an organism (human or animal) multiplied by 100 divided by its maximum length (i.e., in the horizontal plane, or front to back)" (Boas 1899). Franz Boas, distinguished anthropologist at Columbia University, took his students Zora Neale Hurston and Margaret Mead to Harlem in the 1920s to measure the heads of Black people as part of disproving this theory ("Sigerist Circle Bibliography on Race and Medicine" n.d.; Helmreich 2004; Boas 1899; Fergus 2003).

Intelligence testing and IQ theory was a second argument made for Black people being deficient, starting with the British psychologist Cyril Burt and followed notably in the USA by William Shockley, Arthur Jensen, Richard Herrnstein, and Charles Murray. The book by Herrnstein (at that time the former chair of the Harvard University Department of Psychology) and Murray, *The*

Bell Curve (1997), became the magnum opus of this argument. This sparked a debate that produced several volumes of criticism: Jacoby and Glauberman's *The Bell Curve Debate*, Fischer's *Inequality by Design: Cracking the Bell Curve Myth*, and an expanded edition of Gould's *The Mismeasure of Man* (Herrnstein and Murray 1997; Jacoby and Glauberman 1998; Fischer 1996; Gould 1996). Scholars have debated the basis for intelligence: nature (genetic inheritance) versus nurture (social influences). One of the revealing aspects of the research reported in *The Bell Curve* is that a great deal of it was undertaken in apartheid South Africa by racist scholars. Leon Kamin, in his article "Lies, Damned Lies, and Statistics," spells out two disastrous failings of the book:

> First, the caliber of the data cited by Herrnstein and Murray is, at many critical points, pathetic and their citations of those weak data are often inaccurate. Second, their failure to distinguish between correlation and causation repeatedly leads Herrnstein and Murray to draw invalid conclusions.
>
> (Kamin 1995, 82)

The false theories that support the idea that Black people are intellectually deficient are accompanied by false theories that explain that Black people are just fundamentally different. This view has been held even by liberals who have worked in what they thought were in the interests of Black people. Robert Park, a University of Chicago sociologist who served as president of the Chicago Urban League, worked closely with Booker T. Washington and mentored E. Franklin Frazier. Yet, he wrote:

> The Negro is, by natural disposition, neither an intellectual or an idealist like the Jew; nor a brooding introspective like the East Indian; nor a pioneer or frontiersman, like the Anglo-Saxon. He is primarily an artist, loving life for its own sake. His métier is expression rather than action. He is, so to speak, the lady of the races.
>
> (Park and Hughes 2009, 139)

This is not simply a view held by so-called white people (another socially constructed lie), but a fallacy based on limited understanding of how the diversity of experience falls under the universal category of being human (for more on Robert Park, see Raushenbush and Hughes 1992).

Correspondingly, many Black people feel there is something "different" about white people, especially as compared to themselves. The Senegalese artist and politician Leopold Senghor famously stated, "Emotion is Negro as reason is Greek" (Constant and Mabana 2009, 69). His philosophy of Negritude not only argued that Black people were culturally different, but also negated reason for Black people and emotion for the Greeks. Perceptual differences can be found in great diversity between Blacks and whites, as well as among Blacks from different countries and different regions within the USA and different classes. The key is to always find the link between particularity and universality by which every community can be regarded as fully human.

The still-more ominous arguments about difference have to do with differences that suggest antisocial behavior and tendencies toward violence. Some racists argue that Black people have enlarged sexual organs and an uncontrollable lust that predisposes them to promiscuity and rape. This argument has been used to delegitimize Black women with children applying for welfare support. It has also served as a cover for lynching Black men, especially on the charge that their sexual lust leads them to defile white women (see Graves 2005, Chapters 3 and 4).

Deficit and difference feed into the third fallacy about Black people: Black people are dependent on the largess of white people (Fraser and Gordon 1994). This old argument includes claims that colonialism and even slavery were benevolent practices that saved Black people from their savage selves. Today, the argument covers the view that Black people are lazy, don't want to work, and therefore have led the USA in the negative direction of the welfare state. This view argues that if Black people are too lazy to work then they need to starve—so down with all forms of welfare. Of course, this view depends on the false image of welfare recipients being mainly Black people. But the opposite is true: even though Black people are on welfare at a somewhat higher rate than white people, most welfare recipients are white (Tracy 2017).

Black Studies responds directly to these deficit, difference, and dependency theories of Black people's supposed inferiority. The five aspects of the definition above are crucial to the response, and each merits elaboration.

First, Black people are the object of study. African Americans are primary, but this links to Africans and the peoples of the African Diaspora. African Americans are those with the historical experience of the transatlantic slave trade, the Middle Passage to the Americas, living through a slave society and various forms of racist oppression, with a tradition of resistance in struggles for freedom. This study includes comparative research that places Black people in a national and global context. And as with most definitions, this one is challenged by emergent social phenomena, in this case, post-slave-trade African migration to the USA, and Black Studies has responded to this.

Second, Black people are the main agents of research, knowledge creation, cultural creativity, and teaching about the Black experience. This specifies cultural creativity as an important form of intellectual production that is highly visible in Black Studies. And while non-Black scholars have made important contributions, Black Studies must be understood as primarily the intellectual productivity of Black people working on behalf of their own community.

Third, Black Studies is fundamentally anti-racist scholarship that contributes to Black liberation in its analysis and its advocacy for change in higher education and the society in general. The study of the Black experience involves defining the conditions of oppression and exploitation under which Black people have lived, and continue to live, and the forms of resistance to these conditions. As such, Black Studies contributes to the freedom struggle.

Fourth, Black Studies encompasses the cultural celebration of the Black experience, especially as it includes the study of the historical forms of Black culture and the traditional rituals of celebration. This combines theory and research with cultural practice.

Fifth, the study and celebration of the Black particularity functions as one path in the search for a universal understanding of the human condition. It is a legitimate arena for seeking knowledge about humanity. This celebrates diversity and universality, and searches for ways that the Black experience, like all peoples' experience, can be a gateway for grasping the universals that define all levels of human attainment.

To sum up, Black Studies consists of a broad set of intellectual activities generated by Black people in order to rationally and culturally reflect on and celebrate their own experience. An autonomous process, it evolves in dialogue and struggle with mainstream institutions of power. It is the intellectual and cultural manifestation of centuries of Black people's resistance to the racism and national oppression that began with the transatlantic slave trade.

Social forces shape this dialectical process. At every historical moment of Black Studies, three main underlying dialectical processes are at work: (1) the interaction between middle-class forces and working-class forces; (2) the dynamic of formal structures arising out of social movements; and (3) the interplay between dogma and debate. Put simply, Black people created Black Studies, and this book demonstrates and explains how they did it.

OUTLINE OF THIS BOOK

This book consists of three parts comprising a total of fifteen chapters. The three parts are Black Studies as Intellectual History, Black Studies as Social Movement, and Black Studies as Academic Profession. These modes, as I call them, do not quite equate to historical periods. Some activities characteristic of one mode continue across two or three historical periods. Most activity at any given moment reflects the dominant mode, but activities reflecting other modes may be emergent or otherwise present as well. As a result, the book's narrative occasionally departs from the strictly chronological to explain these three modes.

The three chapters of Black Studies as Intellectual History explain the twentieth-century origins of Black Studies. This involved Black scholars in higher education, Black people organized in community-based institutions, and Black activists and theorists of the Freedom Movement. Much of this took place outside of colleges and universities, because Black people were by and large excluded from those campuses. But the early scholars who fought for and won entrance went on to produce foundational knowledge, first as doctoral students in mainstream institutions and then for much longer as faculty in historically Black colleges and universities (HBCUs).

The six chapters of Black Studies as Social Movement bring to light the research and teaching institutions that Black people built as part of six particular forms of struggle. These struggles gave rise to emergent and countervailing organizations such as schools, libraries, museums, and cultural centers.

Finally, the six chapters of Black Studies as Academic Profession trace the emergence and establishment of Black Studies across mainstream higher education. This entailed disrupting earlier academic norms and then negotiating an operating definition of Black Studies. To examine how Black Studies became established in twentieth-century higher education, this part of the book then reviews five core academic activities that together cover teaching, research, and service to the profession.

BLACK STUDIES AS INTELLECTUAL HISTORY

Chapter 1, The Academic Disciplines, demonstrates that Black scholars did the foundational scholarship for Black Studies. The chapter discusses the early Black PhD achievers across fourteen disciplines. These scholars, the clearest evidence of Black intellectual achievement, defeated any racist claims as to their ability. They also laid the foundation for all subsequent research on the Black experience. They were part of the rise of a Black professional class. Their research publications have long been available, thanks to bibliographic documentation, but were for the most part ignored by mainstream scholars until Black Studies in the 1960s.

Chapter 2, The Historically Black Colleges and Universities, explains how the scholars in Chapter 1 led an institutional struggle for Black Studies. Although they were educated at the most elite institutions, racist practices blocked them from mainstream positions. For the most part, they found employment in historically Black colleges and universities, particularly Fisk University in Nashville, Tennessee, Atlanta University in Atlanta, Georgia, and Howard University in Washington, DC. Established after the American Civil War, these institutions featured a Eurocentric curriculum designed to assimilate a Black middle class. The struggle for curriculum focusing on the Black experience first took place at these HBCUs, to be repeated in the 1960s in mainstream institutions.

As the vast majority of Black people had not had access to higher education, they created Black Studies within their communities' own social and cultural institutions. Chapter 3, The Political Culture of the Black Community, argues that libraries, museums, cultural centers, and high schools were bases for Black Studies developing in the community and serving mainly Black and working-class people. Case studies of New York, Chicago, New Orleans, and Los Angeles make this clear.

BLACK STUDIES AS SOCIAL MOVEMENT

Chapter 4, The Freedom Movement, argues that the 1960s Freedom Movement organizations initiated Black Studies in the form of freedom schools, where a new curriculum oriented to the Black experience raised the consciousness of people engaging in movement activity. Examples of this are the 1964 Mississippi Freedom Summer and the school boycott movement in Chicago in 1963 and 1964.

The slogan of "Black Power" signaled a shift in popular consciousness from integration into the mainstream of society toward Black unity and self-determination. Black Power emerged as an ideological concept in 1966, first articulated by Student Non-Violent Coordinating Committee (SNCC) militants Stokely Carmichael (Kwame Ture) and Willie Ricks (Mukasa Dada). The icon Martin Luther King Jr. gave way to the icon Malcolm X. Chapter 5, The Black Power Movement, argues that the Black Power Movement spread the study of Black people's history and culture as a national influence on all other movements and created emergent institutions, conferences, journals, bookstores, and independent schools.

Black-Power-oriented cultural activists led the launch of a new arts movement. Chapter 6, The Black Arts Movement, argues that Black identity and self-determination toward Black liberation created a cultural movement. This chapter presents information on many art forms: music, literature, theater, dance, visual arts, television, and film. Arts organizations, journals, and cultural centers emerged in local communities to carry forward and institutionalize these ideas and practices.

Socialism has long been an active ideological and political influence in Black protest movements. At one point, the global standard was the 1917 Russian Revolution and the USSR. But with the development of revolutionary transformations taking place in China, Vietnam, and Cuba, along with Pan-African socialist movements, Black activists began to look to the former colonial third world for inspiration and guidance. Chapter 7, The New Communist Movement, argues that study groups, newspapers, and a national process of debates within that movement added the serious consideration of socialism to Black Studies.

Black women have always provided critical leadership and essential labor power to every Black social institution and social movement. This includes a history of national organizational development. Chapter 8, The Black Women's Movement, explains how those forces shaped Black Studies by advancing the insight, voices, and agency of Black women and advancing women's experiences as a window into all aspects of the Black experience.

The Black Student Movement exploded after the assassination of Martin Luther King Jr. and the near-immediate surge of first-generation Black college students arriving on campus out of the working class. All of the other social movements aided the development of the Black Student Movement. These students were the original social force who entered the formerly segregated mainstream institutions of higher education as agents of change. Chapter 9, The Black Student Movement, argues that Black students first and foremost articulated the demands that led to Black Studies in mainstream higher education. The primary source of inspiration for these students and for all of the Black-Power-influenced social movements was the ideological leadership of Malcolm X.

BLACK STUDIES AS ACADEMIC PROFESSION

With the background of Part I, Intellectual History, and Part II, Social Movements, set forth, Part III of the book then examines six different aspects of Black Studies in mainstream higher education. Chapter 10 traces how Black Studies took root on campuses by means of social disruptions caused by the Black Student Movement and their allies on and off campus. The well-known national case is San Francisco State University; this chapter also discusses Howard University in Washington, DC, Duke University in Durham, North Carolina, Atlanta University in Atlanta, Georgia, and Cornell University in Ithaca, New York.

As campus student revolts spread across the country, a national dialogue took shape with the purpose of reaching a collective definition and mission of Black Studies as an academic profession. Chapter 11 argues that different class forces in the Black community drove this process of collectivizing a definition of Black Studies: established middle-class Black academics with key positions in mainstream institutions and the HBCUs together with emergent leaders from the Black-Power-inspired social movements, including young faculty and graduate students emerging out of the working class.

Black Studies then undertook a process of institutionalization into a mainstream academic discipline. Chapter 12, Building Institutions, argues that despite its radical origins, Black Studies adapted to the institutional norms of higher education. This was accomplished by a younger generation than the founding generation of Black Studies activists from the social movements. Drawing on 2013 and 2019 surveys, the chapter reviews key areas in the field:

faculty, leadership, curriculum, administrative structure, gender, program activities, and community relations.

Black Studies faculty and administrators faced the challenge of peer review, that is, of meeting the professional standards of their colleagues in similar positions throughout higher education. The process of adapting to mainstream norms included developing Black Studies into a formal academic profession. Chapter 13, Establishing the Profession, argues that this took shape in four ways, centered on the established process of peer review: PhD programs, academic journals, professional associations, and conferences. The chapter looks at Temple University in Philadelphia, University of Massachusetts at Amherst, and Northwestern University in Evanston, Illinois, in particular.

The scholarship of every academic profession is a function of its development of general theoretical tendencies and norms for research methods. Chapter 14, Theorizing, argues that there have been two main theoretical frameworks in Black Studies: Afrocentrism and Black Experientialism. One emphasizes historical continuity with Africa and the African Diaspora, anchored historically in ancient Egypt. The other starts from the study of the African-American experience and draws comparisons to the diversity of the African Diaspora. This chapter also discusses Black Women's Studies and Black Queer Studies, each rooted in Black Experientialism.

Chapter 15, Norming Research, argues that Black Studies research has developed normative methods that focus on documenting the collective works of key scholars, creating genre-based collections of works produced by Black scholars, and studying the major social institutions and movements of the Black community. Central to this process has been refuting racism in mainstream scholarship. A discussion of evaluation research explains how Black Studies developed self-governing evaluation practices in order to maintain the highest standards of an academic profession. The conclusion of the book considers the history recounted here alongside the work of other Black Studies historians to assemble a whole story that others will hopefully fill in and elaborate upon even further.

Relying on a broad definition of Black Studies enables this book to reach deep into recent and earlier history to identify contributions from many generations of scholars, culture creators, activists, and ordinary Black people. The definition of Black Studies, again, is as follows: the study and teaching about African Americans and often Africans and other African-descended people, led mainly by Black people, countering racism and advancing freedom, celebrating the Black experience, and asserting our place alongside the rest of humanity. In response to and in dialogue with dominant social currents, Black people created Black Studies.

This book is at times encyclopedic, because so much of Black people's history making and telling has been devalued and omitted from the record. Likewise, this book works to put the radicals in the record. They too, have been much erased.

One final note about methodology: this volume quotes a few sources at length. With Black Studies continually challenged, not only with regard to academic programs but also library collections, the quotations are not easy for everyone who will read this book to find in totality. As a result, what might seem like lengthy passages are necessary here.

PART I

Black Studies as Intellectual History

Black intellectual history has always been the root of Black Studies. This does not exclude important contributions by, and dialogues with, scholars outside of the Black community. But Black Studies is fundamentally a product of Black intellectuals.

Beginning late in the 1800s, Black people began to earn advanced degrees and establish a record of scholarship focusing on the African-American experience. This spanned most academic disciplines in the social sciences and the humanities. These academic high achievers earned degrees at the most outstanding institutions of higher education. The first scholarly studies of the African-American experience were their dissertations. Many of them spent very productive careers at historically Black colleges and universities, particularly Howard University, Fisk University, and Atlanta University. Their decades of scholarship and institution-shaping form an enormous part of Black Studies as Intellectual History.

The Black community also created its own flavor of intellectual development, including public intellectuals. Organizations of all kinds created documents that were essential reading for the faithful. These documents presented a view of Black history and laid an ideological foundation for the Radical Black Tradition. In newspapers, magazines, and journals, Black intellectuals and artists kept the community informed about the issues of the day, rethinking historical experience and comparing African Americans to the entire African Diaspora and people all over the world. There were bookstores, special library collections, museums, and cultural centers. But, for the most part, mainstream scholars ignored these developments and omitted Black thought from their curriculum materials, even though many of the authors had been their classmates—even in the Ivy League.

Black history itself must be understood as a dialectical unity of, on the one hand, particular social forces that produce ideas and, on the other hand, a tradition of study that fuels knowledge production—in other words, a unity of the people who act and are acted upon with the consciousness of those same people. African Americans have lived through three major periods of social stability, called elsewhere modes of social cohesion: slavery, rural tenancy, and urban industry (Alkalimat 1986, 49–120). These periods of transgenerational continuity have shaped the social life of Black people and seen institutions form and flourish. This has given rise to five main, always evolving, dogmas or ideologies: Pan-Africanism, nationalism, Black liberation theology, feminism, and socialism. Each of these goes into the cauldron of debate when society enters periods of social disruption and change. The emancipation process brought forward the debate over emancipation. The turn-of-the-twentieth-century process of establishing the Black community brought forward the self-determination debate. The urban explosion of the 1960s brought forward the Black liberation debate.

Why embrace this early work as Black Studies as Intellectual History? Sometimes it is thought that people without a past are people without a future—that is, unless other people come along to help. When Black people enter the mainstream for their college experience, they study texts that ignore this historical background. The mainstream, being less informed, sets the standard for what is academic excellence in subjects about the Black experience. Black Studies as Intellectual History sets a different standard—an imperative for intellectual accountability. Moreover, without this history, any scholar or activist risks reinventing the wheel. Intellectual history provides its most valuable service when one generation, after studying and critiquing what previous generations have done, builds on that existing knowledge. This is revealed in literature reviews, footnotes, and bibliographies. The names in this part of the book represent only a sample of the people who need to be considered in each area of scholarship.

Every new scholar has three options when engaging existing research: confirm and agree, contradict and disagree, or fill in a silence. Each of these is valid scholarship on any given aspect of the Black experience. Each generation has to go through this process. With research transformed by new digital tools, people can process larger and larger bodies of digitized texts and other data and use the digital tools to search and find sources on a global level.

Finally, Black Studies as Intellectual History establishes that the field is not limited to the campus or the academy. Black Studies has always been connected to efforts by Black people to study and struggle, to connect knowledge with making life better. This was true, even when Black people were under lockdown during slavery. Even then, everyone knew that reading was a tool to free the mind so that you could then free the body.

1
The Academic Disciplines

This chapter makes the case that Black scholarship from after the American Civil War (1861–1865) through the 1950s constitutes the beginning of the study of the Black experience.

Returning to the thesis of the book as presented in the Introduction, this chapter describes how a growing cohort of Black people began to engage in scholarship about Black people, in resistance to hegemonic opposition and in close relationship to cultural practice. The focus in this chapter is on the activity of a middle-class elite, who were able to gain access to the institutions of scholarship, namely, mainstream universities in the USA. Due to unrelenting racism, these scholars were inside, but also kept outside, as the chapter will show.

Of course, Black people in Africa and Europe had conducted serious academic scholarship well before this time. Just two examples of the earliest speak to the force of that work and how it was received.

The ancient city of Timbuktu, located in what is today Mali in West Africa, became a major marketplace and on that basis also a center of learning. Three large mosques formed the institutional arrangement called the University of Sankore from the twelfth through the fifteenth centuries. Theological study centered on the Quran was the foundation, much as institutions of higher education in the West originated as places for religious study. But a full curriculum of science and math was required as well. Today, 700,000 texts from the University of Sankore have been preserved by families rooted in the cherishing and sustaining of the literary artifacts of their cultural heritage (Clarke 1977; Khair n.d.). The university itself fell victim to the defeat of the central African Songhai Empire by the Moroccans, which took place simultaneous to the rise of the European empires.

A few Africans who made their way to Europe obtained formal education there and subsequently joined institutions of academic scholarship. Among them, coming from an area that later became Ghana, Anton Wilhelm Amo (1703–1759) became the first African to complete a PhD at a European university, the University of Wittenberg in 1734 (J.E.H. Smith 2013; Hountondji 2007, 111–30). He went on to hold professorships in philosophy in universities at Halle and Jena in Germany, and continued to publish. He was an early materialist in his thinking, as shown by his views on the mind–body contradiction:

> Whatever feels, lives; whatever lives, depends on nourishment; whatever lives and depends on nourishment grows; whatever is of this nature is in the end resolved into its basic principles; whatever comes to be resolved into its basic principles is a complex; every complex has its constituent parts; whatever this is true of is a divisible body. If therefore the human mind feels, it follows that it is a divisible body.
>
> (From Amo's "On the Ἀπάθεια (Apatheia) of the Human Mind 2.1," quoted in "Anton Wilhelm Amo" 2018).

Amo soon faced a reactionary turn in Germany. He was forced to leave his position and return to Ghana. Even there, he faced continued harassment and isolation, for fear he would foment a mass uprising against European colonial domination.

So while there had been some early achievers in the mainstream prior to the Civil War in the USA and in Europe, the institutional basis for the Black academic intelligentsia that first generated Black Studies developed as a result of the victory of the antislavery Union army (Anderson 1988). This profound event opened up new opportunities: educational institutions sprang up all over the South and in the North as well.

Early evidence of this leap came just as Black people were beginning to enter the mainstream universities as doctoral students: they created their own networks. The first formal organization of Black scholars and intellectuals was the American Negro Academy, founded and led by Alexander Crummell in 1897, shortly before his death in 1898. The academy, the first professional society dedicated to Black intellectual production, held an annual meeting and published occasional papers until 1928 (American Negro Academy 1969; Ferris 1969). As this organization reflected, people with PhDs and at universities worked alongside of and in communication with leading cultural producers outside of academia.

Not only did these early Black scholars form their own networks, they also began to create bibliographic works that would allow their output to be found and read. Table 1 demonstrates that of the thirteen periodicals that documented and promoted the work of Black scholars, seven were founded in or before 1950: *Negro Year Book* (1912), *Opportunity* (1923), *Journal of Negro Education* (1932), *Crisis* (1936), *The Negro Handbook* (1942), *Negro Digest/Black World* (1943), and *Index to Periodicals by and about Negroes* (1950). Notable among these is Monroe Work's 1912–1937 *Negro Year Book* series (Edwards 1985; M.N. Work 1912, 1913, 1914, 1916, 1918, 1921, 1925, 1931, 1937, 1965 [1928]).

All thirteen of this list of bibliographic sources, but especially the first seven, testify to an unbroken record of Black academic writing, a literature that

Table 1 Works of Bibliography by and about African Americans

Series	*Primary bibliographer*	*1900s*	*1910s*	*1920s*	*1930s*	*1940s*	*1950s*	*1960s*	*1970s*	*1980s*	*1990s*	*2000s*	*2010s*
Negro Year Book	Monroe Work		1912, 1913, 1914, 1916, 1919	1922, 1925	1931, 1937								
Opportunity	Alain Locke			1923 —		— 1949							
**Journal of Negro Education*	Charles Henry Thompson				1932 —								— now
**Crisis*	Arthur Spingarn				1936 —			— 1966					
The Negro Handbook	Florence Murray					1942, 1944, 1946, 1949							
**Negro Digest/ Black World*	John Johnson, Hoyt Fuller					1943 —			— 1976				
Index to Periodical Articles By and About Negroes	Librarians at Hallie Q. Brown Memorial Library, Central State University, Ohio, continued by G. K. Hall						1950 —				— 1998		
Freedomways	Ernest Kaiser							1961 —		— 1985			
Integrated Education	Meyer Weinberg							1963 —		— 1984			
AIMS Newsletter	Herbert Aptheker							1964 —		— 1985			
Black Book Bulletin	Haki Madhubuti								1971 —	— 1981			
**Afro-Scholar*	Abdul Alkalimat									1983 —	— 1991		
*H-Afro-Am	Abdul Alkalimat										1998 —		— 2014
Journal of Blacks in Higher Education	Theodore Cross										1993 —		— now
Number of series in each decade		0	1	2	4	5	4	7	7	7	5	3	3

* indicates currently available online (McWorter 1981; Alkalimat 2008, 2012).

reflects and analyzes the Black experience in virtually every area of scholarship. H-Afro-Am was a discussion list that also contained many bibliography lists.

So Black people were not only intellectually productive, but were also documenting their own intellectual history in such a way as to create a tradition of Black thought. Of course, several of these sources—*Opportunity*, *Crisis*, *Freedomways*, *Integrated Education*, *AIMS Newsletter*, and *Black Books Bulletin*—are connected with the Freedom Movement rather than with academic institutions. This is evidence of what subsequent chapters will elaborate on: Black intellectual production and the freedom struggle have always gone hand in hand.

It is also important to consider this work alongside the experience of the University of Sankore and Professor Amo. These bibliographic reference works grew out of institutions that facilitated intellectual production, distribution, and readership. They also had an appreciative audience. Within the segregated community, there was serious study of the Black experience, and discipline-specific efforts like this emerged as well. Yet, at the same time, mainstream discourse largely ignored this work, because it challenged the dominant racist narrative of Black intellectual inferiority.

One more example is necessary here. There is a general agreement that the preeminent African American scholar of the twentieth century is William Edward Burghardt Du Bois (1868–1963), who was also a historian and a sociologist of Black people (J.H. Bracey, Meier, and Rudwick 1971; A.D. Morris 2015; Meier and Rudwick 1986; Thorpe 1971). Du Bois wrote comprehensive narrative surveys of Black history as well as detailed studies of specific historical periods and social institutions. His contributions will be discussed in several chapters of this book. He used poetry and fiction as well as social science. He took on the Black experience in world context and dared to speak about world events, being concerned with both the welfare of Black people and that of humanity in general (Du Bois 1968).

Du Bois is an exemplar for Black Studies scholarship. He transcended disciplinary boundaries and used various methodologies and intertextual strategies to get at the content of the Black experience. He combined scholarship with activism, pushing the standards of each to their limits, always depending more on how he anchored himself in the historical progress of his people rather than approval he might or might not get from mainstream gatekeepers. He famously summed up his moment of liberation from submission to conventional thinking about being free in America, when he described the staunch opposition to his proposal to undertake a decades-long research program focused on Black people:

> It was of course crazy for me to dream that America, in the dawn of the Twentieth Century, with Colonial Imperialism, based on the suppression of colored folk, at its zenith, would encourage, much less adequately

> finance, such a program at a Negro college under Negro scholars. My faith in its success was based on the firm belief that race prejudice was based on widespread ignorance. My long-term remedy was Truth: carefully gathered scientific proof that neither color nor race determined the limits of a man's capacity or desert. I was not at the time sufficiently Freudian to understand how little human action is based on reason; nor did I know Karl Marx well enough to appreciate the economic foundations of human history.
>
> (Du Bois 1944, 49)

His major work, inspired by his reading of Marx, is *Black Reconstruction: An Essay Toward a History of the Part Which Black Folk Played in the Attempt to Reconstruct Democracy in America, 1860–1880* (Du Bois 2007 [1935]). He recast the social identity of Black people as a Black proletariat, and featured them alongside white workers as the force driving social policy in a democratic direction. Twenty years prior (and one year before Lenin's study of imperialism), Dubois wrote "The African Roots of War" (1915), an economic analysis of World War I with insights into the social and psychological forces driving Europe's colonial policies.

As with much Black intellectual history, each later generation has had to rediscover and reinterpret Du Bois. In the 1960s, when Black Studies was pushing into the mainstream, scholars in that mainstream were especially ignorant of Black intellectual production. Or if they were aware, they lacked respect. So the curriculum typically did not include Du Bois, until young scholars turned to Black intellectual history and began to use and teach his work. Again, a pattern similar to Sankore, Amo, and the bibliographers can be discerned: waves of negation, struggle, and affirmation.

The post-Civil War surge in Black academic scholarship generated enough output to enable a subsequent breakthrough in US higher education curriculum. Data from Greene (1946, 26) and Bond (1966, 564) helps to describe this, taking as the indicator attainment of the doctoral degree. From 1875 to 1962, Black scholars earned 2,331 doctorate degrees. Up to 1944, the leading institutions granting PhDs to Black people were Chicago, Columbia, Pennsylvania, Cornell, and Harvard. (In contrast, from 1955 to 1959, the historically Black colleges and universities [HBCUs] awarded 65 percent of all PhDs granted to Black scholars.) Also, up to 1944, the leading undergraduate institutions attended by those PhD recipients were five HBCUs: Howard University, Fisk University, Lincoln University (in Pennsylvania), Morehouse College (in Atlanta), and Virginia Union University.

Greene (1946) reports that from 1876 to 1943, at least 381 PhDs were granted in thirty-seven fields of specialization. He reported forty-eight women being awarded the doctoral degree, with 60 percent in education, language, and literature. Forty percent of all 381 PhDs were in the social sciences and education. Of

Table 2 First African Americans to Earn Doctorates in Eleven Disciplines

Year	*Discipline*	*Name*	*Sex*	*Institution*	*Title*
1895	History	W.E.B. DuBois	M	Harvard University	The Suppression of the African Slave Trade
1903	Philosophy	T. Nelson Baker Sr.	M	Yale University	The Ethical Significance Between Mind and Body
1906	Sociology	James R.L. Diggs	M	Illinois Wesleyan University	The Dynamics of Social Progress
1920	Psychology	Francis Cecil Sumner	M	Clark University	Psychoanalysis of Freud and Adler
1921	Economics	Sadie T. Mossell Alexander	F	University of Pennsylvania	Standards of Living Among 100 Negro Migrant Families in Philadelphia
1921	Literature	Eva Beatrice Dykes	F	Radcliffe College	Pope and His Influence in America 1715–1850
1925	Education	Charles H. Thompson	M	University of Chicago	An Objective Determination of a Curriculum for Kindergarten Teachers
1931	Anthropology	Laurence Foster	M	University of Pennsylvania	Negro–Indian Relationship in the South East
1934	Political Science	Ralph J. Bunche	M	Harvard University	French Administration in Togoland and Dahomey
1940	Library Science	Eliza Atkins Gleason	F	University of Chicago	The Government and Administration of Public Library Services to Negroes in the South
1942	Music	Oscar Fuller	M	University of Iowa	The Creation: An Oratorio for 12 Parts

the seventy-seven doctoral degrees in the social sciences, 68 percent reported research about the Black experience, with a few expanding out into the African Diaspora. Several of these dissertations became foundational documents in the study of the Black experience and were reprinted based on demand generated by Black Studies in the late 1960s.

Table 2 identifies the first African Americans who earned a doctoral degree in each of eleven disciplines: history, philosophy, sociology, psychology, economics, literature, education, anthropology, political science, library science, and music. Closer examination of these disciplines below will make clear the power of the surge in scholarship during this time.

Seven of the eleven doctorates were earned at Ivy League institutions. (For an understanding of the simultaneous troubled history of Ivy League institutions and slavery, see Wilder 2013.) Three women are among the eleven. Sadie T. Mossell Alexander was the first Black person to earn a PhD in economics (1921), and she went on to be the first Black woman to get a law degree in the USA (1927)—both from the University of Pennsylvania. Eva Beatrice Dykes was the first Black PhD in literature (1921). And Eliza Atkins Gleason was the first in library science (1940).

The research, teaching, and cultural creativity of Black intellectuals and artists have covered virtually every academic area of study. Besides the eleven disciplines listed in Table 2, this chapter will consider five additional areas: language, religion, visual arts, theater, and women's studies. As this will show, Black Studies truly began with the agency of Black intellectuals in the first half of the twentieth century. Each discipline looked at here as a case illustrates that this wave of early doctoral graduates went on to carry out lifelong research activity, often linked with policy as well as teaching. Here is where Black Studies emerges in each of these academic disciplines.

HISTORY

Perhaps reflected in the fact that it was the first discipline to accept a Black person's doctoral dissertation—that of W.E.B. Du Bois in 1895—history has been the leading area for the study of the Black experience. Meier and Rudwick (1986) organize their analysis of Black historians in a chronology of generations. They start with a chapter on Carter G. Woodson, focusing on his organizational work in promoting the study of Black history. They cover two periods: 1915–1960; and 1960–1980. In contrast, Robert L. Harris (1982) organizes his historiography according to five approaches to the study of Black history: revisionism (correcting errors of distortion and omission); hidden hand (describing God's plan); contributionism (how Blacks have helped make the USA great); cyclical (showing alternative successes and failures); and liberalism (showing progress toward some utopian ideal).

In the nineteenth century, George Washington Williams (1849–1891) was the first scholar to write a comprehensive history of the African-American experience (G.W. Williams 1883a; 1883b; for a biography of Williams, see J.H. Franklin 1985). In the twentieth century, Carter G. Woodson (1875–1950) was the leading historian of Black intellectual history (Dagbovie 2007; Scally 1985; Goggin 1993; L.J. Greene and Strickland 1989). After earning an undergraduate degree from the University of Chicago in 1908, Woodson earned the second PhD after Du Bois, also in historical studies from Harvard University, in 1912. He went on to promote the study of Black history in conferences, journals, and public programs. He founded the Association for the Study of Negro Life and History in Chicago in 1915; it continues as the Association for the Study of African-American Life and History. This association is unique in that it embraces academic scholars and community-based practitioners. Woodson also founded the first academic journal in the twentieth century that focused on the Black experience, *The Journal of Negro History* (1916; now the *Journal of African American History*) as well as the mass community-oriented Negro History Week in 1926, which continues every February as Black History Month.

Woodson, a prolific scholar, wrote general surveys of Black history (Dagbovie 2007; L.J. Greene and Woodson 1930; Goggin 1993; Scally 1985; Woodson 1918, 1921, 1936; Woodson and Association for the Study of Negro Life and History 1930; Woodson, Douglass, and Association for the Study of Afro-American Life and History 1926; Woodson and Wesley 1962). He also published collections of speeches and letters to demonstrate the thinking of Black leadership and the general community.

Woodson was an organizer and connected with many scholars, who constituted what many consider to be a school of Black historians. These included A.A. Taylor, Charles Wesley, Lorenzo Greene, Luther P. Jackson, Lawrence D. Reddick, and Rayford Logan, among many others (A.A. Taylor 1973, 1974; C.H. Wesley 1967; D.P. Wesley 1969; C.H. Wesley and Conyers 1997; L.J. Greene 1974; L.J. Greene and Strickland 1989; L.P. Jackson 1971, 2003; Reddick 1944, 1978; Logan 1954, 2011). They created an important body of historical scholarship on African Americans. They used the public outlets and venues created by Woodson to build a strong following in the Black community and beyond. They were sure to be published, as Woodson also established a publishing company, Associated Publishers, in 1920 (Dagbovie 2007).

Several white historians made significant early contributions to the study of Black history. Some of these are William Z. Foster (1881–1961), C. Vann Woodward (1908–1999), Kenneth Stampp (1912–2009), Herbert Aptheker (1915–2003), and August Meier (1923–2003) (Aptheker 1971, 1983, 1990; Foster 1947, 1982; Meier 1992a, 1992b; Meier and Rudwick 1986, 1993; Stampp 1972; Woodward 2006, 2013). Foster and Aptheker were left-wing theoreticians; Woodward and Meier were early civil rights activists. They were friendly with both Du Bois and Woodson. Foster and Aptheker placed the Black struggle for freedom from slavery in the context of the overall class struggle from slave revolts to twentieth-century labor struggles. Woodward and Stampp wrote in opposition to mainstream racist views that denigrated African Americans and blamed them for their own predicament during and after slavery. Meier wrote about Black intellectual history and the civil rights movement and produced a number of anthologies along with John Bracey, Elliot Rudwick, and Francis Broderick.

Certain historians from this pre-1960 period contributed to the development of Black Studies in the 1960s, and their work will be discussed later in the book: John Hope Franklin (1967), Benjamin Quarles (1989), and Lerone Bennett Jr.

(1969, 2000). Numerous scholars have addressed the history of Black historians (Bardolph 1959; Thorpe 1971; R.L. Harris 1982; Hine and American Historical Association 1986; Meier and Rudwick 1986; R.L. Harris and Terborg-Penn 2008).

PHILOSOPHY

African-American philosophers have pursued three main approaches: Africa and the African Diaspora and philosophy; finding philosophy in Black thought, culture, and social movements; and analyzing the Black experience through the lens of mainstream or Marxist philosophy.

The first and foundational Black academic philosopher was Alain Locke, who earned his doctoral degree at Harvard in 1918 (A. Locke 1969, 1971; A.L. Locke 2015; A. Locke et al. 1942; A. Locke and Harris 1989). An even earlier distinction was that he was the first African-American Rhodes Scholar, out of Howard University in 1907, where he was also invited to join the honor society Phi Beta Kappa. Locke returned to Howard University as the chair of the Department of Philosophy. During this period, he began teaching the first classes at Howard on race relations and led a faculty committee to stabilize wages, which resulted in his dismissal in 1925. After being reinstated in 1928, Locke remained at Howard until his retirement in 1953. Locke Hall, on the Howard campus, is named after him. He edited *The New Negro* (1925), which defined a generation of progressive Black thought that swept the country, although it notably did not include consideration of Harlem's Black left. His main work reflected philosophically on Black art and culture, as represented by such works as *Negro Art Past and Present* (1969 [1936]), *The Negro and His Music* (1969 [1936]), *The Negro in Art* (1940), and *When Peoples Meet: A Study of Race and Culture Contacts* (1942), which he edited with Bernhard J. Stern. Leonard Harris has written a valuable biography of Locke, *Alain Locke: The Biography of a Philosopher* (Harris and Molesworth 2010), and edited a collection of his articles, *The Philosophy of Alain Locke: Harlem Renaissance and Beyond* (Locke and Harris 1989). The most recent biography is by Jeffery Stewart (Stewart 2018).

Two important early Black philosophers were Marxists: Eugene Holmes (PhD, Columbia, 1942) and activist-scholar C.L.R. James. The former joined the faculty at Howard University and eventually replaced Alain Locke as head of the Department of Philosophy (Holmes 1959, 1963, 1969; Holmes and Logan 1956). James (1901–1989), one of the most profound twentieth-century Black thinkers of the African Diaspora, was originally from Trinidad but was active in England and the USA. His major work is *The Black Jacobins* (2001 [1953]), a study that locates the Haitian Revolution as a turning point in world history and in the liberation struggles of the African Diaspora (Dhondy 2001;

C.L.R. James 1953, 2001 [1953], 2013, 2018; C.L.R. James, Dunayevskaya, and Boggs 2013). Useful scholarship on Black philosophers includes J.H. McClendon (1980), L. Harris (1983), L.R. Gordon (1997, 2008), Pittman (1997), and Wiredu (2004).

SOCIOLOGY

An early Black PhD in sociology was George Edmund Haynes at Columbia University, who earned his degree in 1912 (Haynes 1945, 2008). He embraced the scholar-activist role, holding down a professorship at Fisk University while being affiliated with the National Urban League. From 1918 to 1921, Haynes served as director of the Division of Negro Economics in the US Department of Labor, thus becoming the first African American to hold a federal subcabinet post. He represents the early connection between sociology and its practical sister, social work.

African-American sociologists in the subsequent generation include Oliver Cox, Charles Johnson, E. Franklin Frazier, Adelaide Cromwell, Ira Reid, and Bertram Doyle (Cox 1970, 1990; Hunter and Abraham 1987; C.S. Johnson 1934, 1969, 1970; Gilpin, Gasman, and Lewis 2014; Frazier, American Council on Education, and American Youth Commission 1967; Frazier 1957, 1997; Frazier and Edwards 1968; Platt 1991; Cromwell 1995; I.D.A. Reid 1930, 1970; I.D.A. Reid, American Council on Education, and American Youth Commission 1940; Doyle 1944, 1971). Johnson (in 1917), Frazier (in 1931), Doyle (in 1934), and Cox (in 1938) earned PhD degrees from the University of Chicago; Reid (in 1939) from Columbia; and Cromwell (in 1946) from Radcliffe/Harvard. This reflects the fact that at the University of Chicago under the influence of Park, and in spite of other more openly racist faculty, Black scholars were recruited and encouraged to focus on the Black experience. Charles Johnson famously did the major study of the racist violence against Black people in 1919, *The Negro in Chicago*, before going to New York to head the research department of the National Urban League and edit its journal *Opportunity*. He then went to Fisk University to lead its social science division, and later became its first Black president in 1946. Johnson contributed major research work on the rural experiences of Black people, especially his classic, *Shadow of the Plantation* (C.S. Johnson 1934).

E. Franklin Frazier worked at Atlanta University (1922–1927), Fisk University (1929–1934), and Howard University (1935–1959). His major research begins with his three-volume study of the Black family: *The Negro Family in Chicago*, 1932; *The Free Negro Family*, 1932; and *The Negro Family in the United States*, 1939 (Frazier and Thompson 2005; Frazier 1966, 1968). Frazier became the first Black scholar to head a major professional association when he was elected president of the American Sociological Association in 1948. He took two major controversial positions. One placed him in opposition to Melville Herskovits and Lorenzo Turner, whose study of the African Diaspora caused them to emphasize the connections between African Americans and African traditions and culture; Frazier sided with his mentor, Robert Park, in this debate, arguing that connection was broken in the Middle Passage. The second was his analysis of the Black middle class, *Black Bourgeoisie*, in which he exposed what he called the failure of the Black middle class to serve the interests of the masses of Black people (Frazier 1997). Frazier was also a scholar-activist who served on many local, national, and international commissions, linking his research to burning policy questions. His early recognition of Marcus Garvey as a legitimate mass leader as well as his service on the board of a left-wing journal, *Science and Society*, kept him under state scrutiny.

The sociologist Oliver Cox carried out detailed empirical work and developed wide-ranging theoretical explanations. His 1938 dissertation, "Factors Affecting the Marital Status of Negroes in the United States," and early work concerned a class analysis rooted in the relationship between the social and technical division of labor and the Black family structure. He went on to write articles such as "Farm Tenancy and Marital Status" (1940) and "Employment, Education, and Marriage" (1941). His major theoretical work is *Caste, Class, and Race*, published in 1948. He went against the grain in voicing strong opposition to the views of the Chicago school of sociology (Robert Park et al.) and Gunnar Myrdal in his *American Dilemma* (1944). Cox was arguing against the use of caste as a concept to describe the African-American condition (as in India); rather, he viewed the issue as fundamentally one of class. He went on to write systemic critiques of US capitalism (*The Foundations of Capitalism*, 1959; *Capitalism and American Leadership*, 1962; and *Capitalism as a System*, 1964). Cox was the most explicitly theoretical of the early scholars in sociology (Cox 1938, 1970, 2006a, 2006b; Cox and Barnes 2006; Hunter 2008; Hunter and Abraham 1987).

Morris (2015) and Earl Wright (2015) contend that as a sociologist, Du Bois created a school of scholars who worked with him and followed his theoretical and empirical path. This included Monroe Work, Edmund Haynes, Richard R. Wright Jr., and Augustus Dill, among others. Work, another University of Chicago PhD, headed a research program at Tuskegee Institute. He created a data set that comprised baseline information and statistics on lynching. Work also produced a regular review of achievements by African Americans in his *Negro Year Book* series, mentioned above.

Many studies have covered the history of Black scholars in sociology (Blackwell, Janowitz, and National Conference on Black Sociologists 1974; Ladner 1973; J.H. Bracey, Meier, and Rudwick 1971; Aldridge 2009; J.E. Conyers 1968, 1986a, 1986b).

PSYCHOLOGY

Psychology stands out as a field in which racist theories were disguised by pseudoscientific illusions of empirical proof. The racists attacked with theories of biology and personality development, measuring brain size and using test scores to demonstrate Black inferiority. To demonstrate the fallacies and intellectual biases of this work, Black psychologists carried out mainstream-standard research, in addition to performing impeccably as graduate students at elite universities.

Guthrie lists a total of thirty-two African Americans awarded the PhD in psychology from 1920 to 1950 (Guthrie 2003, 165–67). The first, Francis Cecil Sumner (Clark University, 1920), was hired at Howard University in 1928 and launched the first degree-granting program in psychology at an HBCU. From 1919 to 1938, Howard University was the only HBCU to have such a program; it had twenty-eight graduate students (Guthrie 2003, 156). Sumner's main interest was in religion, but his lasting contribution was as a mentor of generations of Black psychology graduate students at Howard.

Perhaps the most accomplished scholars in psychology that Howard University produced were the husband-and-wife team of Kenneth Clark (MA, Howard, 1936; PhD, Columbia, 1940) and Mamie Clark (MA, Howard, 1939; PhD, Columbia, 1944) (K.B. Clark 1965, 1988, 1989). Their major research, though controversial today because of contradictory contemporary research, made a substantial impact on policy, including the 1954 *Brown* v. *Board of Education* desegregation case decided by the US Supreme Court. Their experiment used dolls to show that segregated schools perverted the self-image of Black children, demonstrating that segregation produced bad mental health. Black children preferred white dolls and not dolls that looked like them. Much of their work focused on skin color. Kenneth Clark became a major official in higher education, serving on many boards and holding visiting lectureships.

Many Black scholars in psychology had to take nonacademic jobs, because of both the systemic racism that excluded them and their own desire to serve their community more directly. This applies to another husband-and-wife team: Albert Beckham (MA, Ohio State University, 1917) and Ruth Howard Beckham (PhD, University of Minnesota, 1934). He produced professional research papers while being the school psychologist at DuSable High School. She was a psychologist in the school of nursing run by Provident Hospital. Both institutions were primarily Black and located on the South Side of Chicago ("Biography of Ruth Winifred Howard" n.d.; American Psychological Association 2014).

The first major program of research on the psychological state of African Americans unfolded under the direction of the American Youth Commission and the American Council on Education. This resulted in the following books: Ira Reid, *In a Minor Key: Negro Youth in Story and Fact* (1940); Charles Johnson, *Growing Up in the Black Belt: Negro Youth in the Rural South* (Johnson et al. 1941); E. Franklin Frazier, *Negro Youth at the Crossways: Their Personality Development in the Middle States* (1940); and Allison Davis, *Children of Bondage: The Personality of Negro Youth in the Urban South* (1940). As these titles suggest, this was a mapping of the psychological development of Black youth in every social environment, presenting empirical findings on what Kardiner (1951) later called the "mark of oppression" (Kardiner and Ovesey 1962):

> These studies looked at the socialization experiences and environmental contexts which influenced the youths' personality development. They stressed self-hatred, relative to being a Black person—especially one of lower socioeconomic status. The concepts of class and color/race were essential to interpretations of the data.
>
> (Slaughter and Alkalimat 1985, 11)

Two works of literature in particular connect here, reflecting the transdisciplinarity of Black Studies as Intellectual History: the 1896 poem "We Wear the Mask" by Paul Lawrence Dunbar (Dunbar 1922) and the 1940 novel *Native Son* by Richard Wright (R. Wright 1940). Dunbar's "We Wear the Mask" and Bigger Thomas, the protagonist of Wright's novel, cut to the bone with regard to the psychology of Black American life. Scholars widely shared and discussed literature and academic research across these early decades of productivity.

Guthrie authored the major critical study of Black scholars in psychology, *Even the Rat Was White* (2003). Other notable studies include Wispé et al. (1969), Jones (1972, 1999). J.L. White (1984), Slaughter and Alkalimat (1985), Belgrave and Allison (2006), and Boykin et al. (1979).

ECONOMICS

Abram Harris (PhD, Columbia, 1930) blazed the trail for African-American scholars in economics (A.L. Harris 1968; Spero and Harris 1968; A.L. Harris and Darity 1989; Holloway 2002). He was part of the radical core of the Howard University faculty in the 1930s. Greatly influenced by Marxism, he wrote two books that set the foundation for a class analysis of the Black community. The first, the classic text *The Black Worker: The Negro and the Labor Movement* (1968 [1931]), he coauthored with Sterling Spero. Herbert Gutman made the following comments in his preface to the 1968 edition:

> Four general "factors" shaped their study: the interplay between the slave heritage, the structure and policies of craft unions, the recent migration of

> Negroes from the South, and the influence of the Negro middle class and its ideology within the northern ghetto. Their indictment of most trade unions (a few, such as the United Mine Workers of America and the immigrant garment unions, escaped censure) was severe, as was their scorn for the dominant Negro leadership, but what most concerned Spero and Harris was the particular ways in which the Negro lost his place as "an industrial labor reserve" to become "a regular element in the labor force of every basic industry."
>
> (Spero and Harris 1968, viii–ix)

Harris went on to do a study of banking in the African-American community, *The Negro as Capitalist* (A.L. Harris 1968 [1938]), in which he argued that Black capitalism was not a viable approach to solving the economic problems facing Black people. He eventually began to change his views and in 1945 was recruited by the economist Frank Knight to join the faculty at the University of Chicago. At the end of his career, he had completely moved away from his original radical position and studying the economic problems of Black people and was teaching a graduate seminar on John Stewart Mill in the Departments of Economics and Philosophy.

A good example of a scholar who worked outside of an academic department is the economist Robert Weaver (PhD, Harvard, 1934) (Weaver 1967, 1969; A.R. Williams 1978). While a graduate student at Harvard, he connected with law student John P. Davis and they began radical organizing as advocates of policy change to improve conditions for the Black community. This led to an important 1935 conference at Howard University and the founding of the National Negro Congress. Weaver wrote two important books: *Negro Labor: A National Problem* (1946) and *The Negro Ghetto* (1948). His policy orientation led him to be appointed to the informal "Black Cabinet" of advisors to President Franklin D. Roosevelt in 1934 and then to him becoming the first African American to hold a cabinet position as head of the new Department of Housing and Urban Development in 1966.

The most honored Black economist to date is W. Arthur Lewis (PhD, London, 1940), who was awarded the Nobel Prize in Economics in 1979 (W. Arthur Lewis and Gersovitz 1983; W. Arthur Lewis 2013). Lewis was born in Saint Lucia and trained at the London School of Economics. After serving in appointed posts in Ghana and Barbados, he took a position in the Department of Economics at Princeton, where he worked for two decades. He received the Nobel Prize for starting the field of development economics, which concerned what we now call the Global South. His work started with a paper published while he was on the faculty at the University of Manchester, "Economic Development with Unlimited Supplies of Labour" (1954). In this paper, he charted a path for capitalist development by positing a dual labor market in developing countries: a subsistence sector and a capitalist sector.

Three Black women stand out in the early phase of Black scholarship in economics. Male supremacy and racism prevented Sadie Tanner Mossell Alexander (PhD, Pennsylvania, 1921), mentioned above as earning the first doctorate by a Black person in the field, from working in her field. But she went on to law school and to work on policy positions (Epperson 1998; Benjamin 2010). Mabel Smythe (PhD, Wisconsin, 1942) worked as an academic, but her main activity was in international diplomacy, first as the wife of an ambassador to Syria and then as ambassador in her own right to Cameroon and Equatorial Guinea, simultaneously, appointed by President Jimmy Carter. She authored a number of publications, working with her husband Hugh Smythe and Langston Hughes, among others (Smythe, Davis, and Phelps-Stokes Fund 1976; Hughes et al. 1956).

Phyllis Ann Wallace (PhD, Yale, 1948) achieved an unprecedented level of success for a Black woman economist of her era, moving through HBCU appointments and eventually into an MIT professorship from 1972 to 1993. It turned out that her mainstream academic credentials were augmented by the fact that she had worked for the CIA for eight years prior to that appointment (P.A. Wallace, Datcher, and Malveaux 1982).

Key sources on the development of Black scholarship in the field of economics include Boston (1997, 2005, 2018), Quartey (2003), and Price and Allen (2014).

LITERATURE

Among the early contributions from scholars of literature were a series of anthologies that helped to make and keep Black literary production—novels, short stories, plays, poetry, and so on—visible and available. Detailed in Table 3, these anthologies create a trend line for a canon of Black literature that forms the main focus of critical analysis in Black literary theory: (J.W. Johnson 1931; Calverton 1929; Cunard and Ford 1970; Brawley 1970; S.C. Watkins 1944; S.A. Brown, Davis, and Lee 1941; *Anthology of Negro Poets in the U.S.A.: 200 Years.* 2006).

Given the quantity and wide dispersion of Black literary production, these anthologies played a critical role in defining Black literature. Of course, the bias of the editors and the self-interests of the publishers with whom they worked must be taken into account. But most of these editors also served as academics at the leading HBCU institutions and taught courses, as well as mentoring creative writers and literary scholars, while shaping the taste of Black readers in their courses and general public role in the community. They also exemplify the sustained dialogue between scholars and authors, who cannot all be included here. The development of this field demonstrates that Black Studies could only proceed in dialogue with practitioners who were relying on their current experiences; in this particular case, these were the most influential Black writers of the time.

Table 3 African-American Literary Anthologies

Year	*Editor/s*	*Title*
1922	James Weldon Johnson	*The Book of American Negro Poetry*
1929	V.F. Calverton	*Anthology of American Negro Literature*
1934	Nancy Cunard	*Negro Anthology*
1935	Benjamin Brawley	*Early Negro American Writers*
1941	Sterling Brown, Arthur P. Davis, Ulysses Lee	*The Negro Caravan*
1944	Sylvestre Watkins	*Anthology of Negro Literature*
1955	Arna Bontemps	*Anthology of Negro Poets in the USA: 200 Years*

The first major scholar to impact the academic study of Black literature was Benjamin Brawley (MA, Harvard, 1908) (Brawley 1939, 1967, 1968, 1971; Brawley et al. 1998). He was the first dean at Morehouse College before moving to Howard University to head its English Department until 1939. His works include the following: *A Short History of the American Negro* (1913), *The Negro in Literature and Art* (1918), *Paul Laurence Dunbar, Poet of His People* (1936), *Negro Builders and Heroes* (1937), and the anthology mentioned in Table 3.

Sterling Brown (MA, Harvard, 1923) was one of many scholars who began by achieving academic success at Dunbar High School in Washington, DC and then went off to the Ivy League, in his case Williams College (S.A. Brown 1969; S.A. Brown and Harper 1980; S.A. Brown and Sanders 1996; S.A. Brown, Davis, and Lee 1941). Serving on the Howard faculty from 1929 to 1969, his teaching and his accomplishments as a poet formed the core of his academic work. In his teaching, he emphasized the importance of folklore and music. His two most important critical works are *The Negro in American Fiction* (1937) and *Negro Poetry and Drama: and the Negro in American Fiction* (1937). His entire literary work has been collected in two volumes: *The Collected Poems of Sterling A. Brown* (Brown and Harper 1980) and *A Son's Return: Selected Essays of Sterling A. Brown* (Brown and Sanders 1996). Brown became a mentor to many in the arts, where he helped sustain links to the Black folk culture of language, the blues, and storytelling (Tidwell 2013; Tidwell and Tracy 2009).

J. Saunders Redding (MA, Brown, 1932) taught at Black institutions from 1928 to 1955, beginning at Morehouse College and ultimately for twelve years at Hampton Institute (J. Saunders Redding 1969; J. Saunders Redding and

Berry 1992; Jay Saunders Redding 1958; J.P. Reid 1990). His last position was at Cornell as the Ernest I. White Professor Emeritus of American Studies and Humane Letters (1970–1975). His major works include the following: *To Make a Poet Black* (1939); his autobiography, *No Day of Triumph* (1942); *Stranger and Alone* (1950); *They Came in Chains* (1950); *An American in India* (1954); and *Cavalcade*, an anthology of African-American literature he edited in collaboration with A.P. Davis (A.P. Davis, Redding, and Joyce 1992 [1970]).

Hugh Gloster (PhD, New York University, 1943) was one of the early critics of Black literature, with his major work *Negro Voices in American Fiction* having been in print since 1948 (Gloster 1965). Morehouse's seventh president and the first graduate to lead the school, he served from 1967 to 1986. He was a founding member of the College Language Association (CLA) in 1937, the Black organization that stands alongside the Modern Language Association.

If there is one literary figure who rose to the same heights as the social scientist Du Bois, it would be Langston Hughes (Hughes et al. 2001; Hughes and Johnson 2003; Hughes, Miller, and Rampersad 2002; Hughes and Rampersad 2002; DeCarava and Hughes 1991). He wrote in every creative genre, was one of the first to link the performance of poetry to jazz and blues music, and put wonderful prose together with the photographic images of Roy DeCarava in the work *The Sweet Flypaper of Life* (DeCarava and Hughes 1991 [1955]). Hughes led the way in setting the ideological direction of his generation of writers with his essay "The Negro Artist and the Racial Mountain" (1926):

> We younger Negro artists who create now intend to express our individual dark skinned selves without fear or shame. If white people are pleased, we are glad. If they are not, it doesn't matter. We know we are beautiful, and ugly too. The tom-tom cries and the tom-tom laughs. If colored people are pleased, we are glad. If they are not, their displeasure doesn't matter either. We build our temples for tomorrow, strong as we know how, and we stand on top of the mountain, free within ourselves.
>
> (Gates Jr. and McKay 1996, 1314)

The literary debates leading into the 1960s were rooted in the debates that linked three great figures, Richard Wright, Ralph Ellison, and James Baldwin (R. Wright, Wright, and Fabre 1997; Graham 1986; Rowley 2008; J.W. Ward and Butler 2008; Ellison 1964, 2015 [1952]; Ellison and Callahan 1995; Baldwin 1962, 1964, 1995a, 1995b, 1998, 2014; Rampersad 2008). Each achieved the highest status as a Black writer, nationally and internationally.

Richard Wright emerged out of the Depression years focusing on the experiences of Black people facing the terror of racism in Mississippi and Chicago. He affiliated with the Communist movement and was accepted into their network of socially conscious writers, the John Reed Club and *New Masses*. His reputation spread internationally, thanks to support from the USSR and other socialist countries. He earned this support for his writings about the social reality of the Black masses, including his collection of short stories *Uncle Tom's Children* (1938), and his novels of the Mississippi-Chicago experience, *Native Son* (1940) and *Black Boy* (1945). Especially important was his collaboration with two Farm Security Administration photographers to produce the image-rich volume *12 Million Black Voices: A Folk History of the Negro in the United States* (1941), which included a deep look into the Black ghetto of Chicago after the post-World War II Black migration. Testifying to Wright's impact as a writer, The Book of the Month Club selected his novel *Native Son*, making Wright the first African American author to be so honored. He penned the influential manifesto "Blueprint for Negro Writing" (1937):

> Today the question is: Shall Negro writing be for the Negro masses, moulding the lives and consciousness of those masses toward new goals, or shall it continue begging the question of the Negroes' humanity. ... They must accept the concept of nationalism because in order to transcend it, they must possess and understand it... Many young writers have grown to believe that a Marxist analysis of society presents such a picture... Yet for the Negro writer, Marxism is but the starting point. No theory of life can take the place of life. After Marxism has laid bare the skeleton of society, there remains the task of the writer to plant flesh upon those bones out of his will to live... It means that a Negro writer must create in his readers' minds a relationship between a Negro woman hoeing cotton in the South and the men who loll in swivel chairs in Wall Street and take the fruits of her toil.
>
> (cited in Gates Jr. and McKay 1996, 1403–10)

Almost in response to Wright came the ascendancy of Ralph Ellison and James Baldwin. Ellison wrote the iconic novel *Invisible Man* (1952) and made such an impact that he entered the mainstream canon:

> *Invisible Man* won the U.S. National Book Award for Fiction in 1953. In 1998, the Modern Library ranked *Invisible Man* nineteenth on its list of the 100 best English-language novels of the 20th century. *Time* magazine included the novel in its TIME 100 Best English-language Novels from 1923 to 2005.
>
> ("*Invisible Man*" 2018)

Ellison's essays in the collection *Shadow and Act* (1964) are important, especially his review of Gunnar Myrdal's *An American Dilemma* (1944). *Dilemma*, authored by Myrdal, a Swedish social scientist, was the dominant analysis of the African-American experience for the mainstream during the post-war period. Myrdal advocated that Black people would best be served by submitting to Eurocentric cultural norms: "It is to the advantage of American Negroes as individuals and as a group to become assimilated into American culture, to acquire the traits held in esteem by the dominant white Americans" (Ellison 1964, 316). Ellison wrote his review of Myrdal's book in 1944, but it was rejected by *Partisan Review* (then funded by the CIA) and not published until twenty years later (Saunders 2013, 162, 335–43). Ellison presents a Black Studies critique of the mainstream reliance on the lens of social pathology to analyze African American culture:

> Much of Negro culture might be negative, but there is also much of great value and richness, which, because it has been secreted by living and has made their lives more meaningful, Negroes will not willingly disregard.
>
> What is needed in our country is not an exchange of pathologies, but a change of the basis of society. This is a job which both Negroes and whites must perform together. In Negro culture there is much of value for America as a whole. What is needed are Negroes to take it and create of it "the uncreated consciousness of their race." In doing so they will do far more; they will help create a more human American.
>
> (Ellison 1964, 316–17)

Here Ellison is calling for the Black Studies revolution in consciousness that was to come twenty-two years later, after Black Power emerged as a political war cry in 1966.

James Baldwin was sponsored by Wright, who helped him gain access to publishers, only to turn on Wright later when the US State Department awarded Baldwin a contract. At the same time, Baldwin's essays of protest were required reading for the young Black intellectuals of the late 1950s and early 1960s: *Notes of a Native Son*, *Nobody Knows My Name: More Notes of a Native Son*, and *The Fire Next Time* (J. Baldwin 2014 [1955], 1964 [1961]; J.E. Baldwin et al. 2017 [1963]). Baldwin was also a major interpreter of the Black gay experience. He strongly supported the Civil Rights Movement, along with maintaining conversations with Malcolm X (King Jr. et al. 1985). Unlike Wright and Ellison, Baldwin lived to teach in formal Black Studies programs, first at Bowling Green State University and then in the Five College Network of Amherst, Smith, Mount Holyoke, Hampshire, and the University of Massachusetts.

EDUCATION

Education has long been at the heart of the African-American impulse for survival. V.P. Franklin wrote about how this unfolded in the slavery period, which he characterized as formative:

> [This book] utilizes the testimony and narratives of enslaved and free Afro-Americans from the end of the eighteenth century to the beginning of the twentieth, as well as Afro-American folk songs, beliefs, and religious practices, in an attempt to provide a viable explanation of the meaning and significance of self-determination, freedom, resistance, and education in the lives and experiences of the masses of Afro-Americans in this society.
>
> (V.P. Franklin 1992, 4)

Out of the battle to end slavery, those values fused into a political program centered on education. As W.E.B. Du Bois wrote in *Black Reconstruction in America*:

> It was only the other part of the laboring class, the Black folk, who connected knowledge with power; who believed that education was the stepping-stone to wealth and respect, and that wealth, without education, was crippled. Perhaps the very fact that so many of them had seen the wealthy slave-holders at close range, and knew the extent of ignorance and inefficiency among them, led to that extraordinary mass demand on the part of the Black laboring class for education. And it was this demand that was the effective force for the establishment of the public school in the South on a permanent basis, for all people and all classes.
>
> (Du Bois 2007 [1935], 641)

Thus, education is a core value of the Black self-determination ethos that spans African-American history from slavery to freedom. And, in turn, the journey of Black people in education has fueled the Black liberation struggle, from basic literacy to advanced degrees.

Charles Thompson (PhD, Chicago, 1925) was the first Black PhD in the field of education (C.H. Thompson 1928, 1946, 1948, 1959, 1961). He taught at Howard University for forty years. In 1932, Thompson founded the *Journal of Negro Education* and was its editor-in-chief for over thirty years. This is the most important repository for scholarship on the educational experiences of African Americans.

Horace Mann Bond (PhD, Chicago, 1936) achieved his stature as a great educator as both scholar and administrator (H.M. Bond 1966, 1969, 1972, 1976; Urban 1992). He was president of Fort Valley State University (1930–1945) and Lincoln University (1945–1957) before becoming dean of the College of Education at Atlanta University. He wrote several important works on education: *The Education of the Negro in the American Social Order* (1934), *Negro Education in Alabama: A Study in Cotton and Steel* (1939), *Black American Scholars: A Study of Their Beginnings* (1972), and *Education for Freedom: A History of Lincoln University* (1976). In addition, Bond had close ties to Africa. Two of his former

African students at Lincoln became heads of state: Kwame Nkrumah (Ghana) and Nnamdi Azikiwe (Nigeria). Bond helped to establish the American Society for African Culture in 1956.

Important studies of the educational experiences of the African-American people include Woodson (1968), Bullock (1967), V.P. Franklin and Anderson (1978), W.H. Watkins (2001), V.P. Franklin and Savage (2004), and Lomotey (2010).

ANTHROPOLOGY

Even though anthropology has been closely associated with colonialism and the development of state policies of social control over national minorities (often demeaned by the concept of "tribe"), major scholars have resisted the dominant narrative since the beginning of professional study. German immigrant Franz Boas pioneered the field as a professor at Columbia and was a great influence on his graduate students (M. Harris 2001, 250–89). Also working with him was a Barnard undergraduate named Zora Neale Hurston (BA, 1928). She did not choose to become an academic scholar but, after just two years of graduate study, she produced scholarship on the folklore of Black people in the southern USA that continues to shape the field ("Zora Neale Hurston" n.d.).

Following Columbia University under the influence of Boas, the Department of Anthropology at the University of Chicago became the most important training ground. Key scholars who trained there as PhD students include Mark Hanna Watkins (1933), Allison Davis (1942), and St. Clair Drake (1953) (M.H. Watkins 1973). Katherine Dunham was also a Chicago graduate student in the 1930s, and though she was offered a graduate fellowship to finish her studies, she chose to become a professional dancer. In fact, the Dunham Dancers was where she continued her studies and teaching. There, Dunham used her field research in the African Diaspora, especially Haiti, as the basis for her innovative technique, now recognized as the Dunham Technique of Modern Dance (Dunham 1983, 2012; Chin 2014):

> A performance of the Dunham Technique involves the merging of polyrhythmic dance styles in continual motion. Katherine Dunham was the first to combine the individualistic dance movements of Caribbean and African cultures with European-style ballet. She further fused anthropological research into the realm of dance artistry by uniquely including social and cultural rituals into public performances.
>
> ("Katherine Dunham: Dance Technique" n.d.)

Allison Davis was educated on the elite track, graduating as valedictorian of his class at Dunbar High School in Washington, DC, like his father before him.

After graduating on a full scholarship from the Ivy League Williams College, he went on to Harvard to get his PhD in anthropology. When he joined the University of Chicago faculty in 1942, he was the first African American to hold such a post at a major mainstream university. His major work, focused on the social experience of the racist political culture of the US South, resulted in the publications *Children of Bondage: The Personality Development of Negro Youth in the Urban South* (1940) and *Deep South: A Social Anthropological Study of Caste and Class* (1941). He produced one of the earliest social critiques of how IQ tests were being used to falsely argue the mental inferiority of African Americans, *Social-Class Influences upon Learning* (1948); he based this book on the Inglis Lecture he had given at Harvard University (A. Davis 1948, 1983; A. Davis et al. 1940, 1941).

St. Clair Drake had quite a different background from Davis, although Davis became one of his mentors. His father had emigrated from Barbados and become an official in Garvey's Universal Negro Improvement Association (UNIA). After graduating from the Hampton Institute, Drake enrolled at the University of Chicago, getting his PhD based on field research he did in Cardiff, Wales. From then on, he focused on the experiences of the African Diaspora. Along with Horace Cayton, he authored one of the urban sociology classics, a study of Chicago, *Black Metropolis: A Study of Life in a Northern City* (1945). Drake had been involved with the Pan-African movement since his fieldwork days in Wales, when he had met Kwame Nkrumah. Nkrumah asked Drake to come to Ghana after he became president in 1957. Drake answered the call and founded the Department of Sociology at the University of Ghana, serving as its head from 1958 to 1961 (Drake 1959, 1965, 1975, 1987; Drake and Cayton 1945).

Arthur Huff Fauset earned his PhD in Anthropology from the University of Pennsylvania in 1942. His main focus was on religious beliefs and practices in the African Diaspora. His major work is his published dissertation, a survey of urban Black religious organizational forms titled *Black Gods of the Metropolis* (1944) (Fauset 1981, 2002).

Important studies about Black scholars in anthropology include Drake (1978, 1980), Cole (1999), L.D. Baker (1998), F.V. Harrison, Association of Black Anthropologists, and American Anthropological Association (1991), and McClaurin (2001).

POLITICAL SCIENCE

Political science scholars have close connections to the legal profession and in some ways journalism. Ralph Bunche (PhD, Harvard, 1934) was the first Black person to earn a doctorate in political science (Henry 2004; Bunche and Henry 1995). Like many Black scholars, he had one foot in the academic world and one in the community, as a political agent at the local, national, and international levels. One of the radical core members of the social science faculty at Howard University in the 1930s, he argued, from his Marxist viewpoint, the centrality of class struggle as the only strategic path for Black liberation. Bunche served as a staff writer for the Myrdal *American Dilemma* project. Later, he moved to a position at the United Nations, receiving the Nobel Peace Prize in 1950 for his work on the Middle East.

John P. Davis and Henry Lee Moon, a lawyer and journalist, respectively, contributed to the development of Black Studies through organizational work as well as publications. Davis (LLB, Harvard, 1933) as a graduate student joined with others in the process that led to the National Negro Congress in 1935. This new organization grew out of a conference at Howard University; Davis subsequently served as executive secretary of the congress from 1935 to 1942. He was close to Bunche, E. Franklin Frazier, Robert Weaver, and fellow lawyer William Hastie, the first African-American federal judge. One of Davis's major contributions to scholarship on the African-American experience is his edited volume *The American Negro Reference Book* (J.P. Davis 1966). A journalist and staff member of the NAACP, Henry Lee Moon wrote an important early study called *Balance of Power: The Negro Vote* (1948). Of course, the history of Black newspapers is replete with journalists who served the Black community by creating its most sustained source of public intellectual commentary.

Special mention needs to be made of the Howard University Law School. As at other schools, Howard's moot court functioned as an extracurricular training ground for arguing cases. As dean of the law school, Charles Houston (SJD, Harvard, 1923) turned Howard's moot court into a training ground to fight Jim Crow laws. His successes earned him the title as "The Man who Killed Jim Crow" (Houston and Conyers 2012). Thurgood Marshall, one of Houston's outstanding students, took his training to the Supreme Court to argue and win the famous 1954 *Brown* v. *Board of Education* case against school segregation. The political scientists sought to understand the legal system and the lawyers fought to change it (J. Williams 2011; McNeil 1983).

Major research on Black participation in political science includes McWorter (1967), Preston, Henderson, and Puryear (1982), Walters (1988), A.D. Gordon and Collier-Thomas (1997), Pohlmann (2003), Rich (2007), United States Congress et al. (2008), and R.C. Smith, Johnson, and Newby (2014).

MUSIC

Early scholarship on the roots of Black musical traditions came from John Work and James Weldon Johnson (J.W. Work 1969; Richardson 1980). Work, followed by his son, did his scholarship as professor of Latin and history at Fisk University, including his *Folk Song of the American Negro* (1915). James

Weldon Johnson published *The Book of American Negro Spirituals* (Johnson, Johnson, and Brown 1925) while he was the first Black executive secretary of the NAACP (1920–1930). After this, he served on the faculties of Fisk University and New York University. With his brother, John Rosamond Johnson, he wrote the famous song called the "Negro National Anthem" that begins "Lift every voice and sing" (1899). As with literature, the field of music proceeded both inside and outside mainstream institutions.

There have been at least four organic community-based schools of Black music that have sustained these musical traditions: the church, especially its choir; the big band; the small combo; and the singing groups linked into the recording businesses. These schools have been so prominent and influential that they must be considered alongside the mainstream academic music departments and conservatories.

First has been the church with its use of the choir as a school of music. The early example of how the Black church and choir connected with music scholarship was the Jubilee singers of Fisk University. While they started from a European repertoire, they eventually became a sensation—including in Europe—when they took the sacred songs then sung in church and community into the concert halls. This process unfolded through dialogue between faculty and students, as until then the songs did not "belong" there. Another important example of the church and choir as school is the rise of the modern gospel movement out of musical director Thomas Dorsey and his choir at Pilgrim Baptist Church in Chicago from 1932 until the late 1970s (M.W. Harris 1994). One of his main soloists was Mahalia Jackson, for whom he wrote the famous song "Take My Hand, Precious Lord" in 1932.

In the realm of jazz, there have been two kinds of performance-group-based schools, the big bands and the small groups. The big bands have included, most notably, Fletcher Henderson, Count Basie, and Duke Ellington (Magee 2005; Basie, Murray, and Morgenstern 2016; Dance 2000; Ellington 1990). Ellington had a working band from 1923 to 1974, over fifty years. He wrote more than one thousand songs, many with his collaborator Billy Strayhorn. Strayhorn's "Take the A Train" (1939) was the band's signature piece, a testament to people riding the new subway line to and from Harlem, New York's main Black community at that time. Ellington also wrote program music on the history of Black people, notably his three-part suite "Black, Brown and Beige." But Ellington was more than a musician because, from his standing at the commanding heights of the music world, he impacted the status of Black people in the entire society:

> In the era of harsh Jim Crow denigration and violence during the first half of the twentieth century, before the civil rights movement made organized protest a common and relatively safe way for black Americans to register their desire for equality, Ellington subverted and undercut racial stereotypes,

> changing the possibilities for black Americans in the mass media. He did this by carefully cultivating an image of respectability and "genius" in his music, advertisements, shows, and film appearances. Ellington did not fight for civil rights in the manner of political activists, but he contributed much to that cause, most of it unrecognized because it did not fall within traditional forms of racial protest. By focusing on the subject of black history for his heavily promoted inaugural Carnegie Hall appearance and dressing like a classical conductor, Ellington provided a strong counter to the way black Americans were usually portrayed in the mass media. Ellington's beliefs concerning racial equality were molded during his youth in the turn-of-the-century middle-class African American neighborhoods in Washington, D.C., where an emphasis on black identity, pride, and history was imparted to black children in the segregated black school system and in their family lives. According to Ellington and later historians of the period, young blacks in this milieu were taught to command, rather than demand, respect for the race.
>
> (Cohen 2004, 1004)

The smaller jazz combos were often led by one or two masters, who then recruited a new crop of young musicians every few years. These combos provided an internship-like learning experience and launched many careers. One of the best examples is the Jazz Messengers led by Art Blakey (1919–1990) (Gourse 2003; Feather and Gitler 2007). Starting in 1947, Blakey led many iterations of his group, counting more than two hundred alumni ("Jazz Messengers Alumni" n.d.). Among the many whose careers he launched are Art Davis (bass), Benny Golson (tenor saxophone), Bobby Timmons (piano), Branford Marsalis (alto saxophone, baritone saxophone), Clifford Brown (trumpet), Curtis Fuller (trombone), Donald Byrd (trumpet), Lee Morgan (trumpet), Lou Donaldson (alto saxophone), Paul Chambers (bass), Reggie Workman (bass), Sonny Rollins (tenor saxophone), Sonny Stitt (alto saxophone, tenor saxophone), Thelonious Monk (piano), Tony Williams (drums), Wynton Marsalis (trumpet), and Yusef Lateef (flute, oboe, tenor saxophone, cowbell, thumb piano).

A fourth type of school formed as singing shifted from a universal form of recreation to a more specialized form of cultural production. People used to sing with family and friends at home, sometimes a cappella, sometimes with instruments, and sometimes along with records or the radio. In the 1950s, this took to the street with the young people's creation of the doo-wop singing groups, which transformed the genre of Black urban popular music coming out of rhythm and blues. The doo-wop tradition was big in all urban centers (Pruter 2008). People would first imitate the big performers of the day and learn the tunes everyone wanted to hear, but then find their own voice and go for making a hit. It rivaled sports like boxing as a path out of poverty into the "big bucks." Record labels such as Chess Records in Chicago or Motown in Detroit became schools for young artists like the Jackson Five when they were starting out (Callahan and Edwards n.d.; Gordy 2013; Morse 1972).

Historical accounts of scholarship covering the musical aspects of African-American culture include Southern (1972, 1982, 1983), de Lerma (1973, 1981–1984), de Lerma and Reisser (1989), Sheldon Harris (1979), Floyd (1995, 1999), and Feather and Gitler (2007).

LANGUAGE

This and the remaining disciplines discussed in this chapter do not have easily identifiable "first doctoral graduates" such as those in Table 2. Nonetheless, they are each central to Black intellectual and cultural production in the post-Civil War, pre-1960 period.

One obvious difference that has placed the majority of Black people outside the US English-speaking mainstream is how Black people have talked. Mainstream intelligentsia used language as evidence that Black people were incapable of speaking correctly. Black scholars swept aside this racist claim by linking Black language behavior to African retentions and hip cultural developments with an improvisational style.

Mark Hanna Watkins (PhD, Chicago, 1933) launched the academic study of African languages in American linguistics after being a student of Edwin Sapir at the University of Chicago (M.H. Watkins 1973, 1943, 1956). While at Fisk University in 1943, he helped organize the first academic program in African Studies. He then moved on to Howard University and taught in its Departments of Anthropology and African Studies. Lorenzo Turner (PhD, Chicago, 1926) began his career as a scholar in English literature (Dunbar 2014). His career spanned tenures at Howard University (1917–1928, with the last eight years as head of the Department of English), Fisk (1929–1946 as head of the Department of English), and finally at Roosevelt University (1946–1967), where he worked alongside St. Clair Drake. His great work was linking African languages with African-American speech, as exemplified by his classic study *Africanisms in the Gullah Dialect* (1949).

Outside the academy but in dialogue with it, Paul Laurence Dunbar broke the taboo and put Black rural dialect in his creative work. He thus demonstrated that this dialect had the capacity to express ideas and feelings that captured the human experience as richly as any. Some notable examples are his poems in *Lyrics of Lowly Life* (1896) (Dunbar 2014). Unfortunately for Dunbar, he also held very backward views regarding Africa and how Black people needed to meet mainstream standards in order to become middle-class members of US society. In contrast, books about "hip" speech wholeheartedly affirmed the value of generational dialects. Cab Calloway, bandleader and singer with a great talent for inventing language, produced a *Hepster's Dictionary* (1944). Dan Burley was a big-city hipster who assembled a ground-breaking dictionary of the dialect of the bebop hipsters, *Dan Burley's Original Handbook of Harlem Jive* (1944). Calloway and Burley took the oppositional view that the wise ghetto artists were superior to the "squares" of the mainstream from whom they differentiated themselves (Calloway 1944; Burley 1944).

The study of Black language behavior has been summed up in Dillard (1972, 1975), Smitherman (1977, 2000), Rickford and Rickford (2000), and Wade-Lewis (1988, 2005, 2007).

VISUAL ARTS

Artists by and large do not earn doctoral degrees, but they still appear on the faculty of colleges or universities and this was already true in the early period. The work of artists of this era also illustrated and complemented the written words of scholars and writers. The main scholar-artists-in-residence at the historically Black colleges and universities were Hale Woodruff at Atlanta University (1931–1946), James Porter at Howard University (1930–1970), and Aaron Douglas at Fisk University (1939–1966) (J.A. Porter 1937, 1942, 1969; J.A. Porter, Featherstone, and Uzelac 1992; D.B. Porter 1959; Kirschke 1999; Woodruff and Blackburn n.d.; Woodruff and Studio Museum in Harlem 1979). Woodruff established relationships with master painters of the twentieth century, including Henry Ossawa Tanner, Pablo Picasso, and Diego Rivera. After working during the summer of 1937 with Rivera, the master Mexican muralist, Woodruff began his best-known work. This was the three *Amistad Murals* (1938), after which he created three more, all at Talladega College. One of his main projects, apart from his painting, was establishing an annual national exhibition of Black artists at Atlanta University. This created a national transgenerational community of working artists.

Aaron Douglas (1899–1979, MA, Columbia) was one of the main painters of the Harlem Renaissance. His major murals were done in the library at Fisk University and the Cullen branch of the New York Public Library. He illustrated publications by W.E.B. Du Bois, Countee Cullen, Langston Hughes, and James Weldon Johnson, and founded the Art Department at Fisk University.

James Porter (MA, New York University) worked at Howard University from 1930 to 1970. His *Modern Negro Art* (1941) was the first comprehensive study of African-American art published in the US. His biography at the Howard Art Department website states:

> A pioneer in establishing the field of African American art history, James A. Porter was instrumental as the first scholar to provide a systematic, critical analysis of African American artists and their works of art. An artist himself,

> he provided a unique and critical approach to the analysis of the work. Dedicated to educating and writing about African American artists, Porter set the foundation for artists and art historians to probe and unearth the necessary skills essential to their artistic and scholarly endeavors. The canon is borne from Porter's determination to document and view African American art in the context of American art.
>
> ("James Porter's Biography" 2013)

Margaret Burroughs (MA, Chicago Art Institute) achieved prominence both as a poet and as a painter/printmaker (Burroughs 2003). Chicago was her lifelong base; this will be elaborated upon elsewhere in this book. On a broader scale, at Atlanta University's Eighteenth Annual Art Exhibition in 1959, Burroughs led the organizing efforts to form a national organization, the National Conference of Artists. This has remained the pre-eminent annual forum for scholarship on the culture and production of Black art.

The visual arts output of African Americans has been covered in numerous scholarly works, including Dover (1960), S.S. Lewis and Waddy (1969), Cederholm (1973), Gaither (1975), Driskell and Simon (1976), Dallas Museum of Art (1989), Bearden and Henderson (1993), Willis (2000), and S.S. Lewis (2003). Most of these works deal with painting and sculpture, but Willis brings a unique voice on the role of Black photographic arts.

THEATER

As with visual arts, early Black leaders in the theater did not earn PhDs, but they were active on and off campus. Any discussion of Black people in theater needs to begin with Ira Aldridge (1807–1867) (Lindfors 2011; Marshall and Stock 1993). A Black actor who mastered the plays of Shakespeare, Aldridge thus disproved the racist belief that Black people could not grasp, let alone perform, works of so-called "high" culture. He is one of thirty-three people honored with a bronze plaque for their achievements at the Shakespeare Memorial Theater at Stratford-upon-Avon in England. He was a member of the African Company, the first resident African theater company in the USA. That company also built the Grove Theater in New York in 1821 (McAllister 1997). Howard's theater is named after Aldridge.

Owen Dodson (1914–1983; MFA, Yale, 1939) was a teacher and a practicing artist (O. Dodson 1970, 1980; Van Der Zee, Dodson, and Billops 1978). He taught at Howard University, where he was chair of the Drama Department from 1947 to 1970. He wrote six plays, two novels, and two books of poetry. One of his notable works is *The Harlem Book of the Dead* (1978), a collaboration with photographer James Van Der Zee and artist Camille Billops. His students included Amiri Baraka, Earle Hyman, Roxie Roker, Debbie Allen, and Ossie Davis, among others.

James Theodore Ward (1902–1983) migrated to Chicago and became part of the Chicago Renaissance of the 1930s and 1940s (E. Hill and Hatch 2003; T. Ward 2007). Ward composed more than thirty plays and co-founded the Negro Playwrights Company with Langston Hughes, Paul Robeson, and Richard Wright. His work was produced by the Negro Unit of the Federal Theatre Project, part of the Works Progress Administration of the New Deal (Witham 2009). He was part of left-wing cultural production and, after some significant success, he was marginalized and placed on a "watch list" as part of the anti-communist scare activities of Senator Joseph McCarthy. Ward spent his last days teaching Black youth at the South Side Community Art Center in Chicago (Mullen 2015).

Loften Mitchell (1919–2001; MA, Columbia, 1951) was a playwright and theater historian who had one academic appointment at State University of New York, Binghamton, as professor of African-American Studies and theater (1971–1985) (L. Mitchell 1967, 1976). His work began in this pre-1960 period and continued, linked with the Black Arts Movement that is treated more fully in Chapter 6. Among his major contributions are a critical history of Black theater, *Black Drama: The Story of the American Negro in the Theatre* (1967), his editorship of *Voices of the Black Theatre* (1975), and his musical *Bubbling Brown Sugar* (1985).

The history of Black people in the theatrical arts has been summed up in Abramson (1969), E. Hill (1980), A.D. Hill and Barnett (2009), E. Hill and Hatch (2003), H. Young (2013), and H. Young and Zabriskie (2014).

RELIGION

Due to its prominence from early on, the Black church naturally attracted study, with scholars in turn helping to give direction to the church. Howard Thurman (1899–1981; BD, Colgate-Rochester Divinity School, 1925) was a major twentieth-century theologian and religious leader (Thurman 1981, 1996; Thurman and Smith 2006). He wrote twenty-one books and wielded tremendous influence on the religious thinking of the Black community. Thurman served as the first dean of Rankin Chapel at Howard University beginning in 1932, a post he held until 1944, and also on the faculty of the Howard University School of Divinity. Thurman was eventually invited to Boston University in 1958, where he became the first Black dean of Marsh Chapel (1953–1965). He was the first Black person to be named tenured Dean of Chapel at a majority-white university. In addition, he served on the faculty of Boston University's School of Theology.

Benjamin Mays (1894–1984; PhD, Chicago, 1935) studied Black religion as well as being a well-known educator (Mays 1968; Mays and Colston 2002; Mays and Jones 1971; Mays and Nicholson 1969). He served as dean of the School of

Religion at Howard University from 1934 to 1940, and from 1940 to 1967, he served as president of Morehouse College. He published two important works: with Joseph Nicholson he co-authored a study titled *The Negro's Church* (1934), and four years later in 1938 he published *The Negro's God as Reflected in His Literature*. President of Morehouse when Martin Luther King Jr. was a student, for the rest of his life Mays remained King's confidant and advisor.

William Stuart Nelson (1895–1977; BD, Yale, 1924) followed Howard Thurman as dean of the School of Religion at Howard University (W.S. Nelson 1945, 1949; W.S. Nelson, Howard University, and Institute of Religion 1948). He had been the first African-American president at Shaw University (1931), followed by becoming president of Dillard University. While at Howard, he founded the *Journal of Religious Thought*, which remains the major academic journal for studies on the religious experience of African Americans and the African Diaspora. He was an advocate of the strategy of non-violence for social change and put that into practice by marching with Mahatma Gandhi in India and Martin Luther King Jr. in the US South (Warren and Blight 2014).

Substantial narratives or anthologies that sum up the historical experience of Black religious activity and the leading theologians include Wilmore (1972), Wilmore and Cone (1979), Lincoln and Mamiya (1990), and C. West and Glaude (2003).

WOMEN

While women's studies was not yet a discipline in the pre-1960 period, Frances Harper (1825–1911) was an abolitionist educator, writer, and lecturer ("Books by Harper, Frances Ellen Watkins" n.d.). She published six volumes of poetry, several novels, and moving accounts of both slavery and the conditions facing freed people. Most notable were her novel *Iola Leroy* and her work of non-fiction *Sketches of Southern Life* (1872). She founded the National Association of Colored Women in 1896, along with Harriet Tubman, Ida B. Wells, and Mary Church Terrell. Her poem "Learning to Read" (Harper 2018) reflects her love of education:

Very soon the Yankee teachers
Came down and set up school;
But, oh! how the Rebs did hate it,—
It was agin' their rule.

Our masters always tried to hide
Book learning from our eyes;
Knowledge didn't agree with slavery—
'Twould make us all too wise.

But some of us would try to steal
A little from the book.
And put the words together,
And learn by hook or crook.

Anna Julia Cooper (1858–1964) was the fourth African-American woman to earn a doctoral degree (PhD, Paris, 1924) (Anna J. Cooper 2000; Anna Julia Cooper 1925; May 2012). Cooper also studied at Oberlin College and taught briefly at Wilberforce College. She returned to Oberlin for an MA in mathematics in 1887. Her first book, *A Voice from the South: By a Woman from the South*, was published in 1892; for this and other reasons, contemporary scholars often cite her as one of the first Black feminist scholar-activists. Alice Dunbar-Nelson (BA, Dillard University, 1892) followed her (A. Dunbar-Nelson 1988; A.M. Dunbar-Nelson and Hull 1984, 1988). In 1895, Dunbar-Nelson published her first collection of short stories and poems, *Violets and Other Tales*. She married Paul Laurence Dunbar after a courtship of letters that began when Dunbar saw her picture accompanying one of her poems published in 1897.

Ida B. Wells (1862–1931) was an activist who fought against racist violence as well as the patriarchy within the Black community (Wells-Barnett et al. 1995; Wells-Barnett and Royster 2016). Her militancy started during her education at Shaw University (now Rust College) and led to her being expelled. She then attended summer sessions at Fisk University and LeMoyne College. Her most famous writing is a pamphlet titled *Southern Horrors: Lynch Law in All Its Phases* (1892). This was followed by *The Red Record* (1895), a one-hundred-page pamphlet describing lynching in the USA.

Margaret Walker (1915–1998) earned her undergraduate degree from Northwestern (1935) and her MA from the University of Iowa (1942) (M. Walker 1989, 2016; M. Walker and Graham 2002). She won a poetry competition put on by Yale for new poets with her volume *For My People* (1942). The title poem was the signature poem of the Chicago Renaissance of militant Black artists who came of age amid the progressive politics of the 1930s and the New Deal Works Progress Administration (WPA). It ends with these words:

Let a new earth rise. Let another world be born. Let a
bloody peace be written in the sky. Let a second
generation full of courage issue forth; let a people
loving freedom come to growth. Let a beauty full of
healing and a strength of final clenching be the pulsing
in our spirits and our blood. Let the martial songs
be written, let the dirges disappear. Let a race of men now
rise and take control.

(M. Walker 2018)

Scholars have published extensively on the experiences of Black women in recent years, with some of the major works being Bambara (1970), Shockley (1988), R.E. Hill, King, and Arthur and Elizabeth Schlesinger Library on the History of Women in America (1989), J.C. Smith and Phelps (1992), Hine, Brown, and Terborg-Penn (1993) Guy-Sheftall (1992), Hine and Thompson (1998), Page (2007), and Bay et al. (2015).

SUMMARY

The prodigious output of the post-Civil War, pre-1960 Black intellectuals was the start of Black Studies. It was possible in the face of racism, exclusion, and violence, because events and circumstances—the end of slavery, Black people's consequent access to literacy and education, and the Great Migration to the cities—propelled it forward. This survey touching on early exemplars, doctoral graduates, W.E.B. Du Bois, and work across fourteen disciplines demonstrates that Black scholars applied their research interests and cultural creativity to every area of social sciences and the humanities. They studied with leading practitioners. They engaged in policy work. What is more, since only mainstream institutions granted doctoral degrees for the most part, these scholars tended to do their subsequent work at historically Black colleges and universities. Black Studies took shape as self-determination: intellectual production based on self-organization and independent processes of legitimation, without relying on mainstream approval. It took shape as an act of resistance to racism and segregation. It took shape as the only body of work—accessible because it included bibliographic periodicals—that told stories and offered analyses about Black people without recourse to the hegemonic lies. In this way, it was invaluable, as later generations in Black Studies would find.

In line with this activity, the story of Black Studies as Intellectual History continues in the coming chapters. The generations considered in this chapter went on to build institutions of higher education that, through their efforts, ultimately rejected the received wisdom that Black people were not a subject to study in college. This is the story of Chapter 2.

The campus activity in Chapters 1 and 2 was accompanied by community-based and mass-based study and learning, which will be explored in Chapter 3. At that point, it became possible and even necessary to make a break. But before Black Studies as Social Movement, it is necessary to take the next step into the HBCUs and their transformations.

2
The Historically Black Colleges and Universities

This chapter explains how HBCUs were the site of the early battles for Black Studies within higher education. The scholars from Chapter 1 entered these institutions just as they were becoming more Black—for they were founded under white leadership with white staff. That white leadership aimed to educate a Black elite, who would in turn see to and govern the masses of Black people who were just beginning to get a basic education.

The Black scholars arrived with their hard-earned doctorates from elite and rigorous programs. They soon entered into struggle over the curriculum and other aspects of the college or university. In their view, the HBCU curriculum needed to change. It raised up Greek and Latin but overlooked Africa and African America. It was rigorous in the Eurocentric and Christian tradition of early US colleges, but otherwise silent.

The battle for a curriculum and a university that embraced Black people's history and culture had begun. It could only have been so, given the broader activism of the time. What is more, this battle presaged the 1960s struggles for Black Studies that took place across mainstream (white) higher education.

To start with, what are these historically Black colleges and universities? The USA has seen the establishment of more than one hundred colleges and universities that set out to educate African Americans (Bullock 1967). Most were founded in the South after the Civil War. Only four northern HBCUs survive: Cheyney University of Pennsylvania (1837), Lincoln University in Pennsylvania (1854), Wilberforce University (1856), and Central State University (1887). After the Civil War, three main institutions—the Freedmen's Bureau, the American Missionary Association, and various Black churches—established HBCUs. The bureau, founded in 1865 by the US Congress and in operation until 1872, had by the end of 1865 developed a method of schooling for ninety thousand newly freed Black people. By 1872, it had created more than one thousand primary and/or secondary schools and established twenty-five colleges or universities. In many cases, the Freedmen's Bureau and the American Missionary Association worked together, for example, in founding Howard University and Fisk University. Each of these took its name from a leading Civil War general, someone who also helped lead the Freedmen's

Bureau. The United Methodist Church was the first church to found an HBCU, Rust College, in Mississippi in 1866.

Congress kicked off a second wave of HBCU growth thirty years later. The first Morrill Act had passed in 1862. This provided resources, land grants, to found one public university in each state to advance research and development in agriculture and industry. But these institutions were to be segregated. Black people would not benefit from this perverted form of public law. A second Morrill Act in the 1890s set up land-grant institutions for African Americans in each former slave state. Eighteen institutions were the result, including Florida A&M University (1887), North Carolina A&T University (1891), and Tennessee State University (1909).

Among all the HBCUs, three stand out in terms of intellectual production and research on the Black experience: Fisk University, Atlanta University (now Clark-Atlanta University), and Howard University.

James Anderson (1988) makes a distinction between the initial role of the philanthropy of the churches and the later philanthropy of the industrialists. The church founders applied their Abolitionist thinking, harnessing the colleges and universities to the task of emancipation. They were replaced by the industrialists, who backed the Booker T. Washington philosophy of vocational education. This conservative thrust to keep Black people in their relatively lowly place in society profoundly impacted the outlook of HBCU trustees, administrations, and faculty.

This chapter will tell what happened at Fisk, Atlanta, and Howard.

FISK UNIVERSITY (1867)

Fisk University's transformations resulted from the arrival of Black faculty, who had already begun social science and humanities scholarship on Black topics and who were closely attuned to, if not involved in, the antiracism struggles in society and on campus.

John Ogden, Erastus M. Cravath, and Edward P. Smith, who represented the American Missionary Association, and the US Freedmen's Bureau established the Fisk Free Colored School in 1866, which was formally incorporated as Fisk University in 1867. Its first location was in former military barracks of the Union Army in Nashville, Tennessee. John Ogden headed Fisk upon its founding, after resigning from the position of superintendent of education for the Freedmen's Bureau. Fisk University took its name from General Clinton B. Fisk, assistant commissioner of the Freedmen's Bureau for Tennessee, who provided the college's first facility and raised more than thirty thousand dollars to get the school going. All of these people had liberal reasons for helping the ex-slaves become teachers of their people and, by so doing, help create a middle class. The first college students were admitted in 1871, with the entering class of 1873 numbering eight.

From the start, Fisk expressed the contradiction between Eurocentrism and Afrocentrism, meaning deference to the intellectual production of Europe versus affirming the students' own cultural heritage from Africa through the slave experience. Banks reports the following for the first-year curriculum at Fisk:

> *Fall Term* – Latin: Vergil's *Aeneid*, four books. Greek: *Iliad* (Seymour). Mathematics: University Algebra (Wells)
>
> *Winter Term* – Latin: Latin Prose Composition. Greek: *Iliad*, first three books completed; Thucydides, Seventh Book (Smith); Peloponnesian War. Mathematics: Spherical Geometry; Trigonometry (Well)
>
> *Spring Term* – Latin: Cicero's *De Senectute et De Amicitia*. Greek: Thucydides. Mathematics: Surveying, including field work with compass, transit, and Y level (Robbins)
>
> (Banks 1996, 45)

While Fisk adopted this curriculum in order to launch its students into mainstream society as leaders for their people, the university saw an opportunity to generate revenue by actively representing African-American culture, namely, music. As mentioned in Chapter 1, the university launched its Jubilee Singers in order to win national and international recognition and raise needed funds. They set out in 1871 to perform European music, but soon won international fame once they turned to the sorrow songs that came out of the slave experience. Part of an oral tradition, these African-American folk songs did not fit any of the formally recognized song forms of European music. Richardson reports:

> They were beautiful songs, folk songs in the truest sense, songs created by a people giving voice to an emotional life, a life for which America was responsible. These songs were first made available in 1872 when Theodore F. Seward published *Jubilee Songs: As Sung by the Jubilee Singers of Fisk University.*
>
> (Richardson 1980, 29)

Of course, this became a tradition at Fisk and was continued under the leadership of John Work and then his son as described above. So from its earliest days, Fisk University, taken as a whole, contained contrasting cultural paradigms—European and African American.

But the curriculum remained Eurocentric. As a capitalist elite began to replace the abolitionists on Fisk's board, the classical education founded on

Greek and Latin gave way to a more pragmatic curriculum to fit the dynamic economy that they were shaping.

The liberal arts and sciences really took root in the 1920s. Then president Thomas E. Jones consciously undertook to change the composition of the administration, first by hiring two African Americans, historian A.A. Taylor (1893–1955; PhD, Harvard, 1936) as academic dean and Juliette Derricotte (1897–1931; MA, Columbia, 1927) as dean of women. There were many more African-American additions to the faculty:

1. Anthropology: Paul Radin (PhD, Columbia, 1911)
2. Philosophy: Alain Leroy Locke (PhD, Harvard, 1918)
3. Chemistry: St. Elmo Brady (PhD, University of Illinois, 1916)
4. Physics: Elmer S. Hines (PhD, University of Michigan, 1918)
5. Sociology: Charles S. Johnson (PhD, University of Chicago, 1917)
6. English: Lorenzo Turner (PhD, University of Chicago, 1926)
7. Government: Z. Alexander Looby (JD, New York University, 1926)

The proportion of Black faculty was on the rise, increasing to more than 50 percent by 1936, and then to two-thirds by 1945 (Richardson 1980, 114).

A major breakthrough occurred in the Social Science Department, established in 1927 with funds from the Lara Spelman Rockefeller Memorial. After Charles S. Johnson became head, the department's scholars went on to produce a tremendous body of work in a short time:

> In 1935–1936 the Fisk faculty published two books, three songs, and sixteen articles. Four years later thirty-nine books, six songs, and eighty-six articles had been written by Fisk teachers in little over five years. The school was doing research on a larger scale than any other Black college....
>
> A sample of the titles follows: *The Negro in American Civilization, Shadow of the Plantation, The Collapse of Cotton Tenancy: Summary of Field Studies and Statistical Survey, 1933–1935*, and *A Preface to Racial Understanding* by Johnson; *The Negro Family in Chicago* and *The Free Negro Family* by E. Franklin Frazier; *The Education of the Negro in the American Social Order* by Horace Mann Bond; *The Southern Urban Negro as a Consumer* by Paul K. Edwards; *The Etiquette of Race Relations in the South* by Bertram W. Doyle; and a translated *History of Ancient Mexico* by Fanny R. Bandelier.
>
> (Richardson 1980, 137 and 147)

This research won increased support for Fisk. It also impacted public policy. In 1944, the American Missionary Association joined with the university to set up the annual Race Relations Institute. Then, in October 1946, Charles S. Johnson became the first Black president of Fisk. Having led a similar but mainstream institute at Swarthmore College, he was both prepared and powerful enough to do it his way. The mission of the Race Relations Institute was clear:

> The central purpose of the Institute is to advance the all-important science of human relationships by providing knowledge about the complex factors of race and race relations, leading to insight and understanding, intelligent behavior and constructive social action. The incidental, yet perhaps most important value of the Institute is the experience of common fellowship itself.
>
> (Sanders-Cassell 2005, 39)

For the next three decades, every major social scientist and policy maker in the USA, Black or white, attended at least one of the annual institutes. The discussions helped shape elite thinking in both the private and public sectors.

Activist-scholar Johnson presented a clear and consistent message at the national and international levels, and also in the local community. He initiated a People's College to teach literacy and civics to inner-city working-class Black people. It was part of the community program called the Fisk University Social Settlement, which had been launched in 1937:

> The People's College offered courses in business, economics, history, civics, journalism, chorus work, current literature, dramatics, and advanced reading and arithmetic. Handicrafts and workshop classes were given and prenatal and baby clinics held. The settlement was staffed by five full-time and over thirty part-time workers. Part-time employees included a health officer, psychiatrist, psychologist, dentist, and a dietitian.
>
> (Sanders-Cassell 2005, 126)

Other Fisk faculty were also leading figures in Black intellectual history. Arna Bontemps got his masters in library science at the University of Chicago after becoming a well-known writer (Bontemps 1969, 1971, 2003; Bontemps and Conroy 1997). He joined Fisk to head the library from 1943 to 1965, followed by Jessie Carney Smith. She was the first African-American woman to earn a PhD in library science from the University of Illinois (J.C. Smith 1977). Aaron Douglas, a leading painter from the Harlem Renaissance of the 1920s, joined the Fisk faculty to head the Art Department from 1940 to 1966, followed for a decade by David Driskell (Driskell 1985; Driskell and Simon 1976; Kirschke 1999; McGee and Driskell 2006). James Weldon Johnson was hired as an endowed chair in the English Department, the Spence Chair of Creative Literature.

Any Black institution created after the Civil War had to contend with an environment of vitriolic racism and this was certainly true for Fisk. Fisk students faced aggressive racist attacks. In part because of this, student militancy rose alongside the historical progression and intellectual productivity of the larger-than-life scholars. Faculty productivity and student militancy together transformed campus life and intersected with broader social movements for equality. Richardson reports:

> In July 1868 over four hundred members of the Ku Klux Klan hanged a man at Franklin and threatened the Black schoolmaster. Two Fisk students opened a school in Dresden, Tennessee, in July 1869. On the night of September 2 they were taken from their boarding house by armed masked men, forcibly escorted to a nearby woods, and "there severely whipped and under pain of death compelled to discontinue teaching." … Despite numerous difficulties Fisk students continued to advance.
>
> (Richardson 1980, 18)

The Fisk Herald student newspaper was founded in 1883. Du Bois entered Fisk as a sophomore and as a junior became editor. He led the paper in its militancy, writing home that white southerners were "ignorant, prejudiced, repugnant and beyond human redemption" (Lovett 1999, 162). The *Fisk Herald* continued this kind of militant rhetoric, as in an 1891 editorial response to racist mob action indicates:

> "Like unto the savage or the dark and barbarous ages of Europe," the *Herald* stated, "do these blood-thirsty villains roam over the Southern states, bathing the soil with innocent blood … perpetuating deeds upon humanity so heinous … that the very thought of which thrill the soul with horror."
>
> (Richardson 1980, 48)

This student militancy was contained, however, within a campus culture that adhered to the strictest discipline. After visiting Fisk and many other HBCUs, Langston Hughes commented that it was "like going back to mid-Victorian England or Massachusetts in the days of witch-burning Puritans" (Richardson 1980, 88).

The environment would be questioned when a new type of student began to arrive on the Fisk campus in the 1920s. A new politics was in the air, and Black youth were breathing it in. In 1909 the NAACP had formed, following the Niagara Movement (1905–1909) organized by Du Bois and Monroe Trotter. The first Great Migration got underway in 1915. The next year Woodson created the Association for the Study of Negro Life and History in Chicago and Hubert Harrison initiated the New Negro Movement with his Liberty League in New York. Marcus Garvey had formed his Universal Negro Improvement

Association and African Communities League (UNIA) in 1914; it held its first major convention in New York in 1920.

In 1924, the students revolted against campus conditions and began a campaign to force their president Fayette McKenzie to resign. This became a national cause célèbre, backed by Du Bois and the Fisk New York alumni. Du Bois kept in touch with the protest via his daughter Yolanda, then a senior. He campaigned with the students, writing letters, giving speeches, and rallying the alumni. Writing in *The Crisis*, Du Bois concluded:

> Finally and above all at Fisk University today the president and most of the white teachers have no confidence in their students, no respect or hope for the Negro race and are treating them with suspicion and governing them with fear.
>
> (Richardson 1980, 94)

McKenzie had made major contributions to developing Fisk as an academic institution with high standards, but the problems he caused dominated the minds of the students and many of the alumni. He resigned on April 16, 1925, after more than a year of protest.

The Great Depression hit. The challenge of Fisk's tuition fees led to a change in the composition of the student body. More students from the northern Black middle class enrolled. This led to even more student militancy. In 1933, white Tennesseans abducted seventeen-year-old Cordie Cheek just three blocks from the Fisk Chapel, took him back to his rural county, and lynched him. This caused an uproar. Graduate student Ishmael Flory was among those who took action. Originally from California, he had already formed a student group called the Denmark Vesey Forum, named after the leader of an 1822 slave revolt in South Carolina. When President Franklin D. Roosevelt visited Fisk, the students presented him with a petition signed by two hundred-fifty students, urging him to take action. Flory received a warning that he should not lead a planned protest march off campus, so he led the march around the perimeter of the campus. In response, the faculty then voted to expel him. Just as in 1924, this Fisk event became a national scandal (Richardson 1980, 129).

One last indicator of the transformations at Fisk over this period is the inaugural course offerings of Fisk's Program in African Studies, announced in 1943 under the leadership of linguist Mark Hanna Watkins: "The courses and seminars ... include some which have been offered regularly at the University and others which are introduced specially for this project." The courses included:

Introduction to Anthropology
Introduction to African Studies

African Cultures and Institutions
Indigenous African Education
General Linguistics
General Phonetics
The Christian Approach to Africans
The Christian Mission in Africa
Seminar: The New Africa and Its Problems
Survivals of African Culture in America
Research Work in African Linguistics
("Fisk University Program of African Studies" 1943)

The missionary origins of Fisk are visible here alongside social scientific inquiry into Africa as a whole.

The student movement long remained significant at Fisk, and the sit-in movement became a major campaign there as well. It involved key activists such as Diane Nash, a Fisk homecoming queen. Others in Nashville who worked with Fisk students and became leaders in the Student Non-Violent Coordinating Committee (SNCC) were James Bevel, John Lewis, Bernard Lafayette, and Marion Barry.

ATLANTA UNIVERSITY (1867)

This look at Atlanta University focuses on how seasoned scholars of the Black experience came to lead the faculty. At Atlanta, these prominent figures engaged in bold research programs as well as activism and/or public policy debates in the USA and Africa.

Atlanta University is both a school and a center that connects seven historically Black institutions: Atlanta University (founded 1867), Spelman College (1881), Morehouse College (1867), Morehouse Medical School (1975, independent in 1981), Clark University (1869), Morris Brown College (1881), and the Interdenominational Theological Center (1958). As was the case with many HBCUs, white liberals from the North and officials of the Freedman's Bureau established Atlanta University. When Rev. Frederick Ayer, an official of the American Missionary Association, arrived in the city of Atlanta on a mission to develop plans for a school to teach the newly freed African Americans, he found the work had already begun. Clarence Bacote (1906–1981; PhD, Chicago, 1955), the first history professor in the Atlanta University Graduate School, sums this up:

> [He] found two former slaves, James Tate and Grandison B. Daniels, conducting a school for freedmen in an old church building on Jenkins Street, the original home of the present Big Bethel African Methodist Episcopal

> Church. This was the first school in Atlanta for Negro children. Possessed with more zeal and desire than competence, these pioneer teachers readily relinquished the responsibility to better trained teachers from the North.
>
> (Bacote 1969, 4)

In fact, at the end of the Civil War, it was not uncommon for Black Union soldiers to donate some of their mustering-out pay to local efforts to establish schools for freedmen.

Perhaps Atlanta University's most outstanding contribution to Black Studies as Intellectual History was the scholarship of W.E.B. Du Bois (Aptheker 1973a). Du Bois worked at Atlanta for twenty-five years in two stretches: 1897–1910 and 1932–1944. His first appointment was as professor of history and economics. His doctoral dissertation, *The Suppression of the African Slave Trade to the United States, 1638–1870*, had been published the year before as the first volume in the Harvard Historical Series. While at Atlanta, he published two of his most important books: *The Philadelphia Negro* (1899) and *The Souls of Black Folk* (1903).

But, as always, Du Bois combined high-level scholarship with militant activism. He organized the Niagara Movement with fellow Harvard graduate Monroe Trotter, the first Black member of the Phi Beta Kappa Society from that university. The Niagara Movement represented a militant alternative to the more conciliatory leadership of Booker T. Washington. It led to the formation of the National Association for the Advancement of Colored People (NAACP) in 1909.

At Atlanta, Du Bois joined a social science faculty, who were already following a program of rigorous research. But under his powerful leadership, their annual conference and resulting report laid the basis for all twentieth-century scholarship on the experiences of African Americans. As he explained:

> This program at Atlanta, I sought to swing as if on a pivot to one of scientific investigation into social conditions, primarily for scientific ends: I put no special emphasis on specific reform effort, but increasing and widening emphasis on the collection of a basic body of fact concerning the social condition of American Negroes, endeavoring to reduce that condition to exact measurement whenever or wherever occasion permitted. As time passed, it happened that many uplift efforts were in fact based on our studies.
>
> (E. Wright 2005)

In all, there were twenty such studies, Du Bois directing all but the first two:

1. *Mortality Among Negroes in Cities* (1896)
2. *Social and Physical Conditions of Negroes in Cities* (1897)

3. *Some Efforts of American Negroes for Their Own Social Betterment* (1898)
4. *The Negro in Business* (1899)
5. *The College-Bred Negro* (1900)
6. *The Negro Common School* (1901)
7. *The Negro Artisan* (1902)
8. *The Negro Church* (1903)
9. *Some Notes on Negro Crime Particularly in Georgia* (1904)
10. *A Select Bibliography of the Negro American* (1905)
11. *Health and Physique of the Negro American* (1906)
12. *Economic Cooperation Among Negro Americans* (1907)
13. *The Negro American Family* (1908)
14. *Efforts for Social Betterment Among Negro Americans* (1909)
15. *The College-Bred Negro American* (1910)
16. *The Common School and the Negro American* (1911)
17. *The Negro American Artisan* (1912)
18. *Morals and Manners Among Negro Americans* (1914)
19. *Economic Cooperation Among Negroes of Georgia* (1917)
20. *Select Discussions of Negro Problems* (1916)

(Aptheker 1973a, 1973b)

As the first scientific program of empirical research on the African-American experience, these conferences transcended ideological differences. Morris quotes the principal adversary of Du Bois, Booker T. Washington:

> For several years I have watched with keen interest and appreciation the work of these annual conferences, and the whole country should be grateful to this institution for the painstaking and systematic manner with which it has developed from year to year a series of facts which are proving most vital and helpful to the interests of our nation. The work that Dr. DuBois is doing will stand for years as a monument to his ability, wisdom and faithfulness.
>
> (A.D. Morris 2015, 95)

When Du Bois was reappointed to the Atlanta University faculty in 1932, it was as professor of sociology. This was part of a major transition for the entire university, based on the appointment of John Hope as Atlanta University president in 1929. After earning his undergraduate degree from Brown University (where he was invited to join Phi Beta Kappa), Hope had become a teacher and, in 1906, was appointed president of Morehouse College. He had a firm grasp of the necessary connection between academic excellence and social responsibility, so he had joined with Du Bois and Monroe Trotter in the Niagara Movement and the NAACP. As soon as he took over as head of Atlanta University, he reached out to Du Bois to rebuild the sociology department. He said, "I brought him here to be my friend and my companion" (Bacote 1969, 288).

Du Bois had Ira Reid as his colleague in the sociology department. Reid had a PhD from Columbia and had worked as the Director of Research at the National Urban League, so he was already a veteran researcher at a young age. He also greatly admired Du Bois. Du Bois demonstrated his national leadership once again by founding an important journal in 1940, *Phylon, The Atlanta University Review of Race and Culture*. Phylon means "race" in the Greek language, and was a gesture to the classics his generation had been required to master. In his first academic position, Du Bois taught both Greek and Latin at Wilberforce University. Thus, his own career reflects the trajectory of "Blackenization" that this chapter traces.

What is more, during his first stint at Atlanta University, Du Bois attended the first Pan-African Congress organized by the Trinidadian Henry Sylvester-Williams in 1900, and then went on to help organize five such meetings before and after his second stint at the university. Finally, in 1961, Du Bois retired to Ghana at the invitation of the president of Ghana, Kwame Nkrumah.

John Hope filled the faculty with people who would become national intellectual leaders. They included Rayford Logan (history), Hale Woodruff (art), William Stanley Braithwaite (literature), and Clarence Bacote (history). Logan came in as the Slater Board Professor, which required him to teach courses on Negro history. Braithwaite came in to launch a program in creative writing. Bacote became head of the Citizenship School, a community program run by the university and the NAACP for the surrounding working-class community. As described in Chapter 1, Woodruff was a master painter and muralist known for the *Amistad Murals* he painted at Talladega College (1938–1942).

The next president of Atlanta University, Rufus Clement (PhD, Northwestern University, 1930), took the helm in 1937. Clement continued to lead in the hiring of outstanding faculty who advanced scholarship on the Black experience, recruiting Mercer Cook from the faculty of Howard University and bringing Mozell Hill (PhD, University of Chicago) into the Department of Sociology. Hill would later serve as head of that department, as well as consult for the Ghanaian government. Following Hill's arrival, Hylan Lewis (PhD, University of Chicago) joined the department. Whitney Young (MSW, University of Minnesota) arrived to become dean of the School of Social Work in 1954; he resigned in 1961 to become executive director of the National Urban League. Horace Mann Bond (PhD, University of Chicago) came in as the dean of the School of Education in 1957. Having gained valuable administrative experience as president of Lincoln University, Bond was also the leading scholar on the educational experiences of African Americans. During his time as president of Lincoln University, Bond had developed a relationship with Nkrumah while the latter was studying there. Bond became president of the American Society of African Culture and traveled on many occasions for international meetings and consulting in Africa.

As at other HBCUs, the Atlanta University student movement led the push for change at the beginning of the 1960s. Key people were Julian Bond at Morehouse and Ruby Doris Robinson at Spelman. This became especially pronounced as Atlanta became the regional headquarters of the 1960s Civil Rights Movement.

HOWARD UNIVERSITY (1867)

Howard is a unique case, located right in the nation's capital. As at the other two campuses, middle-class leadership engaged in research about Black people as well as anti-racist activism and politics, and followed events and attitudes off campus closely. This included both faculty and students.

Howard University was established in Washington, DC, right after the Civil War. As with other HBCUs, it was a joint project of church and state. Three Congregational ministers initiated the process. They recruited General Howard of the Freedmen's Bureau to support the project. He did, and the institution took his name. National events did not augur well, but the establishment of Howard went forward: President Lincoln was assassinated in 1865, with Vice-President Johnson then becoming president, only to be impeached in 1868 and eventually acquitted. In the midst of this, Congress passed legislation to establish Howard University, and Johnson signed it in 1867.

The curriculum, just as at Fisk, centered on the European tradition of the Greek and Roman classics. To answer the need for a cadre of middle-class professionals to provide services as well as general leadership for the newly freed African-American community, the college was created in 1867, the medical school in 1868, and the law school in 1869. Early on, the university recruited leading Black figures for the Howard board, so that Howard was not an effort by white people alone. The first Black board member was the militant abolitionist Henry Highland Garnet, elected on April 8, 1867 (Logan 1969, 32 and 581). Following him was the great abolitionist Frederick Douglass, serving on the board from 1881 to 1895 (Logan 1969, 71).

As at Fisk, contradiction arose between following the Eurocentric curriculum starting from the classics of Greece and Rome and finding intellectual grounding in Africa and the African-American experience. According to Banks, "By 1900 Howard University required of graduates four years of Latin and two years of Greek" (1996, 45). A course about the Black experience was proposed to the faculty in 1916 and the executive committee rejected it, stating: "The Committee thinks it inexpedient to establish a course in Negro problems at this time." They recorded no reasons for their decision. But when William

Leo Hansberry joined the faculty in 1922, he initiated a course on Africa (Logan 1969, 171 and 208).

The president of Howard, Stanley Durkee, included complimentary words about Hansberry in his remarks opening the 1922–1923 school year. As Winston reports,

> "The ignorant have ever declared," he said, "that the racial group which we at Howard represent, has no past history save that of ignorance and servitude. I am most happy to inform you that we bring to Howard this year, for the winter quarter, a young man who proves himself among the foremost investigators of the history of the race and will, therefore, conduct classes in that history showing great civilizations in the long past, built up and maintained by that race of which you are the proud representatives. I trust you will so shape your courses that next quarter you will enjoy the privilege of working with Mr. Hansberry".
>
> (M.R. Winston 1973)

Howard dean Kelly Miller had already made a move to embrace scholarship on Black people via library work. In 1914, Miller persuaded Howard alumnus Jesse E. Moorland to donate his vast collection of books and materials about the Black experience. Miller's hope was to establish a nationally significant special collection (Logan 1969, 171). Under the direction of librarian Dorothy Porter, another Howard alumnus, this plan took shape. So while the university did not take the step of offering a formal course in the 1910s, the collection helped those social science and humanities faculty studying the Black experience. It also provided material for courses that went forward under less obviously African or African-American titles.

In the 1920s, a new mood took hold on campus and throughout northern cities, summed up as the New Negro. The Moorland collection was a resource that helped to encourage a historic recruitment of scholars who made fundamental contributions to scholarship on the Black experience. First came the struggle for a Black president for this HBCU, which resulted in the resignation of Stanley Durkee. Mordecai Johnson, the first Black president of Howard, took over in 1926. Serving as president for thirty-four years, he was a master politician and a world-renowned orator who was known to rule Howard with a firm grip on leadership in all areas. Johnson had a BA from the University of Chicago and a master's in sacred theology from Harvard University. He hired leading young Black scholars from these and similar schools to join those already on staff. His goal was to create a University of Chicago or a Harvard that would serve Black people.

Most of the people he hired spent their entire careers at Howard, mentoring several generations of Black leaders in their academic careers as well as in virtually every area of social life. Table 4 includes just a sample of the outstanding Howard faculty in the social science and humanities. The scholars Johnson hired, and those already present, held their own against the very best of white mainstream scholars. They could only be held back by racist countermeasures.

Table 4 Key Faculty at Howard University, 1890–1969

Years	*Duration*	*Name*	*PhD Institution*	*Department*
1890–1939	49	Kelly Miller	Howard University (LLD)	Sociology/ Mathematics
1912–1954	42	Alain Locke	Harvard University	Philosophy
1913–1942	29	Charles Wesley	Harvard University	History`
1917–1928	11	Lorenzo Dow Turner	University of Chicago	Literature
1922–1959	37	William Leo Hansberry	Harvard University (MA)	African Studies
1926–1966	40	Charles Thompson	University of Chicago	Education
1927–1944	17	Abram Harris	Columbia University	Economics
1927–1960	33	Mercer Cook	Brown University	Romance Languages
1928–1950	22	Ralph Bunche	Harvard University	Political Science
1928–1973	45	Dorothy Porter	Columbia University (MLS)	Library
1929–1969	40	Sterling Brown	Harvard University (MA)	Literature
1929–1977	48	Lois Mailou Jones	Howard University (BA)	Art
1930–1970	40	James Porter	New York University (MFA)	Art
1932–1944	12	Howard Thurman	Colgate-Rochester Divinity School (BD)	Religion
1938–1965	27	Rayford Logan	Harvard University	History
1940–1976	36	Frank Snowden	Harvard University	Classics
1944–1969	25	E. Franklin Frazier	University of Chicago	Sociology

In 1932, educational psychologist Charles Henry Thompson, who had earned his PhD at Chicago in 1925 and joined the Howard faculty in 1926, founded the *Journal of Negro Education*. It became a leading venue for scholarship about the educational experiences of African Americans, Africans, and the African Diaspora. Together with President Johnson and law school dean Charles Houston, Thompson made sure the journal became the leading source of information on the national program of school desegregation being waged by the Civil Rights Movement.

Howard's faculty included leading activists in the freedom struggle as well as leading scholars. They led from both outside and inside the mainstream, responding to the crisis of the Great Depression that started in 1929. Outside, they formed a united front effort in 1935, the National Negro Congress, mentioned in Chapter 1. This organization grew out of the Joint Committee for National Recovery formed by Robert Weaver and John Davis while they were graduate students at Harvard in economics and law, respectively. A 1935 conference at Howard on the theme "The Position of the Negro in Our National Economic Crisis" provided additional impetus. A group known as the Howard University Radicals helped organize and spoke at the conference. This included Abram Harris, Sterling Brown, Ralph Bunche, E. Franklin Frazier, and several others.

Holloway groups the conference speakers into four categories:

> The conference panelists can be divided into four schools of thought:
> (1) those who believed the New Deal was the ultimate salvation for all workers;
> (2) those who felt that a "workers New Deal" could only exist outside a capitalist society;
> (3) those who sought to reconcile (1) and (2); and
> (4) those who argued that economic security would only develop out of an intraracial consumer cooperative movement.
>
> (Holloway 2002, 70)

The great controversy about this conference was that leading members of the Communist Party, such as James Ford, spoke at the conference. This led the Black congressman from Chicago, Arthur Mitchell, to author a bill to investigate radicalism at Negro universities, although Howard president Johnson protected his faculty. Senior members of the faculty like Bunche and Frazier remained on campus, while younger ones continued to organize:

> [A] younger group of faculty became the NNC's (National Negro Congress) backbone. Doxey Wilkerson and William Alphaeus Hunton, both young professors at Howard in the mid-1930s, helped organize a Howard local 440 of the American Federation of Teachers and advocated that it become more connected with Washington's larger labor movement.
>
> (Gellman 2012, 114)

Meanwhile, political insiders worked toward similar goals within established channels. Howard faculty were members of the informal "Black Cabinet" established in 1936 by President Franklin Delano Roosevelt and facilitated via the relationship between Mary McLeod Bethune and the president's wife, Eleanor Roosevelt. The backbone of the group was forty-five Black officials who worked in various government departments. Some of them had studied at Howard.

Howard University had its share of militant student protests. This was not surprising, given the radical faculty. Students began by forming a student council in 1920 and establishing a student newspaper, *The Hilltop*, in 1924. One of the founding editors of the newspaper was Zora Neale Hurston. The Student Council called a strike that began on May 7, 1925 and lasted one week. The issue was the strict rules set by President Durkee that stipulated the expulsion of students after twenty absences from Reserved Officers Training Corps (ROTC). Eventually, the faculty came around to supporting the students, after they ended the strike (Logan 1969, 220–21).

Howard being located in the nation's capital meant that students were close to the unfolding of national and international politics. In 1927, only Fisk and Howard of all Black institutions sent delegates to the National Student Federation, formed at Princeton the previous year. Kenneth Clark commented on the political culture of Howard when he entered in 1932: "The whole atmosphere of the place was heady and every scholar was eager to relate classroom work to social action" (Holloway 2002, 59). Students were on the move:

> The Student Council on October 19, 1933, sent a letter to President Franklin D. Roosevelt and to the Associated Press protesting the "lax attitude" of the Federal government with respect to lynching. In early 1935, Howard students participated in the picketing of a crime conference … Lionel Florant, one of the most articulate student leaders, was the delegate of Howard's Liberal League to the International Congress against War and Fascism in Brussels, December 29–31 1934…
>
> The 1935–1936 school year was dominated by activities to support the Scottsboro boys, a group of Alabama Black youth falsely accused of raping two white women and sentenced to death. The leading militant student group during the 1930s was the Liberal League. On April 22, 1937 students carried out a one-hour strike (supported by the dean on account of its brevity) against war and fascism in Spain and Ethiopia. This was part of coordinated national actions in response to these crises.
>
> (Logan 1969, 278 and 392)

This tradition of student militancy would reemerge in the 1960s with the formation of the Non-Violent Action Group (NAG) at Howard University. NAG organized before the sit-ins of North Carolina, but then was greatly influenced by those direct actions. Stokely Carmichael reports that running into NAG members led him to enroll at Howard in 1960. The students active in NAG included Ed Brown, Rap Brown, Charlie Cobb, Courtland Cox, Dion Diamond, Ruth Howard, Karen House, Tom Kahn, Mary Lovelace, Bill Mahoney, John Moody, Joan Mulholland, Cleveland Sellers, Mike Thelwell, Hank Thomas, Muriel Tillinghast, Kwame Ture (Stokely Carmichael), Cynthia Washington, and Jean Wheeler (Hartford n.d.). According to Carmichael, faculty who influenced him and other NAG members included E. Franklin Frazier, Rayford Logan, Eugene Holmes, Arthur P. Davis, Sterling Brown, Elias Blake, Conrad Snowden, Clyde Taylor, and Toni Morrison (Carmichael and Thelwell 2003, 129).

SUMMARY

The HBCUs during most of the twentieth century have been the main academic centers for Black people in higher education, both undergraduate students and mainstream PhD holders seeking employment. The leading HBCUs featured faculty with degrees from the highest-ranked mainstream institutions. The first two generations of Black PhDs and artists in these institutions laid the foundation for Black Studies scholarship, and in that respect, they were directly responsible for the genesis of what became Black Studies.

The HBCUs represented the greatest critical mass of Black scholars. They created communities of learning. Their productivity rivaled the mainstream and far exceeded any other scholarship on the Black experience. There is often a silence on this. For example, it is often thought that Herskovits at Northwestern University initiated African Studies (he founded the program in 1954 and then the African Studies Association in 1957) but, as we saw above, Fisk launched its African Studies program in 1943.

The HBCU scholars lived and worked in close proximity and did not limit their discussions to their disciplinary colleagues. There was great intertextuality. Philosophers talked with sociologists and everyone talked with the historians. Key librarians managed important library collections. At Howard, this contribution was made by the librarian Dorothy Porter, married to the historian Charles Wesley and then later the artist James Porter.

The HBCU was by no means an isolated ivory tower. A program of broad outreach to the surrounding community grounded the campus in a service relationship with people's actual needs. The Fisk University People's College, the Citizenship School of Atlanta University, and the Atlanta NAACP testify to this commitment. Of course, this has an even longer history of students working to serve the community: Du Bois as a student at Fisk going into rural Tennessee to teach is one such instance.

The HBCU also created a Pan-African linkage by which Africans and African Americans found ways to be mutually supportive. HBCU faculty scholarship demonstrates this, as does their service in government and other policy positions. Perhaps the most outstanding example of this is when Horace Mann Bond was president of Lincoln University. Two of the most accomplished African graduates of Lincoln became heads of state after liberation from British colonialism, Nnamdi Azikiwe of Nigeria and Kwame Nkrumah of Ghana. Bond sums up how Lincoln served in this way (H.M. Bond 1976, Chaps. 25 and 26):

> It was the first institution to have absolute faith that the African was as susceptible to instruction in the higher intellectual disciplines as any other human being; it was the first institution that was created for that purpose and that sustained it stubbornly through the years.
>
> (H.M. Bond 1976, 509–10)

In sum, the HBCU under the leadership of the first few generations of Black PhD scholars in the twentieth century fully manifested a Black Studies not achieved on mainstream campuses until the 1960s. Black faculty and students as the leading actors achieved critical mass on each campus. They took Black people here and abroad as the subject and concern of their study and teaching, activism, and policy making. They opposed racism as the main line. And they generated research that was used immediately and rediscovered in later decades.

3
The Political Culture of the Black Community

Black intellectual history is often portrayed as the history of the texts of the Black intelligentsia. But these ideas and values also have deep resonance within the popular consciousness of the broad masses of Black people, and frequently even originate with them. It is necessary to draw attention to this tradition, because it helps to contextualize Black Studies as the unfolding of collective intelligence. It counters the mythology of the singular genius of any given member of the academic elite.

And, in fact, Black Studies as Intellectual History unfolded in a second sphere alongside the Black academy, and that was the Black community itself. What does that term mean? Vasquez-Semadi defines political culture as "the set of discourses and symbolic practices by means of which both individuals and groups articulate their relationship to power, elaborate their political demands and put them at stake" ("Political Culture" 2019). The practices of a group attempting to survive, let alone prosper, in the face of every kind of racist practice and ideology, Black America's political culture as discussed here consists of the myriad ways that ordinary (and extraordinary) Black people respond to racism. They respond by not accepting the status quo, but becoming something different and then at times forcing change. This takes form in the social institutions that we live around and through, in our local communities, that is, in what Black people call the community. Their response includes digesting the output of the scholars and other elites discussed in Chapters 1 and 2. It also means creating the new alongside of that, and persisting in doing so.

The vast majority of Black people did not have access to higher education, but that did not stop people from talking, thinking, reading, writing, and producing culture and knowledge of many kinds. The intellectual life of the Black community served as a rich resource for the building and maintaining of community solidarity and a historically based positive identity. Early Black Studies correspondingly drew deeply on this resource. This part of the book will trace the national development of this community-based Black study and learning and then examine four cities that were important centers: New York, Chicago, New Orleans, and Los Angeles.

The institutions underpinning this mass-based approach to learning about and practicing Black history and culture ranged from the somewhat ephemeral to the quite permanent. They included, but were not limited to, literary societies, schools, libraries, churches, fraternal societies, cultural organizations, study circles, community media, publishers of books and pamphlets, and bookstores.

During the earliest periods of American history, Black people who were free and literate formed literary societies. The first such societies date to 1828. Black people linked education to the anti-slavery struggle, and consequently became book collectors and education activists. Howard University librarian Dorothy Porter (1936) put it this way:

> These organizations are indications of the activity of self-educative influences in Negro life. They worked from within the group and showed their results not only in organized action ... working for the improvement of Negro life. The story of the development of Negro education in its broader implications would be incomplete without some reference to these endeavors of the Negro literary societies.
>
> (D.B. Porter 1936, 576)

Over the many decades after the Civil War, the main educational institution for the Black community was the public school, both elementary and secondary. Because of systemic racism and exclusion, until the 1960s, Black PhDs were more likely to find employment in public schools than in higher education. The Black middle class believed that education was the path upward and toward a more complete freedom. They fell in line with the idea that science and creativity drove industrial society. From World War II into the 1960s, the public school classroom was a site of discipline and learning for Black youth.

Almost every community had a high school that was its beating heart of learning. Sometimes it was a school near an HBCU, such as Pearle High School near Fisk University or Dunbar High School near Howard University. Sometimes it was in a major urban center, such as DuSable High School in Chicago or Lincoln High School in Kansas City, Missouri. Black autobiographies make countless references to great teachers and strong school cultures in these segregated institutions. Rituals such as the singing of the Negro National Anthem as well as the Star Spangled Banner affirmed the identity of these schools and their students and teachers (J. Bond and Wilson 2000). Horace Mann Bond did important research that traced Black holders of doctorate degrees back to their high schools of origin and found many high schools that were noteworthy for producing high achievers (H.M. Bond 1972).

Branch libraries were another center for community-based education. Wiegand reports that this activity dates as far back as the 1920s:

> Blacks made "broader use of the branch as a social center." "The Negro's development and increased sense of race pride," branch librarians observed, "is more and more manifest and the branches are working to keep step with this progress." No longer were librarians using the term "slow minded" to describe Black Americans. While Black branches in the South had from their origins established themselves as social centers, in the North migrant Blacks who frequented branches in their neighborhoods turned them into social centers that not only helped assimilate Black readers into their new environments, but they also made it possible for white librarians to experience the richness of the Black cultures these migrants brought with them.
>
> (Wiegand 2015, 126–27)

Religious organizations and fraternal and other societies functioned as places of learning as well. They expected their members to study assiduously the texts that gave their faith or community its particularity. At the top of this list are Christians and their Bible, but it also includes Muslims and their Quran and the Jews and their Torah. The Black Prince Hall Masons and many others had their foundational texts as well (Skocpol, Liazos, and Ganz 2008). Serious members kept book collections and maintained regular study habits. In the Black community, much of this study was interconnected with Black history, including Jesus as a Black man for the Christians and the Ethiopian Bilal for the Muslims (Fulop and Raboteau 1997).

Cultural organizations, both sacred and secular, drew their orientation from Black history, especially in the realm of music, theater, and creative writing. Some reconnected to African origins; others expressed the struggle against racism and national oppression.

In the twentieth century, community-based study circles spread with the Negro history movement, especially activities associated with the work of Carter G. Woodson and Negro History Week. Woodson led a great movement of Black public history, bringing historical scholarship into prominence during annual events in the second week in February, starting in 1926 (Dagbovie 2007). We know this now as Black History Month. Another public history program sponsored by Black churches and fraternal organization has been the oratorical contest: youth contestants compete by giving original speeches and/or by delivering important speeches from the past.

The Black reading public has long relied on their own community media, beginning in 1827 with *Freedom's Journal*, the newspaper created by John Russwurm and Samuel Cornish (Wolseley 1990). Born freemen, they created the tradition of Black media educating the Black public by connecting Black intellectuals to a Black audience. Every Black community has had media that played this role, and it stands today as primary-source information on Black people's tradition of self-education.

There is also the tradition of publishing pamphlets and books. The oldest Black book publisher was the AME Book Concern, which the African Methodist Episcopal Church set up in 1817. Joyce (1991) has researched the historical record of Black book publishers. Connected to this has been the Black bookstore, which has its origins in the nineteenth century (Beckles 1996).

Successive generations of intellectuals and artists—most of them from the grassroots and working ordinary day jobs—drove the development of these community-based organizations as well as of the social movements that this book will turn to in later chapters. In each case struggle arises, sometimes based on differences in the Freedom Movement, sometimes based on generational tensions, and sometimes based on personalities. But a deeper look almost always reveals that middle-class interests pointed one way and working-class interests another. The activities discussed in this chapter represent by and large mass activity, working-class activity, contrasted with the predominantly middle-class, elite activity in the academy (Chapters 1 and 2), but it also interacts with that elite. Dogmas and debates weave their way through this history. This is Black people studying and learning about Black people, linked with cultural practice, resisting the environment of racism, and affirming. It is a key part of Black Studies as Intellectual History. Looking closely at how this unfolded in four cities, one in each region of the USA, makes this clear. Each case in this chapter traces the city's political culture into the recent period. As this book makes clear, Black Studies as Intellectual History is a mode rather than a time period, and the life of Black people in these and other cities conditioned and continues to condition both Black Studies as Social Movement and Black Studies as Academic Profession.

NEW YORK

New York is the largest city in the country (2010 population: 8,755,133) with the largest Black population (2,228,145), making the city more than 25 percent Black. Historically, the main Black population center in New York City has been a northern Manhattan area called Harlem. New York is home to Wall Street, the headquarters of US-based finance capital. The majority of US book publishing companies operate out of New York, and its major newspapers, *The New York Times* and *The Wall Street Journal*, are also national. New York as an entertainment center concentrates major art establishments, performance spaces, and career opportunities for people in the arts. And so the Black community in Harlem has been called the cultural capital of Black America (Osofsky 1996; Clarke 1998). If you take into account the migration flow from the entire African Diaspora, New York is the cultural capital of the African world. The city is also a center of higher education, with students from across the country and faculties that include many Black intellectuals, led by Columbia University,

New York University, the New School for Social Research, City University of New York, and Union Theological Seminary.

In 1917, Hubert Harrison (1883–1927), sometimes called the father of Harlem radicalism, set up his Liberty League and *The Voice* newspaper, which launched the New Negro Movement. Also known as the Black Socrates, Harrison loomed large in Harlem intellectual circles. He helped build a political culture of public speaking, creating what were in effect college classrooms for masses of people (H.H. Harrison and Perry 2001; Perry 2011).

Not long after Harrison created the Liberty League, the USA experienced a wave of violence and race riots against the African-American community called the Red Summer of 1919. That same year eighty-three Black people were lynched, one every four days. In response to the violence against Black people, in New York Cyril Briggs (1888–1966) organized the African Blood Brotherhood for African Liberation and Redemption (ABB). This was a Black militant socialist self-defense organization prepared to meet violence with violence (Haywood 1978, 122–31; Kornweibel 1998, 132–54; Makalani 2014, 45–70).

One key contribution came in 1919 when Claude McKay published his militant sonnet in response to the violence, "If We Must Die." It read in part:

> Oh, Kinsmen! We must meet the common foe;
> Though far outnumbered, let us show us brave,
> And for their thousand blows deal one deathblow!
> What though before us lies the open grave?
> Like men we'll face the murderous, cowardly pack,
> Pressed to the wall, dying, but fighting back!
>
> (Claude McKay 1919)

A great awakening of Black intellectual and artistic creativity began in the 1920s and became known as the Harlem Renaissance. A new militant self-affirmation soon emerged under the name New Negro Movement. This renaissance spanned more than a decade of diverse activities. At its heart were the artists who lived, worked, and collectively experienced this celebration of political culture.

The role of the arts in the Harlem Renaissance has garnered the most attention, and deservedly so, as there was a tsunami of literary production. The signature volume is the anthology edited by Howard professor Alain Locke, *The New Negro* (1925). He included writing by W.E.B. Du Bois, James Weldon Johnson, Angelina Grimke, Langston Hughes, Countee Cullen, Claude McKay, Zora Neale Hurston, Jean Toomer, Arna Bontemps, J.A. Rogers, Arthur Huff Fauset, Charles Johnson, Kelly Miller, E. Franklin Frazier, Walter White, and Arturo Schomburg. Almost one hundred years after it first appeared, *The New Negro* has never been out of print. One reason for this might be that the book did not feature the radical politics of the period. But it did reflect and define a cultural awakening that linked the New Negro Movement to the African Diaspora and to the folk traditions of the rural South.

Langston Hughes was the literary figure of the Harlem Renaissance who made the most lasting impact. He penned a manifesto for his generation of writers, "The Negro Artist and the Racial Mountain," which was published in *The Nation*. It argued for a class identity that the masses of workers and poor people shared:

> But then there are the low-down folks, the so-called common element, and they are the majority—may the Lord be praised! The people who have their hip of gin on Saturday nights and are not too important to themselves or the community, or too well fed, or too learned to watch the lazy world go round. They live on Seventh Street in Washington or State Street in Chicago and they do not particularly care whether they are like white folks or anybody else. Their joy runs, bang! into ecstasy. Their religion soars to a shout. Work maybe a little today, rest a little tomorrow. Play awhile. Sing awhile. O, let's dance! These common people are not afraid of spirituals, as for a long time their more intellectual brethren were, and jazz is their child. They furnish a wealth of colorful, distinctive material for any artist because they still hold their own individuality in the face of American standardizations. And perhaps these common people will give to the world its truly great Negro artist, the one who is not afraid to be himself. Whereas the better-class Negro would tell the artist what to do, the people at least let him alone when he does appear. And they are not ashamed of him—if they know he exists at all. And they accept what beauty is their own without question.
>
> (L. Hughes 2004 [1926], 1312)

During this time, the leading jazz musicians were making music in Harlem, including Fats Waller, Duke Ellington, Fletcher Henderson, Jelly Roll Morton, Willie "The Lion" Smith, Eubie Blake, Bessie Smith, James Johnson, Louis Armstrong, and Cab Calloway. The premiere performance spot for jazz was a Harlem nightclub called the Cotton Club, which operated from 1923 to 1935. The Ellington band was the house band for years. The Cotton Club was an anomaly in Black cultural history: in Harlem, featuring the best artists of the period, but for whites only! They even had a color policy in favor of light-skinned women as dancers and hostesses (H.E. Johnson and Johnson 2014, 26–36). They also called Ellington's musical compositions for his appearances there "jungle music." In fact, Edward "Duke" Ellington was a master musician on top of the charts for fifty years. He was an intellectual who celebrated Black traditions in music and in history: for example, his "Black, Brown, and Beige" from 1946 expresses periodization of African-American history through the metaphor of color.

Artists worked in all media during this long decade of cultural and historical festival. In the visual arts, there were the painters Palmer C. Hayden, Archibald J. Motley, Sargent Johnson, William H. Johnson, Hale Woodruff, and Lois Mailou Jones; the photographer James Van Der Zee; and the sculptors Augusta Savage (who also painted) and Richmond Barthé, among others. The most notable visual artist of the Harlem Renaissance period was Aaron Douglas. He painted local murals and illustrated many literary books of the period (Kirschke 1999).

Harlem was also the staging ground for the two wings of Black radicalism. One wing was Black liberation, as manifested in nationalist and Pan-Africanist tendencies. The other was socialism in diverse flavors. Indeed, in Harlem these were more often combined in some way rather than pitted against each other or mutually exclusive. After forming the UNIA in Jamaica in 1914, Marcus Garvey formed the New York chapter in 1917. The UNIA held an international convention in 1921 at New York's Madison Square Garden that attracted about 50,000 people. Garvey celebrated the life of Lenin and initially attracted key leaders of the Black left to his organizational orbit (R. Lewis 1988; R.A. Hill and Bair 1987; Hill 2005). However, this unity was short-lived. For example, Cyril Briggs and others from the African Blood Brotherhood had tried to organize within the UNIA, but left and moved into the Communist Party USA in 1921 as their first major group of Black recruits (Zumoff 2015, 298–304). The community did support these radicals: a district in Harlem elected the Black communist Benjamin Davis to the New York City Council in 1945 (B.J. Davis 1969).

Out of the UNIA there developed many nationalist organizations, many of them located in Harlem and other large cities. One of the most prominent was the African Nationalist Pioneer Movement started by Carlos Cooks in 1941 (R. Harris et al. 1992). Many leaders of these organizations established reputations in the "university of the streets" as public intellectuals speaking on street corners to audiences of residents. These included James Lawson (United African Nationalist Movement), James Thornhill (African Nationals in America), Bessie Philips (Ethiopia Wisdom House of Judah), Charles Kenyatta (The Mau Mau), Edward "Pork Chop" Davis, and Arthur Reed. Perhaps the two most influential intellectual figures, who emerged out of these nationalist circles are Yosef Ben-Jochannan (1918–2015) and John Henrik Clarke (1915–1998). Both of them started in the community and later emerged as key figures in Black Studies in the academy (K. Smith, Sinclair, and Ahmed 1995; J.L. Conyers and Thompson 2004; Person-Lynn 1996).

In this developing political culture, four publications carried forth both the cultural movement as well as the political radicalism of the time. They included *The Crisis* (1910) from the NAACP and edited by W.E.B. Du Bois, *Opportu-*

nity (1923) from the National Urban League and edited by Charles Johnson, the independent socialist magazine *The Messenger* (1917) edited by A. Philip Randolph, and *Negro World* (1918) from the UNIA and edited by T. Thomas Fortune. In addition to this movement media, the general Black newspaper *Amsterdam News* began publication in 1909. Harlem was becoming a home to a reading public filled with the dynamism of a new political culture.

In addition to this rise of new institutions, pre-existing ones in Harlem contributed to all of these developments. First, the church: there is no better example than the Abyssinian Baptist Church, founded in 1809. By 1930, the church had thirteen thousand members, making it the largest African-American church in New York City and the largest Baptist congregation in the world. Adam Clayton Powell Sr. became the pastor in 1908, and was succeeded by his son Adam Clayton Powell Jr. in 1937. Powell Jr. went on to serve fourteen terms in the US House of Representatives (1945–1971). The father wrote *Against the Tide: An Autobiography* (1938), and the son wrote *Marching Blacks: An Interpretative History of the Rise of the Black Common Man* (1945) and *Adam by Adam: The Autobiography of Adam Clayton Powell, Jr.* (Powell Jr. 1945, 1971).

The Harlem YMCA became a location for study and performance. It opened in 1919 and moved into a beautiful important new building in 1931. The building was declared a National Historic Landmark in 1976; one of its noteworthy features is a mural by Aaron Douglas titled "Evolution of Negro Dance." Many artists and intellectuals stayed for a time in this YMCA, and its spaces were among the main venues in Harlem for local theater groups and literary discussions. The Harlem YMCA tells its history as follows:

> In the generations since it was established, the Harlem Y has been one of New York City's most vibrant cultural hubs. This historic institution has hosted and housed renowned American writers including Claude McKay, Langston Hughes, and Richard Wright; mounted theatrical productions starring legendary actors including Paul Robeson, Ossie Davis, Ruby Dee, and Cicely Tyson; and provided a forum for religious and civil rights leader Dr. Martin Luther King, Jr. to preach his vision of equality and social justice.
>
> ("About the Harlem YMCA" n.d.)

The Schomburg Center for Research in Black Culture originated in 1911, when Arturo Schomburg cofounded the Negro Society for Historical Research, a community-based program for research. The society's members included African, West Indian, and Afro-American scholars (Valdés 2018). In March 1925, Schomburg published his essay "The Negro Digs Up His Past" in an issue of *Survey Graphic* devoted to the intellectual life of Harlem. Alain Locke guest edited this issue, which became his book-length anthology *The New Negro* (1925).

The Harlem branch of the New York Public Library (NYPL) opened in 1905. In 1921, it hosted the first New York exhibit of African-American artists—the library had quickly become much more than a place for books. In 1925, the branch became the site for the library's Division of Negro Literature, History, and Prints. In 1926, Schomburg, who was one of the leading collectors of Black printed texts, sold his library collection to NYPL. In 1932, he became the curator of the Harlem branch special collection. Important changes happened in the 1940s: director Lawrence Reddick named the special collection after Schomburg in 1940, the library branch was named after Countee Cullen in 1942, and Jean Hutson served as director from 1948 to 1980. Members of every major intellectual, cultural, and political movement in New York and for most of the African Diaspora have advanced those movements by doing research at the Schomburg.

Two bookstores were key to the community contribution to Black Studies as Intellectual History. Lewis H. Michaux (1884/5–1976) owned the African National Memorial Bookstore in Harlem from 1932 to 1974 (V.M. Nelson and Christie 2012), and Richard Moore ran the Frederick Douglass Book Center (R.B. Moore, Turner, and Turner 1988). Moore was famous for his book *The Name "Negro": Its Origin and Evil Use* (R.B. Moore 1992 [1960]). Both these men were more than booksellers—they were advocates of many streams of Black resistance. Moore belonged to the African Blood Brotherhood, and Michaux was a close confidant of Malcolm X.

Two New York-based journals, *Freedomways* and *The Liberator*, provided crucial forums for Black thinking in the 1960s. *Freedomways* was a leading African-American theoretical, political, and cultural journal published from 1961 to 1985. Louis Burnham, Edward Strong, and W.E.B. Du Bois founded the journal and Shirley Graham Du Bois served as its first general editor. Esther Cooper Jackson held this position in later years. *Freedomways* was closely associated with the Communist Party. *The Liberator*, edited by Dan Watts, was also established in 1961. Each of these journals published contributions from a national network as well as from the New York area.

Finally, literary circles continued to rise and fall. The end of the 1940s-era Committee for the Negro in the Arts left Harlem writers without a center (Cruse 1967a, 207–20). Sensing a need, John Oliver Killens, Rosa Guy, John Henrik Clarke, Willard Moore, and Walter Christmas started the Harlem Writers Guild in 1950 (L.C. Robinson 2005).

New York's Black community has made major contributions as a national center of intellectual and cultural production. Its unique location as a global port of entry for the USA has enabled it to be a gathering of people from throughout the African Diaspora. It has served as an ideological and cultural cauldron sustained by transgenerational struggles, in which dogma and debate have coexisted to keep alive the many diverse tendencies. Chapter 6 on the Black Arts Movement will further explore the political culture of New York.

CHICAGO

During the Great Migrations of African Americans after World Wars I and II, Chicago was the primary destination from Mississippi and Louisiana. So many Black people settled in Chicago that the name Black Metropolis took hold. The highest immigration was from Mississippi (Drake and Cayton 1945; Grossman 1989; C.R. Reed 2014).

The city was a dynamic industrial center that attracted Black labor with better wages than the rural South offered. Upon their arrival, a Black working-class culture developed quickly out of self-defense. For twentieth-century Chicago—its Black political culture in particular—was baptized by a violent racist pogrom in 1919, after a Black youth ventured onto a "white only" part of a South Side lakefront beach (C.S. Johnson 1923).

On an ideological level, Chicago developed a strong tradition of Black radicalism that provided the worldview for a counter-public sphere rooted in the Black community (Essien-Udom 1962). As in most big-city Black communities, the UNIA led by Marcus Garvey was a great mass influence. Study is a mechanism whereby dogma and debate interact and evolve, and study has always been an organizational process in the Black Liberation Movement across all ideological tendencies. An example is this testimony by Charles L. James, President-General of the UNIA, on what it was like to be part of the African School of Philosophy organized by Marcus Garvey:

> The class became one family. We ate together, roomed together, studied together, recognizing the professor as the chief architect of our intellectual destiny. As for me, it was a dose of humility mixed with the yearning for knowledge. For thirty days and nights, with two sessions per day, mass meetings at 8 o'clock p.m., studying until the early morning hours, we had no time for anything else but study, study, study.
>
> (Marano 2014)

The success of UNIA gave rise to two religious organizations of Black Chicago: the Moorish Science Temple and the Nation of Islam. Noble Drew Ali moved his Moorish Science Temple headquarters from Newark to Chicago, and Elijah Muhammad moved his headquarters from Detroit to Chicago. Each of these three Black Nationalist organizations were the early twentieth-century precedents for the Black Power Movement of the 1960s. They were out-of-the-box manifestations of independent Black thought. They did not take aggressive steps to effect social change, but they did change consciousness and personal behavior, a necessary step toward Black Power in the 1960s.

The best case of ideological debate and discussion in this counter-public sphere was the Washington Park Forum, an open-air democratic space for speaking in a public park on the South Side. This was the Black community's version of the Hyde Park Speaker's Corner in London or what was called Bug House Square on the North Side of Chicago. (Another important example is in Trinidad, where public discussions in a park have been called the People's Parliament or the University of Woodford Square.) In Chicago, people came to hear the ideologists of the community run it down, from Black Nationalists to communists of many flavors. People came to learn about history and current events as well as artistic and cultural developments. For the speakers, it was about what you knew and how well you could communicate with everyday people, not what degrees you had or what level of white acceptance had put you into mainstream visibility.

In one of the most segregated big cities of the USA, Black Chicago had to develop its own autonomous institutions for its information and culture. These included media, a museum, an art center, a special collections library, and bookstores. Each formed an element of a Black cultural grounding, providing for memory of the past, community in the present, and a launch pad for future cultural innovations.

Chicago's major Black media was also the media for the Black community nationwide. Robert Abbott resettled in Chicago from Georgia and founded the *Defender* newspaper in 1905 as a weekly that became a daily in the 1960s (Ottley 1955). John H. Johnson migrated to Chicago from Arkansas and started a media conglomerate: *Negro Digest* in 1942, *Ebony* in 1945, and *Jet* in 1951 (Marsh 2002). Elijah Muhammad, born in Georgia, came to Chicago from Detroit and founded *Muhammad Speaks* in 1960 with the inspiration and legwork of Malcolm X. In diverse ways, these publications represented a Black perspective: Black images, the recognition of achievement, and the celebration of cultural excellence. Even when the focus was on the Black middle class, the impact was to build pride in the community and a general sense that racist oppression could be overcome. This was a form of nationalist consciousness.

The breakthrough in building a memory institution came with the appointment of Vivian Harsh as the first African-American director of a branch public library in Chicago. In 1932, she became head of the George Cleveland Hall Branch Library in Chicago, named after a Black physician who served on the library board and was a co-founder of the Association for the Study of Negro Life and History (Joyce 1988). The special collection that Harsh immediately began to build with Works Progress Administration historical research materials and her own cultural network was later named after her, with librarians such as Donald Joyce, Alfred Woods, and Robert Miller, assisted by Michael Flug, heading it over the years:

> The Chicago Public Library's Hall branch, which opened in 1932, quickly became a community and cultural center for America's new Black capital. Black librarian Vivian Harsh initiated a semi-monthly Book Review and Lecture Forum and organized the DuSable History Club; within a decade fifteen similar groups organized. During that time Richard Wright, Langston Hughes, Zora Neale Hurston, Arna Bontemps, Alain Locke, Katherine Dunham, and Margaret Walker all gave presentations. And while they were in residence, one teenage girl—who as a child listened to Charlemae Rollins read poems and stories about Black people—frequently asked writers to assess her poetry. In 1950 that girl, Gwendolyn Brooks, won a Pulitzer Prize for Poetry.
>
> (Wiegand 2015, 156)

The cultural institutions built in Chicago have anchored Black consciousness over the generations. As part of the WPA, the South Side Community Art Center was founded in 1940. This amazing institution nurtured artists and spread cultural awareness broadly in the community. People who benefitted and contributed included photographer Gordon Parks, painters Charles White, Archibald Motley, Elizabeth Catlett, and Margaret Burroughs, sculptors Marion Perkins and Richard Hunt, and writers Ted Ward, Richard Wright, Gwendolyn Brooks, David Crowder, Vernon Jarrett, and Frank London Brown (Lloyd and Levinsohn 1993).

Margaret Burroughs distinguished herself in so many ways (Burroughs 2003). Her most enduring contribution was the 1957 founding of the DuSable Museum of African American History with her husband Charles Burroughs. First located in their home, the center provided artifactual displays that connected its audience to the history of Black people from their African roots to the present in Chicago. Margaret was a Chicago icon who taught generations of local artists as head of the art department at DuSable High School on the South Side, in the heart of the Black community. Noted historian Sterling Stuckey makes this comment about his personal experience:

> Though I never took a class from Margaret Burroughs while at DuSable High School, I knew very early of her presence and somehow found myself at her home from time to time, drawn there because the beginnings of what was to become the DuSable Museum of African American History were housed there. Consequently, her impact on me was made mainly out of the classroom, and there was no other such influence from any teacher at DuSable. That is how I first came to know Margaret's quietly expressed yet intense

> interest in social justice, which was hardly unrelated to her interest in art. It was many years before I understood what a great artist she is.
>
> (Burroughs 2003)

Music has been the most solid and sustained cultural force in Chicago. The blues came up from rural Mississippi. Jazz jumped up from New Orleans through other cities like Kansas City and St. Louis. In Chicago, DuSable High School served as the training ground for musicians under the tutelage of Captain Walter Henri Dyett. An Illinois National Guard veteran, Dyett taught music at that high school from 1932 until 1962, running his program with military discipline (Gary W. Kennedy 2003). His stellar students speak to his great success: Gene Ammons, Nat King Cole, Bo Diddley, Dorothy Donegan, Von Freeman, Johnny Griffin, Joseph Jarman, Wilbur Ware, Dinah Washington, John Young, Redd Foxx, and scores more. In the community, from 1945 to 1961, the great music elder Sun Ra evolved his unique style partly by recruiting young musicians from Captain Dyett's program. Sun Ra's band was a school and made the most innovative impact since the musical revolution of bebop.

While the local library, as discussed above, served as a major source of books, by no means did it have a monopoly. In the 1920s, F.H. Hammurabi (Robb) after studying law at Northwestern University began a life of public scholarship, publishing and selling books to advance positive knowledge about the world African experience. He was the Chicago equivalent of New York's J.A. Rogers, the most popular African-American public historian (Robb 1951).

As a leading Black militant activist of the Communist Party, Ishmael Flory operated a bookstore in the Englewood neighborhood of Chicago specializing in Black intellectual history and socialist literature about world revolution. In 1960, he founded the African-American Heritage Association and led many activities to raise awareness about the freedom struggles in Africa and key African American leaders like W.E.B. Du Bois and Paul Robeson ("Ishmael Flory" n.d.).

In the 1960s, the most important bookdealer was Curtis Ellis. He began his bookselling on a single rack in a candy store he owned in Woodlawn, just south of the University of Chicago. He grew his business as part of the explosion of the 1960s. At its height, he had three community-based bookstores and several campus bookstores in the Chicago area. His main bookshop became a stopping point for all African-American political and artistic celebrities visiting Chicago, as well as for all local activists in the Black community. He provided the primary commercial outlet for the locally produced literature that built the Black Arts Movement of Chicago.

The two major book publishing ventures started during the 1960s, in addition to Johnson Publications, were Path Press (1961), led by Bennett Johnson and

Herman Gilbert, and Third World Press (1967), started by Haki Madhubuti (Don Lee) ("Bennett Johnson" n.d.; "Our Publisher" n.d.).

The major event, in terms of protecting and extending Black historical consciousness early in the twentieth century, was the 1915 founding in Chicago of the Association for the Study of African American Life and History (then called Negro). On an informal level, people formed literary circles throughout the twentieth century, following the practice mentioned above that began in 1828. One example is the POBLA literary club, based at the Church of the Good Shepard, which has continuously met since the 1950s. This was and is a club of middle-class Black women who loved to read books, especially those about the Black experience.

The senior writers who preceded the 1960s explosion included Gwendolyn Brooks, Lerone Bennett Jr., St. Clair Drake, Allison Davis, and Lorenzo Turner. These scholars and artists of the Black experience led the intellectual life of the community.

Of course, in the 1960s, there was also the grassroots organizing for the study of African-American life, history, and culture. In 1962, an organization was formed in anticipation of the centennial of the Emancipation Proclamation called the American Negro Emancipation Centennial Authority (ANECA). The top leadership of this organization was very much within the political and economic mainstream, with political officials appointing board members and state legislatures and African countries providing grants of money. It was the affiliated youth group called the ANECANS who became the spearhead forces for the Black consciousness movement in 1960s Chicago. These included Jeff Donaldson, Sonja Stone, Russell Adams, and the author. It was an ANECAN, the social worker and University of Chicago doctoral student Russell Adams, who published the popular volume *Great Negroes Past and Present* (1963). This book can be seen as an early reflection of the same focus later taken up by the influential Wall of Respect mural, completed in 1967 (Alkalimat, Crawford, and Zorach 2017).

Adams went on to head the Department of African American Studies at Howard University. Donaldson went on to head the art department and become dean of fine arts, also at Howard University. Sonja Stone, after heading the Center for Inner City Studies in Chicago, went to head African American Studies at the University of North Carolina at Chapel Hill. Their African American Cultural Center is now named after her. The author of this volume went on to head African American Studies programs at several institutions, including Fisk University and the University of Illinois at Urbana-Champaign.

One innovative community and academic collaboration, the Center for Inner City Studies, has focused on the educational experiences of Black, Latino, and poor students in the inner city. In 1966, Northeastern Illinois University created the center located in a building designed by Frank Lloyd Wright in the heart of the Grand Boulevard neighborhood, near the location of the Wall of Respect. It has been a major hub for Black Nationalist activities, including cultural work of all kinds. Key figures at this institution have been Jacob Carruthers, Anderson Thompson, Conrad Worrill, Robert Starks, Nancy Arnez, Carol Adams, and its founding director Sonja Hayes Stone ("Carruthers Center for Inner City Studies" n.d.).

In sum, Chicago's Black political culture featured transgenerational networks, autonomous institutions of memory and cultural creativity, and a militant rhetorical tradition of radical Black thought. It had both a public face and a deeply secure process spanning what seemed like hopeless divides. One example of this is Bennett Johnson arranging for Martin Luther King Jr. to meet with Elijah Muhammad. One can begin to understand unformalized united fronts (unity of action), as both King and Muhammad advocated strongly for Black freedom and against all forms of racism. At that moment in Chicago, as elsewhere, Black consciousness was in the air, for self-defense and for the celebration of self and community.

NEW ORLEANS

New Orleans has a cultural history like no other US city. It was part of the 1803 Louisiana Purchase from France. Its slave past is more like the Caribbean than the cotton plantations of Mississippi or Alabama. After the 1804 Haitian Revolution, a wave of immigration turned the city 63 percent Black:

> New Orleans' large community of well-educated, often French-speaking free persons of color (*gens de couleur libres*), who had been free prior to the Civil War, sought to fight back against Jim Crow. They organized the *Comité des Citoyens* (Citizens Committee) to work for civil rights. As part of their legal campaign, they recruited one of their own, Homer Plessy, to test whether Louisiana's newly enacted Separate Car Act was constitutional. Plessy boarded a commuter train departing New Orleans for Covington, Louisiana, sat in the car reserved for whites only, and was arrested. The case resulting from this incident, *Plessy v. Ferguson*, was heard by the U.S. Supreme Court in 1896. The court ruled that "separate but equal" accommodations were constitutional, effectively upholding Jim Crow measures.
>
> ("New Orleans" 2018)

Four cultural streams gave southern Louisiana and New Orleans its special flavor: European, Cajun, Creole, and Black. While scholars debate the lines between these, differences in language and culture have been real. For Black people, this required adjustment, starting with religion:

> In this striving to maintain unity and to affirm identity in a new land, the Christian God was substituted for the African High God … This African-Catholic syncretism made the transition for Africans to Western culture easier in Latin America and in some parts of the US, particularly New Orleans, and served as support for the continuation of African traditions in the New World.
>
> (Floyd 1995, 39)

Out of the Catholic tradition, the carnival practice known as Mardi Gras was first performed in New Orleans in 1837. The celebration runs from Twelfth Night (Epiphany, January 6) until Ash Wednesday (forty-six days before Easter). Throughout the African Diaspora, this tradition of riotous partying and public mocking of authority was always tied to resisting slavery and racism:

> The historical record of Mardi Gras in many ways resonates with the experience of festivities throughout what was once the "plantation world." These revelries were created out of traditions of resistance as much as they were from activities that enhance life's continuities. These were not simple reflective responses to enslavement. To the contrary they were well-organized moments, complex mnemonic and expansive efforts to maintain face, body, spirit among those still living after the harshness of slavery … From these holidays emerged organized mass escapes into the bush and swamps, especially where Maroon (runaway) communities had already been established. Little wonder that the plantation authorities repeatedly attempted to legislate against these celebrations.
>
> (Abrahams et al. 2010, 6)

For those performing in the parades and balls, Mardi Gras is a school of cultural production. Krewes (associations) spend an entire year planning, practicing, and then performing at Mardi Gras. They represent total theater, with costumes, choreography, music, and a diversity of roles (O'Neill 2014, Chap.17).

Into the nineteenth century, Black people had few options in terms of where they could gather. One place became a site for gathering and cultural performance of both the religious practice of Voodoo and the music that evolved into jazz: Congo Square. It became a tourist site and accepted as having value for the mainstream, but for Black people it remained a site for the freedom impulse in cultural production. In a sense, the square itself was a school, because young people came to learn from the masters of the music and to join formal organizations.

The origin of jazz is usually associated with New Orleans. The city was home to great artists such as Buddy Bolden (1868–1931), King Oliver (1885–1938), Sidney Bechet (1897–1959), and Louis Armstrong (1900–1971). They performed in groups that became intensive schools with young musicians recruited almost as interns to learn the music. In fact, Louis Armstrong is reported to have said that his only real musical mentor was King Oliver (Feather and Gitler 2007).

Another major training ground and place of transmission of the tradition has been the music class in public schools. This represented a contradiction between the cultural policy of the school system versus the popular culture of the community. In 1922, the New Orleans public schools banned jazz from their music instruction, applying this prohibition only to the African-American schools! Students could not even get together and play on their own at school: "Clarence Ford remembered that at one elementary school in the late 1930s, the principal would rush into a group of students holding an impromptu jazz jam session and break it up by brandishing a long leather strap" (Kennedy 2006, 36).

New Orleanians were schooled in musical traditions both sacred and secular. Four names that stand out among the many are Clyde Kerr Jr., Yvonne Busch, Ellis Marsalis Jr., and Danny Barker. On account of systemic segregation in public education, Black students were aggregated and accessible to Black teachers who were also practicing musicians:

> They gave many children their first opportunity to pick up a musical instrument, and they were the first professional musicians many children ever had a chance to meet, hear perform, and come to admire. Students' decisions to become musicians or music teachers often had been made as a result of their classroom experiences with the musicians teachers and jazz mentors who they first met in the New Orleans public schools.
>
> (Kennedy 2006, xxii)

New Orleans was also a center for higher education, including historically Black institutions that helped shape the city's Black political culture. Dillard University, founded in 1935, could trace its origins back to institutions founded in 1869. While Southern University technically opened its doors in 1956, it, like Dillard, was really the latest iteration of several predecessors, in Southern's case, going back to 1880. And Xavier University was founded in 1915. These universities upheld what the Black middle-class ethos would refer to as "being proper." So they applauded scholarship on the Black experience that upheld the highest standards of mainstream scholarship, but did not approve of the cultural production of the masses of poor and working-class Black people. They made one exception: the sacred singing of the church music of gospels and spirituals.

Two institutions merged in 1935 to form the historically Black college of Dillard University. Will W. Alexander was chosen as acting president, serving from 1935 to 1936. At the time of his appointment, he was director of the

Commission on Interracial Cooperation (CIC), which actively campaigned against lynching and conducted research studies on issues pertaining to "Negro welfare" and other southern "problems."

During Alexander's short tenure, one of his most significant contributions was recruiting an outstanding faculty. Drawing from a pool of noted scholars, Alexander assembled a stellar group of educators: Horace Mann Bond, dean of the university and psychology and education faculty; Charles Wesley Buggs, biology faculty; Byrd Dewey Crudup, physical education faculty; S. Randolph Edmonds, drama faculty; Rudolph Moses, English faculty; Lawrence D. Reddick, history faculty; and J.G. St. Clair Drake, sociology and anthropology faculty ("Dillard University" 2018).

Progressive political activists also contributed to knowledge production and cultural creation in New Orleans. Popular Front activity was important:

> The Black Popular Front in New Orleans distinguished itself in the depth of its commitment to recording, analyzing and celebrating the history and cultural life of everyday African Americans in Louisiana and the South. Of course, to some degree such efforts characterized the work of the Popular Front practically everywhere. However, few, if any, places in the South displayed the sustained work in such scholarly and cultural activities during the 1930s and 1940s as New Orleans, due in large part to the Louisiana affiliate of the Federal Writers Project (FWP) of the Works Progress Administration (WPA, renamed the Work Projects Administration in 1939).
>
> (Smethurst 2021, 30)

LOS ANGELES

Black people were part of Los Angeles from the very beginning:

> The origins of the Black community in Los Angeles have been traced to the founding of the city in 1781. Of the 44 original settlers, 26 had some African ancestry. However they quickly lost their majority position. By 1790 the first census of Los Angeles revealed only 22 mulattoes out of a total population of 141; moreover, few Blacks came to the city during the remainder of the Spanish and Mexican periods ... The modern Black community began ... with the land boom of 1887–1888 which increased the Negro population in the city to 1,258, or 2.5 percent of the total in 1890.
>
> (De Graaf 1970, 327)

The dialectic of freedom hit forward, then back, based on this demographic trend: "Admitted as a free state in 1850, California repealed testimony restrictions in 1863 (allowing Black people to appear in court), outlawed de jure racial segregation in California schools, and passed a state anti-discriminatory law in 1893" (Sides 2003, 15).

Then, in the twentieth century, Black people had no choice but to form a Black ghetto, as the aggressively racist Ku Klux Klan became popular in the white community. One important example is Watts, an agricultural community outside of Los Angeles that attracted Black settlers. It was becoming a Black community and represented the possibility of Black agency heading in the direction of self-determination. But that didn't last long:

> This "Watts invasion" was cited by other suburban papers as illustrating the folly of allowing any Blacks to gain title to the land. In 1926, allegedly at the instigation of the Ku Klux Klan, an election was held in which a majority of the voters chose annexation to Los Angeles rather than remaining a separate city which might be predominantly composed of Blacks. The "lesson" of the Watts invasion apparently was heeded, for until World War II the Blacks in Watts constituted a lonely island in an otherwise white southeast Los Angeles.
>
> (De Graaf 1970, 347)

Music was the foundation of cultural activism that brought consciousness of a positive Black identity to LA's African-American community. A good example of the start of this is the 1925 staging of the musical epic written by W.E.B. Du Bois, *The Star of Ethiopia*, which took place at the Hollywood Bowl (Widener 2009, 35). In 1934, a citywide organization called the Committee on Arts of the Negro took off (Widener 2009, 36). Professionals in the teaching of music became a force in the community:

> Music instructors constituted a formidable section of the local Black petit bourgeoisie, accounting by one estimate for between a third and a fifth of the Black professionals between 1920 and 1940. In 1900, one out of every hundred Black Angelenos was a music teacher. Two decades later the proportion had declined, but absolute numbers had more than tripled, growing from 78 to 226 by 1930 … The number of local music students reached into the thousands, and with the most prominent schools enrolling an interracial student body, both the willingness of whites to send their children to study music under the tutelage of Blacks and the obvious quality of the city's Black piano, violin, and choral instruction could not but, in the words of one observer, "help mould sentiment for the uplift of the race."
>
> (Widener 2009, 68–69)

A small number of the many music instructors were in the high schools, for the institution most responsible for cultural excellence was in fact the public high school, especially in the musical arts. The two most celebrated teachers were Samuel Browne and Lloyd Reese, who taught students at two Black high schools, Jefferson and Jordan:

> Browne's teaching career at Jefferson lasted more than two decades, during which time his students included a wide cross-section of local jazz talent. Among his students were Dexter Gordon, Chico Hamilton, Ernie and Marshall Royal, Horace Tapscott, Don Cherry, Frank Morgan, and Roy Ayers. Browne's rehearsals often included former students such as Sonny Criss; students from other schools (Jordan) including Eric Dolphy, Charles Mingus, and Buddy Collette; and the occasional visiting professional.
>
> (Widener 2009, 121)

The visual arts were not far behind the music, following the lead of Alice Tayford Gafford and Beulah Ecton Woodard:

> Woodard was also a driving force behind the short-lived Los Angeles Negro Art Association, which began sponsoring lectures on "Negro Art" in 1937. Woodard and Gafford were members of the Our Authors Study Circle, a book club affiliated with Carter G. Woodson's Association for the Study of Negro Life and History that invited guest lecturers and organized public presentations on Black history and literature. In persuading Mayor Bowron's office to enact the city's first Negro history week celebrations, this all female club opened the initial for Black inclusion within Los Angeles's municipal culture.
>
> (Widener 2009, 84)

Social institutions in the Black community of Los Angeles have their origins in the founding of a church by Biddy Mason, a former slave, in 1872. After successfully fighting for her freedom in a Los Angeles courtroom, Mason was the driving force behind the establishment of the First African Methodist Episcopal Church (Hunt and Ramón 2010, 324–25). She became a successful businessperson and, in time, a millionaire. Her identity became an iconic inspiration for Black community memory and artistic representation.

The vehicle for the public education of the Black community, especially regarding current affairs, has always been the Black press, and Los Angeles is no exception. A notable Los Angeles example is the *California Eagle* newspaper, founded in 1879. Its most powerful owner-editor (1912–1951) was Charlotta Bass. One of its educational efforts was a regular column by T.R.M. Howard titled "The Negro in the Light of History" ("*California Eagle*" 2018). But the paper did much more than that:

> Bass envisioned and utilized the *Eagle* as a vehicle for collective empowerment. She used the paper to inform her readers about terrorist intimidation perpetrated by neighbors determined to maintain (housing) restrictions. She publicized the fire bombings of Black residents' homes and other less violent efforts to maintain a white line in Westside neighborhoods.
>
> (Hunt and Ramón 2010, 329)

Black people exercising their right to live wherever they chose in Los Angeles reflected their understanding of the power of education. Compton, originally a white community with outstanding public schools and Compton Community College, established in 1927, began to gain a Black population in the 1950s. This was when the Black community began to engage with post-secondary education in the city. But, in 2006, it was the first community college in California to have its accreditation revoked, representing a crisis in the support for African Americans in higher education.

As elsewhere, Black autonomy in community-based educational efforts was represented by Black bookstores. The oldest Black bookstore in Los Angeles, The Aquarian Book Shop, was started by Alfred Ligon in 1941 (Luna 2002). He was a Southern Pacific Railroad waiter who started the bookstore with just $100. It was a key spot until it was burned down in the 1992 insurrection. Here is one personal account of its impact:

> For Los Angeles writer Earl Ofari Hutchinson, who started visiting the shop as a Los Angeles City College student in 1963, the store and its resources were a revelation at a time when Southern California was isolated from the civil rights mainstream.
>
> "He created an environment of comfort and intellectual stimulation," Hutchinson said. "There were no pretensions about him, no ivory tower intellectualism. He strongly felt he had a duty to really be a solid mentor to young people and point them in the right direction in terms of understanding their past."
>
> (Luna 2002)

When the Black Nationalist Hugh Gordon died, he left money to open a bookstore that was named after him in the late 1940s. It was affiliated with the Communist Party and connected its programming to every community struggle:

> Perhaps the most important contribution the Communist Party and its local neighborhood clubs and councils made to Black Los Angeles was the political education they dispensed to Black residents … O'Neil Cannon, a Black migrant from New Orleans who owned a small printing shop in Watts, also

> saw the party's political education as a critical moment in the emergence of the modern civil rights movement. "The kind of leadership among people that was encouraged by the party made it possible for people to understand how to struggle. I think that is the most important contribution made by the Communist Party to the world … to teach people how to struggle."
>
> (Sides 2003, 142–43)

The modern organized political life of the Black community was in many ways launched with the founding of the NAACP in 1914. Husband and wife dentists John and Vada Summerville founded the Los Angeles chapter in their home. Its period of greatest growth was from 1941 to 1945, when it went from two thousand to eleven thousand members, making it the fifth-largest chapter in the country (Sides 2003, 140). The Los Angeles Urban League chapter was established in 1921 (Tolbert 1980, 90; Vincent 1981).

The Black Nationalist tradition, meaning all Black organizations organizing for the self-determination of the Black community—a political rather than ideological definition—has long been present in Los Angeles. At every stage, this has involved study programs to orient members to the history of their people and the dangers of the racism and economic exploitation that they face. This starts at the beginning of the twentieth century:

> In 1903 Los Angeles Blacks had organized their first nonreligious community group, the Los Angeles Forum. Unique in both its makeup and purpose, the Forum was designed to provide a space for the discussion of community affairs by Blacks of all strata.
>
> (Tolbert 1980, 27)

Two decades later, the Los Angeles chapter of the UNIA was formed in 1921 (Tolbert 1980, 51–53). The UNIA did not survive internal contradictions, but in Los Angeles this movement tendency was resurrected in 1957 when Malcolm X organized the Nation of Islam's Mosque Number 27 (Sides 2003, 173).

Overall, Hollywood, as an economic force as well as a worldview, has always impacted the cultural life of Los Angeles. Black people were systematically excluded from movie jobs and were portrayed through a racist lens. But the Black community itself provided the counter-narratives. One example is the novelist Chester Himes:

> In 1941, the up and coming Black writer Chester Himes and his wife took a Greyhound bus from Cleveland to Los Angeles. Thirty-two years old and completely exasperated by the racial discrimination he had encountered in Ohio and his boyhood home in Mississippi, Himes hoped Los Angeles would be better … Himes' frustration with racial discrimination in Los Angeles

> informed his first two published novels, *If He Hollers Let Him Go* (1945) and *Lonely Crusade* (1947), both searing indictments of racism, underemployment, and the emasculation of African American men in the 1940s.
>
> (Sides 2003, 54–55)

The major cultural breakthrough at the beginning of the 1960s was Horace Tapscott founding the Pan Afrikan Peoples Arkestra in 1961. At first, this was a vehicle for the musicians to bond and explore new musical directions in the tradition of innovators such as Sun Ra. But, after a couple of years, they turned to the community to spread their message. This is how Tapscott describes some of the motion:

> Some of the members had jobs in the schools around the city and some got jobs as substitute teachers. They'd bring the music into the schools, wherever they taught and whenever they'd sub. We'd sneak it in. We knew it was important to get into the community, deep, real deep, and we wanted to have the schools as our launching pad.
>
> (Tapscott and Isoardi 2001, 94)

Tapscott goes on to describe their Black Studies pedagogical plan:

> We wanted to get the children as early as possible and start playing Black music, and telling them stories about Black folk in history, so they could have something to hook up with, because there was so little for them. Without this, they'd always see the white world as the better world. Straight hair would be seen as good; nappy would be bad hair. Lighter skin would be more beautiful than darker. That's how many in my generation and before grew up, and that's the poison, the dangerous poison, that UGMA (Underground Music Association) wanted to attack. We wanted the children to care about themselves. We even had cats going around teaching older people how to read and write.
>
> (Tapscott and Isoardi 2001, 95)

These activities led to the creation of the Studio Watts Workshop in 1964. The poet Jayne Cortez spearheaded this effort, one outcome of which was the offering of a wide variety of classes, mainly in the arts. Another institutional innovation that same year was led by Samella Lewis, who founded the Museum of African American Art (S.S. Lewis 1973, 1990, 2003; S.S. Lewis and Waddy 1969). The next year, from August 11 to 16, the community of Watts went up in flames during what has been called the Watts Rebellion. One year later, everything changed when the cry for Black Power rang out during a protest march in Mississippi.

Each Black community in this chapter and beyond has its own political culture, created like a stew out of the particularities of geography, history, and local creativity. That political culture involves an extended dialogue and discussion about Black history and culture. This chapter has documented the experience of four major communities: New York, Chicago, New Orleans, and Los Angeles. Examining political culture in this way foregrounds the autonomous agency of Black people using educational programming in many forms to defend themselves against racism and all other forms of oppression. This is the community basis of Black Studies as Intellectual History.

Within the institutional mainstream but under conditions of segregation, the local high school concentrated Black talent, both teachers and students. These schools became advanced musical academies and produced musicians who embraced Black music traditions and achieved a high level of excellence. Outside of the mainstream, Black agency gave rise to media, bookstores, art organizations, museums, library programs, traditions of lectures and discussion, and more. Self-organized cultural practices, especially in the musical and literary arts, advocated for and supported Black consciousness, awareness of Black history, and the desire and capability to combat the evil of racist oppression. Over the generations, out of the antagonism of living and thinking Black under this oppressive system came five particular persistent ideologies of freedom. These are in a sense the main channels of community political culture, even when hidden or unacknowledged.

The ideologies of Black liberation developed in community-based social movements. There have been five main ideological tendencies, always somehow overlapping and never in isolation from each other. Pan-Africanism links together Africa and the African Diaspora in a common search for a unified identity and cultural integrity, free from imperialist colonial domination. Nationalism is a similar ideological position that focuses on nations within the African Diaspora. Black Liberation Theology is the interpretation and use of religion to assert a moral imperative to fight for freedom. Feminism, also called womanism (coined by Alice Walker), is the call for Black women to find common understanding of their experience and fight against male supremacy (patriarchy) in unity with the general fight for Black liberation. And, Socialism targets the capitalist system as the systemic context for all Black exploitation and oppression.

These five ideological tendencies are central to the curriculum focus in Black Studies, especially the main thinkers and writers who have propagated key ideas, and the movements who embodied these ideas in practical struggle. In carrying these ideas forward, key thinkers also provided methodological direction that continues to be important for Black Studies as it is practiced today. Martin Luther King Jr. and Malcolm X are clear examples of this.

Martin Luther King Jr. directly challenged mainstream scholars. Among King's most important speeches, one that explicitly links him to the rationale and program of research in Black Studies, is a 1967 speech he gave to the American Psychological Association, "The Role of the Behavioral Scientist in the Civil Rights Movement." In it he states:

> Negroes want the social scientist to address the white community and "tell it like it is." White America has an appalling lack of knowledge concerning the reality of Negro life. One reason some advances were made in the South during the past decade was the discovery by northern whites of the brutal facts of southern segregated life. It was the Negro who educated the nation by dramatizing the evils through non-violent protest. The social scientist played little or no role in disclosing truth. The Negro action movement with raw courage did it virtually alone. When the majority of the country could not live with the extremes of brutality they witnessed, political remedies were enacted and customs were altered.
>
> (King Jr. 1967)

Going further, he indicates how Black people were not only acting, but were becoming conscious of the bigger social context for their struggle. King explained the resurgence of Black Studies by focusing on the role of the social sciences:

> Ten years of struggle have sensitized and opened the Negro's eyes to reaching. For the first time in their history Negroes have become aware of the deeper causes for the crudity and cruelty that governed white society's responses to their needs. They discovered that their plight was not a consequence of superficial prejudice but was systemic.
>
> The slashing blows of backlash and frontlash have hurt the Negro, but they have also awakened him and revealed the nature of the oppressor. To lose illusion is to gain truth. Negroes have grown wiser and more mature and they are hearing more clearly those who are raising fundamental questions about our society whether the critics be Negro or white. When this process of awareness and independence crystallizes, every rebuke, every evasion, become hammer blows on the wedge that splits the Negro from the larger society.
>
> Social science is needed to explain where this development is going to take us. Are we moving away, not from integration, but from the society which made it a problem in the first place? How deep and at what rate of speed is this process occurring? These are some vital questions to be answered if we are to have a clear sense of our direction.
>
> (King Jr. 1967)

King was speaking to the white academic mainstream, who had no inclination or capacity to respond. But Black Studies was soon to take up this task in the academic mainstream, and somehow he knew this, as James Cone relates: "In Clarksdale, Mississippi (March 19, 1968), he said: 'We're going to let our children know that the only philosophers that lived were not Plato and Aristotle, but W.E.B. Du Bois and Alain Locke came through the universe'" (Cone 1999, 152, n. 20).

In dialectical fashion, Malcolm X made his contribution by directly addressing Black people in what to study and how to think. Malcolm was a revolutionary who thought outside of the box. Keenly aware of the need for study, he directed people to African-American history and world history as well:

> Of all our studies, history is best qualified to reward our research. And when you see that you've got problems, all you have to do is examine the historic method used all over the world by others who have problems similar to yours. Once you see how they got theirs straight, then you know how you can get yours straight.
>
> (X and Breitman 1990, 8)

Likewise, elsewhere he said:

> One of the first things I think young people, especially nowadays, should learn is how to see for yourself and listen for yourself and think for yourself. Then you can come to an intelligent decision for yourself. If you form the habit of going by what you hear others say about someone, or going by what others think about someone, instead of searching that thing out for yourself and seeing for yourself, you will be walking west when you think you are going east, and you will be walking east when you think you are walking west. This generation especially of our people has a burden, more so than any other time in history. The most important thing that we can learn to do today is think for ourselves.
>
> It's good to keep wide open ears and listen to what everybody else has to say, but when you come to make a decision, you have to weigh all of what you've heard on its own, and place it where it belongs, and come to a decision for yourself, you'll never regret it. But if you form the habit of taking what somebody else says about a thing without checking it out for yourself, you'll find that other people will have you hating your friends and loving your enemies. This is one of the things that our people are beginning to learn today that it is very important to think out a situation or yourself. If you don't you'll always be maneuvered into a situation where you are never fighting your actual enemies, where you will find yourself fighting your own self.
>
> (X 1965b, 4–5)

Both King and Malcolm X were charismatic icons who contributed to the mission and method of Black Studies.

PART II

Black Studies as Social Movement

Building on the work of early scholars, the historically Black colleges and universities, the community and the ideologies that they had formulated, Black Studies surged forward in the 1960s through a set of social movements. In other words, Black Studies was how Black activists educated themselves and their communities. They carried this study into all levels of education, especially higher education. It often took place in study circles and organizational meetings, and it extended Black Studies as Intellectual History in new directions.

What is a social movement? It is networks of people who share innovative ideas as manifested in key concepts, slogans, and texts, a desire to work as a collective, following particular methods of communication, acknowledged leaders, organizational forms, and a shared identity. A social movement is not permanent. It has a beginning and an end. But a social movement can give rise to one or more formal organizations that may live on after a movement has subsided. Such organizations formalize membership and usually have rules (for example, a constitution and by-laws) and a financial basis for sustainability. This is in fact how Black Studies grew from an emergent social movement into an institutionalized activity within formal institutions (Rojas 2007; Biondi 2012). That is the subject of Part III of this book.

Part II here identifies educational processes within several movements for social change that have always been driving forces within Black political culture. As this book defines it, a movement begins with a social base in the community—its target constituency. Within this social context, the educational process has both an ideological orientation and an organizational form. It creates roles and an institutional framework in which to carry out the educational process. Intellectual production and educational programs that arose in social movements have become part of the standard curriculum of Black Studies.

This activist manifestation of Black Studies begins off campus in community struggles for social change. Each surge of the Freedom Movement created a new identity for Black people. Each time, that movement also contained the sustained identity of people from an earlier movement or even people who drew on the memory of such movements for inspiration. All manifest the sustained struggles for the strategic goal of freedom.

The identity factor is key, because a social movement exists when people believe they are in it and act accordingly. Identity is made manifest in a person's consciousness. This identity is part of what builds a movement, because people can see it, hear it, and talk to it. There are two key aspects of identity as part of one's consciousness. First is the ability of members to represent the movement. You change your appearance so you look like the movement, and you change your speech so you sound like the movement. Further, you master the movement's catechism, so you can communicate with others as a representative of the movement to win them over and recruit them.

Black Studies as Social Movement advances knowledge about the Black experience. This involves the production, distribution, and use of texts and cultural creativity. This involves the resurrection of previous knowledge, which sparks new consciousness of recreating a tradition of thinking and acting. Reading becomes an imperative, because one of the mandatory starting points of the Black freedom struggle is the reclaiming of Black history to become a living part of freedom consciousness. Part of this is to establish pride in what Black people have accomplished over historical time, and part of this is to affirm that Black people have always fought for freedom and never totally capitulated to the oppressive forces ruling over them. Indeed, this knowledge becomes part of the arsenal of ideas coveted by the Black community for its survival and prosperity.

Why? The important Black historian Lerone Bennett Jr. provides the answer:

> Education for Black people in the US (and throughout the world) is a question of life and death. It is a political question. A question of power. The power to name, to define and to control minds. He who controls minds has little or nothing to fear from bodies.
>
> (Bennett cited in Fuller 1972)

Therefore, a freedom-oriented educational process is a social question that collective social action alone can resolve. Freedom points to the transformation of the society, and such change requires the masses of people, relying on their organizational resources, to take action whether as part of the mainstream system, for example, voting, or in non-institutional ways.

Black Studies as Social Movement owes its origin to what can be called insurgent institutions. They institutionalized educational programs designed to prepare people to struggle for social justice. Insurgent institutions themselves have generally understood their purpose as either to educate cadre or provide forms of mass movement general education. The first is a form of leadership training that involves intensive study of foundational knowledge about society, its history, and the structures of power and control. The goal is to provide core staff with the skills to guide mass movement organizations, be they organizations or forms of mass action such as national mobilizations, sustained local campaigns, and national and international outreach and support work.

The concept of an insurgent institution provides a vital counterpart to mainstream formal educational systems—public and private. Formal educational institutions develop and maintain what they identify as the normalized institutional knowledge of the society sanctioned by the government. For instance, neoliberal policy blurs the distinction between public and private institutions, directing more and more public funds to private and religious schools. At the same time, public policy standards for teacher hiring and evaluation, curriculum development, and evaluation of student achievement are lowered. But social movements create an insurgent institution in order to study the historical development of society and the systemic crisis facing Black people, and then to satisfy the need to imagine an alternative social order, to educate forces to build and expand the movement as the necessary force for change.

Each chapter in this part of the book looks at how one of six movements generated research and/or teaching about Black history and culture. But first, it will help to briefly identify and characterize each of these movements.

THE FREEDOM MOVEMENT

Black people have historically fought for freedom, first from slavery and then from all other types of exploitation and oppression. The Black middle class and their allies appropriated this struggle into a civil rights movement, a reformulation that defined progress as a function of legislation and court decisions rather than the fundamental and actual elimination of racist actions in practice. But within the movement for freedom, while being called a civil rights movement, people were still conscious that they needed to know their own history, especially how people had waged the struggle for freedom from the earliest of times until the present. There was a need for the kind of knowledge that would enable one to navigate the institutional obstacles to full citizenship. People came to realize they had to develop their own point of view, a Black-oriented point of view with freedom as a bottom line.

THE BLACK POWER MOVEMENT

The slogan “Black Power” represented a fundamental break with the dominant position of the Civil Rights Movement, from using persuasion based on reason and morality aimed at the ruling elites managing mainstream institutions of power to aggregating Black people and their autonomous resources in the fight for the power to achieve their desired social change within and outside the system. Militant activists embraced the slogan in their fight for reform, in terms of electing Black public officials and using the large market position of Black consumers to impact local economic developments for Black entrepreneurs and jobs. Those holding a more radical position of systemic transformation advocating revolutionary change also embraced it. Advocates of Black Power began to rethink how society works and situate themselves within the ideological traditions of Black Nationalism and Pan-Africanism. Virtually every social movement expression of Black Studies has taken up Black Power as an essential theoretical concept. As such, Black Studies in all its forms is a Black Power project.

This slogan represented a rupture of class unity. The middle-class movement for reform claimed this slogan as a political lever for advancing their interests within the system. This includes a reinvention of the "buy Black" movement to build Black businesses, to aggregate Black votes to elected Black politicians, and generally to give a new impetus to affirmative action plans for hiring and promotions to advance Blacks into managerial positions. Radical forces appealing to the masses of working and poor Black people did so as well by indicting the system and calling for systemic change. These two contradictory tendencies converged in Black Studies educational activities.

THE BLACK ARTS MOVEMENT

Cultural workers exploded with new forms of creativity aimed at creating a new Black aesthetic. The affirmation was summed up in the slogan "Black is beautiful," a necessary development because the mainstream had always promoted the opposite, arguing, "If you're white, you're all right; if you're brown, stick around, but if you're Black, get back!" The mainstream dominant cultural values held that all aspects of the Black body (hair texture, lip size, skin color, nose shape, etc.) were bad and ugly. The Black Arts Movement carried forward Black Power into visual images, literature, performances, music, and song. This reversed an orientation from how closely one could act and look like a European to discovering an African essence inside whatever improvisational Diasporic form you performed in everyday life.

Black Arts Movement, too, developed two paths of change, one inside the mainstream cultural institutions and the other based autonomously in Black community initiatives. The exposure of patterns of racism in cultural institutions coupled with the rising demand for change from Black people led to greater inclusion. But this inclusion was mainly symbolic, while the greater qualitative impact was the mass mobilization of what amounted to a cultural revolution in the Black community. Black Studies reflects both of these tendencies.

THE NEW COMMUNIST MOVEMENT

As the systemic nature of Black people's oppression became clear in popular political discourse, and as workers began to understand their critical role in the functioning of the economy, activists turned toward Marxism as a theoretical path past capitalism toward socialism. Revolutionary developments in China, Vietnam, and Cuba and in the leading forces within the anticolonial African liberation movements captured progressive consciousness in the world. Marxism became part of the toolkit of those building Black Studies. This laid to rest the question of whether or not Marxist theory has ever been applied to the African-American experience. The theoretical focus was on how the Black freedom struggle was both a national and a class question.

Marxist theory was reborn in its application to the oppression of Black people and the possibility for Black liberation. This led to an awakening of the legacy of socialist thought and its application to Black people from the nineteenth century through the influence of the 1917 Russian Revolution, which in turn resulted in an intense replay of the Marxist-Black Nationalist debate, mentioned in Part I. This debate led to an upsurge in the study of all the relevant literature of Black intellectual history, and had a far-reaching impact on activists in all forms of the Black Liberation Movement discussed in this chapter.

THE BLACK WOMEN'S MOVEMENT

Black women have always been part of every social movement Black people have created to fight against oppression and for justice. Moreover, women have been the main caregivers for the young; hence, they have been the primary educators in the Black community, something that has carried over into formal roles as primary and secondary schoolteachers. A Black women's movement developed because of women fighting against what some have called triple oppression and others call the intersectionality of class exploitation, racism, and patriarchy (male supremacy). This movement has exposed a gender bias in most educational programs and studies of the Black experience, and as such has become a major critical factor in Black Studies.

THE BLACK STUDENT MOVEMENT

The actual social forces that demanded and created Black Studies were nurtured in the community and in the movement. The key catalyst for institutionalization were young people recruited into institutions of higher education as a new generation of students. Students were the main agents of change in the creation of Black Studies, fighting for a new agenda for teaching and research, a new institutional home for Black faculty and students, and a new relationship between the institution and the Black community. Not surprisingly, they encountered hostility and, in response, they created a battlefront for the Black Power Movement.

At the very beginning, students had to create their own study circles before they could penetrate the official curriculum. This led to a reality check on the weaknesses of their libraries' holdings of Black-oriented material, faculty unfamiliar with Black intellectual history, and of institutions reluctant to make moves to facilitate the study of the Black experience as a significant area of scholarship. Again, two paths: one led to the long march through the institutions of higher education, and one left the campus to go back out into the community.

Each of these six movements just described developed a variety of community-based education programs that led to the formal institutionalization of Black Studies, so each merits discussion in some detail. This classification should not be considered as rigid, because these movements were and are learning labs in which groups that differ markedly also learn from each other. However, for the sake of clarity, this framework will help explain how Black Studies has roots as a social movement.

One of the most fundamental points about Black Studies as Social Movement is that many of the first-generation Black Studies activists began their Black Studies experience in this context. Young activists were socialized into the Black radical tradition in study groups and by being mentored by an older generation of activist intellectuals and artists. When they entered college, they became student activists ramping up the national demands for Black Studies, including an increase in Black faculty and Black courses and greater enrollment of Black students. It is important that any consideration of Black Studies take into account the reality of how it started in one or more social movements.

In most cases of Black Studies as Social Movement, a class divide emerged. Black middle-class forces charted a path into the mainstream while the marginalized classes moved in an autonomous direction. Taken to its logical conclusion, this divide represented itself as a difference between reform and revolution, building an educational process to enable Black people to join the mainstream of society or to orient Black people to building a new kind of society altogether.

4
The Freedom Movement

The word "freedom" suggests that Black people conceptualizing their future experience beyond bondage has its origin in Africans being captured and subjected to European-orchestrated slavery. Once enslaved, Black people always longed to be free and struggled to define what that meant at every step in their historical path. There were always three questions: What are the current problems Black people face? What can Black people learn from past freedom struggles? What kind of social change will get Black People free? Answering each of these questions demands some form of study, thus calling forth some manifestation of Black Studies.

The Freedom Movement created pedagogies of protest at every stage. An early manifestation of the Abolitionist movement was the African Free School established by the New York Manumission Society in 1787. Early alumni were Ira Aldridge, Henry Highland Garnet, Alexander Crummell, and Charles Lewis Reason. This school was not without controversy:

> After opening yet other schools with enrollment surpassing a thousand children, a crisis unfolded in the early 1830s when Andrews (a prominent teacher at the school) publicly advocated the idea that American blacks should be colonized in Africa, one of the period's most controversial racial issues. Black students boycotted the schools, leading to Andrews' dismissal in 1832 and the hiring of black teachers to replace whites in each of the city's African Free Schools. By 1835, when the schools ended their run as privately supported institutions, the African Free School had seven buildings in different neighborhoods, and it had educated thousands of girls and boys. At that time the African Free Schools and their facilities were integrated into the public school system. This was several years after all slaves were freed in 1827 (in New York).
>
> ("African Free School" 2018)

Following the Civil War, schooling became more institutionalized throughout the South as a result of the American Missionary Society and the Union army during the great Reconstruction period. One of the little-known facts is the extent to which Black Union soldiers contributed their mustering-out pay for local schools in the South to educate the recently freed African Americans. Just like in the period following the Civil War, the movement in the midst of the Great Depression continued this process of initiating education for liberation:

> In the 1930s and 1940s, the Southern Negro Youth Congress (SNYC) organized labor schools in Nashville, Tennessee; New Orleans, Louisiana; and Birmingham and Fairfield, Alabama. The labor schools educated Black workers and local union leaders "on the present problems of the labor movement, as well as of techniques for improving the effectiveness of their particular union meetings and procedures."
>
> (Payne and Strickland 2008, 177)

A close reading of Black activism reveals that educational programs always were one tactic in the organizing and mobilizing of people to fight against oppression. The sacrifice and agency of Black people themselves propelled all of these efforts. In his book *Black Self-Determination*, Vincent Franklin makes a strong case for education being the basis for the Freedom Movement's roots in the political culture of Black people from slavery on (V.P. Franklin 1992 [1984]). Cedric Robinson makes a similar argument in his *Black Marxism* (1983), when he discusses what he calls the Black radical tradition as based on elements of Black culture:

> It was not, however, an understanding of the Europeans which preserved those Africans in the grasp of slavers, planters, merchants and colonizers. Rather, it was the ability to conserve their native consciousness of the world from alien intrusion, the ability to imaginatively recreate a precedent metaphysic while being subjected to enslavement, racial domination and repression. This was the raw material of the Black radical tradition, the values, ideas, conceptions and constructions of reality from which resistance was manufactured … [I]t was the materials constructed from a shared philosophy developed in the African past and transmitted as culture, from which revolutionary consciousness was realized and the ideology of struggle formed.
>
> (C.J. Robinson 1983, 443)

Several organizations in the Freedom Movement focused both their cadre training and mass-education programs on civil rights, strategically using the US Constitution as the framework for social change within the system. In general, this was when people began to change the name of the movement from the Freedom Movement and replace it with the Civil Rights Movement. The goal of freedom was not only a repudiation of enslavement, but also opened up the question of having the choice to remain in the USA or to repatriate back to the African continent. The goal of civil rights assumed that Black people would remain in the USA, facing a history that bore the burden of the legacy of slavery encoded in the life and culture of that country.

A key insurgent institution for the southern Civil Rights Movement was the Highlander Folk School, founded in 1932 in Tennessee. Black and white trade unionists in the South created it as a liberated zone, one of the rare places where all activists could gather. They set up training programs and facilitated organizing campaigns. One of their major efforts was working with activists to set up what became known as "Citizenship Schools," which were designed to prepare people to organize voter registration campaigns in the South. The focus was not only on the mechanics of voting, but also on the historical obstacles that the racism of the main political parties had developed since the Fourteenth Amendment to the US Constitution. They were re-educating people in the political system and arming them with the methods to build social movements. The Citizenship Schools were subsequently adopted by the Southern Christian Leadership Conference (SCLC) after being led by Septima Poinsette Clark:

> By the time the [SCLC] project ended in 1970, approximately 2,500 African Americans had taught these basic literacy and political education classes for tens of thousands of their neighbors. The program never had a high profile, but civil rights leaders and scholars assert that it helped to bring many people into the movement, to cultivate grassroots leaders, and to increase Black participation in voting and other civic activities.
>
> (Payne and Strickland 2008, 25)

A more comprehensive educational program was developed under the label "freedom school." This insurgent institutional form arose under different conditions in both northern cities and southern states, yet within the dialectics of struggle that defined the Civil Rights Movement. The southern Civil Rights Movement had adopted the philosophy of non-violence of Mahatma Gandhi in constructing a strategy for action. Gandhi called it "satyagraha," meaning the people as a truth force. African-American activists were meeting savage violence by racist forces attempting to halt any progress. Before and after King received his Nobel Peace Prize in 1964, new waves of violence were changing the political landscape of the entire country. Events in Mississippi proved to be a watershed.

In June 1963, Medgar Evers, Mississippi state leader of the NAACP, was gunned down in his driveway. This precipitated plans for a major civil rights campaign in Mississippi to confront racist violence. Mississippi had long been known as the leading state for racist lynching, but now in Mississippi the movement was able to plan a massive response. The civil rights organizations united in a coalition called Council of Federated Organizations (COFO), including SNCC, Congress of Racial Equality (CORE), NAACP, and SCLC.

They launched the 1964 Mississippi Freedom Summer and recruited over one thousand Black and white activists to spend the summer in Mississippi on projects from voter education and registration to freedom schools and other civil rights activities. This was a violent summer:

> Over the course of the ten-week project: 1,062 people were arrested, 80 Freedom Summer workers were beaten, 37 churches were bombed or burned, 30 Black homes or businesses were bombed or burned, 4 civil rights workers were killed, 4 people were critically wounded, and at least 3 Mississippi Blacks were murdered because of their support for the Civil Rights Movement. Most notably three COFO activists were murdered with the support of the local police officials in Neshoba County Mississippi, who were also members of the KKK. Two were from the north with strong family support (Andrew Goodman and Michael Schwerner) and one was a Mississippi Black activist with CORE (James Chaney). This tragedy became a national scandal, fueling 1964 urban insurrections in Harlem, New York, Rochester New York, and Philadelphia, Pennsylvania.
>
> (McAdam 1990)

The best national case of the freedom school movement was in the Mississippi Summer Project in 1964. Jon Hale argues that the Mississippi freedom schools created "pedagogies of protest" that served as a tool to build the movement:

> The Freedom Schools embodied long traditions of an ideology that equated education with freedom and liberation and were therefore ideologically familiar to Mississippi communities. The Freedom Schools were built upon community organization strategies that dated back to Reconstruction. Yet the Freedom Schools were markedly different. They were organized outside of the state's purview, which afforded opportunities to directly combat de jure segregation. Freedom School teachers were independent from the economic system controlled by whites and were therefore free to openly defy the segregated way of life that was cherished in Mississippi. They also adopted a radical and progressive pedagogy and curriculum that cultivated participatory notions of citizenship that were absent from most Mississippi schools. Through both continuity and rupture, the Freedom Schools constitute one of the most unique legacies of the civil rights movement, and indeed, American history.
>
> (Hale 2017, 33–34)

SNCC Field Secretary Charlie Cobb wrote the proposal and plan for the freedom schools during the Mississippi Freedom Summer. He argued that such insurgent institutions as freedom schools were necessary to break through the system of oppression that the government schools in Mississippi represented. His proposal called for a program to include "Political and social studies, relating their studies to their society. This should be a prominent part of the curriculum" (Payne and Strickland 2008, 67–68).

The freedom school curriculum in the Mississippi Freedom Summer implemented pedagogy that was grounded in a theory of getting people to struggle. As a Black Studies manifestation, it centered the articulation of a Black perspective on the need to build a movement for social change. The pedagogical techniques stressed the building of self-knowledge through questions.

Rather than being built around facts to be memorized and answered on standardized tests, freedom schools are based on asking questions. The basic set of questions are:

- Why are we (teachers and students) in Freedom Schools?
- What is the Freedom Movement?
- What alternatives does the Freedom Movement offer us?

And the secondary set of questions are:

- What does the majority culture have that we want?
- What does the majority culture have that we don't want?
- What do we have that we want to keep?

("Freedom School Curriculum" n.d.)

And while the freedom schools were movement-based insurgent institutions that did not become permanent fixtures, they did achieve a clear impact on the generation who participated:

> The curriculum had to work outside the normative parameters of education in order to politically engage disenfranchised youth in Mississippi. Concepts like citizenship, American government, African American history, and civil rights movement philosophy, therefore introduced students to solutions to segregation and unequal opportunity. Organizers reasoned that this would lead to an analysis of freedom, citizenship, and rights in Mississippi. They defined critical thinking in the freedom schools by asking questions fundamental to American democracy that were rarely asked within the confines of the traditional public school.
>
> (Hale 2017, 92)

But freedom schools were not only in the South. One northern city that frequently called freedom schools into existence was Chicago. This was especially true during two major citywide school boycotts in October 1963 and February

1964. During these massive actions of social protest, the movement recruited churches to provide space for students to attend classes it organized. Similar freedom school programs were set up in tandem with other major school boycotts in Boston, Philadelphia, and New York.

Along with the freedom schools were freedom libraries. "Freedom Libraries were originally a product of "Freedom Summer"—the voting registration campaign launched by various civil rights organizations in Mississippi during the summer of 1964" (Selby 2019, 86).

In later years, Marian Wright Edelman, a former civil rights worker and founder and director of the Children's Defense Fund (CDF), brought into being a new iteration of the freedom school. She founded the Black Student Leadership Network (BSLN) in 1991 at a conference at Howard University. This national network of student activists adopted a plan for freedom schools that was implemented in the summer of 1993. The CDF continued the work around the theme "I Can and Must Make a Difference" for children in lower-income Black communities:

> Across the country at more than 80 freedom schools in the summer of 2005, this theme encouraged and empowered African American children to make a difference in themselves, as well as in their families, communities, country, and world. Modeled after the Mississippi freedom schools founded by members of the Student Nonviolent Coordinating Committee in the 1960s, the current CDF summer program arose from the work of the Black Student Leadership work in the 1990s.
>
> (Payne and Strickland 2008, 191)

5
The Black Power Movement

The potent political concept of Black Power jump-started a new form of Black Studies as Social Movement (Joseph 2006, 2009; Bush 2000). This newly articulated slogan announced the transition within the Freedom Movement from a focus on constitutionally based civil rights to a focus on Black liberation based on self-determination—in other words, Black people were organizing themselves rather than depending on white allies. This was a paradigm shift. It changed language. It changed assumptions about society and its political process. It changed the audience who had to approve of leadership and any program for change. Black English became part of the normal speech of political discourse, thus legitimizing mass cultural patterns in the Black community. The starting-point assumption was that racist oppression is systemic and has been for the entire life of the society. So it called into question even the founding fathers and the US Constitution over the barbarism of the slave trade and slavery. Most important of all, for Black Power, the leadership and organizational program now derived their legitimacy from the approval of the masses of Black people and not from mainstream support and mass media visibility.

The cry for Black Power produced a paradigm shift in Black thought. The Black community had, like all other Americans, come to have rising expectations since the end of World War II. The 1960s ushered in a period of advancement, more and better jobs, more income, and hopes for an even better future. However, on a global level, the post-war period led to the "Cold War" competition between the USSR and the USA. An anti-communism passion swept through the USA, led by Wisconsin senator Joseph McCarthy. The culture of fear of the repressive McCarthy period of the 1950s was broken by the Civil Rights Movement, as people began to feel free enough to exercise their rights to speak and assemble freely. The high point of protest was the March on Washington in August 1963, where the eloquent strains of Martin Luther King Jr.'s "I Have a Dream" speech renewed the people's belief that a better life awaited them. The Civil Rights Movement was becoming acceptable to a large section of the mainstream, giving a positive view of itself both to itself and to the world. Martin Luther King Jr.'s being awarded the Nobel Peace Prize in December 1964 made manifest the global symbolism of this.

In 1965, assassinations provoked urban insurrections. The murder of Malcolm X took place in New York on February 21 while the police were lax in their security and appeared to be complicit with the planned assassination (Evanzz 1998). Jimmy Lee Jackson was murdered February 26 by police in Marion, Alabama, while trying to protect his mother from racist abuse. Six months later, the Watts Rebellion erupted in August, resulting in thirty-four deaths and nearly a thousand buildings being either destroyed or severely damaged (Conot 1968). A new militancy was in the air, ready to embrace the message of Malcolm X to fight for freedom by any means necessary.

An ideological shift in the Black Freedom Movement went from "We shall overcome" as a goal to "Black Power" as the strategic tool to get there. The concept of Black Power had been advanced in various forms in all stages of the Freedom Movement from the earliest times. At the core of this tradition is the concept of self-determination, meaning that Black people have a right and must unite themselves to determine their own destiny. This has been a fundamental challenge to the mainstream, because the options have always included both integration into and negation of the mainstream.

The current use of the term "Black Power" for this 1960s movement begins with a book by that title first published in 1954 by Richard Wright about the revolution in Ghana under the leadership of Kwame Nkrumah (R. Wright 1954). Nkrumah, mentioned in Chapters 1 and 2, headed the 1950s independence movement in Ghana. His relationship with African Americans was very close, as he had attended Lincoln University in Pennsylvania and developed a close friendship with its president, Horace Mann Bond. In addition, he had developed a close relationship with W.E.B. Du Bois and many others, including George Padmore from Trinidad, because he had been an activist at the Fifth Pan-African Congress held in Manchester, England, in 1945 (Sherwood 1995).

Nkrumah launched the first Africa-based Black Studies program when he created the Institute of African Studies:

> The Institute of African Studies was established in 1961 as a semi-autonomous Institute within the University of Ghana, and formally opened in October 1963 by the first President of Ghana, Kwame Nkrumah. The mandate of the Institute is to conduct research and teaching on the peoples and cultural heritage of Africa and to disseminate the findings. In addition, the Institute has always emphasized publishing and teaching, particularly at the post-graduate level. At the time of its establishment the notion of Pan-Africanism and nationalism were unquestioned in the academy. The study of Africa and her peoples, both on the continent and in the Diaspora, was considered critical and was pursued with passion.
>
> (Institute of African Studies n.d.)

Nkrumah continued this work in many other ways: he recruited St. Clair Drake, the great African-American social scientist, to lead the establishment of the Department of Sociology at the University of Ghana at Legon. He also convinced W.E.B. Du Bois to relocate to Ghana in order to work on his final major project, the *Encyclopedia Africana*.

Wright published his book, *Black Power*, in 1954, just three years before Ghana achieved full independence. Nkrumah had already become prime minister and, for people around the world, symbolized Africa moving beyond the limitations of European colonial domination. Wright focused on the people he encountered in his reflections and how he interacted with them. It is interesting that when he was explaining to Nkrumah the psychological contradictions he was facing as an African American in Africa, Nkrumah clarified his own position by declaring, "I'm a Marxist Socialist" (Biney, quoted in Lupalo 2016, 46). No doubt, Nkrumah was responding to Wright's own essay rejecting Marxism, published in the CIA-funded anthology *The God That Failed* (Koestler and Crossman 1949; see also Saunders 2013, 64–69).

In November 1965, Lerone Bennett Jr. published an article in *Ebony Magazine* titled "Black Power: Freedmen Seize Reins of Power after Passage of the 1867 Voting Rights Bill" (J. West 2016). Bennett had graduated from Morehouse, where he was classmates with Martin Luther King Jr. He wrote a national best-seller *Before the Mayflower: A History of Black America, 1619–1962*, as well as a biography of King (Bennett Jr. 1964, 1969). Bennett Jr. has been a great contributor to Black Studies as an author, lecturer, and college professor (Northwestern University). His essays in *Ebony Magazine* have been without peer as public history.

His 1965 article uses the concept of Black Power to sum up the 1867 fight for the Voting Rights Bill as one of the major accomplishments of the Reconstruction period following the Civil War. He argues that this is the only time that a radical coalition held sway in the US Congress. But his main focus is on the political agency of Black people:

> It must not be thought that relative freedom came to the Negro unbidden. Throughout this struggle, which raged in the long hot summer of 1865–1866, Negro leaders and the Negro masses were very active, holding mass meetings and parades in Southern cities, sending petitions and pleas to legislatures and Congress ... They clearly saw the close connection between politics and economics, and they realized, better than some of their leaders, that it was necessary to ground political freedom on economic freedom. Repeatedly, in 1865–1866, freedmen demanded confiscation and redistribution of land. Repeatedly, they fought US soldiers who tried to drive them from the land.
>
> (Bennett Jr. 1965, 35)

Adam Clayton Powell, then a congressional representative from Harlem in New York City, raised the concept in spring 1966 in a commencement address at Howard University. Powell was the second-generation minister of a leading church in Harlem, the Abyssinian Baptist Church. Adam Clayton Powell Jr.'s early militancy is reflected in his book about the movement for social justice, *Marching Blacks: An Interpretive History of the Rise of the Black Common Man* (Powell Jr. 1945). In Congress, his style of Black leadership is contrasted with that of William Dawson from Chicago; Dawson was the consummate insider and Powell was the aggressive reflection of the Civil Rights Movement, famous for his Powell amendments that he attached to many bills to advance an anti-racist agenda (J.Q. Wilson 1980).

On June 6, 1966, James Meredith launched a March Against Fear from Memphis, Tennessee to Jackson, Mississippi, but was shot down on the second day of the march. The main Civil Rights Movement organizations picked up the challenge and turned it into a national march against fear. Later in the march (on June 16) Willie Ricks, followed by Stokely Carmichael, leading organizers for SNCC, began the chant for Black Power. By raising the slogan in the midst of this march against fear, they sparked a national debate. SNCC members had already been discussing different courses of action in the face of the hard violent repression against the movement, seemingly without any serious response from the federal government. Once the slogan was popularized during the Mississippi march, a polarization erupted in the overall movement led by Roy Wilkins of the NAACP, who condemned the concept and told *Reader's Digest* "the term 'black power' means anti-white power. [It is] a reverse Mississippi, a reverse Hitler, a reverse Ku Klux Klan" ("Roy Wilkins Facts" n.d.).

The following year, Carmichael and Charles Hamilton published the book *Black Power: The Politics of Liberation in America*. This was an SNCC-based study that advocated a militant program for self-determination. They stated their intention:

> This book presents a political framework and ideology which represents the last reasonable opportunity for this society to work out its racism problems short of prolonged destructive guerrilla warfare. That such violent warfare may be unavoidable is not herein denied. But if there is the slightest chance to avoid it, the politics of Black Power as described in this book is seen as the only viable hope.
>
> (Carmichael and Hamilton 1992)

While the discussion of guerrilla warfare in the USA seems far-fetched today, it becomes more conceivable when put in the context of the urban rebellions of the time. There were at least two massive urban rebellions in 1967: July 12–17 in Newark, New Jersey with 26 dead and 1,100 wounded; and July 23–27 in

Detroit, Michigan with 43 dead and 1,189 wounded (History 2021 [2017]; "1967 Newark Riots" 2018).

THE CONFERENCES

Right in the middle of these collective acts of resistance—from July 20–23—a National Conference on Black Power was held in Newark (Rise Up Newark n.d.). There could not have been a more electric setting for this conference. Masses of Black people were in the streets confronting the police and the National Guard, so the role of the public intellectual at this moment was not to lead the community but to try and figure out what the masses were saying. It is important to point out that this and subsequent conferences carried forward basic contradictions always inherent in Black unity motions, Black Nationalist motions. In general, these events attempt to unify and aggregate the resources of the Black community. On the one hand, there is the drive to aggregate resources to survive and prosper, and on the other the drive to aggregate resources to fight and change conditions of life. Within all of this, there is the class contradiction of what the Black middle class inclines toward, as compared to the masses of poor and working-class Black people. One camp privileges Black businesses and voting—the middle-class option—while quite a different working-class tendency emphasizes economic boycotts and radical street-based protests. By the time of the first Black Power Conference in 1967 in Newark, the differences were becoming sharp.

To some extent, this divergence of interests reflects how historical developments had led to a more complex class structure in the Black community. A shift had moved the Black community from its rural southern agricultural roots to an urban northern industrial base. The independent autonomous Black middle class was being transformed into a professional business comprador element connected to mainstream enterprises—hence no longer autonomous (Landry 1988). For its part, the Black working class was more fully integrated into the general industrial proletariat, though also being exploited at higher rates based on racist practices of being last hired, first fired, and being paid less (Baron 1971). In this 1967 Black Power moment, diverse class forces chose to participate in the conference and debate that ensued.

In fact, massive actions functioned as cauldrons of ideas in which activists imagined and reimagined Black Studies. There are several ways that the Newark Black Power conference connected with Black Studies. During the Newark conference, there were fourteen workshops with twenty chairs and co-chairs. Seventy-five percent of these people ended up being active in Black Studies. Black Studies activists first emerged in the community and then marched on to the campus. They brought the Black Power Movement into mainstream academic settings. The Black Power Movement set the agenda that became the focal point of Black Studies research and curriculum development.

A second Black Power Conference, held in Philadelphia the following year, took a turn toward a more militant political radicalism. And the class contradiction became even clearer. The Newark conference had been called after a planning meeting had been convened by Adam Clayton Powell Jr. in Washington, DC. Nathan Wright, an administrator in the Episcopal Church, was the chair of a planning committee that convened the Newark conference. He was decidedly a reformer with strong corporate ties; in fact, his brother sent out the invitations to the second conference on the corporate stationary of Clairol. They had fifty or more corporations to fund these two Black Power Conferences, a move that proved to be very controversial. The conferences, if viewed in terms of their administrative structure, were controlled by capital, but if viewed in terms of their constituents, reflected the emergent community-based Black Power Movement. Nathan Wright went on to become chair of African American Studies at State University of New York, Albany (Allen 1992, 138).

Another way that these conferences led to Black Studies academic programs is that the debate stimulated every ideological tendency to set up study circles to deepen understanding of the history of their respective positions and to study the other positions as well. The debate was on, and for activists to participate they had to study Black history and the ideological tendencies of the Black Liberation Movement. Many of the first participants in these study circles became the students and faculty in Black Studies on campus.

THE JOURNALS

The emergence of Black journals presenting material that became the curriculum for study in the Black Power Movement fed this turn toward ideological study and debate. In New York, the two most prominent journals were *Freedomways* (1961–1985) and *The Liberator* (1960–1971), discussed in Chapter 3. They represented two different tendencies in the movement, but with some overlap.

Ernest Kaiser, an associate editor of *Freedomways*, explained that:

> the magazine had three specific objectives: to mirror the developments of the Black people's struggles and provide a public forum for the review, examination and debate of all the problems of Blacks in the U.S. and elsewhere; to examine, in terms of Black freedom as well as the nation as a whole, the new forms of economic, political and social systems now existing or emerging in the world; and to provide a medium of expression for serious and talented writers on various levels of craftsmanship. It invited historians, sociologists,

economists, artists, workers, students, and especially activists in the freedom movement to contribute constructively to its search for truth.

(Kaiser 1985)

Freedomways presented a radical analysis by a broad and diverse set of authors. Even such a critic as Harold Cruse admits as much:

> Since its founding in 1961, *Freedomways* has published in its pages samples of the social thought of a larger number of Negro intellects from various levels of status and achievement. This material represents a rather broad consensus of what is actually being thought about the Negro-white situation in America, as of now. Therefore it is not just the old guard leftwing nucleus that is here but the social perception expressed by the articulate Negro intelligentsia as a whole.
>
> (Cruse 1967b, 248)

People working closely with the Communist Party founded the journal, with the first editor being Shirley Graham Du Bois. Ester Jackson, Margaret Burroughs, W. Alphaeus Hunton, and Jack O'Dell also played key roles; and its staff included nationalist-oriented community icons such as John Henrik Clarke, and key researchers from the Schomburg Center for Research and Black Culture-based library professionals such as Ernest Kaiser (J. McClendon 2009).

While the regular issues of the quarterly journal featured singularly important articles, its special issues represented major contributions to Black political and social thinking. Many of them became books and important reference works, which are listed in Table 5.

Table 5 Special Issues of *Freedomways*

Year (issue)	*Topic*
1962 (4)	The New Image of Africa
1963 (3)	Harlem: A Community in Transition
1963 (4)	W.E.B. Du Bois
1964 (3)	The People of the Caribbean Area
1965 (1)	W.E.B. Du Bois
1965 (2)	Mississippi: Opening Up the Closed Society
1968 (4)	The Crisis in Education and the Changing Afro-American Community
1971 (1)	Paul Robeson
1972 (3)	The African-Asian Special Issue
1974 (3)	The Black Image in the Mass Media
1979 (4)	Lorraine Hansberry: Art of Thunder, Vision of Light
1982 (3)	The Information Century
1983 (2 & 3)	The Middle East

Freedomways, describing itself as "a quarterly review of the Negro Freedom Movement," became the main journal of the progressive left-leaning Black intellectual activists. A wide variety of people involved in community circles and in the movements for social justice embraced it as material for study.

Its main competitor was the radical Black Nationalist-leaning monthly edited by a Black architect named Dan Watts, *The Liberator*. Its stated aims were:

> To work for and support the immediate liberation of all colonial peoples
> To provide a public forum for African freedom fighters
> To provide concrete aid to African freedom fighters
> To re-establish awareness of the common cultural heritage of Afro-Americans with their African brothers.
>
> (Tinson 2017, 16)

They maintained this focus in the early years of their publication: "Over the magazine's first five years, the Liberator published nearly one hundred articles and analyses dealing with African liberation movements and independence, and it would continue its coverage through the rest of the decade (1960s)" (Tinson 2017, 45).

The Liberator represented Black Nationalist positions. It was mainly the younger writers who were the driving forces of this tendency, reflecting their embrace of their current generational motion. These included C.E. Wilson, Ossie Sykes, Clayton Riley, Addison Gayle, Amiri Baraka, Larry Neal, and the artist Tom Feelings. I say "mainly," because it also had a range of contributors connected to the Black left, including Cyril Briggs, James Boggs, and Ossie Davis.

The Liberator, as a monthly, tended to feature short commentary articles that reflected on key aspects of current events. But it was a source of theoretical articles as well, by such prominent writers as Cyril Briggs, founder of the African Blood Brotherhood, with his four-part series "American Neo-Colonialism" (Briggs 1966a, 1966b, 1966c, 1967); Harold Cruse, with a three-part article, "The Economics of Black Nationalism" (Cruse 1964a, 1964b, 1964c); and James Boggs, who contributed several articles: "Black Power: A Scientific Concept," "American Revolution," and "The Final Confrontation" (Boggs 1967, 1968a, 1968b).

The Liberator always included a focus on culture, especially music and theater. In almost every issue a review of a play or movie by Clayton Riley appeared. Illustrations by Tom Feelings and lots of photographs filled the pages. *The Liberator* also spotlighted books, through book reviews and its own retail-by-mail book service, as noted in an advertisement in every issue: "Liberator Book Service is a response to the numerous requests by Liberator readers for material on African and Afro-American affairs. We have selected items of interest to our readers, but inclusion in this list does not imply editorial approval."

Though these two journals, *Freedomways* and *The Liberator*, were at odds with each other, both were widely read by Black radicals of all tendencies. They embraced Black radical thought and stimulated debate at the national and local levels, especially in New York. *Freedomways* had the advantage of being connected to institutions, especially the Schomburg, aided by one of its professional librarians, Ernest Kaiser. This helped *Freedomways* penetrate the mainstream, as indicated by WorldCat data showing *Freedomways* in 510 libraries and *The Liberator* in 471, as of November 2019. This is a critical step in the sustaining of important developments in the social movement phase of Black Studies into the institutional academic phase: the collection of documentation in libraries so as to remain accessible and known to succeeding generations of students and faculty.

The main Chicago-based journals that were very much in the debate, often leading it, were *Negro Digest*, edited by Hoyt Fuller beginning in 1961, and *Muhammad Speaks* of the Nation of Islam. *Negro Digest*, founded in 1942, was part of the publishing empire of Johnson publications and as such had national distribution. *Muhammad Speaks*, founded in 1962, is the official organ of the Nation of Islam, a national organization that placed it in the major locations where Black people lived.

Fuller became a major organizer of the literary production of the Black Power Movement years after becoming editor of *Negro Digest*. Black Power impacted his thinking, such that he changed the name of the journal from *Negro Digest* to *Black World* in 1970. His editorial leadership shaped the movement with annual issues on key aspects of the arts and, in each issue, special sections kept a record of key publications, conferences, and all other aspects of intellectual developments of the Black Liberation Movement. He made a tremendous effort to bring the new voices of young activists into public discourse, so that the journal served as a bridge connecting the Black Power Movement with Black Studies as an academic activity on the campus. As part of the Black Arts Movement, Fuller emerged as one of the main theoreticians of key philosophical concepts. Fuller became an active part of Black Studies as an academic profession with faculty appointments at Northwestern and Cornell and speaking on college campuses from coast to coast (Semmes 1998; Fenderson 2011).

Muhammad Speaks was a nationalist-oriented newspaper originally guided by Malcolm X. There were two interesting contradictions in this publication. One was between theology and sociology. The centerfold of the publication was always reserved for a theological essay by Elijah Muhammad for the members and adherents of the organization's belief system, including the origin and the evil nature of white people (the story of Yakub), and the ultimate salvation of Black people (The Mother Ship). On the other hand, there was advice for organizing one's life that spoke to a much larger audience, especially advice on food and health. The Nation of Islam backed this up with a set of businesses named "Your Supermarket," and "Shabazz Restaurant" (Evanzz 2001).

One of the curious aspects of *Muhammad Speaks* is that, for many years, people on the left, for example, Richard Durham and John Woodford, edited the publication. This was the second contradiction that also existed in the wider Black Liberation Movement between Marxists and nationalists. *Muhammad Speaks* had an audience that ranged from Black Nationalists and Pan-Africanists to communists. It was a singular source of material on national and international situations from a Black left perspective. As such, militant activists in the Black Liberation Movement considered it required reading (S.D. Williams 2017; Woodford 1991).

There were two key journals based on the West Coast, *Soulbook* and *The Black Scholar*, that featured the debates of the Black Power Movement (The Black Scholar n.d.; Alkalimat n.d. "Soulbook"). Again, there was a marked difference in terms of penetrating mainstream interest, such that WorldCat reports that *The Black Scholar* is being preserved in 1,443 libraries and *Soulbook* in 5 libraries. *The Black Scholar* was a broadly based journal that Robert Chrisman edited from 1969 to 2012—a total of forty-three years. The editorial board he organized represented all aspects of the tendencies making up Black Studies in 1969. Much like *Negro Digest/Black World* under the editorship of Hoyt Fuller, *The Black Scholar* under Chrisman was essential reading for all sectors of the Black Studies movement. Chrisman also taught as a faculty member in Black Studies academic programs at the University of San Francisco, University of Michigan, Williams College, UC Berkeley, Wayne State University, and the University of Nebraska (Chrisman n.d.).

The Black Scholar was a Black Power journal that served the movement and led the charge of Black Power advocates into the mainstream of higher education. Robert Chrisman, Nathan Hare, and Alan Ross—Ross a white radical activist who owned a print shop—founded *The Black Scholar*: "In June 1969, the three activists moved into office space in Sausalito, California, used by Ross who printed the 20,000 copies of the first issue for $700 in November of the same year" (Henry 2017, 122). *The Black Scholar* published many special issues that stimulated focused study and inclusion into Black Studies course syllabi. Part of this publishing history has been special issues that impacted Black Studies, as shown in Table 6.

However, much like the acrimonious contention between *Freedomways* and *The Liberator* over a Marxist–Nationalist divide in the Black Liberation Movement, within *The Black Scholar* there was a similar conflict between the founders, Robert Chrisman and Nathan Hare, that led to Hare resigning in protest over what he saw as a leftist takeover of a nationalist publication (Henry 2017, 128–29). Charles Hamilton also resigned during this controversy.

However, this 1975 split did not deter the magazine from continuing to publish a variety of Black Cultural Nationalists, including Maulana Karenga—in his case, at least nine articles between 1975 and 2002. Publishing material that directly reflected different sides of the prominent debates in the Black community was the contribution of *The Black Scholar* that endeared it to the main activists of Black Studies as Social Movement.

Table 6 Special Issues of *The Black Scholar*, by Year and Topic

Year	*Topic*
1970	Black Psychology
1970	Black Studies
1971	The Black Woman
1971	Pan-Africanism 1
1971	Pan-Africanism 2
1973	Black Women's Liberation
1973	The Pan-African Debate
1974	The Sixth Pan-African Congress
1974	Black Education: The Future of Black Studies
1980	Black Anthropology Part 1
1980	Black Anthropology Part 2
1984	Blacks in Higher Education
1992	African American Studies in the Twenty-First Century
2001	Black Power Studies 1
2002	Black Power Studies 2
2013	The Role of Black Philosophy

Another valuable function of *The Black Scholar* under Chrisman's leadership was directing the attention of Black intellectuals to the Cuban Revolution (Henry 2017, 129–34). As part of this effort, Chrisman would invite the Cuban poet Nancy Morejon to join the editorial board in 1994. *The Black Scholar* advocated frequently that African Americans needed to embrace Cuba as a vital part of the African Diaspora, which helped the Black Liberation Movement come to appreciate the significance of the Cuban Revolution. *The Black Scholar* published several special issues:

1973 Pan-Africanism and the Caribbean
1977 Report From Cuba
1989 Thirtieth Anniversary of the Cuban Revolution
2005 The Faces of Cuban Culture

Soulbook was a journal of the revolutionary trend in Black Nationalism, at times affiliated with the African People's Party (Alkalimat n.d., "Soulbook"). Over more than thirteen issues (1964–1972), *Soulbook* ran articles by activist intellectuals from the USA and throughout the African Diaspora. It was a crucial venue for the revolutionary tendency of the Black Nationalist movement forces. It was produced via the agency of the movement and mimeographed, while *The Black Scholar* was professionally printed and distributed by mainstream companies.

At least two cities in the South produced journals: Atlanta and New Orleans. A.B. Spellman, working with the Atlanta Center for Black Art, produced three issues of the cultural journal *Rhythm*, beginning in 1970. This was followed in the 1980s by the *Catalyst*, also in Atlanta, which Pearl Cleage edited. The *Wavelength* was a music journal produced in New Orleans from 1980 to 1991.

THE BOOKSTORES

A major community institution for Black Studies as Social Movement was the Black bookstore. Even with high rates of illiteracy among Black people, there has always been a tendency to organize the distribution of reading material. David Ruggles opened the first Black bookstore in the USA in 1834, in New York City:

> Ruggles is generally known as the first African American bookseller. While working at the bookstore he extended many publications and prints promoting the abolition of slavery and in opposition to the efforts of the American Colonization Society which promoted black settlement in Liberia. Ruggles also took on job printing, letterpress work, picture framing, and bookbinding to augment his income. In September 1835, a white anti-abolitionist mob burned his store.
>
> (Larsen 2008)

Another interesting story, almost a century later, speaks of Kathryn Johnson,

> an African American bookseller who used her Ford coupe to transport books to Black people throughout the northern and southeastern US as early as 1922 … Johnson selected materials that she thought Black people "ought to read," including poet Paul Lawrence Dunbar and historian W.E.B. Du Bois.
>
> (Fisher 2006, 85)

The Black bookstore has been a center for education that brought together people engaged in knowledge production with the broad mass of people consuming this knowledge as community-based readers. The person running the bookstore combined the roles of retail salesperson and teacher, and sometimes publisher. These bookstores were anchored in movement-oriented frames of reference, but they were also relatively more stable than any given leader or organization. Each one was an oasis in a desert, a place where all variety of social movement life forms came to get sustenance.

In general, one can consider the Black bookstore as a community-based market for social movement curriculum, both for group study and individual study. They were part of the sustainability of Black intellectual history, especially the texts of the radical Black tradition. They were the main retail outlets for Black publishers and the literature that the organizations of the Black Liberation Movement produced. They were an institutional base for the Black public sphere, a Black third place, like the church, the barbershop and beauty parlor, and the neighborhood street corner. There have been many bookstores at any given time but, in each region of the country, several have been of significance at a regional and even national level.

Maisha Fisher places the Black bookstore in the context of a study of what she calls Participatory Learning Communities (PLCs):

> PLCs are spaces in which people are engaged in reading, writing, and speaking in chosen spaces that include spoken word poetry events, writers' collectives, book clubs, and bookstores. In these learning spaces, written work is created to be shared and performed and to include discussion, debate, and an oral exchange between author and audience.
>
> (Fisher 2006, 86)

This dynamic process before the mid-1960s was a unique experience, because the mainstream was totally segregated, with very few if any Black texts being available in bookstores or college curriculums. The availability of this material was mainly the result of community-based autonomous Black agency. There were key Black bookstores in every region of the country.

East Coast

The most important Black bookstore on the East Coast was the National Memorial African Bookstore, established in 1939 by Lewis Michaux (1895–1976). His brother was the famous religious leader Elder Lightfoot Solomon Michaux. The bookstore was named after a farm set up in 1937 by his brother, the National Memorial to the Progress of the Colored Race in America. Elder Michaux stated: "The land we purchased—over 500 acres in Virginia where slaves of the first white settlers worked—has made this possible. Our project will honor the Negro leadership that has blazed the trail up from slavery. Praise the Lord" (V.M. Nelson 2018, 35).

The bookstore was an institutional conveyor belt for the radical Black tradition of Harlem that mainly consisted of the tendencies of Black Nationalism and Pan-Africanism. Lewis Michaux referred to the bookstore as "The House of Common Sense, The Home of Proper Propaganda," famously located in the heart of Harlem on the corner of 125th Street and 7th Avenue. He was an organic intellectual who embraced the community and challenged them to use the bookstore as their university. (Organic here means based in the masses of people and legitimated by them.) Michaux's wise sayings were powerful messages of truth:

> Don't get took! Read a book!
> Knowledge is power. You need it every hour.
> You are not necessarily a fool because you didn't go to school.
> You go on to school. There are things that you can learn from your teachers, but don't stop thinking for yourself. And don't you stop asking questions.
> Nobody can give you freedom. Nobody can give you equality or justice or anything, if you're a man. You take it.
>
> (V.M. Nelson and Christie 2015)

Right outside the bookstore is famously where street-corner orators of Harlem would lecture crowds large and small. One of the orators and also a devoted customer in the store was Malcolm X. Lewis Michaux was a member of the Organization of Afro-American Unity set up by Malcolm X in 1964. Here is what James Turner, founding director of Black Studies at Cornell University, says about his early experience at the National Memorial African Bookstore:

> I first saw Malcolm X at the bookstore where he comes to talk with Michaux. The corner outside the bookstore is a stage for street speakers in the tradition of Hyde Park in London and Union Square here in New York. Michaux, a major nationalist voice himself, introduces Malcolm at these rallies.
>
> The more I listen, the more their analysis of our lack of power, our people having no sense of their history, those basic nationalist tenets—internal self-contempt, lack of ability to cooperate—begins to resonate.
>
> (V.M. Nelson 2018, 105)

Malcolm X was a singular figure for the development of Black Studies. His autobiography and key speeches have become essential required readings. The key speeches were all given in Detroit as well as in other cities: "Message to the Grassroots" (1963), "The Ballot or the Bullet" (1964), and "The Last Message" (1965a). Together these speeches express his theory of Black liberation.

Michaux was famous for his prophetic words about Malcolm's legacy after the assassination:

Man, if you think Bro. Malcolm is dead
You are out of your cotton picking head
Just get off your slumbering bed
And watch his fighting spirit spread.
Every shut eye ain't sleep
Every good-bye ain't gone.
(V.M. Nelson 2018, 111)

His bookstore was so unique that every young militant and aspiring intellectual found their way to the store, especially from up and down the East Coast. His book stock laid the basis for what was included in the early Black Studies curriculum development.

The other historic bookstore located right around the corner connected the nationalist tradition of Harlem with its working-class Marxist tradition. This was the Frederick Douglass Book Center, run by Richard Moore from 1942 until 1968, when the building was torn down. Moore was born in Barbados and represented a long-standing strain of the Black radical tradition of Harlem of which the progenitors were militants migrating from the Caribbean. Moore had been a member of the African Blood Brotherhood, combining a Pan-Africanist orientation with Marxism. His center was on the second floor in two rooms, one for the sale of books and the other for lecturers and classes:

> In December 1958 Moore instituted Sunday afternoon lectures and book parties at his Moor's Gallery in the Apollo building and later at his expanded store at 23 East 125th Street or the YMCA. Most of the programs were conducted under the auspices of the Afro-American Institute, which he founded in 1969 and served as president until his death. While he was a key lecturer in the Institute series, he played the role of chairperson, provocateur, summarizer, or commentator while taking great pleasure in presenting notable scholars and authors such as Kofi Awooner, Wilfred Cartey, John Henrik Clarke, Alice Childress, Elton Fax, Franklin W. Knight, and Elliot P. Skinner.
> (R.B. Moore, Turner, and Turner 1988, 72)

Yet another Harlem bookstore was the Liberation Bookstore. Una Mulzak (1923–2012) founded it in 1967 and worked there until her death. She had originally been affiliated with the Progressive Labor Party and their Harlem leader Bill Epton, but then took ownership of the bookstore and located its mission in the heart of the Black Nationalist community struggles (D. Martin 2012).

Elsewhere, in Philadelphia, the bookstore that fed the intellectual and political needs of the community was run by Dawud Hakim (1932–1997) beginning in the 1950s (Miller 2014), and in Buffalo, New York, Martin Sostre (1923–

2015) opened the Afro-Asian Bookshop in 1966 (McLaughlin 2014). All four of these East Coast bookstores had the purposes of fueling the political consciousness of the Black community, sustaining Black intellectual history, and serving as third-place study centers for the Black Liberation Movement.

Midwest

The first major Black bookstore in the Chicago area was the beginning of the Ellis Book Centers of Chicago established by Curtis Ellis (1927–2010) in 1960. His first store was actually a candy store near an elementary school just south of the University of Chicago on 61st Street. He had one rack of books, and many activists, writers, and artists made recommendations. His store expanded, based on the demands of the movement and expansion of academic courses focusing on the African-American experience:

> "All of the contemporary writers and discussions that were not represented in the schools and libraries were in that store," recalled the Rev Jesse Jackson, who remembers frequenting the shop. "A lot of people had never been exposed to a bookstore like that. It was at the forefront of Black consciousness."
>
> "It was like an oasis in the desert," said Jackson. "Activists and artists and poets and politicians would come from all over to that bookstore. He was very friendly, very gregarious, always informed."
>
> (Kruk 2010)

Much later, other bookstores opened in Chicago, notably the Institute of Positive Education (IPE) under the leadership of Haki Madhubuti, and Timbuktu, affiliated with People's College. The IPE was part of a broader institutional configuration that included the bookstore as well as a school and a press, Third World Press. The press outlived the bookstore and in 2017 celebrated its fiftieth anniversary (C. Reid 2017). An activist collective engaged in study groups, political actions, and publishing material as part of People's College Press operated Timbuktu. It evolved into 21st Century Books, or TCB, also standing for the Black expression "taking care of business" (Alkalimat n.d., "History of People's College").

There were two major Black bookstores in Detroit: Shrine of the Black Madonna and the Ed Vaughn Bookstore. Vaughn was an activist who later became an elected official:

> Well, Vaughn's book store was certainly something that was new in the community. There had not been a book store here before, and of course I got into the business because I was looking for a book called "A Hundred Years

of Lynchings" by Ginsberg, and I was told downtown that they didn't have the book in stock and I decided that I'd see if I could find it and then when I found it and my friends at the post office said that they'd like to read that and other Black books, so I began to order them and sell them out of the trunk of my car. And then I, about 1962 I had opened Vaughn's book store and we were beginning to sell books rather briskly, people were asking questions, and that was pretty much the mood around the book store. We were mainly oriented toward the people who already were Pan-Africanists and Nationalists or people who were on the left in, in the movement, and they, they came to the store, and soon school teachers, children began to come. There was sort of an awakening in the community from New York, we were hearing about things happening there. I sold a, a magazine called "The Liberator," and so the consciousness was being developed and of course "Mohammed Speaks" and those things were happening then, so there was a consciousness that was being raised throughout the community.

(Pollard 1989)

The Shrine of the Black Madonna Bookstore was started by Rev. Albert Cleage Jr. after the 1967 rebellion in Detroit, serving mainly a Black Nationalist tendency in the movement:

In 1967, he began the Black Christian National Movement. This movement was encouraging black churches to reinterpret Jesus's teachings to suit the social, economic, and political needs of black people. In March 1967, Cleage installed a painting of a black Madonna holding the baby Jesus in his church and renamed the church The Shrine of the Black Madonna.

("Albert Cleage," 2018)

He then renamed the church the Pan-African Orthodox Christian Church and the shrine's services combined elements of the Roman Catholic Church with African traditions. He then renamed himself V Jaramogi Abebe Agyeman. He expanded so that as of 2016 his denomination had nine churches in different parts of the country, each with a bookstore (J.E. Clark 2016).

West

In San Francisco, Julian Richardson established Marcus Books, named after Marcus Garvey, in 1960, after moving from Alabama to set up a printing business in 1942. His wife, Raye Richardson, became head of the Black Studies Department at San Francisco State University. She stated his mission:

In a myriad of ways, his first priority was the fight for freedom, equality, and dignity for Black people … The bookstores and print shop were instruments

> that he used to inform, educate, and empower Black people through knowledge of their illustrious history, art and culture.
>
> ("In Memoriam: Julian Richardson" 2000)

The combination of the print shop and bookstore put Marcus Books at the center of Black cultural and political production in the Bay Area—an oasis of agency for Black identity and social justice struggles.

There were two important bookstores of record in the Los Angeles area, the Aquarian Book Shop and the Hugh Gordon Bookstore. Both of these stores were discussed in Chapter 3, in the section on Los Angeles.

South

An important Black bookstore in Washington, DC was Drum and Spear. SNCC veterans, who also created the Drum and Spear Press and the Center for Black Education, all under the organizational umbrella of Afro-American Resources, Inc. opened the bookstore, located near Howard University, in 1968 (Beckles 1996). After the demise of Drum and Spear in 1974, a local activist, Hodari Abdul-Ali, established Pyramid Books in 1981, also near Howard. After Pyramid closed, Haile and Shirikiana Gerima opened Sankofa Video Books and Café in 1997, again across the street from Howard University and two blocks from Benjamin Banneker High School (Sankofa n.d.).

Faculty and students of the Atlanta University Center together launched Timbuktu the Market of New Africa, a major Black bookstore initiative with its first location being in Atlanta. It eventually had stores in Riverside, California, Nashville, Tennessee, and Chicago under the control of People's College, with the name changing to Twenty-First Century Books, as mentioned earlier.

Nationwide, there were independent radical bookstores that specialized in Black materials as well. China Books, featuring books from the People's Republic of China, had stores in New York and San Francisco. Robins was a major store in Philadelphia. Midnight Special Bookstore opened in Venice, California in 1970 and moved to Santa Monica. There were also bookstores run by political parties: Modern Books, in Chicago and many other cities, was run by the Communist Party USA; The Socialist Workers Party had bookstores; the October League had a bookstore in Chicago; and the Revolutionary Communist Party has bookstores in several cities.

BLACK POWER SCHOOLS

A very important second stage in the development of insurgent institutions became known as Black Independent Institutions. This kind of insurgent institution has a history in the Black Liberation Movement. Rickford identifies this in the UNIA movement organization led by Marcus Garvey:

> The organization's 1920 "Declaration of the Rights of the Negro Peoples of the World" condemned racist materials in public schools and demanded the introduction of Black history curricula. UNIA officials briefly operated a Booker T. Washington University in Harlem as part of their efforts to produce a leadership class devoted to racial advancement and cultural regeneration. In the late 1930s, Garvey personally presided over a School of African Philosophy in Toronto, a rigorous training course for future UNIA organizers. (Rickford 2016, 75)

Rickford goes on to discuss how the Nation of Islam (NOI) schools, under the leadership of Elijah Muhammad, continued in this tradition in the 1940s and 1950s:

> NOI schools attempted to prepare Black children from the age of three to "know self," "love self," and "do for self," a precursor to the Black Power trinity of self-respect, self-determination, and self-defense. Public schools, Muhammad taught, had been "designed by the slave masters" to keep African Americans docile and dependent. The Black man "cannot build a future with white people in his mind" the Messenger (Mr. Muhammad) insisted. African Americans required an education shielded from white control. (Rickford 2016, 77)

A national movement initiated mass school boycotts in major cities, beginning in Chicago and reaching to New York, Philadelphia, and other cities. This included places where the Black community demanded more control over the education of their children in elementary and secondary schools. This led to a level of national organization. In 1968, the Association for the Advancement of Afro-American Educators held its founding meeting in Chicago. This organization's membership consisted of local teachers and principals, faculty from higher education, and other kinds of education professionals. The very next month after the major Pan-African protest of the first US African Liberation Day on May 1972, the Council of Black Independent Institutions (CBI) was formed. This CBI included fourteen organizations focusing on programs aimed at young people ("Council of Independent Black Institutions" n.d.).

Here is a brief survey of some of them, by region:

East

One of the major schools, "The East Educational and Cultural Center for People of African Descent," usually called "The East," was in Brooklyn (Konadu

2005; Rickford 2016). A group of activist teachers, including Les Campbell (Jitu Weusi), Albert Vann, and Herman Ferguson created the school, which lasted from 1969 to 1986. They formed another school in 1970, Uhuru Sasa Shule (Ki-Swahili meaning "Freedom Now School"), which started out as a supplementary program at the high and junior high school level and ended up as a full-time school of over two hundred students. A school publication stated their mission as explicitly political: "We are a Pan-African Nationalist school, meaning that we support and participate in the struggles of Africans worldwide, and, secondly, we are in preparation for Nationhood—ultimate control of our lives" (Rickford 2016, 72).

In Philadelphia, John Churchfield created the Freedom Library School (1965–1978). Churchfield was a SNCC activist who had left the South to join the northern Student Movement. His focus combined the freedom school ethos of those in Mississippi with the Black Nationalist ideology of the Black Liberation Movement in northern cities.

And in Newark, New Jersey, Amiri and Amina Baraka, as part of the general program of the Committee for a Unified Newark, founded the African Free School. It took its name from that of the first school for African Americans in the USA, which had operated in New York City from 1787 to 1835.

Midwest

In Chicago, Shule Ya Watoto (School for Children) opened in 1972 and was in operation until 2003. Hannibal Afrik (Harold Charles) led the effort to found the school, which was on the West Side of the city (Dean 2011). On the South Side of Chicago, Haki Madhubuti (Don Lee) established The Institute of Positive Education (IPE) in 1970, which became the springboard for the New Concept Development Center, a school he and his wife Safisha Madhubuti (Carol Lee) opened in 1974. The IPE website states:

> IPE was founded during the height of the Black Power and Arts movement on 79th Street near Ellis Ave. In 1974, New Concept Development Center (NCDC), now New Concept School (NCS) was established in a storefront on 75th and Cottage Grove. NCDC promoted African-centered education for children Pre-School through 3rd grade and adult. In 1990, NCDC moved to the present location at 78th and Ellis Ave. and gradually expanded to include 8th grade. Today, IPE runs the Pre-school and After-school programs and manages the School Building and surrounding property. During its 46 years of existence, IPE has operated a Training Center and Parent Resource Library. It published quarterly bulletins on education, politics, science, technology and literature. Finally IPE established a parent study group and food co-op.
>
> (Institute of Positive Education n.d.)

A unique educational program was developed in Chicago that was aimed at activists and students, in such a way that the campus was united with the community, hence its name of the Communiversity. It was held at the Abraham Lincoln Center, a Frank Lloyd Wright building that also housed the Center for Inner City Studies of Northeastern University. What was unique is that all major tendencies of the Black Liberation Movement had leading cadre teaching—Black Nationalist and Marxist alike.

South

Independent Black educational institutions also arose in the South. Out of the southern movement former SNCC staff members Charlie Cobb, Courtland Cox, Jimmy Garrett, and others created the Center for Black Education (CBE) in Washington, DC. As mentioned, this was affiliated with the Drum and Spear Bookstore. The CBE was a Pan-Africanist institution combining theory with a focus on skills to work in the community. A significant number of SNCC staff members had relocated to Washington, DC, and became both staff and a support base for the CBE. The educational program had as a foundation the books that they published, such as *A History of Pan-African Revolt* by C.L.R. James (1969b). Their bookstore became a market of ideas and cultural artifacts, a central oasis for people embracing a globally oriented Black consciousness (DC Cultural Tourism n.d.). Another institution based in Washington, DC, was the New School of Afro-American Thought founded by Gaston Neal. This project was also heavily invested in the arts (HumanitiesDC 2011).

In New Orleans, Kalamu Ya Salaam led a group in founding the Ahidiana Work/Study Center. Its special focus was in using the cultural arts to foster Black consciousness and a commitment to serving the needs of the Black community (The History Makers n.d.). In Houston, Texas, the Lynn Eusan Institute (LEI) was founded in 1972, named after a local Black woman activist who had been murdered. She had been the University of Houston's first Black homecoming queen as well as a militant Pan-Africanist. Gene Locke led the LEI. Rickford says this:

> In early 1973, LEI's first cohort of nine full-time students moved into the center's small dormitory, a facility supported by private grants. The pupils, including college students, a welfare mother, and a high school dropout, studied political, economic, and social theory, honing organizing tactics in workshops like "fundamentals of mobilizing." They agreed to become full-time organizers upon graduation, and to perform practical community work while enrolled at LEI. During the institution's first 10-month term, its trainees assisted a tenant group, a high school Black studies club, and the city's welfare rights organization.
>
> (Rickford 2016, 217)

Another educational project, People's College, was founded in Nashville, Tennessee. It resurrected the name used by Charles Johnson in the 1930s for a community education program run by the students and faculty of Fisk University. People's College organized a general community-based curriculum on Saturdays and intensive Marxist study circles during week nights, drawing students from Fisk University, Tennessee State University, Meharry Medical College, and Vanderbilt University. It extended its reach to Black workers as its members left the campus to work in factory jobs and at the local A. Philip Randolph Institute (Benson 2017b).

West

On the West Coast, Bob and Mary Hoover, both activist educators with area colleges, established a major independent school, Nairobi College, in East Palo Alto, near Stanford University. The Hoovers set out to create an institution that identified itself as a Third World College, thus embracing the ethnic diversity of California. Rickford describes its origin and make-up:

> Initial contributions of almost $100,000, including donations from area residents and grants from private foundations, produced a modest but innovative venture. A small private home in East Palo Alto served as the college's "main campus." (The primary and secondary schools of the Nairobi system lay nearby.) As the institution began limited operation that fall, more than 100 working-class, mostly Black and Chicano students, some of them high school dropouts and many of them casualties of the CSM upheaval, enrolled in classes taught by volunteer instructors in area homes, churches, social service agencies, and even a local bank. The faculty consisted of about 40 volunteers, including community organizers and students and professors from nearby universities. An appeal for books yielded 20,000 donated texts from schools, individuals, and publishers.
>
> (Rickford 2016, 205)

THE BLACK UNIVERSITY

The push for self-determination in education had each generation looking for a way to create viable autonomous institutions, including a Black University. A conversation between Abram L. Harris, W.E.B. Du Bois, and E. Franklin Frazier led to this in a 1926 *Opportunity* article signed by Frazier:

> Spiritual and intellectual emancipation of the Negro awaits the building of a Negro University, supported by Negroes and directed by Negro educators, who have imbibed the best that civilization can offer; where his savants can

add to human knowledge and promulgate those values which are to inspire and motivate Negroes as a cultural group.

(Aptheker 1969, 165)

An important theoretical debate and practical struggle focused on creating a "Black University" after Malcolm X was assassinated on February 21, 1965. Roughly sixteen months later, the Black Liberation Movement proclaimed "Black Power" as a national slogan on June 16, 1966. At that moment, a debate emerged that reflected a new polarity between mainstream civil rights forces and Black Nationalist forces: the former were fighting into the mainstream for "first class citizenship," while the latter stressed self-determination based on autonomous forms of organization. While some adherents of each side held fast to their positions, the main trend was a dialectical unity of these two positions, fighting to get inside the mainstream in order to create spaces under Black control. This included the fight for a Black caucus inside mainstream organizations and, of course, Black Studies programs at all levels of mainstream education.

One of the key institutional sources of this practical struggle and debate was Howard University. At issue was a monumental generational conflict. The president James Nabrit, grandson of ex-slaves, had been a lawyer on the team with Howard University Law School Dean Charles Houston, who had built the cases that led to the crucial 1954 Brown Supreme Court decision to integrate the nation's schools. He advocated increasing the enrollment of white students to feature Howard University as an integrated institution. Black students, joined by Nathan Hare, a new Sociology PhD from the University of Chicago who was an assistant professor, took the opposite position, calling for the transformation of Howard under the Black Power slogan into a more ideologically oriented Black University connecting itself to the Black Liberation Movement.

Hare joined the Howard faculty in 1961 as the sit-in movement was awakening militant protest throughout the country (see Chapter 9). The Howard students took up the Black Power slogan and Hare became a mentor of the most militant activists. Mass protests took place during the 1966–1967 school year and, in this context, Hare helped form the "Black Power committee" (Rickford 2016, 195; McWorter 1968, 45). In June 1967, the university fired Hare. This was a shocking development and became a cause célèbre for the movement. Hare then went to San Francisco State University to head the first formal academic college-level Black Studies Program in the country (For more on this, see Chapter 10).

During the spring of 1968, a national conference was held in Chicago to form the Association of African American Educators. This meeting brought together key militant leaders of education struggles in many cities, especially New York

(Preston Wilcox, Al Vann, Jitu Weusi), and Chicago (Anderson Thompson, Barbara Sizemore, Hugh Lane, Abdul Alkalimat [Gerald McWorter]).

In the midst of the nationally discussed crisis at Howard, along with many other campus struggles, *Negro Digest* editor Hoyt Fuller began a three-year set of annual articles exploring the Black University concept along with his guest editor Abdul Alkalimat (Gerald McWorter) (McWorter 1968, 1969, 1970; Rickford 2016, 195).

Here is how Fuller describes the origin of this series in the initial issue of March 1968:

> The special issue of *Negro Digest* devoted to a consideration of the concept of the Black University developed through discussions with Gerald McWorter, a recent Ph.D. graduate of the University of Chicago now an assistant professor of Sociology at Fisk University in Nashville. In his outline letter to the other contributors to this special issue of *Negro Digest*, Mr. McWorter said that the articles dealing with facets of the proposed Black University would concern themselves with "a vision, the articulation of an 'ought' … for the future…" He made it clear that the concept of the Black University, as envisioned by himself and the editors, was concerned with the entire spectrum of social, economic, psychological and cultural imperatives which characterize, influence and control the black community.
>
> (McWorter 1968, 97)

There were twenty-one articles over the three issues, including theoretical formulations and summations of practice. In the first two issues Vincent Harding, Nathan Hare, and Abdul Alkalimat (Gerald McWorter) critiqued mainstream exclusion of Black people and scholarship on Black people, while positing a vision of what Black autonomous self-determination in education might look like. Alkalimat (McWorter) argued for a general vision of a revolutionary transformation to create a new kind of institution linked to the Freedom Movement. Hare presented a rigorous critique of Howard University for being subservient to racist mainstream academic norms. Harding wrote a letter to Black faculty and students in mainstream institutions, calling on them to be mindful that their efforts were leading to white institutions raiding Black institutions, resulting in the decline and even demise of the HBCUs and therefore the foundational path for Black people to get college educations.

Harding's letter hit a nerve and elicited responses assembled in the third *Negro Digest* special issue in 1970. William J. Wilson wrote a defense of his position in a white institution while acknowledging that there were serious issues to be dealt with in this period of transformation. He stated:

> I agree with Professor Harding that the frantic search by white college administrators for black faculty, if left unchecked, will threaten the survival of black schools, and that many northern black students and faculty are either consciously or unconsciously contributing to this precarious state of affairs.
>
> (McWorter 1970, 7)

Wilson went on to anchor his main argument in the general need for expansion of opportunities, because the demand for educating Black students was far greater than the current HBCU capacity.

The March 1970 issue included statements on four important examples. The Institute of the Black World, based in Atlanta, spelled out five key aspects of their project. The Center for Black Education, based in Washington, DC, advocated a community-based program of education and social activism. There were two projects from Chicago. One, the transformation of a mainstream junior college, renamed after Malcolm X, was designed to serve the needs of the Black community, especially on the impoverished West Side of the city. Charles Hurst, formerly a professor at Howard, became president of Crane Junior College and mobilized the community around the name change to Malcolm X. Two, the militant forces of the movement seized the ideological moment and formed a community-based organization that drew from all mainstream campus institutions to form the Communiversity, mentioned earlier. Its unique character was that its faculty and students ranged across the spectrum from Black Nationalist to Marxist.

Another key aspect of the *Negro Digest* three-issue forum on the Black University is that it also solicited contributions from key major HBCU presidents, both current and former: Benjamin Mays (Morehouse College), James Lawson (Fisk University), Samuel Proctor (Virginia Union University), and Benjamin Payton (Benedict College). The debate was a challenge to their institutional history and they engaged in the discussion with a pragmatic counter to movement idealism. As Lawson cautioned, "The important question is: How can the system best be changed?" (McWorter 1969, 67).

Building on this national debate and their local protest activism, faculty at Howard convened a five-day national conference in November 1968 titled "Towards a Black University." This conference brought together social-movement-oriented faculty and students. The major keynote address was a two-hour presentation by Stokely Carmichael (Kwame Ture).

Another instance of the dialectics of theory and practice that pushed the Black University issue forward took place in the Atlanta University Center. Vincent Harding chaired the Department of History and Sociology at Spelman College. He recruited two new faculty members for the 1968–1969 school year: Kofi Wangara (Harold Lawrence) and Abdul Alkalimat (Gerald McWorter). They teamed up to co-teach a course, "Two Continents of African Revolution," during the spring term (Alkalimat and Wangara 1969). After the course met a few times and the students became immersed in Black revolutionary thought, they took up the Black University mission and planned a building takeover to advocate for change. This took place in April 1969, with a takeover of a joint board meeting of Atlanta University, Spelman College, and Morehouse College that became known as the Harness Hall incident (detailed in Chapter 10).

At the same time, the Black students at Cornell University (also detailed in Chapter 10) also took over a major campus building and advanced their program for institutional reform leading to Black Studies in that mainstream institution. The optics of this shocked the country, as the covers of news magazines like *Newsweek* (May 5, 1969) showed Black Cornell students leaving their occupation of Willard Hall armed with shotguns and rifles.

The most developed project for an autonomous free-standing new Black University was Malcolm X Liberation University (MXLU) in Durham, North Carolina, which opened in November 1969. A struggle at Duke University led to students rejecting reforming a mainstream institution and turning to something new and independent. Howard Fuller, a militant social worker turned community organizer, supported the student struggle and became the prime mover for a new institution. MXLU took up the educational paradigm of the Tanzanian Ujamaa village, self-reliance based on the unity of theory and practice in the path for self-determination. So the courses focused on theories of Pan-Africanism and self-determination for African Americans along with the practical skills of agriculture and industrial production.

Benson describes the ideological orientation of MXLU:

> In 1971, MXLU produced a theoretical and ideological manifesto titled, Understanding the African Struggle: A Series of Essays by the Ideological Research Staff of Malcolm X Liberation University. The document articulated four major tenets on which the university would base its operational goals and objectives:
>
> 1. All people of African descent are considered Africans—not Afro-Americans, Afro-Cubans, Afro-Europeans, or any other kind of hyphenated species.
> 2. Common heritage and oppression are inseparable links of all Africans globally.
> 3. The acquisition of land is critical for self-determination and "National building."
> 4. A critique of capitalism and the eventual adoption of a development of an economic system based on the principles of Scientific African Socialism.
>
> (Benson 2014, 160)

The founding of MXLU was a national event in the Black Liberation Movement, as it embraced such luminaries as Betty Shabazz, widow of Malcolm X, and Stokely Carmichael (Kwame Ture). Howard Fuller describes the curriculum in his autobiography, *No Struggle, No Progress*:

> At MXLU, the curriculum strongly reflected our goal to train students who would be willing to go to Africa and help those nations obtain their independence and rebuild. Our program was divided into two parts. The plans called for students first to spend ten months learning about national building through an historical-cultural study of African people, covering the following subjects: Independent African Civilization, Slavery, Neo-Colonialism, Colonialism, and the Independent African World. Students would study an African language (Swahili, Hausa, or Yoruba) and take courses in physical development. Then, students and staff would travel to Africa for two months to get a close-up real-life view of what they had learned. When they returned to the states, the student would move into Areas of Concentration, which would include technical training in the twelve jobs that we believed were most needed to sustain a Black nation: food scientists, tailors, architects, engineers, medics, cadre leaders, communications technicians, physical developers, teachers, Black expressionists, administrators and linguists. The technical training would last up to ten months, followed by internships in the Black community where the student would get to use those skills. While we carried out many of those plans, some proved to be too ambitious for our budget.
>
> (Fuller and Page 2014, 107)

The transformation of an insurgent institution into a stable sustainable institution has proven to be a difficult task for social movements, precisely because the very nature of a social movement is that its intensity has a short lifespan, and the sustainability of an institution requires a stable social base with adequate financial resources to support a facility, a staff, and a program of activities. On the other hand, an insurgent institution can make a big impact, both as a visible alternative to mainstream institutions and as a place to nurture movement cadre.

6
The Black Arts Movement

As explained in earlier chapters, Black Power existed in essence long before its political manifestation in the 1960s. Nowhere is this more evident than in the arts, especially in music. More than any other artists, Black musicians exhibited a powerful Black consciousness with an unbroken lineage back to African origins. At every moment of political resistance, the music and other art forms were instruments of mass education and mobilization. The musicians were in touch with the influences they encountered from the African Diaspora as well as the accompanying anticolonial political ethos. Anchored in the drum as the fundamental musical instrument, Black cultural production has always been the foundation of Black identity.

HISTORICAL DEVELOPMENT

It is important to mention two critical twentieth-century art-based movements that laid the basis for the Black Arts Movement (BAM), each called a renaissance, the Harlem (New York) Renaissance of the 1920s and the Chicago Renaissance of the 1940s.

The 1920s were prosperous times. After a brief period of post-war decline, the US economy soared because of the immense profits earned from the first imperialist war. Black people, as recent arrivals in northern industrial centers, enjoyed this prosperity as well, though the post-war riots and numerous lay-offs revealed that the cities were not free of Black oppression.

As a concept, the New Negro accurately sums up how Black people were transforming themselves. "New" described the migration out of the South, urbanization of Black people into northern ghettoes, and the proletarianization of rural southern Black farmers. As touched on in Chapters 2 and 3, the New Negro also described a wide range of new subjective and ideological developments. There was greater social class stratification of Black people. This included the emergence of a new, more assertive middle class, who were critical of the accommodationist "old Negro" (e.g., Booker T. Washington's leadership). With the NAACP, the Urban League, and the Garvey movement all emerging between 1909 and 1917, there was the tremendous flowering of the organized struggle of Black people for liberation.

The New Negro thus became the credo of the movement of Black writers, artists, musicians, actors, intellectuals, and their patrons who emerged during this period. The cultural expression of this New Negro was authentic and widespread. No longer was Black cultural expression isolated and shunned. Artists like Langston Hughes were inspired to expose the life and culture of Black people in a way that had not been done before. In his 1926 manifesto, "The Negro Artist and the Racial Mountain," he states:

> One of the most promising of the young Negro poets said to me once, "I want to be a poet—not a Negro poet," meaning, I believe, "I want to write like a white poet"; meaning subconsciously, "I would like to be a white poet"; meaning behind that, "I would like to be white." And I was sorry the young man said that, for no great poet has ever been afraid of being himself. And I doubted then that, with his desire to run away spiritually from his race, this boy would ever be a great poet. But this is the mountain standing in the way of any true Negro art in America—this urge within the race toward whiteness, the desire to pour racial individuality into the mold of American standardization, and to be as little Negro and as much American as possible ... But in spite of the Nordicized Negro intelligentsia and the desires of some white editors we have an honest American Negro literature already with us. Now I await the rise of the Negro theater. Our folk music, having achieved world-wide fame, offers itself to the genius of the great individual American composer who is to come. And within the next decade I expect to see the work of a growing school of colored artists who paint and model the beauty of dark faces and create with new technique the expressions of their own soul-world. And the Negro dancers who will dance like flame and the singers who will continue to carry our songs to all who listen—they will be with us in even greater numbers tomorrow.
>
> (Hughes 2004 [1926])

The Harlem Renaissance was not only a movement of the city, but of a particular one—New York, the country's biggest and most cosmopolitan city. This was the first modern twentieth-century art movement of the Afro-American. As such, it had the major task of defeating the racist notion that Blacks were culturally inferior. However, the new Black artists, reflecting their middle-class backgrounds, did not feel bound to the masses in their task of artistic creativity and production. In this sense, the Harlem Renaissance was anchored in the middle class at its height. On the other hand, the artists had to face the capitalist market with their work. Publishing companies and other cultural businesses bought up their products, mass-produced them, and circulated them. Increasingly, this contradiction between the work of the artist and the work of the cultural business began to transform Black art into a more viable commercial product. The mediating social organization was the salon gathering of artists and patrons, with hair industry giant Madame C.J. Walker hosting many.

There were also parties "downtown" frequented by the literary establishment to which some young Black artists would be invited. In this setting, wealthy patrons would meet young Black artists whom they would sponsor, thus providing them with income other than what they could earn from competing in the marketplace.

The Harlem Renaissance was the work of a few talented and highly educated Black people, their white publishers and promoters, and a few others who could afford "Black culture." Thus, while it had an impact on this key sector of the Black population, the Harlem Renaissance was practically unknown to the vast majority of Black people and had little direct impact on solving the problems with which they were most concerned.

Of course, this does not cover the origin of the term "New Negro" in the work of Hubert Harrison, who was in fact speaking of the more working-class and mass-oriented transformation of social consciousness. Moreover, there were two important journals that carried the Harlem Renaissance out to the national community: *The Crisis* magazine (founded 1910) of the NAACP, edited by W.E.B. Du Bois; and *Opportunity* (founded 1923), edited by Charles S. Johnson.

The Great Depression threw many working people out on the street to starve and die and laid bare the racist formula for power in this country. All working people suffered, but Black people suffered even more as the last hired and the first fired. This was devastating proof that the North offered no sanctuary from racism and class exploitation. Rather, life in the northern cities merely represented another, perhaps even more vicious manifestation of oppression because it had held out the hope of being different. The Great Depression affected Black artists as well, since the income derived from selling their art "products" dried up like everything else, shattering the social organization of the artists who grew up during the Harlem Renaissance. This was not limited to New York, but was also experienced coast to coast.

Two forces external to the Black community had a tremendous impact on the development of the arts movement of this period. First, the federal government under Franklin D. Roosevelt set up an unprecedented welfare program that included the hiring of artists. Black artists in every part of the country got Works Progress Administration (WPA) jobs. This changed the social relations of cultural production. Before, the artist had worked as an individual, possibly supported by a sponsor, but the key relationship was with a large capitalist firm that took over the commercial aspects of production. Under the WPA, artists began working collectively (often with social scientists), and the government was the employer (actually acting as a large impersonal employer in the name of the entire country). Many people got jobs, and a lot of work got done.

Second, the overall condition of the masses of people led to a rapid increase in revolutionary political activity, including a significant (at that particular time) role played by the Communist Party USA. This era saw major developments: the unionization of Black workers into the Congress of Industrial Organizations (CIO), the organization of the unemployed in the Unemployed Councils, and militant Black–white unity in the Black Belt South (Southern Negro Youth Congress, Southern Tenant Farmers Union, and the Sharecroppers Union). Economic and revolutionary change consequently emerged as the fundamental question facing both Blacks and whites. This was a political question that made a profound impact on artists, particularly Black artists. As Richard Wright put it: "Today the question is: Shall Negro writing be for the Negro masses, moulding the lives and consciousness of those masses toward new goals, or shall it continue begging the question of the Negroes' humanity?" (Wright 1937, cited in Gates and McKay 1996, 1403–10).

This question was answered as the years wore on. Whereas Alain Locke could say the New Negro in the 1920s was "radical on race matters, conservative on others," Black people in the 1930s and 1940s were increasingly radical in all matters (Locke 1939, cited in Wright cited in Gates and McKay 1996, 990). Black people and their artists began to understand that racist discrimination was a product of capitalism and imperialism. They thus became active as leaders and participants in campaigns for radical and revolutionary changes. These themes of revolutionary class struggle pervaded the work of many Black artists. The best examples of this new proletarian consciousness among Black writers were Richard Wright and Langston Hughes. As cultural artists, they sought: (1) to apply the theory, insights, and lessons of the world revolutionary struggles to the concrete problems of Black people; (2) to expose Black people's experiences with racism and poverty in the USA, and to relate this to the common problem of exploitation facing the entire working class, thereby developing the cultural basis for unity of action among Blacks and whites; and (3) to contribute to the development of a united front of all exploited and oppressed peoples for the revolutionary overthrow of imperialism as a necessary step in the total liberation of Black people.

Richard Wright perhaps best summarized this new revolutionary perspective in his manifesto "Blueprint for Negro Writing":

> Negro writers must accept the nationalist implications of their lives, not in order to encourage them, but in order to change and transcend them. They must accept the concept of nationalism because in order to transcend it they must possess and understand it. And a nationalist spirit in Negro writing means a nationalism carrying the highest possible pitch of social consciousness.
>
> It means a nationalism that knows its limitations, that is aware of the dangers of its position, that knows its aims are unrealizable within the framework of capitalist America; a nationalism whose reason for being lies in the simple fact of self-possession and in the consciousness of the interdepen-

> dence of people in modern society … Every short story, novel, poem, and play should carry within its lines, implied or explicit, a sense of the oppression of the Negro people, the danger of war, of fascism, of the threatened destruction of culture and civilization; and, too, the faith and necessity to build a new world.
>
> (Wright 1937, cited in Gates and McKay 1996, 1403–10)

In what has come to be called the Chicago Renaissance, the cultural workers of the 1940s were cloistered in the ideological interaction of a Black consciousness anchored in a working-class perspective. Much as in New York, the WPA in Chicago hired many artists who led the cultural production of the city. Arna Bontemps, having spent seven years in both Harlem and Chicago, reflected on this after moving to become the head librarian at Fisk University:

> Chicago was definitely the center of the second phase of Negro literary awakening … Harlem got its renaissance in the middle 'twenties, centering around the Opportunity contests and the Fifth Avenue Awards Dinners. Ten years later Chicago re-enacted it on WPA … with increased power.
>
> (Bone 1986, 447)

Alice Browning and Fern Gayden advanced the literary arts in Chicago by starting their journal called *Negro Story* (1944–1946). Bone describes their experience:

> *Negro Story* was published bi-monthly for two years, from May 1944 to May 1946. Toward the end the schedule was erratic, but in all, nine issues appeared. The journal was edited from Mrs. Browning's home at 4019 Vincennes Avenue. It featured not only stories, but poems; not only black, but white contributors; not only young and unknown talent, but seasoned authors as well. At first the staff consisted of Alice Browning and Fern Gayden, co-editors; Langston Hughes and Nick Aaron Ford (then teaching at Langston University, Oklahoma), advisers. With the fourth number (Dec. /Jan. 1944–45), Fern Gayden stepped down as co-editor while Ralph Ellison and Chester Himes were added to the advisory board.
>
> (Bone 1986, 465)

The major Black playwright in Chicago was Ted Ward (1902–1983):

> Ward was well known for tackling controversial topics related to African-American urban life during the Great Depression. His staged works were lauded for their innovative depiction of the black experience, most notably for doing away with the spiritual ballads and feverish dancing that

> dominated "Negro theatricals" of his time in favor of a more nuanced, naturalistic approach to plot and character. A prolific writer, Ward composed over thirty plays and co-founded the Negro Playwrights Company with Langston Hughes, Paul Robeson and Richard Wright. His best known works are the drama Big White Fog (1938), produced by the Negro Unit of the Federal Theatre Project in Chicago as well the musical Our Lan' (1947) which premiered on Broadway at New York's Royale Theatre.
>
> (Wikipedia 2017)

ORIGIN

As with any important new beginning of a social moment, it is usually hard to identify the person or persons who got the ball rolling, but for the Black Arts Movement of the 1960s there is usually some reference to Amiri Baraka and Larry Neal. Baraka was part of the mainstream counterculture scene called the "Beat movement," beginning with his collection of poetry *Twenty Volume Preface to a Suicide Note* (1961) after moving to Greenwich Village. But his life became iconic for the Black Liberation Movement as he experienced three critical turning points that pushed his consciousness and practice ever more deeply into various tendencies of the radical Black tradition.

First, he traveled to Cuba in 1960 and began to delink from his affinity with the American intellectual tradition while gaining more understanding of world revolutionary processes. He makes this declaration in his important essay after his trip titled "Cuba Libre":

> The young intellectual living in the United States inhabits an ugly void. He cannot use what is around him, neither can he revolt against it. Revolt against whom? Revolution in this country of "due process of law" would be literally impossible. Whose side would you be on? The void of being killed by what is in this country and not knowing what is outside of it. Don't tell me about the dead minds of Europe. They stink worse than our own.
>
> (Baraka 1966, 39–40)

A second leap occurred in 1965 as a result of his reaction to the assassination of Malcolm X. He made a definitive turn toward Black nationalism and left Greenwich Village to relocate in the Black community of Harlem. There he founded the Black Arts Repertory Theatre and School, and more directly worked to link Black art to the struggles of Black people. A movement-making position was taken in his poem "Black Art":

> We want a black poem. And a
> Black World.

> Let the world be a Black Poem
> And Let All Black People Speak This Poem
> Silently
> or LOUD
>
> (Baraka 2016)

The critical literary act that centered the Black Arts Movement was an anthology, *Black Fire: An Anthology of Afro-American Writing,* edited by Amiri Baraka and Larry Neal (1968). They featured works in four categories: essays, poetry, fiction, and drama. This gathering of voices placed Baraka and Neal as leaders of the Black Arts Movement.

Baraka's third leap grew out of his involvement in the theory and practice of the African Liberation Support Committee (ALSC), which gave him his most intense exposure to Marxism. The impactful ALSC ideological debate came to a head at a 1974 conference at Howard University. Diverse forces from the Black Nationalist and the Black Marxist tendencies all gave major speeches. Baraka sums up his reaction:

> For my money, nationalism was defeated at that conference at Howard, May 1974. The people on the left who had defeated nationalism did not have all their theoretical gemachts together, but they at least did provide a point of departure, a jumping-off place, and I was ready to jump off.
>
> (Baraka 1984, 308)

This led to his leaving the ranks of Kawaida nationalism on a journey that took him into the diverse world of Marxist-based world revolutionary theory.

Larry Neal came to the origin of the Black Arts Movement by another path, doubling back through folklore, especially the mythical tales of urban street culture, like Shine, Stag-o-lee, and the Signifying Monkey (Smethurst 2005, 163–65). Neal focused on how art was integral to the folk traditions and inherent longing for freedom in the history of Black consciousness. The moment of transformation came when he embraced the Black Power concept. He stated: "The Black Arts Movement is radically opposed to any concept of the artist that alienates him from his community. This movement is the aesthetic and spiritual sister of the Black Power concept" (Neal 1968, 29), and further:

> Our literature, our art and our music are moving closer to the forces motivating Black America. You can hear it everywhere, especially in the music, a surging new sound. Be it the Supremes, James Brown, The Temptations, John Coltrane, or Albert Ayler, there is a vital newness in this energy. There is love, tension and spiritual togetherness in it. We are beautiful—but there is more work to do, and just being beautiful is not enough.

> We must take this sound, and make this energy meaningful to our people. Otherwise it will have meant nothing, will have affected nothing. The force of what we have to say can only be realized in action. Black literature must become an integral part of the community's life style. And I believe that it must also be integral to the myths and experiences underlying the total history of Black people.
>
> (Baraka and Neal 1968, 653)

Malcolm X embodied this new consciousness. In every art form, he was represented as the key figure and voice of the new stage of the Black liberation struggle and therefore central to all forms of Black consciousness. Archie Shepp recorded a major cultural recognition in music, "Malcolm, Malcolm Semper Malcolm," on his album *Fire Music* (1965), one month after Malcolm's death. The editors of the new journal *Black Dialogue* dedicated its first issue in 1965 to Malcolm X (Ya Salaam 2016, 13). The high point of Malcolm X's cultural representation was a collection of poems edited by Dudley Randall and Margaret Burroughs (1969), *For Malcolm: Poems on the Life and Death of Malcolm X*. They announced their plans for this anthology at a Fisk writer's conference in April 1966, a little more than one year after Malcolm X had been assassinated. First, the Black Power divide, and then the iconic Malcolm X, and finally the debate captured the discourse of the artists and cultural workers.

The central ideological debate of the Black Arts Movement concerned the Black Aesthetic. The debate spread like wildfire throughout the country and was the discourse that defined the movement. After challenging the older view that the proper identity was first to be an artist and only secondarily to represent oneself as a Black person, the issue was now: what was distinctive about being a Black artist? The answer was based on the notion that there was a distinctive Black culture and, on that basis, one could theorize the existence of a Black aesthetic. Addison Gayle (1971) of New York edited a book by that name—*The Black Aesthetic*—and it became the next key anthology of the movement following *Black Fire* edited by Baraka and Neal (1968).

The main impresario of the Black Arts Movement was Hoyt Fuller, editor of the journal *Negro Digest*, acting as Alain Locke, Charles Johnson, and W.E.B. Du Bois had done for the Harlem Renaissance and Alice Browning and Fern Gayden for the Chicago Renaissance. Fuller became the most prominent editorial advocate of the Black Aesthetic, Black is Beautiful, movement. He led the OBAC Writer's Workshop in Chicago and directly influenced the young writers emerging there. On a national level, he edited the most widely distributed journal and had far-reaching influence. He helped coalesce the movement, in part because, through the pages of the *Negro Digest/Black World*, each local area was connected to a national audience. He edited annual special issues on poetry, theater, and topical political issues, while also including information in each monthly issue. Every issue featured a column, "Black Perspectives," that chronicled events of the movement, always making note of new publications, performances, and organizational developments (Fuller 1971; Fuller and Randall 1984; Semmes 1998; Fenderson 2011).

The Black Arts Movement encompassed all the arts (Ya Salaam 2016). Each had a local footprint and, because this was a new movement, in most cases, there were educational programs for both aspiring artists as well as their public, since the movement always sought to reproduce itself. More than a spontaneous outburst of raw talent, the Black Arts Movement developed insurgent cultural institutions that systematically linked and integrated ideological content with method. Here is evidence of what was happening in key areas of the arts, highlighting selected examples of local developments.

MUSIC

In music, the foundational art form for the Black Arts Movement, there is a long history to the ideological link between art and politics, between the search for beauty and the search for freedom. There are no better examples of this than the big bands led by Duke Ellington and Sun Ra. As mentioned in Part I, Ellington consistently connected his musical compositions to the historical experiences of African Americans. Sun Ra represented three important themes. He rooted himself in the history of the music. He combined all of the arts into his art, including dance, clothing and set design, and song/poetry. He did the paintings for the covers of each of his early albums. He pulled all of this together in his magical discussion of "space is the place." He challenged people to think past their problems and imagine an existence without exploitation and oppression. All of the musicians of the Black Arts Movement were impacted by Sun Ra. He led the way into what became known as free jazz, the epitome of improvisation (Szwed 2012).

The Sun Ra Arkestra was a school in itself, and it led directly to the Association for the Advancement of Creative Musicians (AACM). The musicians of AACM were all searching for something new and they found each other, mainly pulled together by founders Muhal Richard Abrams, Kelan Phil Cohran, Jodie Christian, and Steve McCall. The AACM was built as an act of self-determination in that the members supported each other and did not base their existence on support from outside their ranks. The AACM was an insurgent institution. It rejected marketing labels for the music, especially the category of jazz, calling their music "Great Black Music!"

The AACM also quickly agreed that it was their responsibility to keep the tradition of Black music alive. Their musicians explore the future in their music and in educating young people:

> Despite the lack of money and materials, the AACM School opened in the fall of 1967 in the basement of Abraham Lincoln Center, moving in 1968 to the Parkway Community House … an idea born in the crucible of the Black Arts Movement—an alternative institution operating in the Black community, facing issues of creativity and innovation through the development of pedagogical methods that combine literature with orature.
>
> (G.E. Lewis 2009, 177)

One AACM member clearly stated the social mission of the school:

> In the AACM we're into more than just the music, so the basic thing is to protect our race, protect our Black children, protect our Black boys and girls and to raise them up to be strong and broad shouldered and proud. This is the undercurrent behind the AACM.
>
> (G.E. Lewis 2009, 179)

The influence of the AACM spread throughout the country. Musicians in St. Louis considered applying to be an AACM chapter but decided to form their own organization. Besides, they wanted to include other art forms, including drama, visual arts, theater, and creative writing, in a way combining the missions of the AACM and OBAC. They formed the Black Artists' Group (BAG) in 1968. Among the first officers were Julius Hemphill as chairman and Oliver Lake as treasurer (Looker 2004, 31).

BAG members launched their version of Black Studies in an inner-city building that they renovated:

> Education was a key tenet of BAG's Black Arts philosophy, and with the Washington Boulevard building as anchor, BAG quickly opened its arts training school … By June 1969, enrollment had climbed to over two hundred students, filling the often-free classes in creative writing, music, drama, dance, and the visual arts. Course in music theory and specific musical instruments were by far the most popular, running every weeknight.
>
> (Looker 2004, 74)

Every large city had some sort of musical expression of the Black Arts Movement. Table 7 lists just a few.

One instance of this organizational process of Black vanguard musicians operating in the jazz idiom presaged the emergence of Black Studies in higher education. Coltrane was complaining about how the music business treated Black musicians and their music. Olatunji, who had left his native Nigeria to do undergraduate studies at Morehouse College before becoming a professional musician in New York, agreed. They met and drafted a mission statement that set forth five goals, including this plan: "To explore the possibility of teaching the music of our people in conservatories, colleges and universities where only European musical experience dominates and is being perpetuated" (Backus 1978, 72; Heller 2017, 22). Unfortunately, Coltrane died shortly after this, in July 1967, and they were not able to implement this very important project.

Table 7 Musicians' Organizations of the Black Arts Movement

Founded	*City*	*Group*	*Founders*
1960	New York	Jazz Artist Guild	Charles Mingus, Max Roach, and Abby Lincoln
1964	New York	Jazz Composer's Guild	Bill Dixon, Sun Ra, Cecil Taylor, Archie Shepp, and Roswell Rudd
1964	Los Angeles	Underground Musicians Association	Horace Tapscott
1965	Chicago	Association for the Advancement of Creative Musicians	Muhal Richard Abrams, Kelan Phil Cohran, Steve McCall, and Jodie Christian
1966	New York	Jazz Composer's Orchestra Association	Carla Bley and Michael Mantler
1966	New York	Olatunji Center of African Culture	John Coltrane, Olatunji, and Yusef Lateef
1968	St. Louis	Black Artists' Group	Julius Hemphill and Oliver Lake
1968	Detroit	Detroit Creative Musicians Association	Doug Hammond and James Blood
1970	New York	Jazz and the People's Movement	Rahsaan Roland Kirk

Particular works captured the mood of the times and became the universal musical soundtrack for the Black Power Movement. In the jazz genre (keeping in mind the AACM's naming of the music as Great Black Music or Black Classical Music), music with political themes was important: John Coltrane, "Alabama"; Charles Mingus, "Fables of Faubus"; and Max Roach, Abbey Lincoln, and Olatunji, "Freedom Now Suite" (1961). And for a larger Black audience, popular music became the score for everyday life: James Brown, "Say It Loud, I'm Black and I'm Proud" (1968); Nina Simone, "Young, Gifted, and Black" (1970); Marvin Gaye, "What's Going On" (1971); Chi-Lites, "Give More Power to the People" (1971); and the O'Jays, "Give the People What They Want" (1974). Many more songs with explicit political themes made the charts. Black music became a soundtrack to everyday life in the USA. The politics of Black Power impacted the artists and they in turn made music that fit the times.

LITERATURE

The Black Arts Movement became a mass movement when poetry became a widely embraced and performed cultural practice. First, the lyrics of popular music were recognized as poems loved by the people, partly because they were married to the music. The output of musicians of Motown in Detroit best expressed this; the sounds coming out of Philadelphia, Chicago, Memphis, and many others locations followed suit. The performers sang, danced, dressed in costume, and sometimes spoke the words of a song. Simultaneous with the theoretical debate, the poets and musicians were demonstrating a Black aesthetic, and theorists paid attention.

As mentioned earlier, the poetic genius of Amiri Baraka was central to the Black Arts Movement becoming more conscious of itself, which added fuel to the fire. His powerful poem "Black Art" (described earlier) named the movement. Baraka personified the collective literary production of three New York area groups: Umbra, the Harlem Writers Group, and the Uptown Writers Group. He had come up as one of the literary stars of the Beat poets, which boosted his visibility. When he left Greenwich Village for Harlem, the mantle of leadership of the literary wing of the Black Arts Movement fell on him. Table 8 lists a few of the literary groups.

Table 8 Writers' Organizations of the Black Arts Movement

Founded	*City*	*Group*	*Founders*
1950	New York	Harlem Writers Guild	John Oliver Killens, Rosa Guy, Dr. John Henrik Clarke, Willard Moore, and Walter Christmas
1960	New York	On Guard	Calvin Hicks
1962	New York	Umbra Writers Workshop	David Henderson
1964	New York	Uptown Writers Movement	Askia Touré and Al Haynes
1965	Los Angeles	Watts Writers Workshop	Budd Schulberg
1967	Chicago	OBAC Writers Workshop	Hoyt Fuller and Conrad Kent Rivers
1969	East St. Louis	Black Rivers Writers Collective	Eugene Redmond

Gil Scott-Heron and the Last Poets were leaders among the masters of literature as curriculum for the Black Arts Movement. These wordsmiths laid the basis for the emergence of the contemporary manifestation of rap, spoken word music. Gil Scott-Heron was a musical political propagandist who called out political figures (e.g., US Vice-President Spiro Agnew [1969–1973]), criticized the media ("The revolution will not be televised"), and called for people to be engaged. He began making his art as a college student at Lincoln University (Scott-Heron 2017). The community-based Last Poets emerged out of the militant street force of New York. They merged a Black Nationalist revolutionary perspective with the conga drums and cultural references to traditional African culture.

Soon writers were emerging and organizing all over the country, especially the Midwest—Chicago, Detroit, and East St. Louis. Chicago's primary literary organization was the OBAC Writers Workshop. It featured strong Black women writers such as Johari Amini, Cathy Slade, Ronda Davis, Alicia Johnson, Carolyn Rodgers, and Barbara Mahone. Later these sisters were joined by Angela Jackson, S. Brandi Barnes, Collette Armstead, and Sandra Jackson-Opoku. Other writers included Sterling Plumpp, Walter Bradford, Mike Cook, James Cunningham, Ransom Boykin, Ebon Dooley, and Cecil Brown.

One OBAC writer, Don Lee (Haki Madhubuti), born in Detroit in 1942, founded Third World Press along with Jewell Latimore (Johari Amini). This press was the major publisher of the OBAC writers and as such was the main vehicle enabling them to make a major impact on the national scene. Lee/Madhubuti and Sterling Plumpp were the most prolific of the OBAC writers. Madhubuti became a highly visible poet in the national Black Arts Movement as well as a major publisher of his own work and that of many others, including almost all of the OBAC writers. He went on to teach at many colleges, including Cornell, Chicago State University, and DePaul University. At Chicago State, he founded the Gwendolyn Brooks Center (Chicago State University 1990).

Sterling Plumpp had the most sustained academic career in Black Studies of all the OBAC writers. Plumpp was born in Clinton, Mississippi, in 1940, moved to Chicago, and worked his way from the post office to a faculty position at the University of Illinois at Chicago. There he worked for thirty years, retiring as a full professor in the Department of African American Studies. He published fourteen books of poems and essays. Plumpp's main focus has been to link literary production with the culture and performance of Black music, especially the blues, anchored in the dialectic of Mississippi and Chicago. He is also known for editing *Somehow We Survive: An Anthology of South African Writing*, as well as authoring other texts (Plumpp 1976, 1982, 1991; Zheng 2016).

Oscar Brown Jr. (1926–2005) was a unique voice in the Chicago scene. The son of a militant Black Nationalist who advocated for Blacks constituting a forty-ninth state, he took his militant activism into the arts. He was a poet–singer who composed his own work, put poems to music (e.g., "Brown Baby" by Paul Lawrence Dunbar) and wrote lyrics as well (e.g., "Afro Blue" by Mongo Santamaria). One of his great achievements was recruiting the Blackstone Rangers, a militant Black gang in Chicago, into a cultural training program to create a musical production called "Opportunity Please Knock." This production, a direct response to the repressive policies of the city administration, proved that with an appropriate educational program alienated Black youth could be motivated to high achievement (Brown Jr. 2005; Brown Jr., Richardson, and Bieschke 2016).

The major Black Arts Movement literary figure in Detroit was the librarian/poet Dudley Randall (1914–2000) (Randall 2014; J.E. Thompson 2005).

He founded Broadside Press and played a key role in promoting Black Arts Movement writers, especially but not only from Detroit and Chicago, and including poetry and fiction. The top four writers he published were Nikki Giovanni, Etheridge Knight, Don Lee, and Sonja Sanchez. Of the eighteen poetry books that Broadside Press published between 1965 and 1969, nine were by women authors. These publications were the intellectual products that fed Black Studies on campus. They also provided an alternative status mechanism that enabled these writers to meet the gatekeeping criteria of colleges to become faculty and writers-in-residence. They were essential in giving the Black writers of the Black Arts Movement legitimacy on their own terms.

Eugene Redmond, from his base in East St. Louis, made key contributions: he founded the Black Rivers Writers Collective and wrote a major survey of Black Arts Movement literary production, *Dreamvoices: The Mission of Afro-American Poetry, a Critical History* (Redmond 1976).

As explained in Chapter 1, the anthology has been the literary form sustaining a national African-American literature. Key anthologies of the Black Arts Movement are listed in Table 9. As an organic social movement, Black art was self-organized in local communities, originating in self-published works by individuals and local organizations. Most of these were distributed locally or at conferences, and otherwise individually through personal networks. An added impetus was when a publication was mentioned in journals such as *Negro Digest*, *Freedomways*, *Journal of Black Poetry*, or *The Liberator*. But anthologies of work by writers from every region and in all literary forms had the widest impact.

Table 9 Literary Anthologies of the Black Arts Movement

Year	*Title*	*Editors*
1968	*Black Fire: An Anthology of African American Writing*	Amiri Baraka and Larry Neal
1969	*For Malcolm: Poems on the Life and the Death of Malcolm X*	Dudley Randall and Margaret Burroughs
1969	*Black Arts: An Anthology of Black Creations*	Ahmed Alhamisi and Harun Kofi Wangara
1970	*The Black Woman: An Anthology*	Toni Cade Bambara
1971	*The Black Aesthetic*	Addison Gayle
1971	*The Black Poets*	Dudley Randall
1972	*Understanding the New Black Poets: Black Speech and Black Music as Poetic Reference*	Stephen Henderson
1972	*New Black Voices: An Anthology of Contemporary Afro-American Literature*	Abraham Chapman
2006	*New Thoughts on the Black Arts Movement*	Lisa Gail Collins and Margo Natalie Crawford
2014	*SOS—Calling All Black People: A Black Arts Movement Reader*	John Bracey, Sonja Sanchez, and James Smethurst

There are clear features of the anthology as a genre of African-American literature. The first point is quantitative: the anthology usually contains a large body of material. A second feature is that the anthology often includes contemporary work alongside historical work, and that argues for the historical reproduction of literary styles, themes, and aesthetics. A third feature is that the anthology includes multiple genres of writing, so that with poetry, fiction, and drama one can more abstractly speak of literature in all its diversity. The study of Black literature has relied heavily on the anthologies, along with key individual works not so included, such as novels.

THEATER

Theater is the literary form that connects with all the other arts, from music to dance to the visual arts in set and costume design and to taking literature into spoken word. Critical to theater, as with all of the arts, is the issue of audience. The Black theater includes plays about Black people aimed at a Black audience. Plays that operated within the Black experience were a major part of the Negro Theater Project of the WPA. Many of the artists who got their start there would be the elders advising the young Black dramatists and actors of the 1960s. They included Harry Belafonte, Ruby Dee, Ossie Davis, Sidney Poitier, Pearl Bailey, Carlton Moss, Claudia McNeil, and Shirley Graham Du Bois. Chicago's leading playwright in this period was Ted Ward. Table 10 lists leading theater groups of the Black Arts Movement.

Table 10 Theater Groups of the Black Arts Movement

Year	*Place*	*Company*	*Founders*
1963	Tougaloo, MS; New Orleans	Free Southern Theater	Gilbert Moses, Denise Nicholas, Doris Derby, and John O'Neal
1965	New York	Black Arts Repertory Theatre/School	Amiri Baraka
1967	Newark	Spirit House	Amiri Baraka
1967	New York	Negro Ensemble Company	Douglas Turner Ward and Robert Hooks
1967	New York	New Lafayette Theater	Robert MacBeth and Ed Bullins
1968	New York	National Black Theater	Barbara Ann Teer
1969	Kansas City	Nyeusi Ujamaa Theater	Toni Escoe
1971	Chicago	ETA Theater	Abena Joan Brown
1968	Chicago	Kuumba Theater	Val Gray Ward

A critical contribution of 1960s Black theater was the emphasis on audience and authors, building a new Black audience for the new playwrights of the period. This was especially true of New York and Chicago theater companies. Many also developed educational programs for actors, playwrights, directors, and set designers.

The New York scene had three important companies that considered themselves part of the Black Arts Movement: Black Arts Repertory Theatre and School (BARTS), New Lafayette, and the National Black Theater. Amiri Baraka founded BARTS after he left the Village for Harlem in 1965. Woodard gives a sense of how BARTS took off:

> Harlem found out about the opening of the cultural institution when Sun Ra and his Myth-Science Arkestra led a parade of writers and artists across 125th Street ... They waved the Black Arts flag designed by one of their artists, a black and gold flag with Afrocentric theater masks of comedy and tragedy. At the cultural center, Harold Cruse taught Black history; Larry Neal, Askia Muhammad Toure, and Max Stanford came as cultural and political advisors, and such musicians as Sun Ra, Albert Ayler, and Milford Graves provided regular jazz performances.
>
> (Woodard 1999, 65)

In addition to being a poet and essayist, Amiri Baraka (LeRoi Jones) was a major playwright, and used BARTS to showcase his work (Baraka 1969, 1978, 1987; Jones 1964, 1967). He lays down his ideas in his essay on revolutionary theater:

> This should be a theatre of World Spirit. Where the spirit can be shown to be the most competent force in the world. Force. Spirit. Feeling. The language will be anybody's, but tightened by the poet's back-bone. And even the language must show what the facts are in this consciousness epic, what's happening. We will talk about the world, and the preciseness with which we are able to summon the world, will be our art. Art is method. And art, "like any ashtray or senator" remains in the world. Wittgenstein said ethics and aesthetics are one. I believe this. So the Broadway theatre is a theatre of reaction whose ethics like its aesthetics reflects the spiritual values of this unholy society, which sends young crackers all over the world blowing off colored people's heads ... The Revolutionary Theatre is shaped by the world, and moves to reshape the world, using as its force the natural force and perpetual vibrations of the mind in the world. We are history and desire, what we are, and what any experience can make us. It is a social theatre, but all theatre is social theatre.
>
> (Baraka 1965, 4–6)

BARTS was relatively short-lived (1965–1966), because Baraka relocated to his hometown of Newark, New Jersey to form a new company, Spirit House.

Barbara Ann Teer then took up the ideological leadership of theater in the Black Arts Movement, founding the National Black Theater in Harlem in 1968:

> We must begin building cultural centers where we can enjoy being free, open and black, where we can find out how talented we really are, where we can be what we were born to be and not what we were brainwashed to be, where we can literally "blow our minds" with blackness.
>
> (J.K. Williams 2008)

Teer led her company into a ritual-based spiritual journey rooted in the tradition of Black religion and in search of a Pan-African consciousness. The mission statement of the National Black Theater places it as a core institution of the Black Arts Movement's role in Black Studies:

> 1. To produce transformational theater that helps to shift the inaccuracy around African Americans' cultural identity by telling authentic stories of Black lifestyle;
> 2. To use theater arts as a means to educate, enrich, entertain, empower & inform the national conscience around current social issues impacting our communities;
> 3. To provide a safe space for artists of color to articulate the complexity, beauty & artistic excellence intrinsic in how we experience the world in the domain of acting, directing, producing, designing, play writing and entrepreneurial autonomy.
>
> (National Black Theater 1968)

A third important Black theater initiative was the New Federal Theatre, founded by Woodie King in 1970. The focus here was more on connecting Black theater to the American mainstream, especially for the employment of professionals working in the field:

> [Our mission is] to integrate minorities and women into the mainstream of American theatre by training artists for the profession, and by presenting plays by minorities and women to integrated, multicultural audiences—plays which evoke the truth through beautiful and artistic re-creations of ourselves.
>
> (New Federal Theatre n.d.)

It is important to include here two Chicago initiatives. After leaving her position in OBAC, Val Gray Ward formed the Kuumba Theater Company in 1968:

> Eventually the company found a home at the South Side Community Art Center before moving to an old warehouse on South Michigan. "During our time there, the gangbangers would break into our cars," says Ward. But before long these same kids took advantage of the cultural opportunities Kuumba had to offer inner-city youths. "Eventually they started building sets for our theater. We became an extended family, and they started going to theater and writers' meetings with us."
>
> (Barnes 1996)

In 1971, Abena Joan Brown and Okoro Harold Johnson formed the ETA Creative Arts Foundation. This was a performance company that featured only original plays with local actors. The foundation for this program was a school with classes for talent development (ETA n.d.).

As Smethurst points out, it is important to include developments in the South as this is a region often neglected when discussing Black intellectual and cultural history. One of the important theater initiatives of the Black Arts Movement, and one of its educational emergent institutions, was the Free Southern Theater (FST) based in New Orleans. It emerged out of SNCC and maintained activities that linked it to the freedom struggle.

The FST was also seriously devoted to the development of a new repertoire, new actors, new playwrights, and new directors rooted in the local Black community, as well as the Black communities of the South generally. It instituted a playwrights' workshop and a writers' workshop in which the participants were almost all local (Smethurst 2021, 68).

DANCE

There were important linkages with the past in the area of dance, including Katherine Dunham (1909–2006) and Eleo Palmare (1937–2008). Dunham's legacy extended into the Black Arts Movement, when she returned to her roots by resettling in East St. Louis. There she focused on making transgenerational connections and mentoring Black Arts Movement cultural cadre, among them Eugene Redmond. Her legacy is performed as her world-renowned dance method called the Dunham Technique:

> What Dunham gave modern dance was a coherent lexicon of African and Caribbean styles of movement—a flexible torso and spine, articulated pelvis and isolation of the limbs, a polyrhythmic strategy of moving—which she integrated with techniques of ballet and modern dance.
>
> (Wikipedia 2018b)

She put it this way: "In short, the Dunham Technique is a series of exercises and forms based on primitive rhythms in dance creating an awareness of time, space, form, and function derived from their most basic interrelation" (Christie Gonzalez 2015). She embodied Black dance and her method is now maintained in a certification program (Institute for Dunham Technique Certification n.d.).

One of the dancers who continued her legacy in his dance company and a school based in the community, mainly serving low-income Black youth, was Eleo Palmare. Palmare reflects the Black Power perspective:

> "I'm labeled … angry … because I will not do what they want from a black dancer. They want black exotics … I have something to say and I want to say it honestly, strongly and without having it stolen, borrowed or messed over."
>
> (Emery, Dixon-Stowell, and Emery 1988, 298)

Three main dance traditions impacted the dancers of the Black Arts Movement: Western classical technique, traditional African dance forms, and popular African-American movement. Innovating with these forms in many ways reinvented modern dance. Alvin Ailey (1931–1989) gained recognition as a major dancer when he formed his Alvin Ailey Dance Company in 1958, which led to his first two major works, *Blues Suite* (1958) and *Revelations* (1960). He consciously designed dance as a reflection of what he called his "blood memories" of growing up in the South, where his community collectively picked cotton and ritualistically celebrated their religion (Ailey and Bailey 1999).

Another important development in New York was the Dance Theater of Harlem founded in 1969 by Arthur Mitchell (b. 1934). Mitchell gained important status in the dance community when he rose to be the first Black man to be principal dancer with the New York City Ballet in 1956. After the assassination of Martin Luther King Jr. in 1968, he returned to Harlem and founded his company and school (A. Mitchell et al. 2016).

Dance has always been part of every Black community, but the Black Arts Movement awakened the need to consciously connect with the fundamentals of Black life, including reconnecting with Africa. In Chicago, this move is very much associated in the 1960s with Darlene Blackburn (b. 1942):

> In 1969, after a performance Blackburn did at DuSable High School, a woman asked her what parts of Africa she'd been to. None, Blackburn said. This was just her impression of African dance. The woman—Dr. Margaret Burroughs, founder of the Du Sable Museum—said, well, then, Blackburn would have to go. She made her first trip, to Ghana, that year; in 1971 she traveled with seven dancers and three drummers to Nigeria. From 1977 to 1980 she lived in Nigeria, teaching dancers there to choreograph and theatricalize the folk

> and ritual dances of their culture. She made the first of her several trips to the Caribbean in 1967.
>
> (Molzahn 1993)

Blackburn became a key force in merging traditional African cultural practices with the improvisational cultural dynamic of the African-American experience. She danced with Kelan Phil Cohran, but most important she became an inspirational cultural performer for Black youth in high schools and community centers. In addition, she taught at Purdue University and in Nigeria at the University of Calabar. As of 2019, she was still teaching dance and yoga in Chicago.

VISUAL ARTS

Visual artists often work alone, but with the impact of social movements for social justice on the consciousness of the artists, unity became imperative. An important example of this was the Spiral Group (1963–1966), organized by Romare Bearden and Hale Woodruff (C.J. Martin 2011; Siegel 2011). Spiral formed "for the purpose of discussing the commitment of the Negro artist in the present struggle for civil liberties, and as a discussion group to consider common aesthetic problems" because "the Negro represents a clear force directed towards the best traditions of a democratic society. As Negro artists, we must determine what we want from American society" (Bearden and Henderson 1993, 401). The group first called artists together to coordinate bus transportation to the March on Washington during August 1963:

> The members of the group were at varying stages in their careers when they first started meeting. While they did agree that their place, as artists, in the civil rights movement was important, they had differing views on what that place would be. The artists in the group were moved to come together and discuss their own engagement in the struggle for civil rights, even though each found engagement in a different way. The collective allowed for a shared response to the courage that defined the struggle for civil rights ... Although the group was active for only a short time, Spiral proved to be important as an historical initiative, and was one of the first artist groups to call for the cultural community's involvement in social change. The group's only exhibition was May 14 through June 5, 1965, titled *First Group Showing: Works in Black and White*. The exhibition was in part a response to the trend of major art institutions to overlook the work of African-American artists. Bearden had suggested the exhibition's black-and-white theme because it comprised both socio-political and formal concerns.
>
> (Wikipedia 2018a)

The Weusi Artist Collective 1965 formed in the wake of the assassination of Malcolm X, and as its members were moving into a Black consciousness that sought to connect to Africa. Based in Harlem, they chose as a name the Ki-Swahili word for blackness.

A major leap for visual artists in the Black Arts Movement took place when the OBAC Visual Arts Workshop painted *The Wall of Respect* in the heart of a lower-income neighborhood on the South Side of Chicago in 1967 (Alkalimat, Crawford, and Zorach 2017). It was explosive, turning Black art from a commodity to a public phenomenon and blasting it into people's consciousness. Black visual artists became mural makers, creating large and complex public images that constituted part of the curriculum emerging from the Black Arts Movement. Every mural was a book for all to see, and read over time, seeking deeper and deeper meaning from symbols and colors connecting to the currents of struggle for Black liberation on a local, national, and global basis. The Wall of Respect spurred a major outpouring of this type of public art, with more than fifteen hundred murals being completed in subsequent years. Table 11 gives a small sample:

Table 11 Key Murals 1967 and After

Year	*City*	*Title of Mural*	*Artists/Organizers*
1967	Chicago	*The Wall of Respect*	OBAC Visual Arts Workshop
1968	Detroit	*Wall of Dignity*	Bill Walker and Eugene Eda Wade
1968	St. Louis	*Wall of Respect*	Leroy White
1969	Oakland	*Leaders and Martyrs*	Shirley Triest and David Salgado
1972	Philadelphia	*Wall of Consciousness*	Bernard Young
1972	Boston	*Knowledge is Power, Stay in School*	Dana Chandler and Nelson Stevens
1975	Atlanta	*Wall of Respect*	Nathan Hoskins, Verna Parks, and Ashanti Johnson

The only art initiative comparable to the murals in terms of a broad impact on Black people was the poster-making genius of the Black Panther Party artist Emory Douglas (Douglas and Durant 2014; Douglas and Roberts 2011). In 1967, he joined the Black Panther Party and became their Minister of Culture. He made art a tool for mass political education:

> Douglas coined the term "revolutionary art" to define his visual politics. He invented much of the paper's iconography: the images of exaggerated Panther warriors with massive armament, the grotesque police and government officials as pigs, the bootlickers' gallery that showed assimilated blacks prostrate before symbols of white power, and the ever-present black fist.

> Douglas fashioned himself as a cultural soldier whose products were a "tool for liberation." "Revolutionary art … gives the people the correct picture of our struggle whereas the Revolutionary Ideology gives the people the correct political understanding of our struggle," he wrote in 1968.
>
> (Rhodes 2017, 101–2)

At the heart of the Black Arts Movement has long been the search for a Black aesthetic. Out of the OBAC Wall of Respect experience, some of the artists regrouped as AFRICOBRA (1968) and made this search their mission.

AFRICOBRA comprised the vanguard of the visual artists in the Black Arts Movement. Jeff Donaldson and Barbara Hogu-Jones defined their experience and approach to art:

> A nucleus of artists felt that a collective effort was possible under a common philosophy and a common system of aesthetic principles. The basic nucleus was composed of Jeff Donaldson, painter-teacher; Wadsworth Jarrell, painter-photographer, Jae Jarrell, clothing designer, Barbara J. Jones (Hogu) painter-printmaker-teacher, and Gerald Williams, painter-student. We had all noted that our work had a message: it was not fantasy or art for art's sake, it was specific and functional by expressing statements about our existence as Black People. Therefore, we began our philosophy with functionalism. Functional from the standpoint that it must communicate to its viewer a statement of truth, of action, of education, of conditions and a state of being to our people. We wanted to speak to them and for them, by having our common thoughts, feelings, trials and tribulations express our total existence as a people. We were aware of the negative experiences in our present and past, but we wanted to accentuate the positive mode of thought and action. Therefore our visual statements were to be Black, positive and direct with identification, purpose and direction. The directness of our statement was to be conveyed in several ways:
>
> A. The visual statement must be humanistic with the figure frontal and direct to stress strength, straight forwardness, profoundness, and proudness.
> B. The subject matter must be completely understood by the viewer, therefore lettering would be used to extend and clarify the visual statement. The lettering was to be incorporated into the composition as a part of the visual statement and not as a headline.
> C. The visual statement must identify our problems and offer a solution, a pattern of behavior or attitude.
> D. The visual statement must educate, it must speak of our past, present, or future…

> Napoleon Henderson, the weaver, joined the group and we moved from five to six which later changed to seven as Nelson Stevens, painter-printmaker came into the group. Yet we continued to grow with Carolyn Lawrence, painter; Omar Lama, a draftsman in pen and ink; and Sherman Beck, a painter and illustrator. During the same period of time we moved from COBRA to African COBRA to AFRICOBRA, an African Commune of Bad Relevant Artists. We moved from a national perspective to an international perspective. All Black people regardless of their land base have the same problems, the control of land and economics by Europeans or Euro-Americans.
>
> (Jones-Hogu 2012)

The Black Arts Movement focused on a search for clarity about a Black aesthetic. The written record of this search has also served as foundational curriculum material for Black Studies. AFRICOBRA codified their aesthetic principles in a creative fashion, based on the philosophy of Black Experientialism that they carried forward from OBAC:

> 1. FREE SYMMETRY, the use of syncopated, rhythmic repetition which constantly changes in color, texture, shapes, form, pattern, movement, feature, etc.
> 2. MIMESIS AT MID-POINT, design which marks the spot where the real and the unreal, the objective and the non-objective, the plus and the minus meet. A point exactly between absolute abstractions and absolute naturalism.
> 3. VISIBILITY, clarity of form and line based on the interesting irregularity one senses in a freely drawn circle or organic object, the feeling for movement, growth, changes and human touch.
> 4. LUMINOSITY, "Shine," literal and figurative, as seen in the dress and personal grooming of shoes, hair (process or Afro), laminated furniture, face, knees or skin.
> 5. COLOR, Cool-ade color, bright colors with sensibility and harmony.
>
> (Jones-Hogu 2012)

TELEVISION AND FILM

Television and film became an important form of mass media for the Black Arts Movement. Early representations on television included the fifteen-minute episodes of *The Nat King Cole Show* (1956), featuring Nat King Cole and his guests, and *Jazz Scene USA* (1962) hosted by Oscar Brown Jr. Major developments took place in the Detroit, New York, and Chicago media markets, places with large Black populations and where there were forces promoting Black consciousness. The Detroit innovation was *Tony Brown's Journal*. This PBS show, which first aired in 1968, featured the Detroit voices of Black Power and the Black Arts Movement and brought this discourse into local mainstream media:

> American Black Journal, originally titled Colored People's Time, went on the air in 1968 during a time of social and racial turmoil. The original mission was to increase the availability and accessibility of media relating to African-American experiences in order to encourage greater involvement from Detroit citizens in working to resolve community problems.
>
> ("Detroit Public Television's American Black Journal" n.d.)

Brown's show was syndicated nationwide in 1978 and popularized a new generation of Black voices.

In New York, also in 1968, Gil Noble launched his weekly program *Like It Is*, and was able to keep the show going until 2011, making it one of the longest-running television shows ever. The show, typically an hour long, allowed Noble to feature in-depth interviews and documentary video coverage of important events. New York provided a context for a more radical orientation than might have been possible in other places, including a strong emphasis on the African Diaspora (Noble 2011).

Popular culture was the focus of *Soul Train*, a television initiative in Chicago. Dick Clark had dominated American popular music and dancing on television with a program *American Bandstand*, started in 1950, which Clark took over in 1956. This show was mostly sanitized, by and large excluding Black performers and certainly Black teens. The big breakthrough for Black popular culture took place when Don Cornelius started broadcasting *Soul Train* from Chicago (1971–1993). Suddenly the popular music and dance styles of Black culture became a national force in the mass media. This program was a weekly class on Black popular culture.

Black painters were featured in key sitcoms and dramas that made television history. *Good Times* (1974–1979) featured a working-class family living in Chicago's Cabrini-Green public housing development. This was a two-parent family with a militant attitude toward any instance of attack against any family member. The oldest son, JJ, was an artist and they used the painting of Ernest Barnes to represent his work. This was the major media representation of Black art in this period (Easter 2019).

Another important use of Black art was in the *Cosby Show* (1984–1992). Bill Cosby hired the artist and art historian David Driskell to curate the art that he featured on this weekly program about a Black middle-class family. Driskell worked at Fisk University and then the University of Maryland:

> His efforts have been augmented most successfully through his art selections for "The Cosby Show," which aired on NBC from 1984 to 1992.

> The show, tapping into heightened cultural awareness established by the black arts movement in the 1960s, and capitalizing on a growing black middle class eager to celebrate itself, brought weekly depictions of black life into American living rooms through the art of Depression-era painter Archibald Motley, postwar painter Ellis Wilson and contemporary collage artist Varnette Honeywood.
>
> (O'Neal Parker 2002)

Film has also been important, with two movies in particular signaling the impact of this medium on the Black Power Movement, *The Battle of Algiers* (1966) and *Finally Got the News* (1970). The anticolonial national liberation thrust of the former inspired Black social movement activists, especially because as visual documentation the film amplified the analysis of Frantz Fanon in his major work *The Wretched of the Earth* (1961). *Finally Got the News* was the pre-eminent documentation of Black workers being a social force that linked the Black liberation struggle to the global anti-capitalist struggle in a major US industrial city, Detroit. Both films were iconic art for the Black liberation struggle.

The Los Angeles School of Black Filmmakers (1967–1989) emerged at UCLA. Film critic Clyde Taylor called them the L.A. Rebellion ("L.A. Rebellion" 2018). They emerged after the Watts uprising in Los Angeles in 1965 and the entry of the Black Power slogan into mass consciousness in 1966. Their films have become permanent fixtures in Black Studies curriculum.

One of the major directors has been Haile Gerima, an Ethiopian filmmaker who makes his home in Washington, DC. He has made many important films: *Bush Mama* (1976) uses a Black woman's hair as the narrative reference for the development of Black consciousness of a working-class woman. *The Wilmington 10 – USA 10,000* (1978) is a documentary expose of racism and violence that focuses on the case of ten movement activists caught up in the criminal justice system. *Sankofa* (1993) is about the transatlantic slave trade, and argues the case for people in the African Diaspora remembering their ancestral roots in Africa.

Another important director to come from the L.A. Rebellion is Julia Dash. She began by making film documentaries, but turned toward narrative film following the lead of the Black female novelists: "I stopped making documentaries after discovering Toni Morrison, Toni Cade Bambara, and Alice Walker. I wondered, why can't we see movies like this? I realized I needed to learn how to make narrative movies" ("Julie Dash" 2018). Her major film is *Daughters of the Dust* (1991):

> The film, set in 1902, revolves around three generations of Gullah women in the Peazant family on St. Helena Island off the coasts of Georgia and South Carolina. Innovative with its use of Gullah dialogue and interwoven story-

lines among the predominately female cast, the film focuses on ancestral and matriarchal story lines as well as the history of former slaves who settled on the island and formed an independent community there. The screenplay was written in the dialect of the island settlers with no subtitles, resulting in an immersive language experience.

("Julie Dash" 2018)

The most celebrated Black film artist out of the East Coast is Spike Lee, who studied film at New York University (McGowan 2017). He explored gender roles in his major debut film *She's Gotta Have It* (1986); he has made over thirty-five films since 1983, including *Do the Right Thing* (1989), *Malcolm X* (1992), and *Chi-Raq* (2015).

A more commercial initiative came out of Hollywood, which came to be called Blaxploitation films because they sensationalized violence and sex and played on Black stereotypes. There were some positive features, though:

Blaxploitation films were originally made specifically for an urban black audience, but the genre's audience appeal soon broadened across racial and ethnic lines once Hollywood realized the potential profit of expanding the audiences of blaxploitation films across those racial lines. The Los Angeles National Association for the Advancement of Colored People (NAACP) head and ex-film publicist Junius Griffin coined the term from the words "black" and "exploitation." The films, though receiving backlash for stereotypical characters all the while, were one of the first instances in which black actors and communities were the heroes and focuses of cinema and/or television, rather than being portrayed as sidekicks or as victims of brutality. The genre allowed the rethinking of race relations in the 1970s. Blaxploitation films were the first to regularly feature soundtracks of funk and soul music and primarily black casts.

("Blaxploitation" 2018)

Films that are sometimes included in this category, although this is sharply debated, are *Sweet Sweetback's Baadasssss Song* (1971), *Shaft* (1971), and *Superfly* (1972).

This commercial trend did not stop others from making great contributions. One such person is St. Clair Bourne (1953–2007):

In a career that began in the late 1960s as a producer for the public-affairs series "Black Journal" on public television, Mr. Bourne launched his production company, Chamba Mediaworks, in New York in 1971. Over 36 years, he produced or directed about 45 works, including documentaries for HBO, PBS, NBC, CBS, BBC, Sundance Channel, and National Geographic.

> Among his most notable films was "Half Past Autumn: the Life and Works of Gordon Parks" (2000), an Emmy-nominated, feature-length documentary about the renowned photojournalist. Other biographical subjects included poet-activist Amiri Baraka, historian and Pan-African activist John Henrik Clarke, and Hughes, the poet and playwright. "Black men who define themselves from an Afrocentric point of view fascinate me—how they succeeded and overcame opposition," Mr. Bourne told American Visions in 1999, the year "Paul Robeson: Here I Stand," his documentary about the singer-actor-political activist, was part of the PBS series "American Masters." (McLellan 2007)

JOURNALS

The Black Arts Movement had advocates and theoreticians who created journals to document and give agency to their cultural creativity (Weissinger 2017). These journals were curriculum materials that spread the experience of

Table 12 Journals of the Black Arts Movement

Founded	*City*	*Title*	*Founders/Editors*
1961	Chicago	*Negro Digest/Black World*	Hoyt Fuller
1961	New York	*Freedomways*	Shirley Graham Du Bois and Ester Jackson
1961	New York	*Liberator*	Dan Watts
1966	San Francisco	*Journal of Black Poetry*	Dingane Joe Goncalves
1967	New York	*Black Theater*	Ed Bullins
1967	New York	*Black Dialogue*	Edward Spriggs and Sam Anderson
1968	New Orleans	*NKOMBO*	Tom Dent and Kalamu Ya Salaam
1968	Newark	*The Cricket*	Amiri Baraka, Larry Neal, and A.B. Spellman
1969	New York	*Black Creation*	Fred Beauford
1969	San Francisco	*The Black Scholar*	Robert Chrisman, Nathan Hare, and Robert Allen
1970	Atlanta	*Rhythm*	Donald Stone and A.B. Spellman
1970	San Francisco	*Black Graphics International*	Julian Richardson and Aaron Pori Pitts
1971	Chicago	*Black Books Bulletin*	Haki Madhubuti (Don Lee)
1972	San Francisco	*Yardbird*	Ishmael Reed, Al Young, and Cecil Brown
1975	Los Angeles	*International Review of African American Art* (was *Black Art: An International Quarterly*)	Samella Lewis

all of the movement, especially the Black Arts Movement. The editors of each journal and the main authors often ended up working on campuses in Black Studies programs. The faculty in Black Studies often used their publications in these journals in their annual reports and applications for tenure. Of course, this became a struggle that will be covered in Part III of this book, because there was an unspoken rule that one had to be accepted by the gatekeepers to mainstream journals to qualify for tenure.

Chapter 5 discussed the important work of *Negro Digest/Black World*, *The Liberator*, *Freedomways*, *Soulbook*, and *The Black Scholar*. There were many other journals of the Black Arts Movement, as Table 12 indicates.

In every area of art, Black people networked and held various kinds of gatherings to become a social movement. As this was still a period in which the mainstream tended to exclude Black artists, this seemed like isolation, but actually provided the context for collectivity toward the norming of cultural activity. Segregation deprived the mainstream of Black talent, but forged greater creativity for Black artists. They created an explosion of Black art production as well as theorizing about the production that took place in these journals. One notable exception is a special issue of *The Drama Review* on Black Theater, edited by Ed Bullins (1968). This was a declaration of something new that opened up the mainstream.

CULTURAL CENTERS

The Black cultural center has been an emergent community institution nurturing the arts. Such institutions as the South Side Community Art Center in Chicago (1940) and Karamu House in Cleveland (1941) loom large in its history. One of the important cultural centers was in Detroit, Boone House, founded by the writer Margaret Danner. It operated between 1962 and 1964. Here is how Dudley Randall, the resident poet-librarian-publisher, describes its origin:

> There were a number of activities at Boone House from jazz sessions to creative writing classes for children. Since the federal government had not begun to fund community projects at this time, Margaret had to rely on membership fees and donations. Boone House was an abandoned parish house lent to Margaret by Dr. Theodore S. Boone, pastor of New Bethel Baptist Church in the inner city of Detroit. In the winter, the place would be insufficiently heated, and we would come early to the meetings in order to break up pieces of wood to make a fire in the fireplace.
>
> (J.E. Thompson 2005, 36)

This description drives home the point that these centers emerged in a period before government and private foundation funding became the driving forces for institutional development. Cultural centers and history museums were two names for similar institutions:

> The first independent, nonprofit museums in the US were the African American Museum in Cleveland, Ohio (founded in 1956), the DuSable Museum of African American History in Chicago, Illinois (founded in 1960), and the International Afro American Museum in Detroit, Michigan (founded in 1965; now known as the Charles H. Wright Museum of African American History). Throughout the 1960s, the energy of the American Civil Rights Movement led to numerous local African-American museums being founded. Between 1868 and 1991, there were about 150 African-American museums established in 37 states.
>
> ("List of Museums Focused on African Americans" 2018)

Two key institutions were established in New York City, The Studio Museum (1968) and the new Schomburg Center for Research in Black Culture (originating in the 1920s but established in its current form in 1980; see Chapters 3 and 5 in this volume). The Studio Museum was a center for the visual arts, but also used its facilities to feature the other arts as well ("The Studio Museum in Harlem" n.d.). The new Schomburg facility became the main venue in Harlem for all of the arts. It has hosted performances, panels and conferences, exhibitions, and residencies for scholars and artists (H. Dodson 1988).

Cultural activists organized cultural centers as places of cultural production, presentation, and instruction. As mentioned earlier, Amiri Baraka first went to Harlem and established the Black Arts Repertory Theatre and School (1965), and then relocated to his hometown of Newark, New Jersey and established Spirit House (1967). In Chicago, the musician Kelan Phil Cohran created the Affro Arts Theater and it became a gathering place for the entire movement in that city. The second f letter in Affro meant "from" (Woodard 1999, 63–68; G.E. Lewis 2009, 165–68).

Elma Lewis (1921–2004) was a leader of Black cultural center activity in Boston:

> Miss Lewis founded the Elma Lewis School of Fine Arts (ELSFA) for black youth in 1950 before foundations and corporations were interested in such projects. The school, which emphasized music and dance, produced many students who found work in Broadway musicals, and who built professional careers in the theater. In 1967, she launched the Elma Lewis Playhouse-in-the-Park, which presented such greats as Odetta, Billy Taylor, and Duke Ellington.
>
> ("Elma Lewis" n.d.)

Then, in 1968, after the assassination of Martin Luther King Jr., she moved to create the National Center of Afro-American Artists (NCAAA), and recruited Edmund Barry Gaither to be the Director and Curator. Gaither has become one of the leading Black art historians:

> For the NCAAA, he [Gaither] developed the Museum from a concept to an institution with collections exceeding three thousand objects and a thirty-two year history of exhibitions celebrating the visual arts heritage of black people worldwide. Formerly, he developed a course on African American art which he taught as a lecturer at Harvard College (1972–75); Wellesley College, 1971–74; Massachusetts College of Art, 1970–71; and Spelman College, 1968–69. Additionally, he taught a special course for Afro-American Studies at Boston University, 1971–83, and also served on the summer faculty of the Arts Leadership Institute, University of Minnesota, 1989.
>
> ("Edmund Barry Gaither" n.d.)

SUMMARY

The Black Arts Movement was the social activity of Black cultural producers who transformed the production of art, but they accomplished much more than this. The Black Arts Movement was a major autonomous force that cultivated the consciousness and everyday cultural practices of the majority of Black people. It was a transformation in aesthetics, morality, spirituality, and social and political consciousness. Most of the innovation was part of an insurgency that created art for the people and only later became embraced by the market and performed as commodity production.

Kalamu Ya Salaam, a scholar activist of the Black Arts Movement, defines the Black Arts Movement as having had three objectives:

> 1. To establish Black leadership of Black cultural expression directed to a Black audience,
> 2. To propagate the concept of the Black Aesthetic, and
> 3. To produce socially engaged art that promoted the Black freedom/liberation struggle.
>
> (Ya Salaam 2016, 1)

James Smethurst, the author of the most comprehensive study of the Black Arts Movement, makes this summary statement: "The Black Arts Movement was arguably the most influential cultural movement the United States has ever seen" (Smethurst 2005, 373).

For Black Studies on campus, this has enabled curriculum, organized campus programs, and the guiding of students to embrace art in their everyday lives.

7
The New Communist Movement

Black Marxists, and their kindred with a particular eye on African Americans, have constituted a small but influential social force for most twentieth-century social movements in the USA. As this book makes clear, study programs have been a central aspect of all movements, based on both primary documents and their application to specific historical conditions. This has certainly been true of Marxist-inspired movements. This chapter explains the origins of applying Marxism to the Black experience, the 1960s emergence of a new communist movement in the USA, and how the Black Power Movement developed a left wing and a curriculum for the Freedom Movement in general. The point is to demonstrate how this is a major tendency that has been part of the origin and development of Black Studies.

In his major work on the political economy of capitalism (1864), Marx connected the slave trade and slavery in general to the initial stage of the development of capitalism:

> The discovery of gold and silver in America, the extirpation, enslavement and entombment in mines of the aboriginal population, the beginning of the conquest and looting of the East Indies, the turning of Africa into a warren for the commercial hunting of black-skins, signalised the rosy dawn of the era of capitalist production. These idyllic proceedings are the chief momenta of primitive accumulation.
>
> (Marx 1864)

Lenin, carrying Marxist theory into the 1917 Russian Revolution, also pointed to the plight of African Americans:

> The Negroes were the last to be freed from slavery, and they still bear, more than anyone else, the cruel marks of slavery—even in advanced countries—for capitalism has no "room" for other than legal emancipation, and even the latter it curtails in every possible way … Shame on America for the plight of the Negroes!
>
> (Lenin 1913)

The emergence of Marxist revolutions in the global south carried Marxism out of Europe and brought forward into world discourse the thought and practice of a new set of revolutionary thinkers, especially Mao Tse-tung, Fidel Castro, Che Guevara, Kwame Nkrumah, and Amilcar Cabral. These developments followed the advances made by the Communist Party of the USSR led by Vladimir Ilyich Lenin and Joseph Stalin, but they were also demonstrable evidence that what Marxists call scientific socialism had universal importance when applied to the countries of Asia, Latin America, and Africa. These revolutionary experiences made a great impact on movement activists in the respective diaspora communities within the USA: Asian Americans, Latinx, and African Americans. A new generational study of Marxist theory and practice thus ensued.

The 1949 revolution in China united the working class and the peasantry in an army under the leadership of a communist party. It was different than the Russian Revolution in that it was rural and based in protracted war rather than urban insurrection. China signaled to Asia, Africa, and Latin America that a socialist revolution was possible. Mao Tse-tung added a popular style to the Marxist texts that were studied worldwide, especially his *Four Essays on Philosophy* (2001) and his methodological essay *Combat Liberalism*.

So Marxism took off even further, as it became the basis for revolutions in China, Vietnam, and Cuba. Mao himself commented on African America:

> I call on the workers, peasants, revolutionary intellectuals, enlightened elements of the bourgeoisie and other enlightened persons of all colors in the world, whether white, black, yellow or brown, to unite to oppose the racial discrimination practiced by U.S. imperialism and support the American Negroes in their struggle against racial discrimination. In the final analysis, national struggle is a matter of class struggle … I am firmly convinced that, with the support of more than 90 per cent of the people of the world, the American Negroes will be victorious in their just struggle. The evil system of colonialism and imperialism arose and throve with the enslavement of Negroes and the trade in Negroes, and it will surely come to its end with the complete emancipation of the black people.
>
> (Mao 1966)

For Black people, and for all of the African Diaspora, Ghana's independence in 1957 was another beacon that promised a future beyond European colonialism and the legacy of slavery. The main leader was Kwame Nkrumah who, following W.E.B. Du Bois and George Padmore, infused a general Pan-Africanist politics with Marxist analysis and as vision of a united socialist Africa. After independence, he contributed to African revolutionary thinking with his works *Neo-Colonialism: The Last Stage of Imperialism* (1965), *Class Struggle in Africa*

(1970), and *Handbook of Revolutionary Warfare* (1968). The clearest examples of Nkrumah's education program are the cadre-training process within the Convention People's Party and his Kwame Nkrumah Institute of Economics and Political Science, also known as Winneba Ideological Institute. At the institute, hundreds of Ghanaian activists studied Marxism.

Following Ghanaian independence, the next revolutionary advance in the African Diaspora was the Cuban Revolution in 1959. Afro-Cubans were central to the Cuban Revolution and had old historical ties to the African-American community in the USA (Alkalimat 2015). There were two very important contributions to the consciousness of the African-American community by the Cuban Revolution, especially through the actions of the leadership of Fidel Castro, Che Guevara, and the Afro-Cuban Juan Almeida. The Cuban Revolution supported and identified with Malcolm X, as demonstrated by the connection Fidel Castro made with Malcolm X when the Cuban delegation visited New York and stayed in the Teresa Hotel in Harlem (Mealy 1993). Cuba also hosted and supported the Black Panthers and the Black Liberation Army activist Assata Shakur, who remains a political refugee in Havana in 2021. The Cuban Revolution was also in the global leadership in terms of giving support to the African liberation struggles, notably in the famous battle that saw the defeat of the South African forces in Angola, the Battle of Cuito Cuanavale in 1987–1988.

THE COMMUNIST MOVEMENT IN THE USA

While the USA has a self-proclaimed identity as the world's leading democracy, its actual political history includes the unceasing suppression of socialist and communist ideas and practice. A fundamental rupture occurred during the anti-communist hysteria led by Wisconsin senator Joseph McCarthy in the 1950s. This created national amnesia about the role that socialism has played at various times in the USA. There is a historic basis for a socialist tendency in Black intellectual history and certainly as a pillar of the Radical Black tradition. This tradition was a context for many diverse programs of education, both propaganda work in mass campaigns and the development of its brand of insurgent institutions.

Socialists advocated for the working class as a whole, but had a troubled record with regard to Black people. Yet, as early as the late nineteenth century, Black intellectual activists helped to lead socialist organizations. Among these activists were Peter H. Clark (1829–1925), George Washington Woodbey (1854–1937), and Hubert Harrison (1883–1927). These three made early connections between emancipating workers from capitalist exploitation and Black people from racist national oppression. Clark was the first, advocating political action. Woodbey, as a minister, connected socialism to Christian teachings.

Harrison was the leading intellectual of his time in Harlem and participated in most of the key debates. All three were distinguished orators (Taylor 2013; Foner 1983; Perry 2011).

Next came a generation who joined the Communist Party USA (CPUSA), following the model of the Leninist party of the USSR, including Richard Moore (1893–1978), Harry Haywood (1898–1985), and Claude McKay (1889–1948). The CPUSA recruited its first wave of Black cadre from the African Blood Brotherhood (mentioned in Chapter 3), led by Cyril Briggs. Their theoretical position that African Americans constituted a nation within the USA was formally adopted by the Communist International in Moscow by resolutions in 1928 and 1930. These resolutions became a frame of reference for Marxist education regarding the Black experience. The core texts for this were the actual resolutions and the explanation of them by one of the authors, Harry Haywood, in his book *Negro Liberation* (1948).

Creating educational programs for the movement became a hallmark of the communist movement. Related to, but quite different from the tradition of insurgent institutions working within the framework of the US Constitution, were insurgent institutions set up by revolutionary socialist forces to fight the system. Their focus was an anti-capitalist curriculum designed to train cadre and promote mass education programs. To understand Marxism, and how to apply it, requires study. The communists in the USA set up various education programs, and often these involved Black people.

African Americans were often among the teachers as well as the students. Perhaps the best example of a school for cadre development is the Jefferson School of Social Science, founded by the Communist Party in 1944 in New York City. Howard "Stretch" Johnson, a dancer who became an educator, ending his career on the faculty of Black Studies at SUNY New Paltz, shares his experience:

> I had been a student of Marxist theory, studying it under the guidance of the best teachers that the American communist movement could produce at two national training schools ... [I became] New York State Education Director, responsible for cadre training schools, including Jefferson School of Social Science, with a student body of 6,000 enrollees per year.
>
> (H.E. Johnson and Johnson 2014, 113–14)

The Jefferson School was in downtown Manhattan, but there was also a school uptown in Harlem, The George Washington Carver School. Harold Cruse shares his memory of how his education in that school led him to join the Communist Party:

> I had met the Harlem communists before, in the YMCA and elsewhere. And I knew these people because in Harlem, nobody gave a damn who you were,

> what your politics were. We used to have those debates in the YMCA, there were Communists debating, black nationalists debating … NAACPers. The whole spectrum of critical opinion was being aired. So in those days—I used to tell people—anybody who couldn't argue Marx or Engels was considered a goddamn dummy! … Anyway, first thing I did, I went to what was then called the George Washington Carver School, on 125th Street, between Seventh and Eight. It's gone, it's wiped off the record. That was the Communist Party's cultural base in Harlem … It was run by Gwendolyn Bennett, the Harlem Renaissance poet, and the wife of Otto Huiswood, who had been exiled in Europe. That's where I first heard DuBois lecture.
>
> (Cruse and Cobb 2002, 285)

Several members of the Communist Party wrote important books and pamphlets relating to Black people, including Herbert Aptheker, James Jackson, Claude Lightfoot, Roscoe Proctor, Pettis Perry, and B.D. Amis. Although not as well known, several autobiographies document the diversity and depth of the Black participation in communist activities (Yates 1989; E. Thompson and Thompson 1976; E.C. Jackson 1953; Painter 1979).

Splits in the communist movement led to a number of organizations independently dispersing members into the mass movements of the 1960s. The Left connected with the student movement, mainly the Students for a Democratic Society (SDS). The Progressive Labor Party entered SDS and fostered a split, with at least four factions developing into organizational formations: The Worker Student Alliance, The Weathermen, The October League, and the Revolutionary Union.

Key veterans of this "old left" that developed out of the tendencies of the Russian Revolution (Leninist and Trotskyist) figured in the development of the New Left organizations that emerged out of the mass movements of the 1960s. Some examples are listed in Table 13.

While our focus here is on the New Communist Movement, it is important to reference the critical role played by leading members of the old Communist Party, especially Herbert Aptheker. Aptheker earned a PhD in history from Columbia University and was a close associate of W.E.B. Du Bois and Carter G. Woodson. As mentioned earlier, Aptheker produced a multivolume documentary history of African-American history that became a foundation text for Black Studies. Other important contributors were Gary Murrell and Bettina Aptheker (2015), Henry Winston (1977), Victor Perlo (1976), Roscoe Proctor (1973), James Jackson (1963), and Claude Lightfoot (1969).

Just as SDS was developing, Black Power developed a left wing and took up the study of Marxism. The Black Panther Party adopted Marxism as an expression of revolutionary thinking from what was then called the third world, especially China, Cuba, and Vietnam. Their study program was grounded in

Table 13 Old Left Veterans in the New Left

Movement Veteran	*Organization Departed*	*Organization Joined*	*Texts*
Harry Haywood	Communist Party	October League (Communist Party-ML)	*Negro Liberation* *Black Bolshevik*
Nelson Peery	Communist Party (Provisional Organizing Committee)	Communist League (Communist Labor Party)	*The Negro National Colonial Question* *African American Liberation and Revolution In the United States*
Leibel Bergman, Vicki Garvin	Communist Party	Revolutionary Union (Revolutionary Communist Party)	*Red Papers #5 National Liberation and Proletarian Revolution in the US* *Red Papers #6*
Raya Dunayevskaya	Socialist Workers Party	News and Letters	*Philosophy and Revolution*
Bill Epton	Progressive Labor Party	Proletarian Cause	*The Struggle of Black People: Where It Is and Where It Must Go*

these texts. Huey Newton, a founder and leading member of the party, stressed political education as the main activity for new recruits, especially the study of third-world revolutionary thinkers like Frantz Fanon. Rhodes points to how Panthers described their experience:

> The memoirs of former Panthers always situate this political education—this process of intellectual struggle—as the formative moment in their decision to commit to the group. David Hilliard recalled feeling utterly frustrated in his early attempts to read *The Wretched of the Earth*, a task Newton urged him to complete. "But if I read and study the book, apply myself, struggle to understand the concepts, rather than just become frustrated by them, I will begin to understand what Fanon is saying. The wretched of the earth—that's not only the peasants Fanon talks about, but us," wrote Hilliard.
>
> (Rhodes 2017, 95–96)

In a practical sense the initial action of the Black Panther Party was a direct result of study, as evidenced in the quote below. Newton discovered a tactic based on California law:

> Newton had been studying law at Merritt College and San Francisco State College, and he also read on his own at the North Oakland Service Center law

> library. He discovered that California law permitted people to carry loaded guns in public as long as the weapons were not concealed. He studied California gun law inside and out, finding that it was illegal to keep rifles loaded in a moving vehicle and that parolees could carry a rifle but not a handgun. In California, he learned, citizens had the right to observe an officer carrying out his or her duty as long as they stood a reasonable distance away.
>
> (Bloom and Martin 2013, 39)

The big breakthrough for a Black Marxist-oriented social movement was in Detroit, when Black autoworkers formed groups based in different factories. After a series of wildcat strikes, an organizational form developed, first as the Dodge Revolutionary Union Movement (DRUM), and then the RUM form spread to many other workplaces. By 1969, these organizations had united to form the League of Revolutionary Black Workers (LRBW). This was crucial, because it not only brought forward a Marxist analysis, but it was also done by a self-organizing motion of Black workers in the heart of a major industrial city. What is more, Detroit was fast becoming a majority-Black city.

The LRBW program emphasized education:

> Our duty is to plan the most feasible means to insure freedom and justice for the liberation of Black people based on the concrete conditions we relate to. In addition, we have the task of training our people for leadership and other special capacities that make a viable organization.
>
> (The League of Revolutionary Black Workers, cited in Marable and Mullings 2000, 465)

They proposed a more general program for the organization to carry out: "Politicizing and educating the masses of Black people to the nature of racism, capitalism, and imperialism, to further outline the solution to these problems in League programs and documents" (The League of Revolutionary Black Workers, cited in Marable and Mullings 2000, 465). For the Black Workers Congress, an organizational form that followed after a split in the LRBW, SNCC veteran James Forman wrote a pamphlet spelling out that workers education be rooted in experience.

> Emphasis must be on sharing experience and learning from each other. We cannot stress this point too much, for too often we do not take the time to learn from each other or to realize that the experiences of working class people are rich in content and very instructive as to how we should deal with reality. Moreover, many of us are not in the habit of summing up our own experiences evaluating them and drawing political lessons for use in the future. We negate the wisdom contained in our own lives and the lives

> of those around us. And in order to win more recruits for the revolutionary ranks we must adopt a consistent attitude that we learn from the people and we share our own experiences which possibly can help others.
> (Forman 1970)

This educational program placed priority on studying the classics of Marxism-Leninism and third-world proponents from China, Vietnam, Cuba, and Africa, then taking that body of literature and applying the principles to the experiences of Black people, especially Black workers. Following Lenin's development of the *Iskra* method—recruiting workers to learn theory by summing up their battlefront experience—the LRBW recruited workers to produce workplace newsletters and then pulled everyone together into a citywide newspaper (Lenin 1901–1902, Chapter 5). The league was able to establish a print shop (Black Star Press) and a bookstore (Black Star Book Store) and to make a movie, *Finally Got the News*. Forman wrote the pamphlet "Control, Conflict and Change" and then formed a mass-oriented Control Conflict and Change Book Club that presented public discussions of key texts. This process led to Forman taking control of a service at Riverside Church in New York and launching the modern reparations movement, which resulted in pledges from major religious denominations of $500 million for social justice.

Out of Black Nationalist tendencies emerged four organizations that took up Marxism, at least to some extent: the Congress of African People became the Revolutionary Communist League, some Revolutionary Action Movement (RAM) cadre formed the African People's Party (APP), some former SNCC activists formed the All African People's Revolutionary Party (AAPRP), and the Junta of Militant Organizations (JOMO) was transformed into the African People's Socialist Party (APSP). The AAPRP focused in particular on mobilizing students and getting them into political education study programs. Their official organization manual states:

> Prospective members must undergo a rigorous process of political education by first joining or forming a work-study group which consists of an average of ten people who voluntarily agree to do some consistent work and study around the issues and problems which affect African people; i.e. correct interpretation of African history, the need for a scientifically clear and precise ideology, a clear objective, scientific socialism, Pan-Africanism, etc.
> (Alkalimat 1980)

The AAPRP reading list for its study program was mainly Black Nationalist texts and some African leaders, but also Lenin, Nkrumah, and Walter Rodney, which gave the program some Marxist content as well.

In general, the fusion of Marxism in the Black social movements that embraced Black Power made use of important books that became required reading for Black Studies activists. Table 14 lists key works emanating from Africa and the African Diaspora.

Table 14 Key Works Fusing Marxism and Black Power

Writer	*Location*	*Text*	*Year*
Frantz Fanon	Martinique, Algeria	*The Wretched of the Earth*	1968
C.L.R. James	Trinidad, England	*A History of Pan-African Revolt*	1969 [1938]
Kwame Nkrumah	Ghana, England	*Class Struggle in Africa*	1970
Walter Rodney	Guyana, England	*How Europe Underdeveloped Africa*	1972
Amilcar Cabral	Guinea-Bissau	*Return to the Source*	1974

Taken together, these five authors come from Africa (two) and the Caribbean (three), and focused on African liberation via history (James and Rodney), contemporary society (Nkrumah), and the armed struggle for liberation (Fanon and Cabral). They represented the agency of the colonized oppressed and were taken up as a liberating force that negated the Eurocentric dominance over Black history and Black consciousness. This perspective is at the heart of all forms of Black Studies: the intellectual agency of Black people themselves.

And while these texts had a great impact on African Americans, they appealed to people throughout the African Diaspora and beyond. For the first time in the historical development of Marxist theory, Black people made major contributions. Of course, as with every important contribution to Marxist theory, these thinkers were theorizing in the context of mighty social movements that brought forward important changes.

Marxist texts by African Americans, particularly those in Table 15, also entered into the necessary curriculum for Black Studies as Social Movement.

Table 15 Key African-American Marxist Contributions to Black Studies

Author	*Text*	*Year*
Harold Cruse	*Crisis of the Negro Intellectual*	1967
Robert Allen	*Black Awakening in Capitalist America*	1969
James Boggs	*Racism and the Class Struggle*	1970
James Forman	*The Making of Black Revolutionaries*	1972
George Jackson	*Blood in My Eye*	1972
Clarence J. Munford	*Production Relations, Class and Black Liberation: A Marxist Perspective in Afro-American Studies*	1978

Within the New Communist Movement, Black activists were writing articles, giving speeches, and leading study groups, ideological production that was of general significance and reached across all organizations and tendencies. Taken together, they constituted a force that transformed a large section of Black intellectuals into a left-leaning progressive force, not unlike what had happened in the 1930s and 1940s. These books, written over a ten-year period, were a reaction to the violent repression of the Black Liberation Movement. Many texts, in targeting the specific attacks against poor and working-class Black people, helped the movement develop a systemic critique of racist capitalist forms of exploitation and how movement forces were responding.

Boggs and Jackson represented the most direct agency of the Black oppressed. Boggs, an autoworker with a background in a Trotskyite tendency of Marxism, made a big impact on Black activists because of his authentic working-class voice. He was joined in this work by his wife, Grace Lee Boggs, who had earned a PhD in philosophy. They worked with C.L.R. James and Raya Dunayevskaya in study circles in Detroit. Boggs placed the exploitation of Black people at the heart of capitalist development in the USA:

> Capitalism in the US is unique because, unlike capitalism elsewhere—which first exploited its indigenous people and then fanned out through colonialism to exploit other races in other countries—it started out by dispossessing one set of people (the Indians) and then importing another set of people (the Africans) to do the work on the land. This method of enslavement not only made Blacks the first working class in the country to be exploited for their labor but made Blacks the foundation of the capital necessary for early industrialization.
>
> (Boggs and Ward 2011, 186)

After the Black Power slogan unleashed a new kind of energy for social change, Boggs took up the mantle as the theoretician of a new moment, a moment driven by unemployed Black youth whom Boggs called a new "street force":

> This force is made up of the new generation of young Blacks who in the past would have been integrated into the American economy in the traditional Black role of unskilled and menial labor. Now they have been rendered obsolete by the technological revolutions of automation and cybernation and driven into the military, the prisons, and the streets. Outcasts, castaways, and castoffs, they are without any future except that which Black Power can create for them.
>
> (Boggs and Ward 2011, 208)

Jackson wrote from the very prison that Boggs spoke about, turning his cell into a personal classroom:

> In prison I met Marx, Lenin, Trotsky, Engels and Mao, and they redeemed me. I also met the Black guerrillas (other revolutionary Black prisoners) George Lewis, James Carr, W.C. Nolen, Bill Christmas, Tony Gibson, and others. We attempted to transform the Black criminal element into a Black revolutionary movement.
>
> (G. Jackson and Jackson 2006, 21)

Jackson asserts the same relationship as did Boggs in how capitalism has impacted Black people:

> Ever since slavery, our principal enemy is and must be isolated and identified as capitalism. The slaver was and is the factory owner, the businessman of capitalist America … It was the profit motive that built the tenement house and the city project. Profit and loss prevents repairs and maintenance. Free enterprise brought the monopolistic chain store into the neighborhood. The concept of private ownership of facilities that the people need to exist brought the legions of hip-shooting pigs down upon our heads … They're there to prevent the entrepreneur.
>
> (G. Jackson and Jackson 2006, 176)

Cruse and Munford were nurtured in the communist movement and made their contribution by launching historical arguments. Cruse wrote a major historical critique of the communist movement and its relationship to Black Nationalism, hitting hard:

> This unwillingness or inability of the Communists to come to grips with Negro national group realities was displayed on both sides of the racial fence among the Party leaders and theoreticians. It was the white Communist leaders who actually laid down the line, but the Negro leaders followed it without deviation. The whites, for the most part confused themselves, were forced to raise many questions and doubts on the Negro issue—questions only Negroes themselves could have answered. Negro leaders, however, consistently failed to answer them. In 1921, when the white leaders were courting the reality of organized Black Nationalism, the Negroes in the African Blood Brotherhood were trying to subordinate nationalism to communism. Later, when the Communists turned their backs on Black Nationalism, the same Negro leaders followed suit.
>
> (Cruse 1967a, 150)

On the other hand, Clarence J. Munford, born in Cleveland, went the route of earning a PhD in political economy from Karl Marx University in Leipzig, East Germany in 1962. He initiated a return to Marxism as a formal academic subject with his book *Production Relations, Class and Black Liberation: A Marxist Perspective in Afro-American Studies* (1978). One of his important interventions was a class he conducted on a monthly basis at the University of Guelph, in Ontario, where he taught for years. African-American militants from the workers' movement in Detroit and students from the Student Organization for Black Unity based in North Carolina would travel to Canada to study with him. He shared his training in Marxism from his doctoral study in Germany with militants who were advancing a class struggle line in the Black Liberation Movement.

Robert L. Allen was a New York correspondent for *The Guardian* newspaper, the most widespread movement media embraced by many diverse forces on the left. His book, *Black Awakening in Capitalist America* (1992), began as a series of articles published in *The Guardian*. It places the Black Power concept in the context of the transformation of the Black Freedom Movement from SNCC through the Black Panthers.

Allen opens with a challenge to movement activists:

> Black America is an oppressed nation, a semi-colony of the United States, and the Black revolt is emerging as a form of national liberation struggle … It must be asked: Are Black militant leaders simply opposed to the present colonial administration of the ghetto, or do they seek the destruction of the entire edifice of colonialism, including that subtle variant known as neo-colonialism?
>
> (Allen 1992, 1)

James Forman, a student of St. Clair Drake while earning an MA in African Studies from Roosevelt University in Chicago, became a major leader in the Freedom Movement in the 1960s as Executive Secretary of SNCC. After the rise of Black Power in 1965, Foreman held unity discussions with the Black Panther Party and then relocated to Detroit and joined the League of Revolutionary Black Workers. His advocacy of a Marxist analysis and a program of working-class struggle made a major impact on the movement.

He sums up the process of struggle this way and answers Allen:

> Our struggle during the early sixties was a struggle against white supremacy and its racist, exploitative manifestations in the area of public accommodations and lack of political representation. Even as we struggled then we were committed to fundamentally changing the political and economic framework of this country in which racism and white supremacy run rampant.

> We see today on many fronts efforts to explain away and to remove the fire from the concept Black Power. There are those who would like to take the revolutionary sting away from Black Power and make it merely another American reform movement.
>
> Therefore it is necessary to state that Black Power is a revolutionary force that seeks the elimination of capitalism and the industrial-military complex which undergirds it. We call upon all our brothers and sisters to intensify the revolutionary consciousness among our people to unite in the fight against racism, capitalism, and imperialism.
>
> (Forman 1970, 179)

What actually spread the study of Marxism was a series of debates. As stated earlier, the main force propelling the movement forward has always been the relationship between social activism and theory building, fueled by debates within the movement to evaluate progress and chart a path forward. It was always a combination of ideology, theory, and political practice. The international communist movement was polarized between the USSR and the People's Republic of China. In the USA, the revolutionary forces emerging out of SDS, the leading student movement organization, and the Black Liberation Movement were attracted to third-world revolutionary forces—mainly China (Mao) and Cuba (Fidel and Che). The Communist Party had abandoned the 1928 position of the Communist International that the African Americans were an oppressed nation, but these forces in becoming what was called a "New Communist Movement" reopened what they called the African American National Question. This was the direct result of the Black Power Movement. *The Guardian* hosted a series of major debates in 1973. Many organizations participated, with audiences of more than five hundred people: the Revolutionary Union, the October League, the Black Workers Congress, the Puerto Rican Revolutionary Workers Organization, I Wor Kuen, Harpers Ferry Organization, Third World Women's Alliance, People's Coalition for Peace and Justice, and the Puerto Rican Socialist Party (Elbaum 2002, 109).

The Revolutionary Union produced one of the most influential documents in the debate on the national question, *Red Papers #5: National Liberation and Proletarian Revolution in the U.S.* (1972). They upheld the 1928 Comintern position as historically correct, but advanced a new line based on their analysis of changes that had turned Black people into mainly an urban industrial working class—hence they coined the phrase that the latter now constituted "a nation of a new type." The Black Workers Congress waged a polemical struggle against this line, based on their view that it would result in the necessary subordination of Black and other national minorities to white workers.

The main debate was in the Black Liberation Movement, as revolutionary nationalists took up active study and debate over the role of Marxism in the fight for Black liberation. This debate spread the study of Marxism to every battlefront and led to splits in every major organization. The main event was a debate organized by the ALSC at Howard University in May 1974:

> The conference was able to achieve its goal of contributing clarity to the ideological struggle. More than 1,000 conference participants were consistently involved in two plenaries (4 hours each) on the conference theme "Which road against Racism—Imperialism for the Black Liberation Movement?," and five workshops (4 hours each), on women in struggle, Youth and Education, Labor, Politics, and Justice. At one point during the question period of one plenary over 50 people were lined up at the two microphones to ask questions of the panelists.
>
> (Alkalimat 1977, 304–5)

The main panel participants engaged in ideological debate:

Panel One:
1. Muhammad Ahmad, Saladin Muhammad, Abner Berry, African People's Party
2. Stokely Carmichael, All African People's Revolutionary Party
3. Abdul Alkalimat, People's College

Panel Two:
1. Kwadjo Akpan, Pan-African Congress (Detroit)
2. Amiri Baraka, Congress of African People
3. Owusu Sadaukai, ALSC (Malcolm X Liberation University)

After this debate, the study of Marxism spread throughout Black Studies curriculum development along with the other main ideological trends: Nationalism, Pan-Africanism, Black Feminism, and Black Liberation Theology. For example, the debate prompted Amiri Baraka's shift to embrace class politics and Marxism: "Owusu's presentation was met with a standing ovation. Alkalimat's was the presentation that was most clearly based on Marxist theory, and as such it was the most orderly presentation, with the most reference to consistent scientific analysis" (Baraka 1984, 308). Ideological differences were sometimes in collaboration and sometimes at odds, but Baraka argued for the Marxist perspective as part of the Black Studies narrative.

8
The Black Women's Movement

Even more influential than the Marxist perspective is the role of Black women. One of the most important ways in which social movements have impacted Black Studies involves Black women. The rise of Black women in social movements has been a crucial and necessary development. Why? One of the main reasons is that women have always been at the foundation of most Black social movements and social institutions in the community. But, in the society in general, and in the Black community in particular, male supremacy and patriarchy have silenced and often made invisible Black women. It has suppressed the fact of the exploitation of Black women as workers and objects of sexual abuse. Another reason is that racism within the general women's movement has marginalized Black women as well. Because of this, the rise of Black women within social movements and that of an independent Black women's movement corrected, clarified, and broke new ground.

The self-organization of Black women has been a consciousness-raising experience out of necessity. Women have had to teach themselves about their own history, especially the struggles past and present to advance women's interests. Sometimes this has been to answer a silence, sometimes to contradict incorrect information, and, in fewer cases, it has been to build on what information has been made available. In most cases, this study has resulted in a major advance in knowledge, illuminating the special role of one or more women who have created a beacon of light for Black women at the grass roots to learn from and be guided by.

One of the ways this has had a direct and national impact has been through gender battles in mainstream contexts. The most comprehensive of those is electoral politics. Black women made a great breakthrough in 1968 with the election of Shirley Chisholm to Congress, where she served seven terms through to 1983. She was a militant Black woman from New York who worked on educational opportunities for Black people. She further distinguished herself in 1972 by being the first major Black presidential candidate in one of the two mainstream political parties. Here was a Black woman at the heart of American politics, clear and uncompromising as far as her voice being heard and her organic base of Black women mobilized.

After retiring from Congress in 1983, Shirley Chisholm took a teaching post at Mount Holyoke, followed by a position at Spelman, both colleges for women. She took her experiences in politics into the classroom to tutor and help develop women to follow in her footsteps. Since she blazed the trail, as of 2018, there have been great electoral victories for Black women: 20 in congress; 3 holding statewide offices; 274 state legislators in 43 states; and 9 mayors in the 100 largest cities.

Another mainstream context for the advancement of Black women is the trade union movement. Jobs in the USA have historically been segregated by gender, with women having less power and fewer roles in leadership. One noteworthy Black woman who rose above this sex discrimination is Addie Wyatt. As a Black woman worker in Chicago, she fought her way up the ranks of trade union leadership. In 1953, Wyatt became the first Black woman to be vice-president of a local branch of the United Packinghouse Workers of America—a major union. She was active as a founding member of the Coalition of Black Trade Unionists in 1972 and of the Coalition of Labor Union Women in 1974. Her greatest achievement was being elected the first Black woman to be an international vice-president of a union, the United Food and Commercial Workers. *Time* magazine selected her as its woman of the year in 1975. She remains a beacon for the 1.3 million Black women members of trade unions, representing 13.3 percent of all employed Black women in 2017 (Bureau of Labor Statistics 2018).

Black women have distinguished themselves in the Freedom Movement. They have done so while male lawyers (NAACP) and ministers (SCLC) had control of the reins. An outstanding woman who changed the face of the NAACP Legal Defense Fund was Constance Baker Motley. She finished Columbia Law School in 1946 and then joined the NAACP legal team. Chosen to work with Thurgood Marshall, Motley wrote the original complaint in the *Brown* v. *Board of Education* (Topeka, Kansas) in 1950. In 1962, she was the first Black woman lawyer to argue a case before the US Supreme Court, defending the right of James Meredith to attend the University of Mississippi. She won this case in 1962, the first of her ten cases before the court—all of which she won. The high point of her career was in 1966, when President Lyndon B. Johnson appointed her to become a US District Court Judge, a post she held until her death in 2005.

Ella Baker was a militant woman who made a great impact on the Freedom Movement through her involvement with three major organizations: the NAACP, SCLC, and SNCC. From 1938 to 1953, she served in leadership positions in the NAACP, including as director of branches and president of the New York chapter. She went to Atlanta to join Martin Luther King Jr. as a key staff person in the national office of SCLC. Her organizational skills institutionalized a movement organization driven by charismatic orators. At an SCLC-sponsored youth conference, she advised the sit-in activists to form their own organization and not become a youth affiliate of SCLC, and so SNCC was born. She resigned from SCLC and became a key advisor to SNCC and mass actions like the Mississippi Freedom Summer and the Mississippi Freedom Democratic Party. Barbara Ransby makes the case that Baker decisively shaped the freedom schools during the Mississippi Summer Project:

> It was almost poetic that radical education had assumed center stage in a movement inspired by the reluctant but relentless teacher Ella Baker. The establishment of the Freedom Schools was an amazing accomplishment … Indeed, they embraced a radical pedagogy and a radical philosophy that were an extension of Baker's teaching style and method, which had been reinforced and popularized through her interactions with SNCC activists every day for four years.
>
> (Ransby 2003, 327)

One of the great advances made by SNCC was the value it saw in the women who joined the staff in the offices and as field organizers. Among the many were Diane Nash, Ruby Doris Robinson, Joyce and Dorie Ladner, Prathia Hall, Jean Wiley, Doris Derby, Gloria House, Karen Spelman, Ethel Minor, Judy Richardson, Bernice Reagon, and Gwendolyn Zoharah Simmons.

The Black Power slogan in 1966 signaled a shift in the Black Liberation Movement, but that did not stop Black woman from making their advances. SNCC was in the midst of a transformation as its leadership took up the slogan during the March Against Fear in 1966 initiated by James Meredith. But the militancy of women members of the Black movement was well established before the Black Power slogan gained wide acceptance. Gloria Richardson joined SNCC in 1962 in Cambridge, Maryland; by the summer of 1963, she had moved beyond the tactical stance of non-violence. Armed conflict broke out and she defiantly led demonstrations against the occupying forces of the National Guard. She joined forces in a new organization named ACT affiliated with Malcolm X and other leaders of militant movements in Chicago (Lawrence Landry), New York (Adam Clayton Powell), and Chester, Pennsylvania (Stanley Branch). Kathleen Cleaver moved from SNCC to the Black Panther Party one year after it formed in 1967, becoming part of the national leadership as communications secretary. Cleaver talks about her transition:

> Joining SNCC led me directly to the Black Panther Party for Self-Defense … We studied the ideological, psychological, political, and military methods of liberation young insurgents were deploying around the world and developed an analysis of how imperialism constrained our freedom.
>
> (Marable 2005, 279)

Assata Shakur (Joanne Chesimard) moved from the Black Panther Party to the Black Liberation Army. These last two have become symbols of the most militant expressions of the Black Power Movement.

Black women continued to participate in the communist movement in the 1960s, with two of the key activists being Charlene Mitchell and Angela Davis. Mitchell joined the Communist Party (CPUSA) in the 1940s when she was sixteen years old, and rose to be the Communist Party presidential candidate in 1968. As a protégé of Herbert Marcuse, Davis rose to join the faculty in philosophy at UCLA while also being a member of the Communist Party. She joined the Che-Lumumba Club, an all-Black CPUSA-affiliated collective in Los Angeles and then worked with Jonathan Jackson in his effort to free his brother George Jackson from prison. After being wrongfully charged as an accessory to an attempted murder, she went underground and was placed on the Ten Most Wanted List of the FBI. A worldwide campaign launched to free her succeeded and her image became the most recognized image of a Black woman in the struggle for Black liberation. "Free Angela" was a repeated slogan in every gathering of the Black Liberation Movement.

A big breakthrough came with the Black Arts Movement. As expressed in Chapter 6, Black women in the movement excelled and attained national prominence. As has been mentioned in discussions already, the major figures included Jayne Cortez, Barbara Ann Teer, Sonja Sanchez, Mari Evans, Carolyn Rogers, and Johari Amini.

The most recent explosive social movement for Black women has been their expression of Gay Liberation. Key figures here are Audre Lorde and Pauli Murray. Lorde emerged as a poet and theoretician of the life journey of a Black lesbian woman, formulating her last theoretical reflection out of her final death dance with cancer. Murray became the first Black woman to be ordained as an Episcopal priest, and went on to be the first Black woman to get a doctorate from Yale Law School. Yale honored her by naming a new residential college after her.

Key social movement organizations for Black women include the National Welfare Rights Organization (1966–1975), the Third World Women's Alliance (1968–1980), and the Combahee River Collective (1974–1980). Each of these organizations mobilized a sector of Black women and built on the work of the key women mentioned above. Of course, all of this takes place in the context of the overall political dynamic after the mid-1960s.

Men initially led the National Welfare Rights Organization, notably George Wiley, a former national leader of CORE. However, Black women on welfare and living in public housing projects formed the base of membership. There was a revolt and a new leadership emerged, led by Johnnie Tillmon. She was a welfare mother of six and embodied what the organization was all about. She was a theoretician in her own right, as evidenced by her famous 1972 essay, "Welfare is a Women's Issue," published in *MS* magazine:

> Maybe we poor welfare women will really liberate women in this country. We've already started on our own welfare plan. Along with other welfare recipients, we have organized so we can have some voice. Our group is called the National Welfare Rights Organization (N.W.R.O.). We put together our own welfare plan, called Guaranteed Adequate Income (G.A.I.), which would eliminate sexism from welfare. There would be no "categories"—men, women, children, single, married, kids, no kids—just poor people who need aid. You'd get paid according to need and family size only and that would be upped as the cost of living goes up.
>
> As far as I'm concerned, the ladies of N.W.R.O. are the front-line troops of women's freedom. Both because we have so few illusions and because our issues are so important to all women—the right to a living wage for women's work, the right to life itself.
>
> (Tillmon 1972)

The Third World Women's Alliance (TWWA) emerged out of the Freedom Movement, especially under the leadership of the SNCC activist Fran Beale. First, there was the Black Women's Liberation Committee within SNCC, based in New York City. With the development of connections to Puerto Rican activists and an interest in socialist thought, the TWWA was founded as a separate organization. The organization carried out rigorous and sustained political education. This was expressed in their newspaper, *Triple Jeopardy*, with the masthead identifying the issues of "Racism, Imperialism, Sexism":

> They envisioned the paper serving three primary functions. First, it was to be informational. To "clarify what the realities are," the paper would disseminate facts and interpretations of development in the United States with particular emphasis on those issues that concern Third World women. The second function of *Triple Jeopardy* was to engage in current ideological struggles. This included ideas within the Black Power Movement—such as the call for Black capitalism coming from some conservative elements—as well as the women's liberation movement where "some are proclaiming that men are the major enemy and completely reject any analysis based on the class or race to which women belong." Finally, the publication was used as an organization tool by spreading TWWA's ideology to women across the country and recruiting members.
>
> (Ward 2006, 138)

The TWWA published a collection of essays they titled "Black Women's Manifesto." Soon after came another very influential document written by the

Combahee River Collective. Barbara Smith did much to facilitate the development of this organization, naming it after the place of the only slave insurrection planned and led by a Black woman, Harriet Tubman. Seven hundred and fifty people were freed!

The Combahee River Collective Statement brought the voices of Black lesbians to the forefront and into clear and open leadership of the Black Liberation Movement. They located their thinking in a challenge to the capitalist system:

> We realize that the liberation of all oppressed peoples necessitates the destruction of the political-economic systems of capitalism and imperialism as well as patriarchy. We are socialists because we believe that work must be organized for the collective benefit of those who do the work and create the products, and not for the profit of the bosses. Material resources must be equally distributed among those who create these resources. We are not convinced, however, that a socialist revolution that is not also a feminist and anti-racist revolution will guarantee our liberation. We have arrived at the necessity for developing an understanding of class relationships that takes into account the specific class position of Black women who are generally marginal in the labor force, while at this particular time some of us are temporarily viewed as doubly desirable tokens at white-collar and professional levels. We need to articulate the real class situation of persons who are not merely raceless, sexless workers, but for whom racial and sexual oppression are significant determinants in their working/economic lives. Although we are in essential agreement with Marx's theory as it applied to the very specific economic relationships he analyzed, we know that his analysis must be extended further in order for us to understand our specific economic situation as Black women.
>
> ("The Combahee River Collective Statement" n.d.)

Some of the women in the Combahee River Collective, along with Audre Lorde, founded the Kitchen Table: Women of Color Press (1981–1992). This press created curriculum material for the Black Women's Movement. Barbara Smith makes their intention clear:

> We have always considered Kitchen Table to be both an activist and a literary publisher; we are committed to producing work of high artistic quality that simultaneously contributes to the liberation of women of color and of all people. We publish a work not simply because it is by a woman of color, but because it consciously examines, from a positive and original perspective, the specific situations and issues that women of color face.
>
> (B. Smith 1989)

9
The Black Student Movement

This chapter links with the next. It tells about the protagonists of the movement; the next chapter lays out the full impact of their struggles. The student uprising of the 1960s also fused elements of all the social movements in the preceding chapters, building to a confrontation with the institutional racism in higher education.

First, though, the Black Student Movement of the 1960s had precedent. Aptheker points to an earlier demographic shift in higher education:

> It is the Twenties which begin the universalization of such (higher) education. But while in this decade the general enrollment in colleges doubled, among Negro youth it quintupled. And while in 1920 a total of 396 Negro youth received bachelor's degrees (118 in northern colleges), in 1925 the total had reached 832 (224), and by the end of 1929 the figures stood at 1,903 (374). This means that the graduates from Negro colleges had increased six-fold in ten years, and Negro graduates from northern colleges had increased three times.
>
> (Aptheker 1969, 152–53)

The main historical precedent for the 1960s student motion was a 1930s organization, the Southern Negro Youth Congress (SNYC). This organization grew out of a youth caucus of the National Negro Congress. They declared:

> We, the Youth Section of the National Negro Congress, realizing the vast possibilities in the millions of young people, unawakened and uninformed; the disinherited sharecropper, the tenant farmer, the workers of the field, young people whose future outlook is one of monotonous toil without any hope of security or happiness, resolved that we cast our lot with Southern brethren knowing that ultimate success will not be achieved until the South is free.
>
> (Richards, in McWorter, cited in W.E. Martin n.d., 3)

The SNYC was a force of Black agency that gathered youth from on and off the HBCU campuses to play a key role in community and labor struggles. Some of these youth took up the arts: their Caravan Puppeteers used puppet shows across the rural South to educate communities about such issues as the poll tax, the necessity of labor unions, and building the Black Liberation Movement organizations like the SNYC (Rogers 2012, 52–53).

The modern student movement also emerges from continued success in ending segregation in higher education. Critical court decisions, shown in Table 16, facilitated Black enrollment in higher education (Congressional Quarterly 1968, 6–7).

Table 16 Key Court Cases Ending Segregation in Higher Education

Year	*State*	*Case*	*Outcome*
1938	Missouri	*Missouri ex rel. Gaines* v. *Canada*	The court held that the State of Missouri could not exclude a Black person from its public state law school when the only alternative was to send the student out of state. This began a rethinking of equality.
1949	Texas	*Sweatt* v. *Painter*	The court examined the law school education at an HBCU and the University of Texas and held this did not meet the standard of equality of "separate but equal." Texas was ordered to admit Black students to the law school.
1950	Oklahoma	*McLaurin* v. *Oklahoma State Regents*	The court went further in this decision to state that the institutions could not segregate Black students in separate classrooms, in the library, or in dining halls. This would deny students equal protection under the law.
1954	Kansas	*Brown* v. *Board of Education of Topeka, Kansas*	This was the critical decision that overturned the doctrine of "separate but equal" by deciding that doctrine violated the Fourteenth Amendment of the US Constitution.
1957	Pennsylvania	*Pennsylvania* v. *Board of City Trusts of Philadelphia*	The court decided that a private institution was not allowed to segregate, even if their initial gift of money required that policy. This case involved Girard College.

College students then began moving off campus, becoming foot soldiers in the sit-in movement that reignited the Freedom Movement in Greensboro, North Carolina, on February 1, 1960. Four students from North Carolina A & T State University took the lead: Joseph McNeil, Franklin McCain, Ezell Blair Jr., and David Richmond. The movement in Nashville, Tennessee, including Fisk students, actually began in 1958, when Rev. Kelly Miller Smith and

James Lawson began workshops in nonviolence in preparation for a campaign of mass civil disobedience. They were spreading the strategy and tactics of Gandhi. The North Carolina sit-in jumped on February 1; that was quickly followed by the Nashville movement's sit-ins on February 13. The leaders of the latter were Diane Nash (a Chicago resident who had transferred from Howard to Fisk), James Bevel, Bernard Lafayette, and Marion Barry. Before this ended in the desegregation of public facilities in Nashville, thousands of students and community youth had thrown themselves into the battle for justice.

Students in the sit-in movement convened at Shaw University in April 1960. Ella Baker, Executive Secretary of the Southern Christian Leadership Conference, provided $800 to fund the conference and gave the key advice to form their own organization rather than become a youth wing of SCLC led by Martin Luther King Jr. SNCC formed that same year (Ransby 2003). It became the most activist-oriented formation of student militants, leading the Freedom Bus rides to integrate interstate transportation and public accommodations and a wide range of efforts including voter registration.

SNCC went on to initiate freedom schools during Freedom Summer in Mississippi and cities such as Chicago. At this time, another formation developed out of radical Black student organizing at Central State University in Ohio: The Revolutionary Action Movement (RAM, 1962–1969). Key leaders were Max Stanford (now Muhammad Ahmad) and Don Freeman.

A big transition was about to take place. Rogers targets a critical turning point:

> The year 1963 proved to be the seminal year of Black nationalist organizing at prestigious and urban HWCUs (Historically white colleges and universities), with moderately large African American populations stimulated and angered by the southern civil rights atrocities, colonial struggles, and northern and western racism. Meanwhile, HBCU students moved away from off-campus demonstrations and civil rights that year as well. By 1964, they were noticeably headed toward campus activism and Black Power, with campus protests at Jackson State, Alcorn State, Norfolk State, and Howard. From May 1 to 4, the Afro-American Student Movement, a radical affiliation with SNCC headed by Michele Paul and Betty Rush, convened the first Afro-American student conference on Black Nationalism at Fisk. To RAM's Stanford, who attended and helped plan it, the conference "was the ideological catalyst that eventually shifted the civil rights movement to the Black Power Movement."
>
> (Rogers 2012, 70–71)

The general impact of the student movement on the development of Black Studies was a two-step process that consisted of fighting for:

1. an increase in Black enrollment and institutional changes to accommodate their presence, and
2. a change in curriculum and associated faculty and staff hiring, along with a change in the institutional relationship with the local Black community.

The assassination of King in 1968 led to a massive enrollment by Black students in institutions of higher education. At the beginning of the 1960s, there were more than two hundred thousand Black students enrolled in higher education; at the end of the 1960s, more than one million. Many of them were the first college student in their family. They brought with them a heightened political consciousness that reflected the state of the struggle gripping most communities, especially working people.

Black students were leading struggles on campuses:

> An American Council on Education study found that 57 percent of all campus protests in 1968–69 involved Black students … A study conducted by the Urban Research Corporation, for example, found that in the first half of 1969, Black students were involved in 51 percent of all protest incidents, yet accounted for less than six percent of the nation's total college enrollment … In 1967 and 1968, over 90 percent of sit-in demonstrations instituted by Black students occurred on college campuses, not in segregated facilities in neighboring communities.
>
> (Van Deburg 1992, 67–68)

An important example of what happened on a campus is the Project 500 experience at the University of Illinois. The University of Illinois is a land-grant institution that was established in 1867 through the 1862 Morrill Act. Despite Illinois being a northern state, the first African American student enrolled only in 1887, followed by very slow increases: 2 in 1900, 68 in 1925, 138 in 1929, and 148 in 1944 (Williamson-Lott 2003, 17). The campus and most of the community remained segregated into the 1960s. Black Power then came to the campus in the mid-1960s, since most of the Black students came from Chicago, bringing with them a consciousness shaped by militant urban struggles.

By 1967, there were 372 Black students enrolled at the University of Illinois out of 30,400. The barbershops in town would post pictures of Black All-American athletes like football star J.C. Caroline while refusing him service. Militant students rose up and forced the campus administration to implement a new program called the Student Education Opportunities Program (SEOP), which started with a major leap in enrollment. Project 500 resulted in 565 new Black and Latino students being enrolled for fall in 1968. The university brought the new students to campus and set them up in dorm rooms. But when the semester was about to begin, administrators asked them to vacate the rooms as the "regular"—white—students were returning. There were no extra rooms. Cots were set up in dorm lounges and the student union. The new students rejected this, leading to protest and confrontation with the administration and local police. The crisis led to

> one of the largest arrests of college students in American history. Most of the 248 arrested were freshmen in the SEOP program. The students were arrested at 3am for occupying and causing damage to the Illini Union lounges. After a week of orientation, students were unsure of where they would be living in the fall and how much a University of Illinois education would cost them. Much like University housing, the cities of Champaign and Urbana were not prepared to hold the suddenly large amount of SEOP students and temporarily held them in Memorial Stadium as a makeshift jail. All of them were released on bail within the next day by members of the black community in Champaign-Urbana. The school year had not even begun.
>
> (Project 500 n.d.)

This kind of program was part of a national response to militant student demand for an increase in Black and Latino student enrollment. A good case of this was in New York:

> In 1967, then first-year Assemblyman, Arthur O. Eve, of the 141st Assembly District, gave further force to the principles of access and opportunity by developing the appropriation bill that gave birth to the Educational Opportunity Program. Modeled on the SEEK (Search for Education, Elevation and Knowledge) program that had been instituted by Percy Sutton in the City University in the prior year, the first unit of what would become a university-wide opportunity program enrolled 249 students at the State University College in Buffalo, New York. In the following year, Assemblyman Eve was able to obtain sufficient funding to permit expansion to ten campuses. By the 1970–71 academic year, thirty campuses had enrolled more than 4,600 opportunity students and New York State Education Law §6452 had formally established the provisions of SEEK at the City University of New York, the Educational Opportunity Program in the State University of New York and the Higher Educational Opportunity Program at the independent colleges in New York.
>
> (Educational Opportunity Program n.d.)

With a critical mass of Black students now on a campus, struggle broke out against the institutional racism of the classroom: what was taught and who was teaching. This began a general period of social disruption on campus to end de facto white supremacy. Sometimes concerned faculty and/or staff supported the students' efforts, and sometimes community members and/or alumni, usually but not only Black people, did so. All this resulted from first-generation Black and Brown college students facing the institutional racism and the inability of the campus to change its social norms and past discriminatory practices. This has been documented as part of the general pattern of how Black student movements developed in New York, Oklahoma, New Jersey, and Pennsylvania (Glasker 2002; Bradley 2012; McCormick 1989; Exum 1985; G. Henderson et al. 2010).

A major aspect was the dynamic of movement experiences, both victory and defeat, interacting with advances of the student movement on campus. A wave of deaths and assassinations took elders who were in a position to give theoretical and visionary leadership: Richard Wright (d. 1960), E. Franklin Frazier (1962), Medgar Evers (1963), W.E.B. Du Bois (1963), Malcolm X (1965), and Martin Luther King Jr. (1968). Of these, at least three were assassinations: Evers, Malcolm X, and King. Movement activists were killed as well, with just a few being Herbert Lee (1961); Andrew Goodman, James Cheney, and Michael Swerner (1964); Jimmie Lee Jackson (1965); James Reeb (1965); and Viola Liuzzo (1965). In addition, urban rebellions were sites of mass killings: Watts (1965: thirty-four reported dead), Newark (1967: twenty-six reported dead), and Detroit (1967: forty-three reported dead).

In this context, although this will be discussed later, it is important to mention the African-American college students who were killed during the struggles of the 1960s and after:

1966, Tuskegee: Sammy Younge Jr.;
1968, South Carolina State University: Samuel Ephesians Hammond Jr., Delano Herman Middleton, and Henry Ezekial Smith;
1969, UCLA: Bunchy Carter and John Huggins;
1970, Jackson State University: Phillip Lafayette Gibbs and James Earl Green; and
1972, Southern University: Denver Smith and Leonard Brown.

Students saw their struggles become a matter of life and death. Most student martyrs were killed in the South—eight out of every ten. Most of these killings were at the hands of the police, but the UCLA murders in the West revealed a deep and deadly division within the campus movement.

In this heightened climate, the student movement waged struggles that took on different forms reflecting the political culture of each campus and community. Because this took place over one or more decades, in each case the sequencing of events cannot be precisely ordered. Biondi raises critical questions:

> [H]ow did Black students all over the country, without formal organizational links, express such similar grievances and demands? Why did the call for Black Power become increasingly popular among Black youth in the late 1960s? And why were students at historically Black colleges also up in arms? In fact, this phase of the Black student movement actually began on Black college campuses. Why?
>
> (Biondi 2014, 13–14)

One answer is the organizing activity of RAM. Its main organizer, Muhammad Ahmad, makes this point:

> RAM organized a student wing called ASM, the Afro-American Student Movement. It organized chapters in Nashville, Tennessee, Fisk University, Detroit, Michigan and Los Angeles, California. ASM called a student conference on Black Nationalism in May 1964. The convening of the 1st National Afro-American Student Conference on Black Nationalism held May 1st to 4th in Nashville, Tenn., was the ideological catalyst that eventually shifted the civil rights movements into the Black Power movement.
>
> (Muhammad 1978, 5)

In addition, there were many local organizational forms of Black student activism at the high school level:

> Black and Latino students in Los Angeles, Kansas City, Iowa, Chicago, Detroit, Cleveland, New York, Crystal City and Houston, Texas, and Philadelphia and York, Pennsylvania, participated in boycotts (walkouts or blowouts) for desegregation, community control of schools, and better curricular options, among other issues. They were fundamentally interested in acquiring a better education and helped transform individual schools and districts.
>
> (Danns 2018)

STUDENT WING OF THE BLACK LIBERATION MOVEMENT

The two national organizations that best represented national Black student activism after SNCC were the National Association of Black Students (NABS) and the Student Organization for Black Unity (SOBU). In both cases, these student organizations connected to broader forces of the Black Liberation Movement, linking struggles on campus to community and workplace struggles (Patton 1981, 274–91).

NABS grew out of criticism Black student leaders leveled at the mainstream National Student Association. Benson provides the details:

> NABS was established in August of 1969 after a controversial split from the US National Student Association (USNSA/NSA) denounced the actions and programming of the NSA as racist and dismissive of Black student lives and societal challenges. Headed by Gwen Patton, the spokesperson and student leader of the dissident group, Black students announced that the association was no longer relevant to the significant problems of Black students who sought the following: organizational independence from the NSA, financial reparations from the NSA, and that the new organization was to be known as NABS.
>
> (Benson 2017a, 58)

Patton had been elected student body president at Tuskegee Institute (1965–1966) and represented her school in the NSA until the split. She was a militant activist who connected with SNCC organizers, especially James Forman, the SNCC Executive Secretary. During her presidency, fellow student Sammy Younge Jr. was murdered by a racist gas station attendant. Forman recalls her reaction:

> They called me at three o'clock in the morning to tell me that Sammy was dead, and I laid the phone down and went upstairs to my room in the dormitory. I stayed up, 'cause I realized that even though Sammy was my friend, there was something I was supposed to do, and I had to figure out what it was I could do. So I sat there and sat there, and about five-thirty I decided that I would have a meeting in the gym at eight o'clock in the morning. And we decided to march that same day—Tuesday. About three thousand people turned out.
>
> (Forman 1968, 197)

Patton was from Detroit and had become familiar with the League of Revolutionary Black Workers, assisted by Forman who was also connecting with them. The LRBW were investing in students in Detroit, and had developed a study program for them, especially high school students:

> The group's leadership identified Black students as a reserve army of activists and soon-to-be members of the Black working class. The League supported Black high school activists by organizing non-hierarchical spaces where they could explore radical ideas, formulate political analyses of social and political conditions, and reflect on the ways in which these ideas might function in practice. The students who participated, in turn, founded the citywide high school organization, Black Student United Front (BSUF) … The rigorous examination of concrete conditions and an intellectual hunger to study actionable and applicable revolutionary theories and praxis were hall-

> marks of the League's political education (P.E.). The League's classes helped high school students make sense of their world and the relationship between oppression abroad and at home. Early political education classes featured a diverse range of works that examined the history of chattel slavery, the rise of capitalism, and social movement theory and practice … The students who comprised the BSUF, however, soon began self-organizing and expanding student organizations in individual schools. Members of the BSUF, for example, constructed a rigorous political education program under the guise of a freedom school at Northern High School in 1969. At this after-school program, students taught action-oriented courses on activism, self-criticism, and comparative Black history.
>
> (D. Walker 2018)

Following the LRBW and their work with the BSUF, NABS developed their concept of the "student-worker." This concept pointed to two social realities of most Black Students: they were mostly from the working class and would likely remain in that class, albeit with more skills; and while building their own movement, their greatest strength would come through a student-worker alliance. NABS evolved from a mass student organization into a more disciplined form of what they called a cadre organization by 1972:

> With the objectives of consciousness building, NABS developed study groups with the intentions of developing a politically shaped cadre orientation toward anti-imperialist struggle. NABS emphasized study and development of revolutionary principles. While it conducted political education on topics such as the Vietnam Revolutionary Youth Association, Marx, China, Fanon, Cuba, Nkrumah, and Cabral, its leadership grappled with the role(s) that students and youth should play in the general movement.
>
> (Benson 2017a, 70)

SOBU also followed this developmental pattern. SOBU came into existence in 1969 in order to fill a void created by the decline of SNCC, as did NABS. SOBU began with a base of HBCU student government leaders, Nelson Johnson, who had been elected vice-president of the student government at North Carolina A & T State University, led a coalition of student groups to unite in SOBU and was subsequently elected national chairperson. SOBU allied itself with the Pan-Africanist orientation of Malcolm X Liberation University, based on a long association between Johnson and Owusu Sadaukai. Morris sums up the aims of SOBU:

> From its inception, SOBU had four main goals: promoting Pan-Africanism among Black students; saving Black colleges; building an independent Black

> political party; and supporting anti-colonial and anti-apartheid African liberation struggles. SOBU looked upon Black students primarily as participants in the Black liberation struggle.
>
> (V. Morris and Freedom Road Socialist Organization 1991, 21)

SOBU was active in organizing Black students throughout the southern network of HBCU institutions, but also at some institutions in the North such as Harvard, the University of Wisconsin, and the University of Kansas. They were ideologically oriented and began an intensive program of educating student leaders they called cadre. Their emphasis was on an American university organizer forming a group of people, first a dialogue group to maintain a conversation about the struggles they participated in, and then a more disciplined political education study group. They were successful in building a major Black student organization of the late 1960s and early 1970s.

They advanced the slogan "Save and Change Black Colleges." This was a very dialectical slogan promoting unity and struggle. They sought unity with as many forces as possible, within institutions and the surrounding communities dependent upon them. At the same time, they advanced the critique that these institutions had to change internally to become more effective agents of societal change. They targeted state governments, as they controlled the public HBCUs, and religious denominations, as they mainly controlled the private HBCUs.

SOBU took a strong position against the co-optation of Black Studies in mainstream (white) institutions of higher education. Johnson stated their position:

> Many serious, hard-working and well intentioned Brothers and Sisters set out to force the educational institutions of this country to develop an educational process meaningful to Black people. The contradiction here was soon revealed, for an educational process really meaningful to Black people would have been a prescription for the destruction of the American way of life, i.e., exploitation (capitalism and imperialism) and racial oppression … Brothers and Sisters now involved in Black Studies programs must resist all forms of co-optation. The task must be to continue the struggle of our people in whatever way possible even if this means the destruction of a particular program. The revolutionary spirit that inspired Brothers and Sisters to sacrificial struggle in the early and mid-sixties must not be exchanged for material comforts and concentrated study in the three r's—ripple, reefers, and rappin.
>
> (N. Johnson 1971)

With an anti-imperialist focus on African liberation, the leading members of SOBU turned to Marxism, following the leading organizations of African liberation movements and theorists like Kwame Nkrumah. They changed the name of their newspaper to *The African World* and used it as curriculum for their forces and the movement in general. It rivaled *Muhammad Speaks* in its coverage of Pan-African affairs, networking student/youth activists as reporters following the strategic orientation that Lenin spelled out in his essay "Where to Begin" as the way to build the working-class movement (Lenin 1901). They included a column for political education that focused on key theoretical concepts, a column designed to promote the formation of study groups.

Their greatest impact came when they joined forces with other militant Pan-Africanists, especially the MXLU, to launch the African Liberation Day mass demonstration in 1972. This protest led to the formation of the African Liberation Support Committee, which in turn sparked a major ideological surge in the Black Liberation Movement characterized by a new version of the Marxist-Nationalist debate. Activists circulated documents and held debates, but most of all they turned to study. Fresh air blew into the radical Black tradition.

This led to a rethinking of their social role to include Black youth in general, and a name change to the Youth Organization for Black Unity (YOBU). This also signaled the move from a mass organization to a cadre organization. People's College was another important organization in this process (Benson 2017b). It published a study program in a special issue of *The Black Scholar* on "Black Education: The Future of Black Studies" titled "Imperialism and Black Liberation: A Study Program." Finally, YOBU reorganized as the February First Movement and aligned with the newly formed Revolutionary Workers League (Elbaum 2002, 122 and 199; People's College 1974).

SUMMARY

While Part II of this book has discussed six movements in six chapters, their actual development was quite interdependent. Key individuals were moving in and through several movements, carrying the Black Power debate into different discourses involving critical commentary on both historical and contemporary writings. They all focused on making change, sometimes building institutions and other times impacting pre-existing mainstream institutions.

The mass movements and especially the ideological slogan "Black Power" unleashed a new identity and a new vision of how to fight back and win for the majority of Black people. This changed the model of change from upward mobility into the middle class as the path to a better life to one of self-determination by the masses of poor and working people. This was a new beginning that led to massive processes of organized educational activities.

One aspect of this was a generational paradigm shift stimulated by Malcolm X that created a new normal for Black orientation toward social change. Malcolm was the symbol of this new drive for education; he called for it and people responded. But each of the movements described took on a life of its own. Not only was this a manifestation of Black Studies itself, but also the texts, works of art, and documentary evidence of movement activity became the essential basis for Black Studies curriculum as it took hold in formal educational institutions.

PART III

Black Studies as Academic Profession

In the 1960s, Black Studies became an academic profession. First, what is that? A profession is an occupational category that requires its members to earn a credential and maintain standards of conduct. Members have to be certified and are subject to approval by an appropriate peer group, because a profession is to some extent self-governing. A profession often requires some kind of certification by a state agency. Usually a profession has institutional contexts of practice and training, for example, lawyers have courts and law schools, doctors have hospitals and medical schools (Abbott 2010).

Black Studies became an academic profession when it became a formal part of an educational system, a structured bureaucracy. In the USA, this meant the four-year colleges and universities.

The process of Black Studies becoming an academic profession is a case of how a social movement can penetrate and become part of a bureaucracy (Biondi 2012; Rojas 2007). This dialectical process includes elements of change imposed by the social movement as well as aspects of how the social movement was co-opted and subordinated to pre-existing institutional norms (Rooks 2006). Revolutionary aspirations of a social movement, when successful, are implemented as a process of institutional reform. This may help one to understand the general process of how society is usually changed, a leap in power relations and a march through history one step at a time, although some steps are actually leaps as well. This is the practical process of social change.

There has been a debate over what organizational category fits Black Studies, or more specifically, whether it is a legitimate academic discipline or an ad hoc aggregation of activities. Established disciplines defend their status, but permit degrees that are transdisciplinary, multidisciplinary, or interdisciplinary. There are also lesser categories like field of study or area studies. However, the seemingly fixed nature of established academic disciplines is no longer a safe space for disciplinary dogma. The hard sciences are converging into big research in which biology, chemistry, and physics find ways to merge, to work together. English is transforming into cultural studies in which film plays a major role. Theory and method have long moved easily from one field to another. And so, despite words to the contrary, the debate over whether Black Studies is a discipline is reducible to turf, budgets, and administrative control. When Black Studies attained departmental status, it became a de facto academic discipline.

This part of the book looks at six forms of activity that characterize the history of Black Studies as Academic Profession. These are disrupting, building consensus, building institutions, professionalizing, theorizing, and norming research. This general framework provides a structure for examining diverse experiences of individual institutions. Local cases can then be understood in light of national developments. Hundreds more such cases need to be studied, and the framework can facilitate their comparative analysis. To better explain the framework, here are the six aspects.

1. Disrupting

The typical campus in the USA was a case of institutional racism for most of its history. Sometimes, this was a matter of legal practice. Always, it was one of long-standing custom. When court cases and social pressure after World War II led to the integration of higher education, a new generation of students entered colleges. Later, in the 1960s, Martin Luther King Jr. was assassinated, and another large college enrollment of first-generation Black students ensued. This new generation of Black college students became the social force advocating for Black Studies in the academic mainstream. Militant student action confronted institutional racism, especially with tactics like the occupation of campus buildings, sometimes for a few hours, sometimes overnight. The students made diverse demands that included the development of Black Studies. They created a process of negotiation that included a dialectical process of unity and disunity with faculty, administrators, and trustees. While each campus history is different, it is possible to summarize the histories taken together into a general model.

2. Building Consensus

Campus actions led to national discussions and debates. Debate is very much the main expression of a canon in Black intellectual history. The canon of an insurgent social force is necessarily debate rather than textual dogma. Many contradicting voices rather than a list handed down from on high. An elite definition of a canon leans too far toward the great person theory of history. Debate means a process to construct a consensus, not concerning any individual iconic text but a generational gathering of diverse forces welding together alternative ideologically based programs of change. This certainly took place at the end of the 1960s, as militant activists and academics forged a definition of Black Studies. There were two kinds of discourse: one that was primarily among Black activists themselves, and another that was primarily the scholar-activists in dialogue with mainstream faculty, administrators, and agency heads. Of course, there were key books that summarized these processes as well.

3. *Building Institutions*

Transforming student demands into conceptual designs for Black Studies became imperative for campus faculty and administrators. The main aspect of this was how to manage the implementation of conceptions drawn from national inspiration within the context of diverse campus norms and historical precedents. There were many issues relating to faculty, curriculum, administrative structure, degrees, activities, and funding. The permanence of the field is built on faculty achieving tenure, an undergraduate major and minor in a department, and sustainable funding.

4. *Establishing the Profession*

The professionalization of Black Studies was and is a national process implemented at the individual and campus levels. The main national instruments for professionalization are organizations and journals. The process is peer review, by which established scholars in the field evaluate the credentials and research of prospective candidates. This peer review process represents the consensus of the profession. The main credential for an academic profession is the doctoral degree, as this degree demonstrates through a major research project that one has the skill set to perform at the expected level of professional excellence. Each profession has a way of evaluating performance, and for academic departments the tenure process usually takes six years.

5. *Theorizing*

The content of any field follows from the dominant theoretical frameworks utilized and created by faculty. The main ideological themes of Black intellectual history have guided this process: Pan-Africanism, Black Nationalism, Black Liberation Theology, Black Feminism, and Socialism. These basic perspectives led to general theories of the field. The two major theoretical orientations are Afrocentrism and Black Experientialism.

6. *Norming Research*

The lifeblood of an academic profession is research. Curriculum development is the codification of published research. The critical issue is methodology, the process by which knowledge is socially constructed. Publishing research—

scholarship—is the main activity that qualifies faculty and graduate students for degrees and promotion. Again, the critical process is peer review, professional evaluation by established professionals.

The evaluation of Black Studies is research that takes place within the discipline as well as in general. The evaluation process is manifest in many ways: recognition of success or failure within the profession and the general public, choices made by prospective students and faculty, and funding agencies. The main indicators in evaluation are faculty achievements, leadership roles in the profession, and research productivity. Regarding research productivity, it is not sufficient simply to publish in quantity; the peer response to published research is measured in terms of the number of times a publication is cited. A third factor has to do with self-promotion and popular media recognition, especially the role of what have been named public intellectuals, meaning scholars who get television face time and are promoted in the popular press.

The social forces that launched and influenced all these aspects can be organized into a conceptual map of the rise of Black Studies in mainstream higher education, shown in Figure 1.

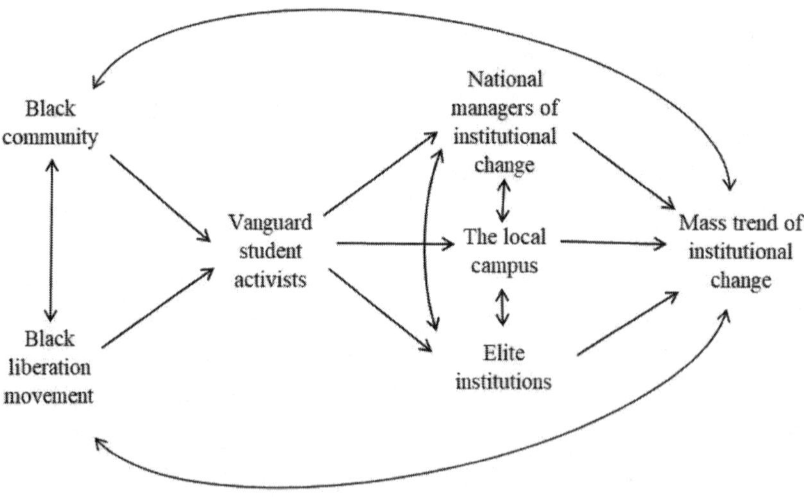

Figure 1 Model of the Rise of Black Studies in Mainstream Higher Education

Of course, this general model has room for regional and institutional differences, and even differences in timing on any given campus. The background to the rise of Black Studies as Academic Profession is the Black community in all its diversity, as well as the state of the Black Liberation Movement. The combined effect of these two phenomena—each of them macro-sets of variables—helps to define the quantity and quality of Black college students, their class origin, and their consciousness. This, in turn, helps to explain the propensity of Black students to become activists in the struggle for Black Studies.

The driving force for Black Studies has been the militant Black Student Movement and its direct actions, demands, and general ideological campaign for change. Sometimes the students go into action because of an incident of campus racism, and sometimes because of the ideological influence of Black Liberation Movements community-based activists. As Chapter 9 recounted, students were vital participants of the wider Black Power Movement.

Student activists influenced three main institutional formations: the local campuses, the nationally recognized elite institutions (which were the pacesetters), and the institutions that set policy for colleges and universities. The dynamic interplay of these three formations leads to a national consensus that provides the rationale for what is acceptable or not to the mainstream. Militant action from 1968 to the early 1970s led to experimentation with faculty hiring and curriculum development. Soon after, a consensus defining alternatives developed. The alternative forms of development represent the mass trends of institutional change. The process begins with the militant action of students.

10 Disrupting

Institutional racism was an accepted historical feature of mainstream higher education. It was how the system worked. White academics considered it normal to have a homogeneous white environment on campus, including students, faculty, and administrators, based on the exclusion of African Americans and other people of color. This extended to knowledge itself. The fallacy of Eurocentrism blinded scholars, such that they thought European particularity was itself universal. To be beautiful, everyone had to look like a European. To be rational, everyone had to think like a European. To be cultured, you had to have cultural values like a European. The experience of Black people from throughout the African Diaspora was considered by many mainstream scholars to be a lesser form of the human experience. Based on this assumption, their research focused on how to explain this difference as Black inferiority.

Huggins describes mainstream biased faculty attitudes toward a Black perspective this way:

> Few scholars were sympathetic, most were condescending, and some were actively hostile to the suggestion that the Black experience in any of its manifestations was worthy of study. Many were heard to comment that the very idea of Black economics, Black sociology, or Black literature was ludicrous. All of which is to say that the problem implicit in the student complaint—the blind ethnocentrism of American higher education—was for the most part ignored.
>
> (Huggins and Ford Foundation 1985, 34)

This was the environment that student activists encountered when they entered mainstream campus institutions. The previous experience had been that Black students came in very small numbers and frequently ended up being the only Black person in a class. They were forced to accept segregated facilities on campus from housing to hair care. As Chapter 9 detailed, the situation changed dramatically in the late 1960s. The 1968 assassination of Martin Luther King Jr. brought about a surge in Black student enrollment in higher education. The new challenge for a campus was that these students came as a social expression of the Black Power Movement.

Black students developed a consensus that campus needed more Black people, and a new academic focus on the Black experience in terms of both curriculum and research. White faculty were usually uninformed about and apathetic to these concerns. The few who considered themselves informed often felt they were experts in what was accepted knowledge. Usually the few white faculty ignored Black intellectual history. Most of these students were first-generation college entrants and had a community orientation. They were not accustomed to being subservient to these forms of institutional racism. They were in the institution to earn the right to be part of the middle class, but on their own terms, and that included being committed to the freedom struggle just like people elsewhere in the African Diaspora. Both E. Franklin Frazier (1962) and W.E.B. Du Bois (1903) spoke to this.

The first action was some form of social disruption, upsetting the normal life on campus to bring Black issues to the forefront of policy deliberations on campus. Rojas sums up his findings: "Much evidence shows that disruptive tactics do correlate with a movement's goal attainment … There is a significant correlation between Black student activism and the creation of an African American Studies program" (2007, 173 and 177), sometimes these actions were a defensive action in response to some kind of racist attack, sometimes it was an ideological offensive, and sometimes both.

For example, the year 1968 was a year of tumult. Police killed students at South Carolina State in Orangeburg (February 8), Martin Luther King Jr. was assassinated (April 4), and Robert Kennedy was assassinated (June 5). On the other hand, Tommy Smith and John Carlos raised fists during the Olympics in Mexico City (October 16). Shirley Chisholm was the first Black woman elected to Congress (November). Motown led the popular music charts, with Diana Ross and the Supremes' "Love Child" and Marvin Gaye's "I Heard It through the Grapevine." The Fair Housing Congressional Civil Rights Act (April 11) and the Poor Peoples March (May–June) were significant steps forward. In this context, Black students swung into action.

THE SAN FRANCISCO STUDENT STRIKE

One of the major examples of student struggle that led to Black Studies is the San Francisco State University Strike, the longest such strike in the history of higher education (Rojas 2010; T'Shaka 2012; Biondi 2012).

The state of California had been a state of extremes ever since the colonial wars over who would rule over land expropriated from the indigenous people. California history has had five stages: Native Americans, the original people; European exploration (1542–1769); Spanish colony (1769–1821); Mexico (1821–1848); and US territory/state (1848–present). Based on agriculture, military installations, entertainment (especially Hollywood), and the technology of Silicon Valley, California today has become a major home of the top capitalists, with 131 billionaires—more than any country in the world except the USA as a whole and China (Savchuk 2015). On the other hand, California leads the country in homeless people with 25 percent of the US total (Levin and Botts 2019). There is a class polarity in California. What happens in this state is no secret, as it has a major media industry, including all the conventional forms of media, including the film and television industry in Hollywood.

There are three levels to higher education in California: a community college system, a state university system, and a University of California system. This is a hierarchy of status and funding, with Black and Latino student enrollment proportionately greater in institutions meant for the working class and people of lower status. San Francisco State joined the state system in 1961.

Heading into the 1960s, there was a struggle from civil rights to labor in industry and in the fields, as well as within the more ideologically focused left-wing and nationalist organizations. By the 1960s, people were in place who had come out of this history of struggle. Ronald Reagan was an opportunist politician who vacillated between the Republican and Democrat parties before becoming an outspoken anti-communist. After the 1964 Free Speech Movement at University of California, Berkeley, he was elected governor of California as a Republican as part of a conservative backlash:

> Ronald Reagan launched his political career in 1966 by targeting UC Berkeley's student peace activists, professors, and, to a great extent, the University of California itself. In his successful campaign for governor of California, his first elective office, he attacked the Berkeley campus, cementing what would remain a turbulent relationship between Reagan and California's leading institution for public higher education.
>
> (Kahn 2004)

Reagan became governor on January 2, 1967. The previous year, Huey Newton and Bobby Seale had founded the Black Panther Party in Oakland, California. On May 2, 1967, the Black Panther Party marched into the California statehouse bearing arms to proclaim their determination for self-defense. This was legal, based on an old California law, but it shook the establishment and set up a basic political struggle that was to play out on the campus of San Francisco State College, as it was then called. Cultural activists were also busy in the Bay Area, and much of it at San Francisco State. Students from San Francisco State founded the journal *Black Dialogue*, and one of the editorial staff, Joe Goncalves, went on to establish the *Journal of Black Poetry*.

At the heart of this political drama were the students who led the fight to enroll more Black students, who in turn formally registered the Black Student Association as an officially recognized student organization in 1963. As the students moved in a more militant Black Nationalist direction, they faced the crisis of a decline in Black student enrollment:

> As the Black Student Union began to grow from 12 to 400 members, the Board of Trustees developed new SAT (Scholastic Aptitude Test) requirements. Students applying for admissions to state colleges had to score in the top third of their graduating class. This worked to reduce the number of Black students admitted to state colleges. By 1965 and 1966 the Black student body was reduced from ten percent to four percent. The admission of more Black students was a necessity.
>
> (T'Shaka 2012, 19)

Black students began to act both on and off campus, taking established college programs and repurposing them to fit a Black Power program. Influenced by the Free Speech Movement at Berkeley, students at San Francisco State began what they called the Experimental College. Biondi explains:

> Black Studies first got under way in the Experimental College, a student-run, highly innovative program that began in 1965 and quickly became a national prototype … The first Black studies course at SFSC was titled Black Nationalism, taught by Aubrey LaBrie in the spring of 1966. In the fall the BSU launched a Black Arts and Culture series within the Experimental College, which stood as an exemplar of what Black studies might offer. Poets Leroi Jones and Sonia Sanchez, luminaries of the Black arts movement, taught courses. Jones, who soon afterward took the name Amiri Baraka, also ran a theater company that staged plays in Black neighborhoods … The following year, eleven Black studies courses were offered in the Experimental College.
>
> (Biondi 2014, 46–47)

The off-campus program was the Tutorial Center, also established in 1966. Its mission was to offer educational programs for students in poor neighborhoods to support their academic achievement. It opened a community office that was located a couple of blocks from a Black Panther Party office, and people began to mingle in and out of both places. Students and Panthers got to know each other and share a common militant perspective.

Two student leaders made critical contributions. Jimmy Garrett, a SNCC activist from Los Angeles, enrolled in 1966. Bringing skills as an organizer and the consciousness of a militant Black Nationalist, he initiated a transformation. In a 1970 interview, he stated:

> We began to set up, well, we call it internal education program, where we would [meet] at my house, or someone else's house and we would talk about

ourselves, seeking identity, and stuff like that. A lot of folks didn't even know they were Black. A lot of people thought they were Americans. Didn't feel themselves that they were Black people. We discussed that a great deal.

(Rojas 2010, 53)

Garrett led the effort to change the name of the Black Student Association to the Black Student Union. The other key figure was soon to be a graduate student in English, George Murray. He taught a course in the Experimental College and served as director of the Tutorial Center. Murray became the Minister of Education for the Black Panther Party and an outspoken militant active in spreading their ideology.

Garrett wrote and submitted a proposal for a formal Black Studies program in March 1967. With a campus political culture transformed by militant Black Nationalist students, a faculty committee met and quickly agreed to place it on their agenda to start the several steps required for formal adoption as institutional policy. By the fall semester—November 6, 1967 to be precise—all hell had broken out. The editors of the student newspaper, the *Daily Gater*, had written articles criticizing the militant Black students. A posse of ten Black Student Union militants confronted them in the *Daily Gater* office and physically assaulted the editorial board. George Murray was involved in the entire episode. Afterwards, Murray started being harassed by the San Francisco police.

Through the spring, summer, and fall of 1968, the debate over suspending and removing Murray from campus continued. Governor Reagan put intense pressure on the campus administration to make an example of Murray, to expel him. They finally suspended Murray on October 31, 1968. The Black Student Union moved quickly: they demanded that the administration reinstate Murray or they would strike on November 6, the one-year anniversary of the *Daily Gater* incident. They were ignored, so the Black Student Union (BSU) made a list of ten demands for a Black Studies Department, faculty, and increased student enrollment. They also demanded that Nathan Hare, formerly at Howard University, be hired as acting head of Black Studies in February of that year, and get an appointment as a full tenured professor with appropriate salary. Two days later, a coalition called the Third World Liberation Front of non-Black students, closely allied with the BSU, added their five demands for a comprehensive School of Ethnic Studies.

Almost immediately, the strike began. Black students were leading what became the longest campus strike in American history, from November 6, 1968 to March 20, 1969. On several occasions, police entered the campus, and this led to large-scale physical battles with serious injuries. President Smart resigned in November after the strike started, having only been resident since February when the previous president Summerskill resigned. Right then the trustees appointed president S.I. Hayakawa president, a long-time professor at the institution. This created the same kind of polarity that existed in the community, Reagan versus the Panthers. On campus, it was Hayakawa versus Nathan Hare. By February 1969, Hayakawa had fired Hare. Then Hayakawa accepted all of the student demands except for two. He was not willing to bring back either Murray or Hare.

The San Francisco strike was path-breaking, because it involved so many aspects of national developments. The fight with Reagan linked the fight for Black Studies to the role of government policy about Black people. The role of the Black Panther Party linked Black Studies to the Black Liberation Movement. The role of Nathan Hare linked Black Studies in mainstream institutions to critical developments at HBCU institutions. The refusal to reinstate George Murray and Nathan Hare points to the sacrifice of the militants who were in the vanguard of the Black Studies struggles. The role of Jimmy Garrett points to the critical importance of the Black Student Movement. And, finally, the roles of key cultural figures point to the link between Black Studies and the Black Arts Movement, including Amiri Baraka, Sonja Sanchez, and Marvin X. In sum, the militancy of the San Francisco State strike was a spark for national developments.

BUILDING SEIZURES

The boldest form of social disruption that spread nationally was the seizure and takeover of a campus building (Table 17). A group of students would enter a building and inform the occupants that they were seizing control: they would limit entry and sometimes not allow people to leave, thereby taking hostages. There was a wave of building takeovers in 1968 and 1969 focused on the demands of Black students.

The main period of these takeovers was from spring 1968 to winter 1969. The actions were concentrated in the South and East, mainly in public institutions. In the context of major social movements, Black students, willing to take great risks while fighting to improve the quality of their education, considered this kind of militant action as viable. The risks were clear to the students, as seen when considering the demands that emerged from the actions.

This is better understood by examining how things happened on four different campuses: Howard University, Duke University, Atlanta University, and Cornell University.

HOWARD UNIVERSITY, MARCH 20, 1968

Howard University is the most prestigious historically Black college and university. Its law school faculty, students, and alumni had led the legal battle

Table 17 Building Takeovers

Date	*Campus of Building Occupation*	*HBCU*	*All*
Fall 1967	Grambling State University	1	1
Winter 1968	South Carolina State University	1	1
Spring 1968	Columbia University Tuskegee University Colgate University Ohio State University Bowie State University Northwestern State University Brooklyn College Trinity College Boston University University of Chicago	2	10
Fall 1968	LeMoyne-Owen College California State University at Northridge San Fernando Valley State College University of California, Santa Barbara University of Notre Dame Rutgers	1	7
Winter 1969	Swarthmore College Brandeis University University of Minnesota Duke University Wiley College	1	5
Spring 1969	Atlanta University Cornell University Hampton City College of New York Voorhees College Howard University	4	6
Winter 1970	Amherst College	0	1
Spring 1970	Colby College	0	1

for the Civil Rights Movement. In the 1960s, militant students there formed Non-Violent Action Group (NAG), which included activists who went on to be leaders of Student Non-Violent Coordinating Committee (SNCC). The Black Power slogan entered mass consciousness on the Howard campus, especially since it was associated with an alumnus, Stokely Carmichael (Kwame Ture). The symbolic high point was in the election of Robin Gregory as homecoming queen in October 1966. She wore a natural hairstyle, a fashion statement that negated the historical Black middle-class bias in hairstyles for Black women. Moments after her coronation was announced, the student body went up in wild cheers and spontaneously led a march onto the campus with students chanting "Um-Ga-Wa Black Power." As Chapter 2 indicated, Howard had seen struggle, but it was not sufficient for the 1960s generation.

The students had one militant faculty ally, Nathan Hare, discussed in Chapter 5 and in this chapter. He became a faculty catalyst for student struggle:

> In the year of the emergence of Black Power, he wrote a letter to the campus newspaper, "*The Hilltop*" challenging Howard's president's desire to make Howard 70% White, and joined the students in writing a Black Manifesto criticizing "the negro college" and calling for a Black university with a relevant education. This earned Dr. Hare a delay in and ultimate denial of the renewal of his contract, even though the faculty committee had voted unanimously to renew his contract.
>
> (Karenga 2015)

Hare left Howard in 1967. Muhammad Ali spoke on Howard's campus during April 1967 and lit a fire in the consciousness of the students. On March 20, 1968, after three terms of agitating for change, the students announced their plans to seize the administration building and sit in. Adrienne Manns, a student editor of *The Hilltop*, made this announcement to a student rally:

> Many of us will stay in the administration building and be arrested. We feel that the administration must give us some public indication that they will move to establish democracy and a Black oriented curriculum before we can discontinue our protest. Our position is legitimate and we must continue to push for all of our demands.
>
> (Invisible Bison n.d.)

The students occupied the building for four days, but left after some negotiations with members of the board of trustees, including Kenneth Clark. The militancy on campus simply deepened and led to more action. Rogers describes what happened on May 8, 1969:

> Six buildings were occupied by Black campus activists, compelling President James Nabrit to close the college. The students not only barricaded themselves inside the building but also barricaded the main gate with boards, chairs, and desks to repel a police invasion. Students who were not inside buildings broke into the campus restaurant and smashed doors, windows, and vending machines. Litter pervaded the campus. A fire gutted the ROTC building … In all, during the sweep of the six buildings, twenty-one students were arrested and charged with "criminal contempt of court." Two of those students ended up serving two weeks in jail. But that did not stop their activism. At the end of the month, twenty Howard students pushed past

> two policemen into a trustees' meeting and suggested they appoint Kwame Nkrumah, the deposed president of Ghana as Howard's next president … The trustees passed on Nkrumah. But they did replace the disliked Nabrit with James E. Cheek, who endorsed aspects of the Black University concept. In the summer, Cheek outlined a program for the future of Howard that included "creative and imaginative ways to deal with the problems of the cities, the economically disadvantaged, health care, Black Americans and Black people throughout the world."
>
> (Rogers 2012, 146–47)

Russell Adams, a University of Chicago PhD, was hired as Director of Afro-American Studies, serving from 1971 to 2005.

DUKE UNIVERSITY, FEBRUARY 13, 1969

Duke University is a private institution, as of 2018 ranking twenty-first among world universities. A southern institution, it had all the historical norms that implies. It is located in Durham, North Carolina, having been founded in 1838. The first known African-American student entered in 1961, and the first Black faculty was hired in 1966. In November 1967, thirty-five Black Students staged a sit-in at the president's office to protest racism and the use of segregated facilities by university employees including the president. During the summer of 1968, Chuck Hopkins, then president of the student Afro-American Society at Duke University, interned with Howard Fuller (soon to be Owusu Sadaukai), a militant activist working as a community organizer in Durham. He mentored Hopkins and reinforced his militancy and Black consciousness.

The crisis demands of the struggle at Duke University continued with a focus on the condition of the Black workers at Duke. This was an elite southern university:

> Nevertheless on Friday evening, April 5, 1968 the day after the assassination of Dr. Martin Luther King, some 450 students and a handful of younger faculty members marched to the house of President Douglas M. Knight and presented him with four demands: 1) that he sign an advertisement to appear in the Durham newspapers calling for a day of mourning for Dr. King and asking Durham citizens to do all they could to bring about racial equality; 2) that he resign from the segregated Hope Valley Country Club; 3) that he press for the $1.60 minimum wage rate for non-academic employees (the existing minimum of $1.15 was not scheduled to rise to $1.60 until 1971); 4) that he appoint a committee of students, faculty, and non-academic employ-

> ees to make recommendations concerning collective bargaining and union recognition.
>
> (Kornberg and Smith 1969, 104)

In October 1968, the Afro-American Society presented President Knight with demands to increase the number of Black students and faculty as well as to end university participation in the segregated institutions of the Durham community, and in response "the university agreed to make a few changes. Such as hiring a Black barber and no longer playing 'Dixie' at its events, and a month later a committee was appointed to research a curriculum for a Black Studies Program" (Fuller and Page 2014, 92).

This turned out to be just a dress rehearsal. Duke's February "Black Week" was the turning point. The students brought the following speakers to campus: Fannie Lou Hamer, Dick Gregory, Maynard Jackson, James Turner, Ben Ruffin, and Amiri Baraka. On February 13, 1969, more than sixty members of the Afro-American Society seized Allen Hall and renamed it Malcolm X Hall: "'A turning point for all of us was Fannie Lou Hamer being here,'" said Bertie Howard, who helped take over a Duke building on February 13, 1969. "For a lot of us it caused us to stop and pause and think about what we were going to do" (Rogers 2012, 81).

Fuller was out of town, but when he heard about the student action, he rushed back and joined the students. Here is his account:

> By the time I arrived on campus … I walked around to the side of the building, climbed through a first-floor office window, and the students let me into the main hallway where they were gathered. They were calm, pretty well organized, and determined. There were meetings throughout that long afternoon … The faculty was split. While most of them either supported Knight's hard-nosed stance or remained quiet, a sizeable and vocal contingent of them backed the Black Students … Unbeknownst to me at the time, the faculty members rushed to the Allen building, and formed a human barrier at the door.
>
> (Fuller and Page 2014, 93–94)

The campus was in turmoil, but a faculty committee along with President Knight continued to meet and discuss what changes were possible. Fuller commends Knight:

> He stayed at the table, he listened and he was reasonable. When we finally emerged from the meeting three hours later, we had worked out a tentative agreement to make Duke the first university in the South to offer a Black Studies Department.
>
> (Fuller and Page 2014, 95)

ATLANTA UNIVERSITY, APRIL 18, 1969

As Chapter 2 recounted, Atlanta University has been a major center for Black intellectual history. It appeared to be continuing that tradition when Vincent Harding was hired to chair the Department of History and Sociology at Spelman College. Working with his colleague at Morehouse College, Stephen Henderson, he began designing the Institute of the Black World (D.E. White 2011). As part of his planning, he hired Kofi Wangara (Harold Lawrence) from Detroit, and Abdul Alkalimat (Gerald McWorter) from Fisk University. They were soon joined by A.B. Spellman and Council Taylor. Their plan was to design a major think-tank to serve the emerging Black Studies Movement and anchor developments in the HBCUs.

Wangara and Alkalimat taught a course together, Two Continents of African Revolution, that was taken by students from both Morehouse and Spelman, including the SNCC veteran and musicologist Bernice Reagon returning to finish her college degree. The course covered and compared the struggles for national liberation on the African continent and the Black Liberation Movement in the USA. One of the course activities was to hold a community-wide discussion on Black liberation issues, which included a review of the role of the Atlanta University Center in relation to the movement. Wangara was a veteran of African Nationalism, based on his activism in Detroit and West Africa. Alkalimat had been the editor of the special issues of *Negro Digest* on the concept of the Black University. They were both critical of the current state of the Atlanta-area HBCUs (Wangara and Alkalimat 1969).

An opportunity came when the boards of trustees of Morehouse, Spelman, and Atlanta University were meeting together in Harkness Hall. Students from the Wangara–Alkalimat class decided to take action. They stormed the meeting, locking the trustees in the conference room with student leaders while other students secured the building. Debates took place inside and outside of the building, including presentations to students who had gathered outside of the building from a balcony of the conference room. The trustees were held for thirty-six hours, except for Martin Luther King Sr., who was released when he complained of bad health.

There were two main demands. One demand was that a framework be created for the coordination of every academic department, so that basic courses would be open to all students of the five colleges of the Atlanta University Center (Morehouse, Spelman, Clark, Morris Brown, and Atlanta University). This would enable faculty to have the opportunity to teach advanced courses in their areas of specialization, and not have to repeat basic courses on each of the five campuses. The other was to embrace a Black identity, starting with renaming the entire complex Martin Luther King University, as this was his hometown and Morehouse was his college. This went hand in hand with the students' demand that the overall institution shift its focus more in the direction of being a single unified major Black university.

The trustees finally agreed to seriously consider the demands, and the takeover ended without further incident. As soon as the trustees left Harkness Hall, they announced that the agreement was made under duress and therefore had no validity. There were meetings on and off campus, but there was no further action on the demands. Later, the Ford Foundation advanced the students' demand for more institutional coordination, and provided funding to incentivize the trustees to agree. As a result of the protest, Wangara and Alkalimat did not get contract extensions. The Institute of the Black World was forced to sever ties with Alkalimat and Spellman and make concessions to the institutions, to the King family, and to the Ford Foundation for its continued existence and funding (Rojas 2010, 152; D.E. White 2011, 42–44).

CORNELL UNIVERSITY, APRIL 19, 1969

Cornell has the unique identity of being both an Ivy League institution and a land grant institution. It was also part of the American norm in terms of not fully including Black people. In 1963, there were only twenty-three Black students in a total student population of eleven thousand. A new president in 1963, James A. Perkins, set up the Committee on Special Education Projects (COSEP) to increase the number of Black students, so by 1969 the number had increased more than tenfold to two hundred and fifty. In addition, Perkins, who had been chairperson of the United Negro College Fund, agreed to a Black Studies initiative.

Change was in the air. The new students were highly qualified and from urban working-class backgrounds, reflecting the zeitgeist of Black Power. The Afro-American Society had been established after the cry for Black Power in 1966. James Turner was a graduate student at Northwestern University; students recruited him and convinced the university to hire him. He met with students at the November 1968 Howard conference, and by late February had accepted the position as head of Black Studies, even without a PhD. Three others had been teaching courses in the area in advance of his hiring—Don Lee, Michael Thelwell, and Cleveland Sellers.

Black students responded to racist comments by Professor Michael McPhelin, who in Economics 103 made comparisons to surviving in the urban ghetto with surviving in the jungle. This and other remarks upset Black students, who thought they reflected a racist perspective. After some deliberation, the students began a protest action in the office of the Department of Economics on April 4, 1968. That same day, Martin Luther King Jr. was assassinated.

Several protests took place on the campus over the next several months. A major incident occurred during a sit-in at the president's office in December, when some students turned over a vending machine, causing material damage. A student conduct board met to consider what penalty should be applied for breaking campus rules. The day that the student conduct board decided to reprimand the students, the Black women at Wari Cooperative House woke up to a burning cross on their front lawn. Wari Cooperative House had been established in 1967 for Black women in the COSEP program, based on Black demand. Black students were enraged by both actions and met late into the night.

A militant contingent of Black students, led by the leadership of the Afro-American Society, marched to the student union, Willard Straight Hall, and took it over. They seized the building keys from the janitorial staff and fanned out into the residential section to evict parents who had come to a parents' weekend, forcing them to pack and leave within an hour. The society had tipped off the Cornell chapter of the Students for a Democratic Society (SDS) that an action was eminent, so by 9 a.m. they were marching fifty strong to Willard Straight and took positions to protect and defend the building seizure. SDS led the chant: "Fight racism! Meet the Black demands now!"

The campus went into shock at what was viewed as an arrogant transgression by Black students. The Delta Upsilon fraternity of white students decided to invade the building and end the occupation. They entered the building through a first-floor window, but were repelled by Black students prepared to fight and not yield in what they perceived as a battle royal between advocates of white power versus them as advocates of Black Power. However, the threat remained. Hundreds of police had been gathering, fully armed. Reactionary racists began calling into the campus threatening violence to end the occupation. The students were alarmed, and decided to bring in guns to defend themselves. The stage was set for a campus bloodbath.

Doug Dowd was a professor in the economics department. This is how Dowd remembered the scene:

> Pretty much all of SDS and the draft resisters and a fair number of faculty ringed the student union (not an easy thing to do, for it is a very large building sitting on a fairly steep hill). A crowd of frat boys remained outside, booing and cursing. And got a few back.
>
> Inside, the Black students had good reason to fear that the worst might yet be on its way. The tension in there, in what was something like a bunker, must have been almost unbearable; it certainly was on the outside. And it rose in the building when the students heard of armed white students and arranged then to have guns smuggled into the building. (To this day I have never known by whom or how.)
>
> To make matters worse, something like anarchy was developing on the campus. At one point, for example, a committee of the faculty reluctantly

> asked me (because of my relationship with the Black students up to that point) to act as a go-between between the Black students and the university president. I sought out the president, only then to learn that he was then—and for the remainder of the crisis—hiding out, unable to be found for several days … VP Muller had the courage and good sense to enter the building to try and work something out.
>
> (Dowd 1997, 161–62)

The administration acted quickly, set up a negotiation process, and quickly came to an agreement with the students. When they marched out, they held their weapons high and were accompanied by administrators and protected by campus police. The students led, as they refused to be led by the white administrators. After the faculty senate held two contentious meetings, no actions were taken against the students for the December infraction or the building seizure.

These militant socially disruptive actions carried forth demands for institutional change. Of course, in every case, one demand was to protect the students and faculty from any reprisals for their action. In many cases this was achieved, but not at San Francisco State, Howard, or Atlanta University, among others. Ballard sums up the general trend with fifteen specific student demands that fit under general five themes:

1. Increase Black participation (students, faculty, staff, administration)
2. Support Black student success
3. End racism on campus
4. Better community relations
5. Black Studies

(Ballard 2004, 72–73)

A NATIONAL DISCOURSE

In the main, these demands followed the self-determination mode of political action. The demands sparked controversial debates, which then polarized opinion. All this structured national discourse, both within Black intellectual circles and within the mainstream. In part, this was a general conflict within Black intellectual circles. The emerging 1960s cohort, socialized by the Black Power consciousness of mass movements, was impatient and somewhat delinked from the earlier generation socialized in an integrationist ethic of besting the mainstream on its terms. Many leading scholars from an older generation were in opposition, as the movement seemed to reject the raison d'être of their careers: to integrate and attain the highest standards of the mainstream. Cornell was a good case in point involving Thomas Sowell. Sowell was a conservative Black economist with degrees from Harvard (BA, 1958), Columbia

(MA, 1959), and the University of Chicago (PhD, 1968). He was on the Cornell faculty from 1965 to 1969 (Sowell n.d.).

Sowell viewed Black Studies as outside the mainstream, where he located himself:

> It is significant that demands for black studies were most insistent at white institutions, particularly at the most academically demanding ones. The demands for black studies differed from demands for other forms of new academic studies in that they (1) had a strong racial exclusionary tendency with regard to students and/or faculty; (2) restricted the philosophical and political positions acceptable, even from black scholars in such programs; (3) demanded larger areas of autonomy than other academic departments or programs; and (4) sought a voice or veto on the admissions of black students and the hiring of black faculty in the institution as a whole. In short, black studies advocates sought a withdrawal of blacks from academic competition with whites and rejected traditional academic standards, whether exemplified by white or black scholars.
>
> (Sowell 1974, 191)

Sowell was explicitly against what happened at Cornell: the creation of Black Studies as a victory of Black Power Movement activists:

> When Black Studies are a pay-off to prevent campus disruption, however it may be disguised by liberal rhetoric, it is not going to be an honest effort to seek out the whole truth at all costs. The personnel, reading material, and everything about the program is bound to reflect this fact. When Black Studies is simply one more issue raised by campus "leaders" who need a series of "issues" and "victories," psychologically or for empire-building, then its status as a pawn in a great game almost insures that nothing worthwhile will come of it, whatever its real potential.
>
> (Kilson, Rustin, and A. Philip Randolph Educational Fund 1969, 35)

He targeted the students with criticism, as if they simply didn't belong with scholars like him in such an elite institution:

> Writing thirty years later about the 1969 violent takeover by black Cornell students of Willard Straight Hall, Sowell characterized the students as "hoodlums" with "serious academic problems [and] admitted under lower academic standards," and noted "it so happens that the pervasive racism that black students supposedly encountered at every turn on campus and in town was not apparent to me during the four years that I taught at Cornell and lived in Ithaca."
>
> (Sowell 1999)

Andrew Brimmer, another Harvard-educated economist (PhD, Harvard Business School, 1957), served as the first Black member of the Federal Reserve Board (1966–1974). He was worried about Black students choosing Black Studies:

> In particular, I am greatly disturbed by the proliferation of programs variously described as "black studies" or "Afro-American Studies" and by the growing tendency of numerous Negro students to concentrate in such areas or to substitute such courses for more traditional subjects in undergraduate programs (especially in the social sciences and humanities).
>
> (Kilson, Rustin, and A. Philip Randolph Educational Fund 1969, 41)

Finally, a 1979 Nobel Prize-winning Black economist from Saint Lucia, W. Arthur Lewis (PhD, London School of Economics, 1940) warned that future careers would be in jeopardy if students went into Black Studies. Lewis spoke from his faculty position at Princeton University:

> The principal argument for forcing black students to spend a great deal of their time in college studying African and Afro-American anthropology, history, languages and literature is that they need such studies to overcome their racial inferiority complex. I am not impressed by this argument. The youngster discovers that he is black around the age of six or seven; from then on the whites he meets, the books he reads, and the situation of the Negro in America all combine to persuade him that he is an inferior species of *homo sapiens*. By the time he is 14 or 15 he has made up his mind on this one way or the other. Nothing that the college can do, after he reaches 18 or 19, is going to have much effect on his basic personality. To expect the colleges to eradicate the inferiority complexes of young black adults is to ask the impossible. And to expect this to come about by segregating black students in black studies under inferior teachers suggests some deficiency of thought.
>
> We are knocking our heads against the wrong wall. Every black student should learn some Afro-American history, and study various aspects of his people's culture, but the place for him to do this compulsorily is in the high school, and the best age to start this seriously is even earlier, perhaps around the age of ten. By the time the student gets to a first-rate college he should be ready for the business of acquiring the skills which he is going to be able to use, whether in his neighborhood, or in the integrated economy. Let the clever young black go to a university to study engineering, medicine, chemistry, economics, law, agriculture, and other subjects which are going to be of value to him and his people. And let the clever whites go to college to read black novels, to learn Swahili, and to record the exploits of Negro heroes of the past: They are the ones to whom this will come as an eye-opener.
>
> (Lewis 1969)

These Black critics (Sowell, Brimmer, and Lewis) did not take the racist position that there was nothing important about studying the Black experience, but they were opposed to the Black Power initiative positing a Black perspective that challenged the fundamental basis of knowledge of all mainstream disciplines. They had achieved within their discipline, overcoming the obstacles of prejudice and discrimination, and called for Black students to follow their lead. They also made the pragmatic point that occupational success required conforming, acquiring the skills offered in the traditional disciplines. Thus, Lewis argues that Black Studies is a topic that should target mainly white students:

> I yield to none in thinking that every respectable university should give courses on African life and on Afro-American life, which are of course two entirely different subjects, and I am very anxious to see such courses developed. It is, however, my hope that they will be attended mostly by white students, and that the majority of Black students will find more important uses for their time; that they may attend one or two such courses, but will reject any suggestion that Black studies must be the major focus of their programs.
>
> (Blassingame 1973, 141–42)

On the other hand, some of the white critics were confused about whether such courses were even important. Some held the notion of Gunnar Myrdal that African Americans were a reflection of European Americans. Ralph Ellison makes this point about them by quoting Myrdal: "The Negro's entire life and, consequently, also his opinions on the Negro problem are, in the main, to be considered as secondary reactions to more primary pressures from the side of the dominant white majority" (1964, 315).

This was the basis for many institutions only dealing with the Black experience by means of courses titled "Social Problems" or "Race Relations." Even worse, there was the racist view that no cultural, moral, or rational behavior anywhere in the African Diaspora, including African Americans, merited being the main focus of an academic field of study.

A key aspect of how Black Studies survived was the strong backing that came from some established Black scholars. St. Clair Drake, first mentioned in Chapter 1, was a vigorous supporter (Alkalimat 2011). He was born into a family engaged in the freedom struggle, with his father an official in the UNIA with Marcus Garvey. Drake was also an activist with the Quakers in the Civil Rights Movement. His summation of the relationship of the rise of Black Studies to mainstream scholarship defended the ideological orientation of the militant student activists:

> The very use of the term Black Studies is by implication an indictment of American and Western European scholarship. It makes the bold assertion that what we have heretofore called "objective" intellectual activities were actually white studies in perspective and content; and that corrective bias, a shift in emphasis, is needed even if something called "truth" is set as a goal. To use a technical sociological term, the present body of knowledge has an ideological element in it, and a counter-ideology is needed. Black Studies supply that counter-ideology.
>
> (McWorter and Bailey 1984b, 22–23)

Drake had been teaching at Roosevelt University in Chicago, an institution that had distinguished itself by including Blacks and Jews without quotas. His inclusive views put him in tension with Black students, who argued for a degree of Black autonomy in the Black Studies program they were fighting for. (He had not wanted an all-Black program, having white colleagues at Roosevelt he respected and wanted to recruit.) In spite of this, Drake was recruited to head Black Studies at Stanford, winning the respect of students and faculty alike.

Likewise, Vincent Harding (1980, 1981) supported what the activists were demanding in the creation of Black Studies. Like Drake, he had an activist background, as a Mennonite lay leader and civil rights activist, especially so as a close associate of Martin Luther King Jr. Harding's support for Black Studies seems to suggest that his very own agenda was being advanced by these militant students:

> The students sense the bankruptcy of American higher education (to say nothing of the high schools, which are also facing major student rebellions), and understand that its failure to deal with blackness is a sign and signal of its profound illness, the illness of the entire society. They know that scores of abrasive criticisms of the American university were being published many years before the black movement began its offense. So they are not impressed by the black and white (but mostly white) academicians who ask them to respect the great traditions of the university, to do things in its honored style, to submit their black studies programs to the wisdom of the faculties. They know that these are the same faculties who had never heard of Horace Mann Bond, Charles S. Chestnutt, Martin Delany, or Charlie Parker five years ago, who never thought the black experience was worth one course three years ago. So they fight to protect their experimentation against the deadly rule of the faculty, to say nothing of that of the administration. This is part of the meaning of the struggle for autonomous black studies program.
>
> (Harding 1970, 84–85)

There were many others, including the economist Robert Brown, who founded the Black Economic Research Center in Harlem in 1969 and directed it until 1980, as well as publishing a journal, *The Review of Black Political Economy*. Also following the earlier work of Sterling Brown at Howard University was Stephen Henderson, first as a colleague of Harding at Atlanta University and then as a leader of the Institute for the Arts and the Humanities at Howard (1973–1985) (Cook and Henderson 1969; S.E. Henderson 1980).

There were critiques of Black Studies activists from Black intellectuals who challenged the ideological thrust of radical students while defending the importance of scholarship on the Black experience. Two major figures stand out here: Martin Kilson and C.L.R. James. James was a Trinidadian scholar activist (1901–1989) who made great contributions as a Marxist scholar (C.L.R. James 2018; C.L.R. James, Dunayevskaya, and Boggs 2013). James began his statement on Black Studies by criticizing the position of W. Arthur Lewis, whom he locates within the ranks of bourgeois thinkers arguing that Black people should focus on becoming a proportionate part of the society as it is. He then clarifies his position:

> I do not know, as a Marxist, Black Studies as such. I only know the struggle of people against tyranny and oppression in a certain social and political setting and, particularly, during the last 200 years, it's impossible to me to separate Black Studies from white studies in any theoretical point of view. Nevertheless, there are certain things about Black Studies that need to be studied today. They have been ignored; we are beginning to see a certain concern about them. I believe also that certain of these studies are best done by Black people, not by professors as such, but by the same people who are engaged in the struggle in which those people were engaged then. That will make them better understand them and illustrate them. And that is how I see Black Studies.
>
> (James 1969a, 31)

James' critique of the Black Studies initiative is from a left viewpoint, with his ideas being rooted in the need for building a movement against the entire oppressive structure of capitalism. Kilson, the first tenured Black member of the Harvard faculty, did much in the beginning to build Black Studies at his institution, but had cautious words for the militant students advancing the demand. He explained his unique position:

> It happened that during the struggle for an Afro-American Studies curriculum at Harvard during that school year [1968–1969], I was the only African-American faculty member in Harvard College, having been

> appointed an assistant professor in political science in 1964, voted to tenure in the department of government in 1968, and officially appointed a full professor in the spring term of 1969. From the start of my teaching as a lecturer in 1962 and in my subsequent appointments, I was hardly a typical faculty member. That is, in addition to being African American, I was a leftist intellectual, a Civil Rights and anti-Vietnam War activist, interracially married, and engaged with the active sector of Harvard's Black students as faculty advisor to their association, the Harvard African and Afro-American Students Association (HAAASA), and its journal the *Harvard Journal of Negro Affairs*, which I helped to organize and pay the printing bills between 1963 and 1965.
>
> (L.R. Gordon and Gordon 2006b, 60)

Kilson, a defender of the mainstream, argued for joint appointments, so that African American Studies faculty would have the legitimacy of approval by an established discipline's faculty. His view was that Afro-American Studies did not possess a disciplinary framework, and thus needed to rely on the rigorous theory and method of the established disciplines:

> When it comes to the problem of the formal academic organization of Afro-American studies programs, the militant advocates of Black studies have little to contribute. They have failed to recognize that Afro-American studies is an interdisciplinary field of the first order, and like other such fields (e.g., East Asian studies, Middle-East studies, African studies, American studies) it is important to require that a student first ground himself in an established discipline such as history, economics, political science or sociology before attempting to move between disciplines.
>
> (Kilson, Rustin, and A. Philip Randolph Educational Fund 1969, 13)

This ran counter to the demand by militant Black students at Harvard for institutional autonomy and opened up Kilson to their criticism. Unfortunately, this has led to a general view that Kilson opposed Black Studies in general, which he did not. In any case, the controversy over what this new field of study was going to be generated a broad far-ranging national debate. In the end, Harvard implemented Kilson's idea; joint appointments with an established department became the norm for African American Studies faculty.

The most interesting discussion of the rise of Black Studies, as it made the transition from a social movement to an academic profession, occurred during a meeting at Haverford College. A transcription of what was said was finally published in 2014 as *The Haverford Discussions: A Black Integrationist Mani-*

festo for Racial Justice. The editor of the discussion sums up its purpose and compositions:

> By the spring of 1969, black separatist ideologies and movements were proliferating so rapidly, especially among young college blacks, that it was simply impossible to ignore them, so [Kenneth] Clark invited a number of prominent African American intellectuals to meet at Haverford College in Pennsylvania in order to identify flaws in the black separatist philosophy, to define a black integrationist position, and to formulate a comprehensive program of action. The coordinator of the meeting and one of the participants was Anne Cooke Reid, a professor of drama and the wife of Ira de A. Reid (1901–1968), a sociology professor at Haverford. By any standard of judgment, the list of participants is impressive: St. Clair Drake, Stanford University professor and coauthor of *Black Metropolis*; Ralph Ellison, author of *Invisible Man*; John Hope Franklin, University of Chicago professor and author of *From Slavery to Freedom* (among many other books); William Hastie, chief judge of the U.S. Court of Appeals for the Third Circuit; Robert Weaver, the first African American to hold a cabinet level position (he was the secretary of housing and urban development); Adelaide M. Cromwell, director of the African Studies Program at Boston University and author of *An African Victorian Feminist: The Life and Times of Adelaide Smith Casely Hayford, 1868–1960* (among other books); and J. Saunders Redding, author of numerous books and the first African American to hold an endowed chair at an Ivy League university to name only a notable few. The group met on May 30 and 31, 1969, and their meeting was taped.
>
> (Lackey 2014, xiii–xiv)

They spoke from positions within the mainstream won against formidable odds. So they had a generational aversion to the confrontational political movement that was creating a new campus crisis. Not only did they feel threatened and disrespected, they were worried that the Black Studies Movement would lead to a reversal of the gains of their generation. The major voice urging a position of engagement with the students was that of St. Clair Drake. He had the most direct experience, having been at Roosevelt University in Chicago, and was shortly to be taking a new position as director of African American Studies at Stanford University. He felt the students were dealing with some of the same problems as had been taken up in the Haverford discussions, and in any case felt the most radical positions were not viable and would not have a lasting impact. He wanted to keep the debate going:

> I think what we need to worry about, or think about, is how the dialogue that's already going on can be sustained. I don't like to see this in terms either

> of "saving" the kids from something or an attack on militancy. Rather I see it in terms of giving people a range of opinions—a range of material that they can use as their own dialogue goes on.
>
> (Lackey 2014, 87)

Eddie Williams, then vice-president of the University of Chicago, was most prescient in his summary:

> I think it's a waste of the intellectual's time—those intellectually qualified by all of the qualifications that have been enunciated today—to talk about the immediacy of the situation in terms of black protest, or black studies, or Afro-American studies. As Dr. Clark said a few years ago about black power, that was the Watusi (dance) of the civil rights movement, i.e., a fad, I think that must of what we're seeing today will pass. It perhaps will move into some of the more bureaucratic, more institutional, more disciplinary aspects of the academic community; and I think this is very good. That's what we'd like.
>
> (Lackey 2014, 52)

This describes much of what has happened, as Black Studies has become an academic profession. But the crux of the Haverford discussions is an affirmation of what can be learned about Black Studies as Intellectual History. Here are three clear statements:

> Ralph Ellison:
> In summing up what I tried to say in our discussion I would emphasize my personal affirmation of integration without the surrender of our unique identity as a people to be a viable and indeed inescapable goal for black Americans.
>
> (Lackey 2014, 111)

> Adelaide Hill:
> Afro-American Studies should take its rightful place in the body of knowledge available to all those who seek a complete education. It goes without saying that Afro-American Studies, as with all knowledge, must be built upon truth—recording accurately the experience of the past, analyzing precisely the present in order to educate students for the world of the future.
>
> (Lackey 2014, 120)

> John Hope Franklin:
> It is very important that in these days of heated debate we do not lose sight of the fact that the integrity of the field of Afro-American Studies rests on its

> validity as an intellectual discipline and not on its importance as a rallying point for some abstract proposed reordering of society. If it has value in the reordering of society, as I very much believe that it has, its claim must be argued from the position that it tells the truth and does not engage in myth-making.
>
> (Lackey 2014, 114)

The debate was on—launched by the students' bold and defiant actions—Black Power in action—and so the next step, since their demands were acknowledged, if being not met, was to develop a national consensus out of the many unique campus battles.

11
Building Consensus

Black Studies in the 1960s sprung from the energy of the Black Power Movement. Advocates for Black Studies were in general agreement that racism saturated virtually all mainstream institutions of higher education. This institutional racism had many specific manifestations. It limited Black people as faculty, staff, or students. Hardly any curricula dealt with the Black experience, much less from a Black perspective or based on texts by Black activists, intellectuals, white faculty and students were hostile. And the university was predatory toward the Black community. So with the consciousness of the Black Power moment, the students were prepared to reject the norm of submission to an anti-Black assimilation process.

At first, the articulation of ideological demands for change was abstract and in the language of values, of a social movement. Demands referenced Black liberation, service to the community, the end of racism, and affirmative action. The system's generic reply to the ideological demand was "Exactly what do you people want?" The spontaneous answer was a "Blackenization" of the institution. This meant Black students, Black faculty, Black administrators, Black courses, Black culture, and Black community programs. This reflected forms of Black consciousness, and this includes what Dawson calls "linked fate," the belief that Black people are under common forms of oppression and therefore have to unite in collective action (Dawson 1994, 76–80). This was anchored in the belief that campus activity had to connect with the action programs of the Black Liberation Movement, while also making changes to transform institutions of higher education. In some sense, it was navigating the relationship between reform and revolution.

The national discourse toward a consensus took two forms: one was within the collective discourse of Black people; and the other was between Black academics and activists and their mainstream counterparts. The high point of this discourse was 1968 to 1971, but it continues to this day.

As previously mentioned, three special issues of *Negro Digest* on the Black University played a key role in the discourse among Black people (McWorter 1968, 1969, 1970). The primary question was over self-determination for Black people. *Negro Digest* published pieces by ideological advocates of Black Studies (Nathan Hare, Gerald McWorter, Vincent Harding, and J. Herman Blake) alongside ones by pragmatic Black faculty and administrators in HBCUs and mainstream higher education (Darwin Turner, Benjamin Mays, James Lawson, Benjamin Payton, and Samuel Proctor). Strategic visions contrasted with reforms administrators saw as feasible. All writers saw the Black experience as a necessary subject for academic research and curriculum development. Within that, the conflict was between institutional sustainability with mainstream support versus the radical transformation demands of the militant Black social movement.

Simultaneous with the publication of these three special issues of *Negro Digest* came a national organization initiative, also out of Chicago. The National Association of Afro-American Educators (NAAAE) was a national organizing effort linking higher education with K–12. Militant educators came from many cities, especially Chicago (Barbara Sizemore, Anderson Thompson, Hugh Lane, Abdul Alkalimat [Gerald McWorter], and Harold Pates, among others), and New York (Preston Wilcox and Al Vann, among others). Wilcox, elected president of NAAAE, reported after the 1968 founding meeting in Chicago: "At its first meeting in June, 1968 [NAAAE] engaged the following issues: higher education, blackening the curriculum, black educator, black student, school and black community, materials of instruction" (Thonvis 1971, 100). Connected to this work, self-determination emerged as an ideology within the movement for the community control of schools, as with Ocean Hill—Brownsville and I.S. 201 in New York City. In the full sense of the term, these were struggles for Black Studies.

One of the main scholar-activists advancing this national discourse was Vincent Harding at Spelman College in Atlanta. In 1969, he was a lead organizer of a national television series of lectures sponsored by Columbia University, CBS, and the Institute of the Black World. The *Black Heritage* television series was serialized weekly to a national audience and shown in repeats. This popularized much of the content that was being fought for in Black Studies curricula. The Black community was being stimulated in new ways, because new scholarship based on the radical framework of Black Power was there to be viewed on television. In fact, the audience far exceeded the Black community. A diverse group of Black scholar-activists were on full display to a national television audience for the first time. These lecturers were from mainstream institutions and HBCUs, were activists and academics, representing multiple generations and ideological orientations:

Keith E. Baird
Lerone Bennett Jr.
Lloyd Best
James Boggs
Horace Mann Bond
Ray Brown
Robert Browne
Vincent Browne
Toni Cade Bambara
James Campbell
John Henrik Clarke
Albert B. Cleage Jr.
St. Clair Drake
James Farmer
James Forman
James Garrett
Addison Gayle
Joanne Grant

Charles Hamilton
Vincent Harding
Joseph Harris
Linda Housch
LeRoi Jones
Julius Lester
Elsie M. Lewis
C. Eric Lincoln
Staughton Lynd
Gerald McWorter
Julian Mayfield
Richard Moore
Larry Neal
Jack O'Dell
Benjamin Quarles
Charles L. Russell
Betty Shabazz
James Shenton
A.B. Spellman
William Strickland
Sterling Stuckey
Barbara Ann Teer
Earl Thorpe
Edgar Toppin
James Turner
Essien Udom
Voices, Inc.
Andrew Young

Harding also served as a leader of a new organizational think-tank for Black Studies, The Institute of the Black World (IBW, 1969–1983). The original planning group headed by Harding included Stephen Henderson, A.B. Spellman, Council Taylor, Larry Rushing, and Abdul Alkalimat (Gerald McWorter). They were faculty at Spelman and Morehouse Colleges, as well as the Southern Education Program:

> The IBW emerged from the Black Studies movement as a key evaluator of it. Henderson described the institute's objective as giving "direction to the Black Studies Movement." He added that the IBW was "acting as a catalyst, a kind of obstetrician to a new way of thinking about integration, of art, humanities and political struggle." As leading theoreticians of the Black Studies movement, IBW associates Harding, Henderson, McWorter (Alkalimat), and [Lerone] Bennett collectively promoted the Black University perspective of intellectual opposition, structural autonomy, and research relevant to the needs of Black communities. In essence, the Black University perspective was a first step in facing the challenge of Blackness during the long 1970s.
> (D.E. White 2011, 50)

It is important to point out that the IBW was developed initially as a unit within the Martin Luther King Center. As a result of the Harkness Hall building takeover, in which they had participated, Alkalimat and Spelman were removed from the IBW staff at the insistence of Coretta Scott King and Benjamin Mays. Even more sinister was the demand by James Armsey, a program officer of the Ford Foundation, that Alkalimat be purged because he was thought to be a revolutionary (Rojas 2010, 162 and 264). Even after submitting to those demands, however, Harding continued to move forward and hired Joyce Ladner, Robert Hill, Bill Strickland, and Howard Dodson. They were joined in advisory roles by leading activist intellectuals: St. Clair Drake, C.L.R. James, Harry Haywood, Sterling Stuckey, Walter Rodney, and Lerone Bennett Jr.

Two major conferences at Howard University summed up the ideological developments of this 1960s renaissance of Black Studies. The first was quite an event, as described by George Davis: "During a balmy five-day weekend that started on Nov. 13, 1968, more than 1,900 students, scholars and artists from 40 states and more than 100 colleges and universities gathered at Howard University called, 'Towards a Black University'" (McWorter 1969, 44). This conference was heavily ideological, having been organized by students who had led the building takeover earlier in the year and opening with a two-hour keynote address by Stokely Carmichael.

The second conference was the 1969 founding meeting of the African Heritage Studies Association (AHSA) (Clarke 1976; Rowe 1970; Skinner 1976). At the level of professional associations, AHSA's birth was right in line with the militancy of Black students. It began as a Black caucus in the African Studies Association (ASA) during its 1968 meeting in Los Angeles. This was necessary, because the ASA functioned more as an auxiliary for the US State Department. It wasn't until ASA's tenth meeting, in 1967, that they scheduled any panels on how to teach African Studies. This was the opening for their Black members to connect their work in the ASA with the emergence of Black Studies activism. The Black Caucus transformed itself into AHSA, leading to conflict at the Twelfth Annual ASA meeting in Montreal, when Black members of AHSA walked out.

The first annual conference of AHSA at Howard was based on these aims and objectives:

> Education
>
> 1. Reconstruction of African history and cultural studies along Afrocentric lines while effecting an intellectual union among Black scholars the world over;
> 2. Acting as a clearinghouse of information in the establishment and evaluation of a more realistic African or Black studies program;
> 3. Presenting papers at seminars and symposia where any aspect of the life and culture of African people are to be discussed;
> 4. Relating, interpreting, and disseminating African materials to elementary and secondary schools, colleges, and universities.
>
> International
>
> 1. To reach African countries directly through embassies in order to facilitate greater communications and interactions between Africans and Africans in the Americas;
> 2. To assume leadership in the orientation of African students in the U.S. and orientation of Afro-Americans in Africa by establishing contacts;

3. To form a committee to monitor American foreign policy toward Africa, to strengthen and support Congressman Diggs as Chairman of the House Subcommittee on African Affairs.

Domestic

1. To inform all other Black associations and organizations of the existing responsibilities in the area of Black studies;
2. To solicit their influence and affluence in the promotion of Black studies and in the execution of AHSA programs and projects;
3. To arouse social consciousness and awareness of these groups;
4. To encourage their financial contribution to Black schools with Black studies programs.

Black Students and Scholars

1. To encourage and support students who wish to major in Black studies;
2. To instill in Black students and scholars the necessity for involvement in Black studies programs at all levels to the extent of their expertise;
3. To make sure that Black scholars attend national and international conferences relating to Black studies and persuade them to read papers at these conferences;
4. To ask all Black students and scholars to rally around AHSA to build it up as a sturdy organization for the reconstruction of our history and culture.

Black Communities

1. All Black studies programs should be relevant to the Black community near the school and should in turn be supported by the Black community;
2. The Association [AHSA] should act as a liaison between Black communities and funding agencies;
3. AHSA should compile a list of Black scholars who need financial support for their community projects or their academic research;
4. The Association will edit a newsletter or a journal through which its activities should be known.

(Clarke 1976, 7)

In sum, the discourse among Black people was not without struggle, but in the end won a broad consensus that Black Studies was needed as an expression of Black self-determination, and that Black leaders should by and large lead the creation and study of knowledge about the Black experience.

The discourse between Black Studies activist-scholars and the higher education mainstream unfolded simultaneously. Key organizational managers of higher education led the national search for a mainstream consensus concerning both intellectual and financial issues. A bellwether of how higher education is managed is through the leadership of elite institutions. One of the first such efforts was a 1968 conference at Yale University. Armstead Robinson, then an undergraduate and later a distinguished historian, led students in calling for and organizing a conference to discuss the content of the new field of Black Studies (Roper 2006). It was an early and at times sharp discussion between mainstream academics and foundation officials and militant representatives of the Black Studies movement (Hall 1999, 18–29).

The national debate over Black Studies was also taken up by mainstream agencies whose function was to support and manage new initiatives in higher education. Two examples are the Social Science Research Council (SSRC) and the American Academy of Arts and Sciences. The SSRC formed a committee that had marginal African-American participation, as it chose to invite Black Studies scholars from outside the USA to participate. The committee rejected the Black Studies scholars working on and in the USA. The committee's first conference, held in Jamaica, was steeped in controversy. Joyce Ladner, one of the Black scholars who refused to participate, made this critique:

> I deeply regret that the Social Science Research Council is sponsoring a conference on Afro-American Continuities, while allowing the major presentations to be made by non-blacks … I consider it an affront to black intellectuals who are "authorities" in the areas which are being dealt with in the conference to have these presentations made by white people, whose perspectives, regardless of empathy, are frequently alien to the black community—and often racist.
>
> (Yelvington 2018, 417)

The American Academy of the Arts and Sciences held an invitational meeting at their facility in Massachusetts on the subject of the HBCUs. What resulted was another confrontation between mainstream white faculty and Black faculty, who operated on the basis of mainstream thinking, albeit as representative of the HBCUs, and representatives of the self-determination orientation of the Black Studies Movement. Both the SSRC and the American Academy of the Arts and Sciences' efforts ended in stand-offs.

These issues were hotly debated in the popular press, and continue to crop up today. *The New York Times* in the early stages of Black Studies focused in particular on problems and its possible failure, although their news coverage does give some data on campus events, especially in the state of New York. Here are some representative headlines:

1969 "In the Colleges, 'Separate' Could Mean 'Inferior' for Blacks"
"New Challenges to the Value of Separatism and 'Black Studies'"

"Black Curriculum Opposed"
"Black Studies Draws Censure of Wilkins"
'Negro Professor Quits Cornell, Charges Leniency Hurts Blacks"
"A 'No' to Separatism"
1970 "Black Studies Take Hold, But Face Many Problems"
1971 "Black Program Cut in Hempstead"

In 1974, *The Wall Street Journal* tried to slam the door shut on Black Studies with this headline: "Disrupted Discipline: Black Studies Flounder as Student Interest Declines and Faculties Grow More Skeptical."

The Chronicle of Higher Education, the main trade newspaper for higher education, has also tended toward negative coverage of Black Studies. A good example is Robin Wilson's article titled "Are Black Studies Programs Obsolete?"

> Black-studies programs at many public universities are having trouble attracting students and are suffering from budget cuts that have whittled down their faculty ranks. Meanwhile, classes with African-American perspectives are cropping up in departments like history, women's studies, and English, diluting the need, some say, for separate black-studies departments … Some black professors outside the discipline, however, question whether it is worth the effort, and whether black-studies programs have simply grown obsolete. Established in part as a symbolic gesture of academe's commitment to diversity, the programs may have run their course, as multiculturalism and diversity have become concerns throughout higher education.
>
> (Wilson 2005)

Many people raised their voices to challenge Wilson's methods and conclusions (e.g., M. Christian 2007; Okafor 2007). A major forum discussion in *The Chronicle of Higher Education* featured responses to Wilson from more than fifty Black Studies scholars. One scholar wrote:

> I spoke with the reporter Robin Wilson several times in response to her phone calls and my return calls to her, yet apparently the facts that I gave her did not fit the net she was throwing out for negative fish. I spoke of our strong Black Studies dept. here at San Francisco State Univ. and I made it clear to her that the name change from Black Studies to Africana Studies was about evolving, and reflecting where the discipline is today; it has nothing whatsoever to do with struggling to stay alive. I expected better of the Chronicle than a sensational attack on Black Studies, with the writer going after what she wanted … So in the year 2005 mainstream prejudices are still slanting the evidence according to their fishing for negatives regarding African Americans.
>
> (*Chronicle of Higher Education* 2005)

Shirley N. Weber, then president of the National Council for Black Studies, laid out the criteria for any evaluation of Black Studies:

> Robin Wilson was invited to come to New Orleans for the 29th Annual Conference of The National Council for Black Studies in March, and she chose not to come and observe dialogue about research, curriculum, students, outreach, graduate study, etc. taking place among the hundreds of scholars who have dedicated their professional lives to this discipline. No other discipline would be treated with such disrespect!
>
> (*Chronicle of Higher Education* 2005)

The actual experiences of specific institutions were critical reference points for the early development of Black Studies. It was a contentious process, leading many to think that the fight for Black Studies would be a losing battle. Open conflict broke out at highly visible Ivy League institutions such as Harvard and Yale. After the 1968 Yale conference, it was time for implementation. In 1969, the Ford Foundation granted Yale $184,000 to launch an African American Studies program, which it followed twelve years later with a grant of $300,000 to add graduate-level studies (Rojas 2007, 138; J. Bass 1978). This was a major step toward legitimacy. However, the campus administration ignored the politics of self-determination that were a principal demand of the Black Studies Movement. The Yale administration appointed Sidney Mintz, a white anthropologist, to head the committee to plan the program, but at least included three Black committee members as well, James Comer, Dean Paul Jones, and Houston Baker.

The three Black committee members made a plan, and the next day brought it to the full committee meeting. Mintz apparently opened the meeting in full control. Baker jumped to his feet after the committee chair had announced his plans as a fait accompli and launched into a rhetorical representation of the prior days' agreement:

> I was on my feet faster than Muhammad Ali on Sonny Liston, saying: "Having read the plans and consulted with 'the people,' we blacks on this committee do not feel the current Black Studies plan meets the minimum requirements for a first-rate program in the university. We therefore demand [it was, of course, fashionable in the 1960s to demand, from Free Speech to Attica] autonomy, independence, tenured faculty, and a proper research and community component for the Black Studies Program at Yale. We also demand a budget commensurate with the goals of the program, and space in which to house it. We demand a program sufficient to address the black urban needs of 'the people' of New Haven and the United States as a whole. Furthermore [and here, I was totally improvising and way beyond the 'groundings' with

> my brothers of the day before], we demand *black* leadership of the present committee."
>
> (H. Baker 2006, 15)

Mintz was shocked, but Baker reports that he gained back control once Comer and Jones indicated they were with him and not the young assistant professor Baker. However, Baker makes it clear that while the Ford money and faculty action was part of the process, the main causal force was militant advocacy of a Black Studies Movement:

> By the fall of 1970, Afro-American Studies was firmly established at Yale. But—and everyone *must* know this—it had not come into being *solely* as an effect of Ford Foundation sponsored symposia, eager and accommodating Black undergraduate efforts, Comer/Jones "brokerage blackness," or white anthropological cocky conviviality. No, Black Studies at Yale was *instituted* effectively and powerfully by men and women who were black, urban, street—and downright brilliantly organically intellectually funky CRAZY. Polite, placating, and palliating white men in tweeds and casually expensive shoes there were, but even they dressed differently for May Day.
>
> (L.R. Gordon and Gordon 2006a, 17)

So Yale had a contentious conference, and then faculty conflict, but in the end a Black Studies program was established and given early leadership by the young historian John Blassingame.

Harvard was no different. In 1968, it took two steps forward: it formed a committee to explore the possibility of African and African American Studies, and added a special year-long course to focus on the Black experience. On January 20, 1969, the committee presented its findings as the Rosovsky Report, named after its chairman, the Dean of Harvard College:

> [The Report] was a strong affirmation of change that validated the many grievances of Black students at Harvard and endorsed their ideas for change. But it did make two recommendations that would become points of contention. The Rosovsky Report recommended that majors (concentrators at Harvard) in Afro-American Studies also complete a second major, and that faculty in Black Studies also hold appointments in other departments.
>
> (Biondi 2012, 181)

So only existing academic disciplines would be legitimate, but a topical focus on the Black experience would now be possible. To oversee this, the Rosovsky Report proposed setting up a faculty committee and a Center for Afro-American Studies. Black students rejected this, and militantly expressed their views to faculty. On April 22, 1969, the faculty voted to reverse its position and approved the student demand to form a Department of Afro-American Studies. By early fall the department was established, and also the W.E.B. Du Bois Institute for Afro-American Research. They hired nine faculty and named professor Ewart Guinier as the first chairperson (Dalton 2000, 15–20). Also in 1969, student protests led to the hiring of Derrick Bell as the first African American tenured member of the Harvard Law faculty.

Guinier was a 1933 graduate of Harvard College and a distinguished labor attorney with progressive left politics. He was the kind of person the students wanted, but not the kind of person who would move smoothly into ruling-class Harvard faculty culture. He led the department for seven years (1969–1976). His views as expressed in a 1975 *Freedomways* article clearly place him as an outsider at Harvard:

> Why is the struggle for Black Studies at Harvard so crucial? Because here one encounters the high priests of white supremacy and class privilege. And here the academic leadership has abandoned any pretense of manners, of courtesy, of civility in relating to the Afro-American Studies Department. As these leaders face the department, it is clear that their intent is to hold Black people up to ridicule and humiliation and, finally, to isolate and to pistol whip us into submission as the entire Harvard community watches. Once and for all they want to teach us a lesson, to show us our place.
>
> (Guinier 1975, 3)

So with a great deal of struggle, a consensus was developing that Afro-American Studies would have a place in higher education. How it would be implemented on any given campus was shaping up as quite contentious. Several texts have presented important summations of the processes that shaped the national consensus, shown in Table 18.

Table 18 Early Books about Black Studies

Author	*Title*	*Date*
Sid Walton	*The Black Curriculum: Developing a Program in Afro-American Studies*	1969
Armstead Robinson et al.	*Black Studies in the University*	1969
John Blassingame	*New Perspectives on Black Studies*	1971
Nick Aaron Ford	*Black Studies: Threat or Challenge?*	1973
Rafael Cortada	*Black Studies: An Urban and Comparative Curriculum*	1974

Sid Walton's (1969) account reflects Black militant discourse. Sid Walton was on the faculty of Merritt Junior College in California and together with Sarah

Fabio helped establish the first associate of arts degree program in African American Studies. Huey Newton and Bobby Seale had begun the process in 1964 by their agitation for courses in Black Studies. Seale relates how this came about:

> Huey took an experimental sociology course. I guess he'd been at Merritt a few years then. This experimental sociology course: he was running down to me about how the course was for those in it to deal with some specific problem in society, and he swung the whole class to the need for Black History in the schools. Huey P. Newton was one of the key people in the first Black history course that was developed at Merritt College, along with many of the other people in the experimental sociology course. I remember him telling me about it, and I was enthused about it, because I had been doing quite a bit of Black History study myself.
>
> (Seale 1991, 20)

Walton's book presents a documentary history of the struggle of the organizational development of Black Studies at Merritt and its relationship to the University of California, Berkeley. It was a self-published book, reflecting the militant demand for self-determination, with a forward by Preston Wilcox, president of the National Association for African American Educators. In it, Walton captures the basic positions of the militant activists for Black Studies. The emphasis was on Black leadership, relevance to the Black community, the use of writings by Black scholars and artists, the importance of confronting the language of racism, and ample funding and staffing of Black Studies.

Armstead Robinson et al. (1969) contains selected presentations and commentary from the 1968 Yale conference. The volume contains contributions from Black Studies advocates, including Harold Cruse, Maulana Karenga, Abdul Alkalimat (Gerald McWorter), Nathan Hare, and Alvin Poussaint, as well as the responses and questions of Yale faculty, who took a variety of positions. Boniface Obichere of UCLA made a case for African Studies based on his experience in Africa, Europe, and the USA. The Black agnostic in the event was Martin Kilson, who, as discussed earlier, was skeptical of the Black Studies Movement:

> Now, to some extent in my brief remarks on the intellectual validity of the Black experience this is what I shall attempt to do: to smell a rat. Indeed, it is a common fallacy to believe that what is momentarily politically serviceable is *ipso facto* intellectually virtuous. I personally understand this viewpoint as held by Black nationalists. Indeed I am compassionate toward it. But my intellect rejects it. Like Mary McCarthy, I begin to smell a rat and feel compelled to dissect it for all to see.
>
> (A.L. Robinson et al. 1969, 13 and 15–16)

Robert Farris Thompson gave an extraordinary talk on the African Diaspora anchored in his mastery of language and musical skill based on years of fieldwork. He demonstrated Diasporian connections in Missouri, South Carolina, Georgia, and New York. McGeorge Bundy, a Yale alumnus and president of the Ford Foundation, followed Thompson and commented on various aspects of what the Black Studies activists had said and subtly indicated his willingness to support Black Studies.

The second book out of Yale was an anthology edited by John Blassingame (1973), then an assistant professor in the history department. His stated goal for the book was realized in its impact on the national discourse:

> The different ideologies represented in the essays and the seriousness of the contributors will, hopefully, create the atmosphere for a meaningful dialogue on Black Studies. The disagreements among the contributors accentuate many of the controversial aspects of the programs. Yet, in spite of their disagreements, many of the contributors agree on several essential points: Black Studies is a legitimate and long overdue intellectual enterprise; it should and will produce change in the attitudes of Blacks and whites; it will lead to improvements in the Black community and train more sophisticated leaders for it; and the program should stress scholarship and the solution of pressing social problems. The various positions taken by the essayists provide important new perspectives on Black Studies.
>
> (Blassingame 1973, xx)

Two additional books made strong contributions to the discussion of Black Studies. Nick Aaron Ford (1973) used NEH funding to investigate the state of the field in the early 1970s. After twenty-five years as head of the English department at Morgan State University in Baltimore, he became their first Alain Locke Professor of Black Studies (A.V. Young 1992, 473). His method combined a mailed questionnaire with campus visits; he also formed a national panel of advisors. He argued that Black Studies had a history in the HBCU institutions and was spreading as a legitimate academic field of study. Ford explained the title of his research report, *Black Studies: Threat or Challenge*? in the following way:

> [Black Studies] are a threat to blatant ignorance of well-meaning people who are supposed to know the truth about the entire history and culture of their country and its people. They are a threat to prejudice and bigotry nourished by fear of the half-truths and unadulterated lies that miseducation has produced. They are a threat to apathy and inertia in vital matters that require action now. They are a threat to false and distorted scholarship that has flourished without condemnation or shame in the most prestigious

> bastions of higher education in this nation … *Are Black Studies a threat or a challenge*? The answer is BOTH.
>
> (Ford 1973, 188–89)

Rafael Cortada (1974) comprehensively reviewed how Black Studies had flourished in the urban experience. He traces its early development at the K–12 levels as well as in higher education, both two- and four-year institutions. For comparison purposes, the book includes an extensive bibliography on African Americans.

The development of a collectivized consensus within the Black Studies movement activists was not without debate and a clash of ideas. The key polemic at this very time was written by Harold Cruse, *The Crisis of the Negro Intellectual* (1967a). His biting criticism of Negro intellectuals was crucial in creating a rationale for Black Studies. Cruse took issue with both nationalist and Marxist intellectual tendencies:

> When the intellectual output, the level of social insight, and the lackluster quality and scarcity of the Negro intellectuals' creative enterprises are stacked against the potentialities of the Negro ethnic group in America, the Negro intellectual class is seen as a colossal fraud. The Negro intellectual may have been sold out in America, but he has participated all too readily in the grand design of his own deception.
>
> (Cruse 1967a, 375)

At last, when the dust had somewhat settled, the consensus both among Black people and within the academic mainstream was to design and establish Black Studies on campus in order to reach the potentialities Cruse wrote of and teach them broadly.

12
Building Institutions

Moving from concept to reality involved navigating institutional landscapes of rules and tradition, negotiating the decision-making politics of faculty and boards of trustees, and protecting early victories in the face of years of budget realignments, faculty changes, and mood swings of student advocacy. While different forms of Black Studies had existed before the 1960s, as recounted in earlier chapters, there was little to build on inside mainstream institutions. Furthermore, what did exist was not based on research or scholarship carried out by Black scholars, creative thinkers, and cultural activists in the Black community. When Black Studies emerged out of the 1960s, many aspects of an academic discipline in mainstream institutions of higher education demanded attention. This chapter examines eight: faculty, leadership, curriculum, administrative structure, culture, programs, community relations, and sustainable funding. But first, how far did this institution building go? In other words, what has been the result?

THE RESULT

Especially given the relentless media reports of the decline or death of Black Studies, the empirical description of the institutionalization of Black Studies must be presented and affirmed. Several different surveys done in the USA, plus some new data, help here. They show a leap in courses at two-year colleges during 1968–1970; steady growth in degrees earned since 1986; Black Studies courses and/or units at three-quarters of all four-year institutions as of 2013; and that remaining the case as of 2019.

Lombardi presented early data on how many two-year colleges were offering Black Studies courses. He surveyed 543 such colleges to find out when they first started offering any such course, either a more traditional course that looked at African Americans or a more recently designed course starting from the Black experience. Table 19 shows that these colleges joined the Black Studies surge in the years of 1968–1970, confirming the narratives in Chapters 10 and 11 (Lombardi 1971, 3).

The National Center for Educational Statistics has for many years published data on degrees awarded by field. Figure 2 shows the number of bachelor's, master's, and doctoral degrees in African American Studies awarded annually from the 1987–1988 academic year to the 2016–2017 academic year. The three decades show steady growth, with the only disruption being correlated with the 2007–2010 mortgage crisis and recession, and the resumption of growth since then. An appendix provides a table of these numbers and a gender breakdown; more women than men have been earning degrees at all levels in Black Studies.

Table 19 Two-Year Colleges' Introduction of any Black Studies Course

Year introduced	*Number of colleges*
1966–1967 or earlier	23
1967–1968	24
1968–1969	100
1969–1970	92
All	239

Note: Data from 543 colleges surveyed by Lombardi (1971)

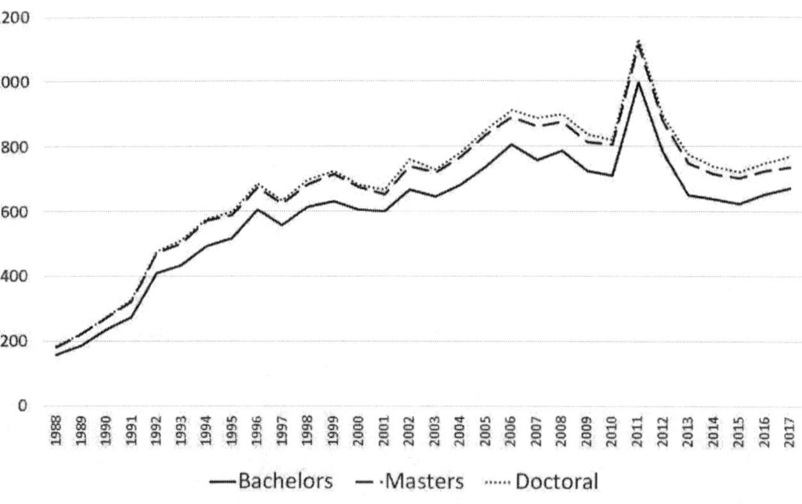

Figure 2. Black Studies Bachelor's, Master's, and Doctoral Degrees Earned Each Year in the US from the 1987–1988 Academic Year to the 2016–2017 Academic Year.
Source: Data from the National Center for Education Statistics (Cristobal de Bley, email message to author, September 20, 2019)

Alkalimat et al. (2013) reported to what extent the four-year colleges and universities in the USA have implemented Black Studies courses and academic units. As Table 20 shows, a full 76 percent of all 1,777 institutions have courses and/or units in the field. Here Black Studies courses are defined as those with titles that reflect the Black Studies consensus, so "Sociology of the Black Experience" but not pre-1960s-type courses such as "Racial and Ethnic Relations." Black Studies units are any academic department, program, center, institute, and so on; those units are typically the institutional home for Black Studies course offerings, with dedicated staff and faculty.

The 2013 data also indicates that institutions in the South, which has the highest proportion of African-American residents of all regions in the USA, are the most likely to offer courses (71 percent), but lag behind other regions when it comes to academic units (16 percent). Public institutions are more likely than private or for-profit ones to offer courses or have a unit. Private institutions are the most likely to have established a Black Studies unit. Larger institutions are also more likely to offer Black Studies in some way.

Table 20 Percentage of Four-Year Institutions with Black Studies Courses or Units

	N	*Percentage with Black Studies courses*	*Percentage with Black Studies units and courses*
By region			
Midwest	449	57%	22%
Northeast	426	51%	23%
South	587	71%	16%
West	295	33%	23%
By ownership			
Public	571	54%	37%
Private	991	62%	15%
For profit	215	34%	0%
By size			
Large (10,000+ students)	268	25%	69%
Medium (3,000–9,999 students)	448	64%	22%
Small (1,000–2,999 students)	640	69%	11%
Very small (<1,000 students)	401	49%	1%
Size unknown	20	25%	0%
All	1,777	56%	20%

Source: Data from Alkalimat et al. (2013)

Updating this data in 2019 entailed re-examining those 361 units. A full 99 percent of them continue to operate. (A closer look at these 356 units is provided in Tables 21, 22, 25, 33, and 34.) Only 1 percent of the 361 have disappeared: four were either combined into other units or discontinued, and one was at a university that closed. It is highly likely that at least a few of the colleges or universities beyond the 361 found with Black Studies units in 2013 launched

Black Studies units during the same period, especially with so many of them already offering courses. So further work would certainly indicate Black Studies holding steady or continuing to grow.

There is no evidence that Black Studies is on the decline. Undergraduate and graduate education in the field continues to grow. Barring cataclysmic change—and all students and educators should remain alert—the field has achieved a permanent place in US higher education. Now we can look at how this came about by considering eight aspects of the institutionalization of Black Studies as Academic Profession. These include faculty, leadership, curriculum, administrative structure, culture, events, community relations, and funding.

FACULTY

One step in the establishment of a program is the selection of a person to lead this development and faculty to create and teach a new curriculum. Decisions about the first faculty produced diverse options. The obvious cost-effective measure was to reach out to any existing faculty who were so inclined, sometimes with expertise and sometimes not. This didn't stop administrations from moving forward. Connected to reaching out to existing faculty for a joint appointment in Afro-American Studies was the general point of view that for a hire to be safe, it should have the approval of an existing academic unit. Rojas points out this tendency in a case study of a Midwestern research university:

> The Department started offering courses during the academic year 1970–1971 and awarded its first bachelor's degrees in 1973. The chair, Dr. Glee, an African American social scientist with a Ph.D. and an established scholarly reputation was already tenured in another department. Until her death in the 1990s, she held a joint appointment in Black Studies and Speech … [While she was] successful in recruiting some permanent lecturers and two senior faculty members with joint appointments in other departments, bureaucratic delays prevented the recruitment of junior and senior scholars.
>
> (Rojas 2004, 184–85)

There was also an attempt to involve the community in negotiating the possibility of a new innovative Black Studies program with faculty and administrators. The University of Chicago tried and failed at this. James Bruce, then an African American assistant professor of German, headed a committee that brought together consultants from the Chicago community, several Black alumni, and nationally renowned Black Studies advocates. The self-conscious elite education at the University of Chicago had produced Black scholars with a community orientation, but the university itself did not embrace such an approach. The meeting of the committee on May 8, 1968 was quite contentious:

> The meeting's outcome shows the importance of political skill. Black studies advocates at Chicago formulated demands that contradicted the culture of the University of Chicago. When an opportunity arose to define an agenda and build a coalition, nobody was able to interpret the interests of the university administration and Black activists in a way that would lead to a consensus and a new curriculum. The prestige of African American intellectuals and business leaders was not sufficient to force the creation of a new agenda. The crucial step from grievance to agenda was never taken.
>
> (Rojas 2007, 104)

Another approach was to create visiting faculty positions that did not require meeting the institutional requirements for a tenure-track position, usually a PhD and a publication record. This was also true for adjuncts hired on a course-by-course basis, constituting the most cost-effective way of offering courses without having to pay a full salary with benefits. These options allowed the opening up of faculty roles to graduate students and local community-based experts. An example is the hiring of local ministers to teach courses on Black religion, as at the University of California, Santa Barbara and the University of Toledo. This has also been done with journalists, musicians, and lawyers.

The fundamental issue for faculty recruitment over time was whether there were ample numbers in the PhD pipelines of the various disciplines, until such time as there would be PhDs in the field itself. Two foundations developed programs to expand this process, the Ford Foundation and the Woodrow Wilson Foundation:

> In 1985, the Ford Foundation committed resources to address the pipeline problem by adding predoctoral and dissertation fellowships to their post-doctoral fellowship programs for underrepresented minorities. This program, administered by the National Academy of Sciences, joined a long line of Ford Foundation initiatives devoted to developing Black faculty. Earlier programs provided resources for faculty development at historically Black colleges and universities, but by 1969 eligibility was expanded to include Black faculty at any institution of higher education. Also in 1969, a doctoral program was established offering up to five years of support to Black students holding the bachelor's degree.
>
> (Griffin 2007, 7–8)

One of the most impactful scholars funded by the Ford Foundation was the historian John Blassingame, who spent most of his career at Yale University.

The Woodrow Wilson Foundation initiated two important programs. The Woodrow Wilson Teaching Internships (1963–1990) funded graduate students to spend a year teaching at HBCUs, and "[b]y 1970, 303 Teaching Interns had been placed at 62 institutions." Contradiction developed between those who fit the local campus culture and those who functioned as colonialist know-it-all saviors of the unfortunate. A more impactful program was the Martin Luther King Jr. Fellowships (1968–1974), which funded "two years of support for black veterans pursuing graduate and professional degrees in preparation for careers in the service of society. Augmented by a counseling service, the program supported 250 Fellows during its six years of awards" (Woodrow Wilson National Fellowship Foundation n.d.).

As with society in general, Black Studies faculty should be understood within their generational context. The founding generation was necessarily a young activist social force who challenged institutional racism to create Black Studies. This meant that undergraduates, graduate students, and non-tenured faculty were risking their careers as part of the general motion of the Black Power Movement, often in alliance with community-based activists. To some extent, this generation founded Black Studies and advanced the view that Black Studies was part of the movements for Black Power. They shared this position with their students, who were by and large first-generation students coming from working-class families. Black Studies continues to be a potential site of struggle, as has been seen with the response of the discipline to the Katrina disaster (August 2005) and Black Lives Matter (2013–present).

With time, a new generation emerged with full credentials, but without the direct social-movement experience of the founding generation. A new profession was formed according to the social norms of US higher education. There was always the need to fight racism and inequality, but now it was within the system and usually not by rallying forces in the community outside of institutions of higher education. This new generation is well qualified, highly productive, and has often been recognized with the highest honors. However, this delinking from the Black community as well as the Black Liberation Movement forces remains one of the greatest challenges for Black Studies faculty.

Faculty by gender, shown in Table 21, indicates male–female parity across the 2,614 faculty teaching in the 356 Black Studies units examined in 2019. This remains consistent across regions and ownership. It does appear that women are more likely to be hired as the college or university gets smaller.

Research on faculty rank in Black Studies programs reveals a significant pattern of academic achievement. Table 22 demonstrates that the majority of faculty in Black Studies units are tenured, that is to say, professors and associate professors. But men dominate among the full professors, while women dominate among assistant professors. It remains to be seen whether fuller gender equality with respect to tenure will come, with the women assistant and associate professors moving up.

Table 21 Faculty by Gender in 356 Black Studies Units (2019)

	N	*Men*	*Women*	*Nonbinary*
By region				
Midwest	632	51%	49%	0.2%
Northeast	864	49%	51%	0.1%
South	725	48%	52%	0%
West	393	49%	51%	0.3%
By ownership				
Public	1,505	49%	50%	0%
Private	1,109	49%	50%	0%
By size				
Large (10,000+ students)	1,630	50%	50%	0.2%
Medium (3,000–9,999 students)	546	49%	51%	0%
Small (1,000–2,999 students)	418	47%	53%	0%
Very small (<1,000 students)	20	45%	55%	0%
All	2,614	49%	51%	0.1%

Note: Methodology detailed on [opening of Chapter 13]. Alkalimat and Williams, "African American Studies 2019: A National Web-Based Survey."

Table 22 Faculty Rank by Gender of 2,614 Individuals in 356 Black Studies Units (2019)

	N	*Men (n=1,288)*	*Women (n=1,323)*	*Nonbinary (n=3)*
Professor	814	37%	25%	33%
Associate professor	873	30%	37%	3%
Assistant professor	509	16%	23%	33%
Other	321	13%	12%	0%
Rank not available	97	4%	3%	0%
All	2,614	100%	100%	100%

Note: "Other" are the non-tenure-track positions ranging from visiting or clinical positions to adjunct. Methodology detailed on [opening of Chapter 13]. Alkalimat and Williams, "African American Studies 2019: A National Web-Based Survey."

Since higher education in general, and Black Studies in particular, is a job market for faculty and an institutional market for recruiting students, branding, or a vivid and persistent public image, is an urgent task. This has led to the "star" system of hiring people who have public recognition and a strong market position. Such a system becomes a resource in recruiting additional faculty, not unlike a sports team, sometimes even involving a salary bidding war. In fact, as faculty are gathered into an ensemble, this itself is something to use to enhance market position. The best example of this is when the Harvard Black Studies faculty, which included Henry Louis Gates Jr., Cornel West, Anthony Appiah, Evelyn Higginbotham, and William Wilson were named a "dream team" by its chair (Trescott 1996). While not named as such, a much earlier example was the faculty assembled at the University of Massachusetts Amherst: Michael Thelwell, Esther Terry, Chester Davis, John Bracey, Max Roach, Nelson Stevens, Shirley Graham Du Bois, Johnnetta Cole, Paul Carter Harrison, William "Bill" Strickland, Julius Lester, Ernest Allen, Diana Ramos, and Archie Shepp. Later, they were joined by James Baldwin. These are just two examples, but other schools have brought major scholars together as well. It all depends on who is doing the dreaming.

LEADERSHIP

One approach to leadership was to select a high-profile nonacademic as the first director of Black Studies. Two good examples of this are the first directors Lerone Bennett Jr., a public historian and journalist, hired at Northwestern University in 1971; and Ewart Guinier, a Harvard-educated lawyer, hired at Harvard University in 1969. Neither of these choices fit seamlessly with local faculty culture. A second approach was to install an untenured assistant professor, such as at Loyola University in Chicago: Milton Gordon, assistant professor of mathematics, became director in 1971; and University of Illinois at Springfield: Daryl Thomas, assistant professor of political science, became director in 1983. All this resulted in weak directorships, in that they were people unfamiliar with the political culture of the institution, and without tenure, so without any job security, lessening their ability to fight for resources and withstand attacks. Academic status is a critical asset for a unit director, and that usually means at least being tenured.

Another critical issue is the length of time a person serves as chair or director. When faculty governance is a democratic process, elected leadership rotates every four to six years. This has not been the case in most Black Studies units. Partly this has to do with maintaining a positive working relationship with administrative officials, often at their discretion, and partly with having to take the time to build and maintain a stable tenured faculty. After a period of start-up, during which there tended to be many short-lived leaders, many individuals held leadership posts for several decades, such as Russell Adams (Howard University), James Turner (Cornell University), Molefi Asante (Temple University), Maulana Karenga (California State University at Long

Beach), Henry Louis Gates Jr. (Harvard University), and William Nelson (Ohio State University).

There is also the question of gender difference in Black Studies unit leadership. The 2006–2007 research found that women led 50 percent of units in the state of New York and 42 percent of the units in California (Alkalimat 2006, 2007). From 1967 to 2018, women have been three of eleven heads at Harvard (Department of African and African American Studies n.d.). In 2018, in Illinois, women were heads of 38 percent (N = 24) of Black Studies units.

One interesting difference in some institutions, for example, the University of Illinois, is between having a chair or a head of a department. A chair is a democratically elected leader voted on by the tenure track faculty. A head is appointed by a dean and rules without needing faculty support. The general tendency for departments across the USA is to shift from the chair system to the head system, from faculty governance to administrative fiat. It is the way that continuity in compliance with administrative policy has been achieved.

As Table 23 shows, as of 2013, women had achieved near parity in the leadership of Black Studies. This is more true in the Northeast and less true in the West. Women were slightly more likely to lead units in private colleges and universities (48 percent) than in public ones (45 percent). Size of college or university seems to have little relationship to gender of the unit head.

Table 23 Gender of Black Studies Unit Heads and Chairs as of 2013

	N	*Men*	*Women*
All	366	54%	46%
By region			
Midwest	104	54%	46%
Northeast	100	49%	51%
South	95	56%	44%
West	67	60%	40%
By ownership			
Public	213	55%	45%
Private	153	52%	48%
By size			
Large (10,000+ students)	186	54%	46%
Medium (3,000–9,999)	101	55%	45%
Small (1,000–2,999)	75	53%	47%
Very small (<1,000)	4	50%	1%

Note: The number of unit heads/chairs was slightly larger than the number of units, due to co-directors and co-heads.

CURRICULUM

In general, at the beginning in the 1960s, there was not much Black-oriented curriculum to build on. A Carter G. Woodson report shows where things stood forty years earlier:

> In 1919, prior to the influx of HBCUs offering black history courses as a part of their curriculum, Woodson issued the first report on African-American studies courses offered in Northern colleges. He reported the following courses:
>
> 1. Ohio State University, Slavery Struggles in the United States
> 2. Nebraska University, The Negro Problem Under Slavery and Freedom
> 3. Stanford University, Immigration and the Race Problem
> 4. University of Oklahoma, Modern Race Problems
> 5. University of Missouri, The Negro in America
> 6. University of Chicago, The Negro in America
> 7. University of Minnesota, The American Negro
> 8. Harvard University, American Population Problems: Immigration and the Negro
>
> Furthermore, Woodson reported that a small number of HBCUs were offering courses in sociology and history pertaining to the Negro experience. Woodson stated that in spite of the lack of trained teachers, Tuskegee, Atlanta University, Fisk, Wilberforce, and Howard offered such courses, even at the risk of their becoming expressions of opinions without the necessary data to support them.
>
> (Land and Brown n.d.)

Ford describes the curriculum on Black people taught at Fisk University:

> It is a remarkable fact that Fisk University has offered a total of eighty-five different courses in Black Studies during the past fifty years, three having been offered as early as 1921, and forty-two before the Black student revolution of 1967. Despite its past history of emphasis on Black Studies, it acknowledged a still greater need for additional emphasis by adding forty-three new courses between 1967 and 1971.
>
> (Ford 1973, 52)

There was increased interest in Black people from many disciplines after the 1954 Supreme Court decision on school integration and the rise of the Civil Rights Movement with the 1960 sit-ins. A good example is sociology. Gordon

(1963) surveyed the literature on race as a biological category and the nature of prejudice, drawing on then new data sources like the *Race Relations Law Reporter* and the reports of the US Civil Rights Commission. Rose (1968) reported data on a survey of curriculum in sociology departments, with an emphasis on race, minority group, and ethnic group relations. For both, there was no specific focus on Black people, only the relationship that nonwhites had with whites. Most important, neither of these scholars mentioned any Black scholars in their summation. This gross omission points to the need for Black Studies.

There have been three stages of curriculum development in Black Studies: (1) experimentation; (2) development of alternative models; and (3) emergence of national trends.

The first curriculum initiative was to "Blackenize" the existing curriculum, practicing the dialectic of antiracism. If there was literature, the demand was for Black literature; history led to the demand for Black history; and so on throughout the course offerings. This led to demands for Black authors, as what little was in the mainstream was inadequate. There was a need to learn from the self-reflective scholarship of Black authors in an effort to escape the Eurocentrism encoded in mainstream scholarship.

What this meant was subject to the disciplinary background of the faculty assigned to teach each course. This resulted in the initial course offerings using one of three frameworks: historical, cultural, or social. This was also reflected in the appropriation of faculty from other departments to teach cross-listed courses available to students for credit in either that discipline and/or Black Studies. This first stage was temporary, because each campus had an administrative process by which courses were proposed and then approved by a faculty-review process, a sort of peer review. It typically took several years for Black Studies faculty to get courses permanently approved. This often led to the first courses being temporary offerings under a special topics rubric. This period of experimentation was funded: the Ford Foundation invested $2,168,500 in Black Studies over a three-year period, 1969–1971. A total of twenty grants were made, including seven to HBCUs. Of the grants that targeted curriculum development, eleven were at the undergraduate level and two at the graduate (Rojas 2007, 138).

After a few years of experimentation, faculty and administrators made attempts to advance models for an undergraduate major. There had been suggestions about such a development, but now there were some years of practice on which to base models. A basic concern was the standardization of an introductory course. Two major texts paved the way, Alkalimat (1975; originally published in 1973), and Karenga 2010 (originally published in 1982). The Alkalimat text grew out of a study guide to a two-volume anthology into an original text written by the Black Studies political collective called People's College discussed in Chapter 5. Its core theoretical framework is called a Paradigm of Unity in Black Studies (Alkalimat 1986).

Logic of change	Social cohesion	Traditional Africa		Slavery		Rural life		Urban life
	Social disruption		Slave Trade		Emancipation		Migrations	
Units of analysis	Ideology	A1	B1	C1	D1	E1	F1	G1
	Nationality	A2	B2	C2	D2	E2	F2	G2
	Class	A3	B3	C3	D3	E3	F3	G3
	Race	A4	B4	C4	D4	E4	F4	G4

Figure 3 Paradigm of Unity in Black Studies

Figure 3 is a Cartesian conceptual space in which to locate experiences using a variety of sources in order to get comparative clarity on data and theory. The design posits a theoretical space of historical periodization of the African-American experience that is a lens through which to see and understand all aspects of social, cultural, political, and economic life. The study guide was first created to compare seven widely used texts (Bennett Jr. 1969; Fishel and Quarles 1968; J.H. Franklin 1967; Huggins, Kilson, and Fox 1971a, 1971b; McPherson 1971; Frazier 1957). This People's College volume is included in the permanent exhibit of the Smithsonian National Museum of African American History and Culture in recognition of it being the first textbook in the field to be nationally adopted.

Karenga (2010 [1982]) is the other popular text. Karenga organized the text around what he calls the seven core subject areas of Black Studies: Black history, Black religion, Black social organization, Black politics, Black economics, Black creative production, and Black psychology. There is a specific focus on Black Studies as an academic discipline.

In addition to these two texts, a number of anthologies have been and are being used in introductory courses. Three of the most comprehensive represent the humanities, edited by Gates Jr. and McKay (1996); the social sciences, edited by Marable and Mullings (2000); and *Afrocentricity*, edited by Asante and Abarry (1996). Another approach was to use a few key texts as a canon of Black intellectual history. However, there seemed to be a disconnect between what were considered canonical texts and those actually being assigned in courses. In most cases, curricula have not included the iconic texts (Rojas 2010, 202). One outstanding exception to this is the curriculum of the University of Massachusetts Amherst.

The year 1981 stands out, for the launch of several curriculum projects. The initiative with the greatest impact was the release of the report by the National

Council for Black Studies (NCBS) on a model curriculum. Joseph Russell, executive director of NCBS, gives the rationale for this report, prepared by a committee chaired by Perry Hall, then at Wayne State University and including the following members: Vivian Gordon, John Indakawa, William Jones, Abdul Alkalimat (Gerald McWorter), Joseph Russell, and James Stewart:

> The question of what constitutes an academically sound Black Studies Curriculum has been answered in various ways by a variety of persons over the past several years without closure. About one year ago, the National Council for Black Studies placed the curriculum question on its "top priority" list and named a nationally representative committee of scholars to develop a "collective" core curriculum for Black Studies ... NCBS is most pleased to share the final report of the Curriculum Standardization Committee which was formally adopted by the Executive Board in July, 1981. We especially call the reader's attention to our wish "to provide a standard model which operates as a yardstick for determining what is to be included or excluded in a program of study as well as providing criteria for criticizing and evaluating alternative pedagogical models" in Black Studies.
>
> (Hall 1981, iii)

The NCBS national newsletter, *Voices in Black Studies*, spells out the main goals of the NCBS report on curriculum standardization:

> The Curriculum Standards Committee of NCBS has articulated the rationale and particulars for a core curriculum in a model Black Studies Program. The overall goals of standardization which emerged from the Committee's deliberations are as follows:
>
> 1. Articulation of the rationale of a core curriculum in Black Studies
> 2. An outline of the academic substance of a core curriculum in Black Studies
> 3. Identification of the body of knowledge and literature which defines the parameters of Black Studies
> 4. Identification of the skills and methods of Black Studies as well as the relationship of Black Studies skills associated with general education on the post-secondary level
> 5. Facilitation of the institutionalization of Black Studies as a discipline of study in U.S. higher education
>
> (NCBS 1981, 1)

Figure 4 is the first NCBS model for a Black Studies core curriculum. It has the same intention as the People's College "Paradigm of Unity" and Karenga's core subject areas; diverse ideological and theoretical positions can coexist,

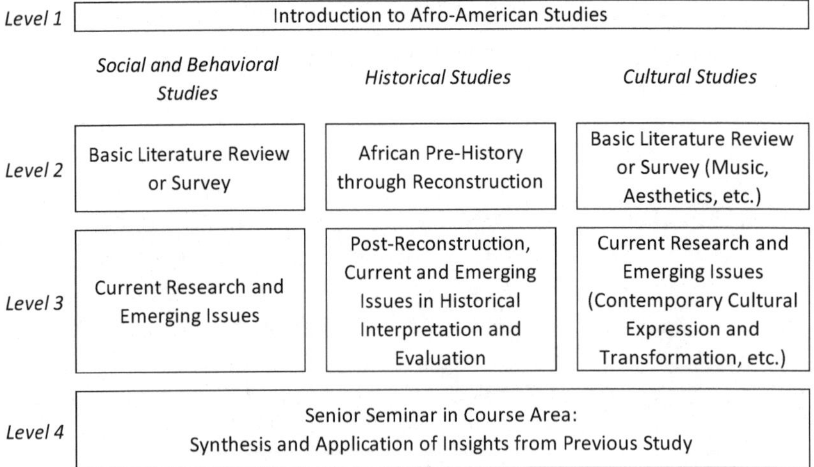

Figure 4 NCBS Model for a Core Curriculum in Black Studies
Source: Norment (2007, 736)

thus enabling Black Studies to survive its contentious ideological origins, for example, it includes approaches of both Cultural Nationalism and Marxism.

In addition to the NCBS report, four scholars launched different national curriculum projects, with funding from the Fund for the Improvement of Secondary Education (FIPSE) or the National Endowment for the Humanities (NEH): (1) Johnnella Butler, Smith College (FIPSE); (2) Ron Bailey, Chicago Center for Afro-American Studies (NEH); (3) Abdul Alkalimat (Gerald McWorter) University of Illinois at Urbana-Champaign (FIPSE); and (4) Vincent Harding, Institute of the Black World (FIPSE). The Smith project brought together activist scholars from two academic movements for innovation, Black Studies and Women Studies, and it identified areas for cooperative curriculum development in the Five Colleges of Amherst, Massachusetts (Amherst College, Hampshire College, Mount Holyoke College, Smith College, and the University of Massachusetts Amherst). The Chicago Center's project focused on the People's College text, *Introduction to Afro-American Studies*, as a case study. It organized an intensive discussion among a national panel of scholars and activists. Key to this was a comprehensive discourse on Black intellectual history by St. Clair Drake. The University of Illinois project developed text material for a set of courses to be included in a core curriculum. Participants in the Chicago curriculum workshop included Russell Adams, Delores Aldridge, Ronald Bailey, Thomas Boston, Al Colon, St. Clair Drake, Howard Fuller, Maryemma Graham, Abdul Alkalimat (Gerald McWorter), Sterling Plumpp, Eugene Redmond, William Sales, Rosalyn Terborg-Penn, and Carlene Young.

The Institute of the Black World convened a group of important scholars to evaluate a collection of syllabi in three areas—history, social science, and culture—coordinated by Douglas Davidson (D.E. White 2011, 194–97). Henry sums up the IBW curriculum project:

> Under the leadership of historian Vincent Harding and staff director Howard Dodson, IBW surveyed some 250 Black Studies units asking them for sample syllabi and teaching methods. They discussed the results of the survey in three conferences from 1981 to 1982. Six goals were put forth by the project's organizers: (1) to provide Black Studies faculty with new material and approaches; (2) to encourage the exchange of materials, ideas, and methodologies in the discipline; (3) to supply faculty members with effective course materials; (4) to promote novel approaches to teaching Black Studies; (5) to encourage a higher level of "critical self-evaluation in the field"; and (6) to refine issues and problems in the field of Black Studies. The conferences revealed the virtual absence of attention to the contributions and issues of Black women—a finding that would be repeated in the work of the NCBS. Unfortunately, IBW did not survive long enough to implement its work.
>
> (Henry 2017, 107)

A general set of content issues emerged from these projects for Black Studies courses.

Following considerable discussion a consensus emerged as to the general content for Black Studies curricula foci:

> 1. Theoretical Review of Literature
> a. Critique of mainstream scholarship
> b. Review of radical thought
> c. Survey of Black intellectual history
> 2. Summation of practical experience
> a. Summation of empirical data analysis
> b. Review public policy on key issues
> c. Survey of the Black liberation movement
>
> (McWorter and Bailey 1984a, 1984b)

Simultaneously, it was possible to address these content areas in curricula thanks to an upsurge in the publishing of Black-authored texts, both new and older works that were out of print. The three major houses publishing reprints were the New York Times-Arno Press, Mnemosyne Publishers, and Atheneum Press, with the Arno Press publishing two series of 210 volumes in total. Molefi Asante (then Arthur Smith) summed up the importance of this reprinting effort:

> As well as capturing in the reprint series the factual history of the Black American, the volumes more properly must be viewed as reflecting the intellectual development of Black scholars. There are several books which should have enjoyed greater circulation and longer lives at their first publication. In fact, the majority of the books reprinted in this collection had limited circulation in their day. The writings of Blacks were often looked upon as nonessential to an understanding of the scholarly traditions of American education, nor were those writings thought to add to that tradition. However, Lorenzo Turner's *Africanisms in the Gullah Dialect* has never been excelled as a study of American linguistic behavior, and Carter G. Woodson's *The Education of the Negro Prior to 1861* is a classic document.
>
> (A.L. Smith 1972, 118)

Of course, there has always been the agency of Black intellectuals publishing on their own. The two most critical sources for the early stages of Black Studies are the self-published work of J.A. Rogers and the Associated Publishers created by Carter G. Woodson. Rogers was outside of the formal academy and only received official recognition in Europe. His entire body of work was self-published and distributed with the assistance of his wife Helga Rogers (Turner 1975; Asukile 2010). Woodson created Associated Publishers to launch his school of African-American historians, which included Lorenzo Greene and A.A. Taylor: the output of this school impacted an entire generation. Meier and Rudwick describe the importance of Woodson as a leader among scholars:

> By the early 1930s, Woodson had thus gathered about him a highly productive band of black scholars. Of the fourteen Negroes who were awarded Ph.D.s in history and the history of education before 1940, eight were in the ASALH circle. Among these black doctorates, nine had done significant publishing by the end of the 1930s; two-thirds of these were in the Woodson group. In short, it was the first generation of professionally trained black doctorates associated with Woodson who were chiefly responsible for laying the foundation for the study of the Afro-American history as a genuine scholarly specialty.
>
> (Meier and Rudwick 1986, 94–95)

With a flood of old and new texts, the question became which to include in a standardized curriculum at the national level. One important approach was described in the third edition of the People's College's *Introduction to Afro-American Studies*:

> A work of Black social analysis is considered a classic when it does the following: (a) definitively summarizes the existing knowledge of a major Black

> experience; (b) represents a model of methodology and technique that serves to direct future investigations; (c) draws from the analysis theoretical concepts and propositions that contribute to our general theoretical grasp of the USA and the Afro-American people; (d) stands the test of time by not being proven incorrect or inadequate and replaced by a superior work; and (e) guides one to take an active role in the struggle to liberate Black people and to fundamentally change the nature of American society.
>
> (Alkalimat 1975, 46)

After a subsequent ideological consolidation of the board, NCBS issued a second curriculum report that more fully embraced the Afrocentric model. Dr. William Little chaired the committee, funded by the Ford Foundation, that developed the Africana Studies Holistic Curriculum Model. Henry describes this development, after noting the changes from the 1981 Perry Hall report, *Introduction to Black Studies*, in the 1985 Little report, *Introduction to Africanology*:

> The NCBS final report to the Ford Foundation explicitly compares the new "Holistic Afrocentric Curriculum Development model" to Hall's earlier Black Studies Model. Whereas Hall's model introduces three subfields … Social/Behavior Studies, History, and Cultural Studies—the new model … has five subfields—African Aesthetics and Expressive Arts and Tradition; African Peoples, Civilization and Social Development; African World Views and Belief Systems; African Power and Organizational Relationships; and Science and Technology in the African World.
>
> (Henry 2017, 109)

These two curriculum reports demonstrate a marked polarity in Black Studies between Afrocentricity and Black Experientialism, including the difference between leading with ideology and leading with research practices, which is discussed in Chapter 14.

ADMINISTRATIVE STRUCTURE

One crucial way to answer the question of whether Black Studies is permanent is to identify the administrative structure of the unit. Data in Table 24 shows the patterns as to what units were departments, programs, or some other structure, as of 2013 (Alkalimat et al. 2013). While 38 percent of the units are departments, 56 percent of Black Studies units are programs. The department is a unit that has been approved at the faculty and board level, and thus a more permanent feature of the budget and the institution as a whole.

Table 24 suggests that Black Studies has achieved more permanence (departments over programs) in public colleges and universities than in private ones. As of 2019, a full 42 percent of Black Studies units in public colleges and universities have achieved departmental status, but only 33 percent in private institutions have. The West has proportionately more departments and the South proportionately more programs than other regions. Programs are more typical across all sizes of colleges and universities, with large institutions more likely to have departments.

Table 24 Black Studies Units by Region, Ownership, and Size of College or University

	N	*Department*	*Program*	*Other*
By region				
Midwest	101	44%	52%	4%
Northeast	99	41%	53%	6%
South	90	21%	71%	8%
West	66	50%	48%	2%
By ownership				
Private	146	33%	62%	5%
Public	210	42%	53%	5%
By size				
Large	186	46%	48%	6%
Medium	100	34%	62%	4%
Small	66	26%	73%	2%
Very Small	4	25%	50%	25%
All	356	38%	56%	5%

Note: "Other" includes areas, centers, committees, concentrations, institutes, and intercollegiate departments. Data as of 2019; for methodology, see [opening of Chapter 13]. Alkalimat and Williams, "African American Studies 2019: A National Web-Based Survey."

Another aspect of administrative structure is a dedicated space, where the unit can build a culture of academic productivity and socialization for faculty and students. Many units are dispersed because they are dominated by joint appointments, with people being housed in their other academic and hence more-important appointments. Outstanding examples of buildings devoted to Black Studies are at Cornell University in New York and Wabash College in Indiana.

Finally, Black Studies as academic profession must submit to annual evaluation, both the individual faculty and the complete academic unit. There are different evaluation procedures, with some taking place on the local campus and others being completed by nationally distributed peers and professional organizations.

Individuals are evaluated, first and foremost, within the Black Studies unit: students by their classroom instructors and faculty by each other. Black Studies faculty evaluation takes place based on faculty rank. Tenured faculty vote on untenured faculty, and the opinions of full professors have greater weight. However, if the Black Studies unit is not sufficiently self-governing, then senior faculty in other departments are sometimes called to make evaluations. When the person has a joint appointment, the crisis is the relative weight given to each unit. Final evaluation always takes place at the college and campus-wide level, being up to the board of trustees.

Institutions use some mix of the following criteria: (1) subjective evaluation of senior scholars in the field; (2) rankings based on national surveys; (3) empirical trend metrics, especially the scholarly productivity in terms of publications; and (4) focus on elites, the number of individuals who have outstanding reputations. Ray (1976) and Slater (1993) present a general discussion of criteria used for evaluation. Ray notes that at Western Michigan University:

> The model for the study, evaluation and assessment of Black Studies is in Du Bois. His carefully designed studies provide a base and foundation for methodology. His predictions for reference and scheme, his ideas for creativity and spirit, his nobility for credibility, and his style for legitimacy, all give direction to appropriate research designs. He is everywhere in the Black movement. He commented on all topics and all communities including the international community. Du Bois gives definitions, evaluative criteria, and style. His thoughts and values support the search for truth.
>
> (Ray 1976, 389)

Slater uses the quantitative method based on citation analysis:

> The citation ranking technique was first developed by the Institute for Scientific Information (ISI) in Philadelphia. ISI surveys over 3,200 academic journals from around the world in most major disciplines from social science to arts and humanities to clinical medicine, and almost everything in between. Each year, ISI enters into its massive database all footnote references and biographical information from over 600,000 papers and records over 12 million citations annually … Through the use of its database search technology, ISI is then able to rank authors, research papers, universities, or academic departments by a number of variables including the number of papers cited, the total number of citations received, or the number of citations awarded per paper.
>
> (Slater 1993, 38)

McWorter (1986) argues for a model of professional achievement that includes leadership positions in journals and professional organizations, as well as a publication record in Black Studies journals specifically. Broussard takes issue with limiting the scholarship to only Black Studies journals, in a 1984 article in the *Journal of Negro Education* (McWorter 1986). The focus on journals and organizations in the discipline is critical to the survival and sustainability of Black Studies as a professional field of research and teaching.

In general, there are four audiences to consider in any comprehensive approach to evaluation: (1) the faculty and students within Black Studies, as the formal unit in higher education; (2) Black academics and intellectuals in general; (3) the mainstream academic establishment; and (4) the popular media with its mass audience. However, it is critical to keep these separate, as all too often the general public is given priority over professional assessment and trends within the profession. Sometimes the public has a view that does not accurately reflect what is actually happening in terms of national trends on campuses. There are also universal issues that have emerged in the general evaluation of Black Studies units and individual faculty, examples being sexual harassment and the improper granting of academic credit to athletes, although these scandals have not been any more widespread in Black Studies than other disciplines (Davies 2018; Wikipedia 2010)

CULTURE

The universal cultural program connected to Black Studies is the gospel choir. This is a secular form of a Black religious cultural practice. One of the most successful such programs was founded in 1969 by Russell Knighton at Macalester College in St. Paul, Minnesota. The group was originally called the Macalester College Black Voices but, in 1971, the group changed its name to Sounds of Blackness. They continued to work together after graduation and earned three Grammy Awards, four Stellar Awards, one Emmy nomination, and an NAACP Image award ("Sounds of Blackness" n.d.). Another important practice has been artist-in-residence positions or tenure-track appointments of practicing professional artists. A high point here was the appointment of master musicians such as Max Roach and Archie Shepp at the University of Massachusetts Amherst. Another approach, that of the University of Chicago, features an artist-in-residence program for young up-and-coming artists (University of Chicago Arts n.d.).

The foundation of Black culture is music, but there is so much more. Another major aspect of cultural production by Black Studies faculty and students is the promotion of public art. This was mural making, following the path-breaking 1967 Wall of Respect in Chicago (Alkalimat, Crawford, and Zorach 2017). Outstanding examples of this are Nelson Stevens at the University of Massachusetts Amherst and Dana Chandler of Northeastern University bringing student mural making into Black Studies courses (Prigoff and Dunitz 2000, 129–31, and 203).

Edmund Barry Gaither, director of the Museum of the National Center of Afro-American Artists, said of murals,

> When the Organization of Black American Culture (OBAC) brought about the creation of the Wall of Respect in Chicago in 1967, it precipitated a seminal event … As the number of urban murals grew, their visual language widened and became richer. Regional differences appeared, and the range of subject matter again broadened, reaching well beyond political and nationalist polemics. Several Black museums embraced these fresh works and in time the visual arts canon began to shift admitting to the existence of a distinct tradition of Black murals. Historically Black colleges and universities retained their place as leading sites for the commission of narrative murals, as demonstrated by comparatively recent unveilings in Winston-Salem State University, Texas Southern University and Hampton University.
>
> (Prigoff and Dunitz 2000, 5)

Higher education institutions embraced Black culture and it was common for them to establish a Black Cultural Center as an administrative form of physical space or home for Black students and for those interested in a multicultural experience. This was so even at institutions without an academic Black Studies unit. The centers were usually autonomous and operating within their university's Student Affairs. This is a separate from the academic side of a college institutional structure.

Such centers became so numerous that the Association for Black Culture Centers formed. Fred Hord, director of Africana Studies at Knox College in Illinois, founded the organization in 1988 for reasons that were central to the original mission of Black Studies: "Black Culture and Multiculture Centers rose out of the student protest and other activist movements of people of color in the United States for social justice and cultural recognition on the college campus" (Association for Black Culture Centers [ABCC] n.d.). Sanders sums up the functions of the typical Black Cultural Center:

> Black culture centers provide important university support and services, such as tutoring, academic advising, career development, mentoring, and leadership skill building (Bankole, 2005; Hefner, 2002; Hord, 2005a; Patton, 2010; Princes, 2004). Typically housed in either academic affairs or student affairs divisions of universities (Bankole, 2005), they are described as a safe space for Black students to retreat from the "perceived hostility of an unwelcoming campus community" (Young & Hannon, 2002). Studies indicate that culture centers aid in recruiting and retaining students from historically mar-

> ginalized racial and ethnic groups, provide a "home away from home," help students cope with marginalization, and serve as a source of cultural pride and education (Patton, 2006a, 2006b; Jones et al., 2002; Jones & Williams, 2006; Strayhorn, Terrell, Redmond, & Walton, 2010). In their examination of the African American Student Center (AASC) at a Northwestern university, Jones and Williams (2006) report that undergraduates at this institution considered the center "a safe haven," "a home away from home," a place to talk about problems," and "a place [of refuge] from PWI [predominantly White institutions] stress." Jones and Williams (2006) reason that culture centers and other initiatives targeted toward supporting these populations can be viewed as factors that contribute to both the quality and quantity of students of color on campus. The sentiments shared amongst the interviewees in this study are indicative of the significant role the AASC played in student success at this university.
>
> (Sanders 2016, 30)

One of the main assets of the Black Cultural Center is the space it provided. More so than academic units, the Black Cultural Center has often had a separate building all its own. Some examples include The Sonja Hayes Stone Center for Black Culture and History at the University of North Carolina at Chapel Hill, the Lonnie B. Harris Black Cultural Center at Oregon State University, and The Bruce Nesbit African American Cultural Center at the University of Illinois.

An excellent example is the Black Cultural Center at Purdue University (BCC). It gained its stature on campus because one of its directors, Tony Zamora, a musician who led the center from 1973 to 1995, was also the Assistant Director of the Purdue Student Union and in a position to leverage strong budget support for the BCC. By 1999, the student union was able to raise $3 million dollars to build a new BCC building. The building design was an African visual style, with the following elements:

- A geometric brick pattern based on a design used in wall mats found in Zaire and the Democratic Republic of the Congo;
- Window openings that work within the overall pattern of the walls, in keeping with the traditional African architecture;
- An entrance that resembles a portal, often used as the path into a traditional village. The keyhole-shaped portal enhances the identity of the building. The lattice design of the cast stone medallions embedded in the portal represents a typical African ornamental motif;
- An octagonal lobby that acts as the village courtyard, while the surrounding "cells" or rooms create a true ordering system. The lobby encourages community living rather than seeking exclusion within an isolated room;

- A wrought-iron balcony on the second floor that represents the early 1700s enslaved Africans who were commonly employed in the metal trades and blacksmithing; and
- The center of the entrance that reflects the geometrical and symbolic patterns in African design. The "windmill" pattern is reminiscent of an Adinkra motif, which means "ability to face difficulty in life."

(Black Cultural Center n.d.)

PROGRAMS

Black Studies units host events that follow the political culture of the African-American community as well as conventional practices in higher education. The main activity on every campus is the annual Black History Month, which is the month of February:

> Every campus, with or without a Black Studies unit, does programs on the Black experience in February, now universally recognized as Black History Month. The story of Black History Month begins in Chicago during the summer of 1915. An alumnus of the University of Chicago with many friends in the city, Carter G. Woodson traveled from Washington, D.C. to participate in a national celebration of the fiftieth anniversary of emancipation sponsored by the state of Illinois. Thousands of African Americans travelled from across the country to see exhibits highlighting the progress their people had made since the destruction of slavery. Awarded a doctorate in Harvard three years earlier, Woodson joined the other exhibitors with a black history display. Despite being held at the Coliseum, the site of the 1912 Republican convention, an overflow crowd of six to twelve thousand waited outside for their turn to view the exhibits. Inspired by the three-week celebration, Woodson decided to form an organization to promote the scientific study of black life and history before leaving town. On September 9th, Woodson met at the Wabash YMCA with A.L. Jackson and three others and formed the Association for the Study of Negro Life and History.
>
> Going forward it would both create and popularize knowledge about the black past. He sent out a press release announcing Negro History Week in February 1926. Woodson chose February for reasons of tradition and reform. It is commonly said that Woodson selected February to encompass the birthdays of two great Americans who played a prominent role in shaping black history, namely Abraham Lincoln and Frederick Douglass, whose birthdays are the 12th and the 14th, respectively. More importantly, he chose them for reasons of tradition. Since Lincoln's assassination in 1865, the black community, along with other Republicans, had been celebrating the fallen President's birthday. And since the late 1890s, black communities

across the country had been celebrating Douglass'. Well aware of the pre-existing celebrations, Woodson built Negro History Week around traditional days of commemorating the black past. He was asking the public to extend their study of black history, not to create a new tradition. In doing so, he increased his chances for success.

(Association for the Study of African American Life and History 2017)

Major events in Black Studies units celebrate academic achievement, namely, special graduation ceremonies for Black Studies majors and minors, as well as for African-American graduates in general. These activities give special recognition and a cultural experience for families and friends of the students and an opportunity for families to socialize with the African-American faculty and

Table 25 Selected Annual Events Sponsored by Black Studies Programs

Institution	*Annual Lecture*
Claremont Colleges	Annual Intercollegiate Black Studies Conference
Colby College	The Marion Osborne Matheson Black History Month Lecture
Columbia University	Annual Zora Neale Hurston Lecture
Harvard University	The W.E.B. Du Bois Lectures
Medgar Evers Community College	National Black Writers Annual Conference
Northwestern University	The Allison Davis Lecture
Olive Harvey Community College	Annual Black Studies Conference
Princeton University	The Toni Morrison Lecture
Purdue University	Symposium on African American Culture and Philosophy
Stanford University	The St. Clair Drake Memorial Lecture
Syracuse University	The John L. Johnson Lecture
Temple University	Cheikh Anta Diop International Conference
University of Florida	The Ronald Foreman Lecture
University of Illinois Chicago	The Grace Holt Lecture
University of Illinois Urbana-Champaign	The Annual Malcolm X Lecture
University of Kentucky	Annual Black Women's Conference
University of Louisville	National Conference on the Black Family
University of Missouri	Annual Fall Conference on Black Studies
University of North Carolina at Charlotte	Annual Africana Studies Conference
University of Northern Iowa	Annual African American and Children and Families Conference
University of Texas at San Antonio	Annual Black Studies Symposium
Yale University	The Henry Louis Gates Jr. Lecture

staff. At many institutions, these are long-standing traditions; Harvard held its first Black-only graduation ceremony in 2017 (McIntyre 2017).

Other ways that institutions celebrate achievement is through annual awards for faculty and students and publications. For students in particular, this boosts admission to graduate programs and increases the possibility of being hired. Publications of student scholarship and cultural creativity build a tradition of publishing as a precursor to future professional productivity.

Some institutions showcase scholarship via annual conferences and special named lectures. These are social occasions when the entire program's faculty and students can invite the entire campus to a noteworthy performance of scholarship. The documentation of these activities often amounts to the best trend data of their academic activities. Examples of special named lectures and annual conferences are provided in Table 25.

COMMUNITY RELATIONS

Some Black Studies departments have established and maintain connections to the community as an integral part of their programs. In areas where the institution is in close proximity to a Black community, it is common for course credit to be allocated for service learning projects. An especially well-developed approach to community programming is that of the Black Studies department at Ohio State University, which established a Community Extension Center (CEC) in 1972, located off campus in the community. The department did this with money allocated by the state legislature, and now the CEC has a building constructed for its use in the heart of the Black community. This effort was ahead of its time:

> When the CEC was first established the slogan "outreach and engagement," which now characterizes a critical aspect of the university's mission, was not yet in vogue. However, extending the university's resources and capital to the community has always figured prominently in Black Studies as a discipline. Yet, when the department announced it would create a Community Extension Center, it was ahead of its time in pioneering a new role for a major Research 1 university, located in an urban setting. Again, the idea of a Community Extension Center was in-keeping with the mission of Black Studies … The CEC's goal was to help uplift the Black community by providing educational and other opportunities that enhance the life chances of those who live, work, play and attend school on the near eastside. However, it also sought to discover ways of making the activities and programs, through which it actualizes its mission, responsive to the relative needs and realities identified by residents. Over the years, the CEC has had to necessarily

> remain dynamic in its effort to be responsive to economic, political, social and even demographic changes over time. The CEC helps bridge the gap, and sometimes disconnect, with the real world that has so often characterizes academia. Among the kinds of activities and programs that the CEC has offered over the years include credit and noncredit courses, lectures, computer literacy training, leadership development, income tax assistance, legal counseling and college prep seminars for high school students.
>
> (Albright, Jeffries, and Goecke 2013, 41)

A second type of community program was initiated at Brown University under the leadership of George Bass and Rhett Jones. The program, Rites and Reason, transforms faculty academic scholarship into a theatrical presentation for the broad community:

> In the Fall of 1973, Jones and Bass began to prepare for the formal bringing together of the two kinds of knowledge: one with its origin in the community and the other with its origin in the university. Jones and Bass decided to begin with a research topic they knew residents of greater Providence's black community could discuss with authority and ease. The project was called "Oral History as an Index to Change" and focused on race relations in Providence between 1920 and 1940. Study began when Bass and Jones offered a seminar in which nine black and seven white students enrolled. Jones gave the students some elementary training in interview techniques, worked with them in constructing an interview schedule, and with support provided by a number of community agencies, was able to arrange for students to interview senior citizens, both black and white, who had lived in Rhode Island in the twenties and thirties. White students interviewed the white informants, and black students interviewed the black informants. All interviews were audiotaped, and excerpts from them were played in meetings for discussion in the seminar. Bass participated in all meetings of the seminar and after it was completed took the interviews conducted by the students, their working papers, summary papers completed by Jones, as well as data gathered from newspapers, census information, and other published sources and began to work on the play.
>
> (G.H. Bass and Jones 2004, 8)

Study travel to the African Diaspora is another popular type of program. Typically, programs facilitate students' study abroad in English-speaking countries like Ghana, Nigeria, Tanzania, South Africa, and Jamaica. Afrocentric programs tend to organize student trips to Egypt (for more on this, see Chapter 13).

FUNDING

Institutional success requires a stable sustainable budget, from both internal institutional sources and external sources as well. Internal institutional funding can be soft or hard, temporary or permanent. Black Studies usually begins with a campus-based or soft-money allocation from the administration requiring annual renewal. Historically, this would keep the unit in an unstable insecure position, and given the polemical origin of the unit in student protest, pressure was needed every budget cycle. Administrations allocate soft money at their discretion, so with every new administrative official a new round of negotiations is necessary to secure continued funding.

The federal government has been and remains a source of grant funding, especially through the National Endowment for the Humanities, the National Endowment for the Arts, and the Fund for the Improvement of Post-Secondary Education, as well as other agencies. The main private-foundation source of funding has been the Ford Foundation: "In the 25 years since the first Ford Foundation report on African American Studies was commissioned, the foundation has made almost $31 million in grants to African American Studies programs, departments, and organizations" (Griffin 2007, xxii).

The most notable fund-raising effort has been by Henry Louis Gates Jr., who has adopted an entrepreneurial style in leading the program at Harvard. This has not been viewed as a success by everyone (Watson 2013). A Ford Foundation report in 2000 states:

> Winning support from both foundations and individual donors, Gates established Afro-American Studies as one of the most successful fundraising units on campus. (At Harvard, every unit raises its own money.) Indeed, as of late 1998, Afro-American Studies had raised roughly $17 million in the decade, including a $2 million endowment. In addition, the Alphonse Fletcher Chair was established and used to recruit Cornel West from Princeton; and the DuBois Institute library was named for Harvard alumnus, Franklin Raines, director of Fannie Mae, and director and former director of the U.S. OMB (Office of Management and Budget), who had contributed money to the unit. (Griffin 2007, 179)

The Du Bois Center itself at Harvard was renamed in 2013 when it took on the name of a new major donor:

> With the help of a $15 million gift from one of the University's most active donors, Harvard will create a new, fully endowed research center for African and African-American Studies next month, financially uniting seven existing initiatives and funding a handful of new programs in the field. The new cen-

> ter, named the Hutchins Center for African and African American Research after the project's chief donor Glenn H. Hutchins '77, will officially launch on Oct. 2 with a ceremony in Sanders Theatre. Construction will begin shortly thereafter to expand and remodel the current home of the W.E.B. Du Bois Institute for African and African American Research and the other existing initiatives at 104 Mt. Auburn Street to house the Hutchins Center.
>
> (Clarida and Fandos 2013)

The majority of Black Studies programs exist on local funding. In public institutions, this is tied to enrollment, as government funding is usually allotted based on class size. An additional factor is that the major agencies that fund higher education have funding streams aimed at specific disciplines, for example, the National Science Foundation provides grants for work in sociology, but none target funds for Black Studies except on an ad hoc basis.

13
Establishing the Profession

In order for Black Studies to become a legitimate academic profession, it had to implement a process by which it became a self-governing network holding its members to the highest standards. There are at least four main aspects of this: the doctoral degree, professional journals, professional organizations, and the conferences around which those organizations are constructed.

THE DOCTORAL DEGREE

Professionalization in the academy relies on the highest level of academic certification, the PhD degree, and its activity being evaluated through peer review. This entails two things: faculty members with earned PhDs and a pipeline for graduating doctoral students. Once again, it must be emphasized that historically, Black academic professionals were at the HBCUs: "As late as 1936, more than 80 per cent of all Black PhDs were employed by Howard, Atlanta and Fisk Universities" (Henry 2017, 26), and "for the 15-year period from 1932 to 1947, about 85% of the 2,535 MA theses and 359 PhD dissertations on Negro subjects accepted by American universities were done by Blacks" (Henry 2017, 42).

Peer review is the legitimation process for status recognition in an academic discipline. The historical dilemma is that the small number of Black PhDs in mainstream institutions meant that peer review for Black faculty was often by white faculty not in Black Studies. In the first stage of Black Studies, the legitimation of Black Studies was controlled by faculty in other departments or by administrative fiat. This was true while Black graduate students were still having a difficult time navigating what was a racist path without sufficient support from faculty or administration (Davidson 1970; J. Bracey 1971).

As of the academic year 2006–2007, the Black Studies faculty was well credentialed at the PhD level. A full 88 percent of New York Black Studies faculty and 87 percent of those in California had earned doctoral degrees (Alkalimat 2006, 25; 2007, 16). It is highly likely that other states, which we did not analyze in such detail, would show similar results. But, most of their degrees were not in Black Studies; they were typically scholars whose doctoral work had focused on some aspect of the African Diaspora, but within some other departmental discipline. This is beginning to change.

Table 26 reports the data from a 2005 survey of doctoral programs in Black Studies (Evans 2006, 3).

Table 26 History of Several Black Studies Doctoral Programs

Institution	*Department founded*	*PhD program started*
Temple	1971	1988
Massachusetts	1969	1996
Berkeley	1970	1997
Harvard	1969	2001
Michigan State	2002	2002
Northwestern	1971	2006

Source: Evans (2006, 3).

The National Center for Education Statistics reports that from 2005 to 2017, 270 PhDs were awarded in African American Studies, an average of 22.5 per year.

One of the common features of these PhD programs is the qualifying exam, a process to certify one's general level of understanding before moving on to the specialized research of a doctoral dissertation. Evans reports this finding on the comparative study of the comprehensive PhD exam in Black Studies:

> The structure of the tests include the following: (Temple) a two-day test, including four sets of questions, with two three-hour sittings per day in a designated classroom; (UMass) a three-day written take home general exam after the "Major Works" courses and a three day written exam on the student's area of specialization before construction of the dissertation prospectus; (Berkeley) two written papers, one on theories and methodologies in the field and one on the students area of specialization along with a two-hour oral exam which measures familiarity with literature, critical engagement from a disciplinary and interdisciplinary perspective, and mastery of major issues; (Harvard) a two-hour exam no later than the third year, then development and defense of a prospectus; (Michigan State) a three-day take-home exam with three questions measuring knowledge of content and theory in both a general area and specialization, then the answers evaluated by two full professors in the program and one professor from the advisory board; and (Northwestern) oral general exam that includes questions tailored to the students' specialization accompanied by a take-home exam of three questions with a one-week allotment for completion. Though the schools vary greatly on form and function of exam, the gist is the same: to test students'

> mastery of the program's content and to measure readiness for the student to move forward with independent research.
>
> (Evans 2006, 4)

So what are the main differences in the PhD programs? There are three types, with some institutions having more than one type:

1. Autonomous PhD-degree-granting unit: e.g., Temple, Massachusetts-Amherst, Pennsylvania, Berkeley, Pennsylvania, Brown, Northwestern, Harvard, Cornell, Brown, Louisville, Indiana, Ohio State, Michigan State University, Texas-Austin
2. Partnering of Black Studies department with another PhD-granting department: e.g., Yale, Florida International, Pennsylvania State
3. A Black Studies concentration/certificate in another discipline PhD program: e.g., Virginia Tech, Missouri-Kansas City, Princeton, Duke, Maryland, Wisconsin-Madison, UC Santa Barbara, University of Illinois

There is a great need for these doctoral-degree programs in Black Studies to convene annual discussions, not only to standardize the basic content of the PhD degree, but also to build a job market for their graduates. One step in this direction was a 2012 summit organized by the Department of African American Studies at Northwestern, "A Beautiful Struggle: Transformative Black Studies in Shifting Political Landscapes." A closer look at three campuses helps make real the achievements and issues. Temple University was the first to offer a PhD in Black Studies. University of Massachusetts at Amherst offered the strongest program oriented toward Black Experientialism. And Northwestern University's program grew up alongside early programs on Africa itself. After considering each campus, this chapter looks at three indicators of scholarship: scholarly journals, professional associations, and academic conferences.

TEMPLE UNIVERSITY

The first formal PhD program in Black Studies was launched at Temple University in 1987. Molefi Asante was the author of the proposal to create the program and its first head. Asante explains its significance:

> In 1987 when the Temple University Board of Trustees approved the proposal for a doctoral program in African American Studies it represented one of the most historical developments in American higher education. There were three reasons that came readily to mind at the time: (1) it represented a major breach in the structure of white supremacy, (2) it introduced a new paradigm, and (3) it minimized the significance of race in theoreti-

> cal and conceptual innovation. In the first place the proposal to create a new doctoral program in a major white institution in the United States was a bold act. I knew it then and believe it now.
>
> (Asante 2018)

•

By 2006, the Temple program had nine full faculty and nine listed as affiliates. In 2019, the number of full-time faculty was six and the core curriculum included five courses. The Temple program is open to part-time working students, as most of its courses are taught after 4:30 p.m., and a few financial assistantships are available.

The orientation of the program is clear in the title of one of the required courses: The Afrocentric Paradigm. Two of the five required courses are in methodology: Theories and Methods in African American Studies and Ethnographic Methods. Its name is the Department of Africology and African American Studies. The term "Africology" originated at the University of Wisconsin at Milwaukee and has been adopted by the advocates of Afrocentrism (Asante n.d.).

The Temple department has awarded more PhD degrees than any other program. They have granted about 170 PhD degrees, including three in 2019 and four in 2020. While 159 have been of African and African-American backgrounds, there have been seven whites and four people from the global south. Women have outnumbered men 101 to 69. Beginning in fall 2020, there will be twenty students working on their PhDs (data from correspondence with the Department chair Molefi Asante).

Its graduates are leading Black Studies programs at Howard University, Princeton University, University of Houston, and the University of Pittsburgh. Another PhD graduate, Ibram X. Kendi, is the founding director of Boston University's BU Center for Antiracist Research, and a 2016 winner of the National Book Award.

In addition, the department established an annual conference to honor the famed scholar Cheikh Anta Diop and continue his research tradition. The Temple department convened the conference until 1996, when it became affiliated with the Association of Nubian Kemetic Heritage (ANKH). In 2009, the conference was transformed into one presenting professional activity when it was taken over by the Diopian Institute for Scholarly Advancement (DISA).

UNIVERSITY OF MASSACHUSETTS AMHERST

Afro-American Studies at the University of Massachusetts Amherst established itself as a major academic department at the undergraduate level and on that basis developed its PhD-level degree. Bernard Bell wrote a memoir (2012) of his experiences during 1968–1971. He focuses on their manifestation of the key

Black Studies motto, "Academic Excellence and Social Responsibility," carried out by himself and Michael Thelwell, the founding chair of the department:

> UMass Amherst's W.E.B. DuBois Department of Afro-American Studies, named for the Massachusetts native who believed social justice must be rooted in exemplary scholarship, began as a program in the university's English Department in the late 1960s and became an independent department in 1970. Although a predominantly White university located in a somewhat rural White community, the department attracted renowned Black intellectuals and artists such as James Baldwin, Chinua Achebe and Dr. Johnnetta B. Cole, who were all on the faculty across the decades.
>
> In the early 1990s, [John] Bracey says the members of the department realized they had a new mission: to train their successors. In 1996, he outlined his vision for a graduate program.
>
> All first-year graduate students in the W.E.B. DuBois Department of Afro-American Studies at the University of Massachusetts at Amherst take a year long course of study titled "Major Works in Afro-American Studies," a team-taught seminar in which they read more than 50 books spanning a diverse range of subjects.
>
> (Elfman 2017)

This is a unique feature of the University of Massachusetts Amherst PhD program. It is the total immersion of an entering class. There are no assumptions about any prior undergraduate preparation. The first-year students thereby familiarize themselves with the basic literature and absorb the political culture and lifestyle of the department. They are exposed to the core faculty as the process is team taught. Bracey makes clear why this comprehensive introduction is necessary:

> "We didn't want to fragment Black people's lives into the little chunks that the academy does with White people's lives," says Bracey. "People don't live that way. It doesn't make sense to talk about somebody's economic life absent a discussion of who they are politically or what music they listen to or what clubs they belong to—the whole person. We wanted to establish an institution that would allow a student to come into an African-American oriented environment and see how all the pieces flowed into each other," he adds. "We wanted to obliterate those distinctions and open up a way of looking at things that was fairly rare in the academy."
>
> (Elfman 2017)

Currently, after the basic first year, students are guided to choose one of two tracks for greater specialization, either literature and culture, or history.

The last seventeen years of granting the PhD degree (2002–2018), has produced fifty-three graduates. Of the first sixteen (2002–2007), ten have tenured faculty positions and four are currently assistant professors. From 2008 to 2018, thirty-seven PhDs were awarded, of which twenty-nine (78 percent) have faculty positions as assistant professors. This includes two department chairs and one journal editor (University of Massachusetts Amherst n.d.).

NORTHWESTERN UNIVERSITY

Northwestern University is distinguished by having one of the major programs of African Studies in the USA, which was established under the leadership of anthropologist Melville Herskovits. He founded the Department of Anthropology in 1938 and the African Studies Program in 1948. Northwestern offers a graduate certificate in African Studies to people enrolled in a departmental PhD program, based on at least six courses taken with African Studies content.

Northwestern University issued a press release during the first year of its new PhD degree in Black Studies (2006–2007):

> "The margin forced the center to change and has altered the very ways we produce knowledge," says Dwight McBride, Leon Forrest Professor and chair of Northwestern's African American studies department. "Much of what we now understand as cutting-edge scholarship could hardly have been imagined before the advent of African-American studies, ethnic studies and gender studies … According to McBride, rumors of the field's demise have swirled since the first undergraduate programs were established decades ago. "However, few scholars today seriously consider cutting-edge scholarship without thinking about the impact of race." … Under McBride's leadership, Northwestern's Black studies faculty has grown from three to 14 core members and from six to 22 affiliates. In recruiting Darlene Clark Hine—who helped shape Michigan State University's Black studies doctoral program—McBride brought to campus a leading scholar of the African American experience and pioneer of Black woman's history.
>
> (LeNoble 2010, 451)

The former department chair of African American Studies, Patrick Johnson, describes the PhD program:

> We are especially pleased to offer a doctoral degree in African American Studies. Launched in 2006, our program seeks to train the next generation of African Americanists in the areas of Expressive Arts and Cultural Studies; Politics, Society, and Culture; and Historical Studies.
>
> (Northwestern University n.d.)

The current chair is Martha Biondi.

According to the NCBS (2018), there has been an increase in graduate-level degree programs in Black Studies.

JOURNALS

There are several important studies of Black Studies journals (McWorter 1981; Alkalimat 2008; Weissinger 2010, 2017; Zulu 2017). Connecting back to Black Studies as Intellectual History, six Black Studies journals that were established prior to the 1960s are still being published: *Journal of Negro History* (now *Journal of African American History*), founded 1916; *Journal of Negro Education*, founded 1932; *Phylon*, founded 1940; *Negro Educational Review*, founded 1950; *Howard Law Journal*, founded 1955; and the *College Language Association Journal*, founded 1957.

Today, thirty-one journals concern themselves with Black Studies, and their self-definition puts them into any of three categories: disciplinary, cross-disciplinary, or thematic. Eight define themselves as representing the academic field of Black Studies. Of these, one, *Phylon*, pre-dates the 1960s and another, *Black Scholar*, reflects the social activist orientation of the founders in the late 1960s. The remaining six fit a more conventional model for an academic journal. These eight are:

African American Review
Afro-Hispanic Review
Black Scholar
International Journal of Africana Studies
Journal of African American Studies
Journal of Black Studies
Phylon
The Western Journal of Black Studies

Sixteen Black Studies journals are linked to one other academic discipline:

Anthropology: *Transforming Anthropology*
Art: *International Review of African American Art*
Economics: *Review of Black Political Economy*
Education: *Journal of Negro Education, Negro Education Review*
History: *Journal of African American History*
Law: *National Black Law Journal*
Literature: *CLA Journal, Obsidian III*
Latinx: *The Afro-Hispanic Review, PALARA*
Local history: *Afro-Americans in New York Life and History*

Music: *Black Music Research Journal*
Philosophy: *Philosophia Africana*
Political Science: *National Political Science Review*
Psychology: *Journal of Black Psychology*
Women's Studies: *Black Women, Gender, and Families*

Seven journals take a broader multidisciplinary perspective, across either the humanities or the social sciences:

Humanities: *Callaloo, Langston Hughes Review, Drum Voices, Black Renaissance*
Social Science: *Trotter Review, Souls, the Du Bois Review*

sponsored by or based in academic institutions (including one with a nonprofit organization as its publisher), and four are based in professional associations, as Table 27 shows.

Table 27 Black Studies Journals and their Editors and Editorial Board Members, by Type and Publisher (2008)

	Disciplinary journals	*Bidisciplinary journals*	*Multidisciplinary journals*	*All*
Journals				
Type of publisher				
University	3	10	4	17
Commercial publisher	3	3	3	9
Professional Association	1	3	–	4
Nonprofit Organization	1	–	–	1
Region of publisher				
East	–	7	4	11
Midwest	2	4	1	7
South	2	4	2	8
West	4	1	–	5
All	8	16	7	31
Editors and editorial board members				
Humanities	38	63	45	146
Black Studies	34	39	24	97
Social Sciences	28	37	27	92
History	7	20	8	35
Other	6	11	5	22
Outside academia	9	8	5	22
Not known	61	51	14	126
All	183	229	128	540

More can be learned by analyzing the editorial board membership, as these are the people who link the journals to the broad community of academic scholars. Each editor and editorial board has an academic identity. They stand collectively as a definition of their respective journal. A good example of this has been the advisory editorial board of *The Black Scholar*, which until 2012 was dominated by senior scholar-activists of the founding generation of Black Studies, including the two editors, Robert Chrisman and Robert Allen.

Each of the three longest-serving editors of Black Studies publications, Robert Chrisman, Molefi Asante, and Charles Rowell, guided their respective journal from social movement to the top tier of academic achievement. Chrisman edited *The Black Scholar* for forty-three years, from its founding in 1969 until shortly before his death. Molefi Asante edited *Journal of Black Studies* for forty-nine years, since he founded it in 1970, and now he and Ama Mazama are co-editors. And, Charles Henry Rowell has edited *Callaloo* for forty-three years since its founding in 1976.

Women make up 40 percent of the editors and editorial board members of academic journals in Black Studies. On the positive side, four of the journals have a majority of women on their boards: *Afro-Hispanic Review* (thirteen men, seventeen women), *Black Women, Gender and Families* (no men, eighteen women), *Du Bois Review* (four men, nine women), and *Journal of African American History* (eight men, fifteen women). On the negative side, at least three can be singled out for gender imbalance in terms of men to women: *Western Journal of Black Studies* (seventeen men, two women), *Afro-Americans in New York Life and History* (twenty-one men, four women), and *Philosophica Africana* (nineteen men, one woman).

Of 540 editorial positions, 321 are held by tenured or tenure-track faculty, and of these, 90 percent are tenured (professor or associate professor).

Of the four main divisions of academic disciplines, the humanities are by far the dominant connection and context for Black Studies editors, especially if one adds history. An interesting pattern emerges, when one looks for tendencies linking one's affiliation with the type of journals. Black Studies scholars are more likely to be associated with disciplinary journals, while historians are more likely than the others to be associated with the cross-disciplinary journals. Scholars in the social sciences and the humanities are more closely tied to the thematic journals. While editorial board members in the three categories of journals come from all fields, in each type there is a greater tendency for scholars affiliated with that subject area to be on the boards. This is reassuring, as it suggests that there is a subject-specialty division of labor—expertise dominates.

A total of 184 universities are represented on the boards of these 31 journals. Of the top five universities in terms of the number of faculty members on these journals' boards (see Table 28), two are HBCUs, two are from the Ivy League, and the fifth is a major public research university. This reflects the inclusion of scholars from diverse institutions, the hallmark of institutionalization of Black Studies in higher education.

Table 28 Top Five Universities in Terms of Black Studies Journal Editorial Positions (2008)

University	*Faculty with Black Studies editorial positions*
Atlanta University Center	26
Harvard University	17
Columbia University	15
Howard University	15
University of Illinois at Urbana-Champaign	12

The 540 editorial positions are filled by 487 people, 447 of whom hold only 1 position. Ten people hold at least three editorial board positions (see Table 29).

Table 29 Faculty Holding Three or More Black Studies Journal Editorial positions (2008)

Faculty	*Number of Black Studies editorial positions*
Conyers, James L., Jr.	4
Aldridge, Delores P.	3
Cha Jua, Sundiata K.	3
Davis, Angela Y.	3
Guy-Sheftall, Beverly	3
Karenga, Maulana	3
Kelley, Robin D.G.	3
Staples, Robert	3
Williams, Lillian	3
Williams, Vernon J.	3

As Part I recounted, Black intellectual productivity was historically based in the Black community and manifested self-determination. With Black Studies as Academic Profession, this is not the only approach, but it is still visible, as Table 30 shows. Some journals are published by the mainstream and others by Black Studies or other Black organizations.

Individual campuses and Black Studies units have published journals. Important examples are *Black Lines*, associated with the University of Pittsburgh, and *Contributions in Black Studies*, associated with the Five Colleges, Inc.: Amherst, Hampshire, Mount Holyoke, and Smith Colleges and the University of Massachusetts. Neither of these are still being published.

Table 30 Contexts for Black Studies Journals (2008)

	Mainstream		*Black community*	
	Journal	Publisher	Journal	Publisher
Disciplinary	*Journal of Black Studies*	Sage International	*Journal of Afro-American Studies*	NCBS
Cross-disciplinary/ humanities	*African American Review*	MLA	*Journal of African American History*	ASALH
Cross-disciplinary/ social science	*Du Bois Review*	Cambridge University Press	*Journal of Black Psychology*	Association of Black Psychologists

Two other important publishing activities in Black Studies are working paper series and departmental newsletters. The former serve as a preliminary step to formal journal submission. Examples include those of Johns Hopkins University (Shell-Weiss 2007), and St. Cloud State University (n.d.).

Departmental newsletters promote scholarship and other program activities campus-wide and across the profession. Typical content may include recent faculty and student achievements, information about past and future programs, curriculum announcements, alumni news, and a statement from the chair or director. Particularly informative newsletters have included, among others, *Akwaaba* at Temple University, *The Drum* at Georgia State University, *Africana Newsletter* at University of Maryland, *CAAS Newsletter* at UCLA, *Vibrations* at UC Santa Barbara, *Nommo* at Purdue University, *Pan African Newsletter* at University of Akron, and *Afro-Scholar* at the University of Illinois. *Afro-Scholar* started out as a campus newsletter and grew into a national source of bibliographic references (1983–1992; see Alkalimat n.d. "Bibliographies").

ORGANIZATIONS

The three main African-American professional associations in existence prior to the 1960s were the ASALH (founded in 1915), the College Language Association (founded in 1937), and the National Conference of Artists (founded in 1959). The new organizational form of the 1960s was the Black caucus in a mainstream organization. This was widespread across the humanities and social sciences. Some of the caucuses became free-standing organizations that implemented a Black Studies agenda in a particular discipline, for instance:

1. Association of Black Sociologists: http://associationofblacksociologists.org/
2. Association of Black Psychologists: www.abpsi.org/
3. Association of Black Women Historians: http://truth.abwh.org/
4. Association of Black Anthropologists: http://aba.americananthro.org/

5. National Economic Association: www.neaecon.org/about/
6. National Conference of Black Political Scientists: www.ncobps.org/default.aspx
7. National Society of Black Engineers: www.nsbe.org/home.aspx

Of the three professional organizations within Black Studies, ASALH and AHSA have been discussed in other chapters. The NCBS merits consideration here.

NCBS became the main professional association of those established in academia in the decade following the rise of the Black Power Movement. The scholar central to its founding was Bertha Maxwell:

> Bertha Maxwell Roddey, often referred to as "Mother of the Black Studies Movement," was the person responsible for convening the group in 1975 in Charlotte, North Carolina from March 18 to March 21. This group had as its goal to review and analyze the structure and goals of Black Studies programs across the nation. A follow up meeting was held in July of that year at the Educational Testing Service (ETS) in Princeton, New Jersey. It was at this meeting, convened by ETS's William Harris, that the organization (NCBS) was created, with Maxwell elected temporary chairperson.
>
> (M.K. Asante and Mazama 2005, 359)

Herman Hudson, vice-chancellor for Afro-American Affairs at Indiana University, was instrumental in hosting the meeting to formalize the organization. The NCBS constitution was adopted by the executive committee, July 7–9, 1976, in which it stated:

> The purpose of this Council is to promote and strengthen academic and community programs in the area of Black Studies. The Council believes that Black Studies academic programs should include any subject area that has the World Black experience as the principal object and content of study. The council is composed of educators, interested citizens, and students who are committed to the advancement of Black Studies.
>
> (NCBS 1976)

The motto adopted by NCBS was "Academic Excellence and Social Responsibility." This slogan was originally created for a statewide Black Studies conference convened at the University of California, Santa Barbara in 1977, a conference that had brought together all of the major ideological tendencies in the Black Studies movement, including nationalists like Karenga and Marxists like Bill Epton and Bill Sales. The conference program chair, Abdul Alkalimat, had designed the conference to demonstrate what kind of unity was possible in building a foundation for Black Studies without ideological factionalism. The conference attracted scholars from programs at over twenty California institutions, as well as community-based participants from Santa Barbara and Los Angeles.

As a legacy of the militant struggle that had taken place at public institutions to create Black Studies, NCBS has been led mainly by scholars from public institutions. Different from ASALH, NCBS has not involved a high level of participation on the part of HBCU institutions or educators and librarians serving the community and K–12 educational levels. However, at the college level, it has been a great venue for networking and building relationships between faculty and graduate students on a national basis. This is crucial, as national meetings serve as informal job markets. NCBS has also been a major source of awards and public recognition of high achievement in Black Studies for students and faculty.

NCBS has given voice to both sides of the ideological debate between Black Nationalists and Marxists that raged in the Black Liberation Movement. This came to a head in 1982, when the conference in Chicago was hosted by the University of Illinois and the Illinois Council for Black Studies. Here is a report by Rhett Jones:

> The NCBS board, then dominated by nationalists, raised questions about the election. At the next annual conference, held at Berkeley, the NCBS leadership called for a re-vote to determine whether or not Alkalimat was legitimately the new chair. The meeting during which the vote was called was confusing and, many felt, illegitimate, but Alkalimat was voted out, a decision confirmed by the executive board, which later met at Princeton. Voting rules were changed so that the outcome became retroactive and Alkalimat would not become chair. This was rightly perceived as an illegitimate coup by leftists and integrationists. Some nationalists were also outraged. Many who did not see themselves as located in any particular camp thought Alkalimat had been unfairly treated. The careful work and unity that had created a strong NCBS was shattered by the board's action. Some abandoned organized Black Studies entirely, others left the national organization—now viewed as nationalist controlled—and concentrated their energies at the state level or on individual African-American Studies units.
>
> (L.R. Gordon and Gordon 2006a, 41)

State and regional organizations formed in New England, Missouri, Ohio, California, and Illinois as affiliates of the national organization. These were valuable contexts for networking between faculty in programs in close geographic proximity. The Illinois Council for Black Studies (ICBS) was a strong example of a statewide affiliate of NCBS. The founding conference was at the University of Illinois in Urbana on October 13–14, 1979. An opening panel included professor Joseph Russell, executive director of NCBS, who described the organization's activities and commended the formation of ICBS as a state affiliate. Perry Hall, at Wayne State University in Detroit and chair of the NCBS Curriculum Committee, and T.K. Daniel of Northern Illinois University, a member of the NCBS Accreditation Committee, described other NCBS activities. Delegates from sixteen institutions were at the meeting, after which the number of member institutions grew to twenty-three.

An important activity of ICBS was an annual meeting in the state capital, Springfield, with the staff of the Illinois Board of Higher Education. *The Chronicle of Higher Education* described the 1981 meeting:

> Here in Illinois, last month's meeting between the Black Studies council and Robert Walhaus, deputy director of the state board of higher education, was called in response to what Mr. McWorter, chairman of the council, described as a "statewide crisis" in Black Studies…
>
> After a lengthy and heated debate, Mr. Walhaus left the meeting promising to support a proposal for a statewide survey of the status of Black Studies. "I think I now have a better appreciation of the problems and potential role of Black Studies," he told a reporter when the meeting was over. "Their principal struggle seems to be one of gaining recognition as legitimate part of the academic experience."
>
> (Middleton 1981, 1, 7)

The utility of a statewide organization was expressed by Johnetta Jones, Director of Black Studies at Eastern Illinois University. Her program had survived a proposal to end Black Studies at the university:

> Fortunately, the Illinois Council of Black Studies (ICBS) was founded at the same time we were struggling to find a way to preserve the program. This statewide organization proved to be an invaluable resource in terms of creative ideas, potential guest speakers, grant expertise, and entry into a network of experienced Black Studies professionals. Utilizing the resources of ICBS and the opportunities provided by the February meetings in Springfield to develop and maintain a statewide profile with agencies and the state legislature, we implemented a major revision of the program structure. After two years of struggling and support from other ICBS schools undergoing similar reviews, the IBHE recently (May 1982) approved a recommendation placing the program's major back into a regular five year review cycle.
>
> (ICBS 1982, 31)

One of the major accomplishments of ICBS was the conference "Black People and the 1980 Census," which convened at the University of Chicago on

November 30, 1980. The census is the basis for mapping all electoral districts for local, state, and national elections, and for all federal and state appropriations. The undercount is a major issue. ICBS published a seven-hundred-page volume of the conference proceedings. The issue was clear:

> The main problem with the census is the disproportionate undercount of Black people and other oppressed people. After the 1970 census, the Census Bureau itself admitted that it missed 7.7 percent of the Black population in the U.S.—almost 2 million people, or about equal to the combined 1970 Black population of Chicago, Atlanta and Detroit. A similar percentage of Hispanics was missed. This compares with only 1.7 percent missed among whites. This statistical genocide, as it has been called, results in the loss of political representation for Black communities, and in a reduction in the amount of public tax monies that flow into cities with large Black populations. These political and economic losses are no small matter in the face of mounting social and fiscal problems facing urban areas, where 81 percent of all Black people lived in 1970.
>
> (ICBS 1980, 4)

ICBS was community oriented, convening, for instance, a 1984 conference on the topic "Black Studies and Community Development: Search for a Partnership." David Johnson, the mayor of Harvey, Illinois, who was also the Director of Black Studies at Thornton Community College, gave the plenary speech, in which he reinforced this commitment:

> We say that Black Studies should be about academic excellence and social responsibility. And when we speak of academic excellence, we are talking about challenging our students to become the best intellectuals that they can possibly be. That means they have to acquire skills, they have to develop critical thinking, they have to become marketable individuals in a technologically advanced society. That puts a premium on individual development and advancement. On the other hand, we say that these students must be socially responsible. This is a value orientation. I think this gets to the heart of what Black education has been about historically, that education must serve the needs of our people. Education must contribute to the community.
>
> (ICBS 1984)

CONFERENCES

The main Black Studies professional associations meet annually, with participation based on peer review of scholarship. A very important professional responsibility is serving as the annual program chair to direct planning for and implementation of the annual conference. This is often the role of the organizational chair or the chair-elect. The year's Black Studies conferences are ASALH in October and NCBS in March. A good example for NCBS is the 1982 conference (Henry 2017, 101; Alkalimat 1982). The largest NCBS conference to date, it produced a 126-page program and was summed up in six volumes of proceedings.

One-off conferences have also been organized to take stock of Black Studies. For example, the Ford Foundation has been a funder of Black Studies conferences since the 1960s. Table 31 starts with the first one in 1968 at Yale, as discussed in Chapter 11 (A.L. Robinson et al. 1969). The most recent major such conference was in 2006, an invitation-only symposium held at the Ford Foundation headquarters. These proceedings were also published, in a special issue of the *International Journal of Africana Studies* (Thomas-Houston 2008). The Ford-funded conferences of the 1990s were designed to move beyond Black Studies as social movement to defining Black Studies as an academic profession (Griffin 2007, 150, 153, 188, 197, 213, and 216).

Table 31 Ford Foundation Conferences on Black Studies

Year	*Host*	*Title*
1968	Yale	"Black Studies in the University: A Symposium"
1991	Michigan	"Reflections and Revisions: Twenty Years of Afro-American and African Studies"
1991	Wisconsin	"Afro-American Studies in the 21st Century"
1995	Michigan State	"Comparative History of Black People in the Diaspora"
1996	UCLA	"Race, Class, and Citizenship"
1998	UC Berkeley	"Conditions in the African Diaspora"
1999	Michigan	"Black Agenda for the 21st Century"
2006	Ford Foundation	"Conversations for Sustaining Black Studies in the 21st Century"

One of the best examples of a major conference is "The State of Black Studies: Methodology, Pedagogy and Research," a conference organized by the African American Studies Program at Princeton University and co-sponsored by the Schomburg Center for Research in Black Culture and the CUNY Institute for Research on the African Diaspora in the Americas and the Caribbean (IRADAC). It took place in New York City, February 6–8, 2003; key organizers were Howard Dodson (Schomburg), Colin Palmer (Princeton), and James De Jongh (City University of New York). There were 1,200 conference participants and 125 speakers in 27 sessions over three days (Alkalimat.org/eblackstudies). The pre-eminent measure of the value of a particular conference is whether or not the proceedings merit publication. Good examples of this are Yale (1969), Wisconsin (1991), Illinois (2004), and Ford Foundation (2008) (see Table 31) (Thomas-Houston 2008).

14
Theorizing

The ideologies of Black Studies as Intellectual History continue to influence Black Studies as Academic Profession: Pan-Africanism, Nationalism, Black Liberation Theology, Feminism, and Socialism (Chapter 3 discusses these ideologies). They have been translated into theoretical frameworks. But, most scholars in Black Studies use what Robert Merton (1968, 39–72) called theories of the middle range. This means conceptual explanations of a specific set of phenomena, rather than fixed, fully articulated theoretical frameworks spanning history and society.

Theorizing in US scholarship is typically grounded in a Eurocentric paradigm. In other words, the highest achievements of human civilization and culture originate in Greece and Rome, and their descendants remain superior to all other human groups (Kuhn 1996; Amin, Membrez, and Moore 2010; Blaut 2000). One can say this is the theory behind the institutionalized racism of higher education. Black Studies itself directly confronts this. That said, five particular ways that Black Studies has answered this assault merit consideration here: Names, Afrocentrism, Black Experientialism, Black Women's Studies, and more recently Black Queer Studies.

NAMES

Black was in many ways the received name for African-descended people (and also, for some time, South Asian migrants to the UK). Capitalizing the word was an early way to assert Black people's own culture and history. The naming of Black Studies reveals a complex of social forces and points of view in play. The names are in fact a conceptualization of the discipline, a way of theorizing. Our 2013 survey of Black Studies units found three names that reflect the US national reality: African American, Afro-American, and Black. Other names reflect a diasporic reality: Africana, African and African American, Pan-African, and so on. Diasporic names acknowledge the African Diaspora and sometimes also the different waves of arrivals from Africa to the USA. A third type of name uses the term "ethnic" or something similar and reflects a multinational reality. Multinational or multicultural names group African Americans in the USA with other immigrant communities and with Native peoples. Table 32 shows the variety of names of the 356 Black Studies departments, programs, centers, and institutes that were identified in a 2019 update of the 2013 survey of 1,777 four-year colleges and universities across the USA. Only four Black Studies units include people in their names: Carter G. Woodson, W.E.B. Du Bois, Frederick Douglass, and St. Clair Drake. (This survey examined teaching units, not research units or cultural centers.)

Table 32 Names of 356 Black Studies Units, as of 2019

Africa and African American Studies
Africa and the African Diaspora
African American and African Diaspora Studies
African American and African Studies
African American and Africana Studies
African American and Diaspora Studies
African American Studies
African American Studies and American Cultural Studies
African American/African Women's Studies and History
African and African American Studies
African and African Diaspora Studies
African and Africana Studies
African and Black Diaspora Studies
African and Diaspora Studies
African Diaspora and the World
African Diaspora Studies
African Studies and the African Diaspora
African, African American, and Diaspora Studies
African, Black, and Caribbean Studies
African/African American Studies
Africana/Black Studies
Africana and African American Studies
Africana and Black Studies
Africana and Latin American Studies
Africana and Latino Studies
Africana and Puerto Rican/Latino Studies
Africana Studies
Africana-World Studies
Africology and African American Studies
Afroamerican and African Studies
Afro-American Studies
American Cultural Studies
American Ethnic Studies
American Multicultural Studies
American Studies
American Studies and Ethnicity
Black and Latino Studies
Black Studies
Black Studies/Africana Studies
Black World Studies
Comparative Race and Ethnic Studies
Critical Race and Ethnic Studies

Critical Race, Gender, and Sexuality Studies
Culture, Race, and Ethnicity
Cultures, Societies, and Global Studies
Diversity and Gender Studies
Diversity, Culture and Inclusion
Ethnic and Cultural Studies
Ethnic and Gender Studies
Ethnic and Racial Studies
Ethnic and Women's Studies
Ethnic Studies
Gender, Race, and Identity
Global African Studies
Global Studies
History, Languages, Critical Race and Women's Studies
Indigenous, Race, and Ethnic Studies
Intercultural and Anthropological Studies
Intercultural Studies
Interdisciplinary Studies
Languages, Cultures, and Race
Multicultural and Gender Studies Program
Pan African Studies
Race and Ethnic Studies
Race, Ethnicity, and Migration Studies
Social and Cultural Studies
Studies in Race, Colonialism, and Diaspora
Transnational Studies

Table 33 shows that, as of 2019, diasporic and national unit names or identities dominated. Diasporic names are the most common in the Northeast (71 percent) and least common in the West (32 percent). This suggests a connection with recent African immigration into those states. By a slight margin, the South is the most likely to have units with national names (30 percent). Units in the West are most likely to have multinational names (45 percent). This suggests a connection with the larger Latino and Asian-American populations in those states. Units in private colleges and universities are slightly more likely to have diasporic names (59 percent versus 54 percent) and those in public colleges are slightly more likely to have multinational names (20 percent versus 16 percent). Unit names and identity do not show any strong patterns that correlate with the size of the college or university.

Regional differences exist with respect to the naming of Black Studies units. Those in New York are more likely to have a Diasporic name (71 percent). This reflects the West Indian and African populations of the state. California's Black Studies units are more likely to have a multinational name (46 percent). This reflects the Latino and Asian American populations of the state. These names also reflect the campus and community alliances that pushed Black Studies into the academy and defended it there. A good example is the San Francisco State University Third World Liberation Front.

Table 33 Black Studies Units by Type of Name and Region, Ownership, and Size

	N	*Diasporic*	*National*	*Multinational*
By region				
Midwest	101	49%	28%	24%
Northeast	99	71%	22%	7%
South	90	66%	30%	4%
West	66	32%	23%	45%
By ownership				
Private	146	59%	25%	16%
Public	210	54%	27%	20%
By size				
Large	186	55%	28%	17%
Medium	100	52%	24%	24%
Small	66	64%	21%	15%
Very Small	4	75%	25%	0%
All	356	56%	26%	18%

Note: Diasporic are those programs called Africana, African and African American, Pan-African, and similar; national are those programs called African American, Black, and similar; multinational are those programs called Ethnic and similar.

Source: Data from 2019; methodology explained below Table 20, on page [198].

AFROCENTRISM

The main theoretical contention in Black Studies is between two contrasting paradigms: Afrocentrism and Black Experientialism. Each of these contains various theoretical positions and research practices. But the bulk of Black Studies research does not proclaim allegiance to any one dogma. These two alternatives in essence serve as guides for Black Studies practitioners—lighthouses in the storm of ideas.

Afrocentrism is the theoretical position that counter-attacks Eurocentrism in search of a paradigm shift. It posits a battle of ideas advancing ancient Africa to contest the Eurocentric focus on Greece and Rome as sites of origin. A number of key scholars have advanced Afrocentrism. The debate has been intense, disrupting mainstream discourse in the field of classics and creating a school of thought in Black Studies.

Three scholars wrote the early texts establishing the basis for Afrocentrism: John Jackson (1907–1993), Chancellor Williams (1893–1992), and George G.M. James (1893–1956). Mostly self-educated, Jackson studied independently with Arturo Schomburg, J.A. Rogers, and Hubert Harrison in the library and lecture halls of Harlem in the 1930s. He focused on the African origins of Christianity, especially through a comparative analysis of the Egyptian *Book of the Dead* (also called *The Book of Coming Forth by Day*) with the King James translation of the Bible. Jackson wrote two introductory volumes on African Civilization (1970), detailing the origin of civilization in the experience of North Africans, alternatively called Ethiopians and Egyptians:

> A number of scholars, both ancient and modern, have come to the conclusion that the world's first civilization was created by a people known as the Ethiopians. The name "Ethiopian" we owe to the ancient Greeks. When the Greeks came in contact with the dusky inhabitants of Africa and Asia, they called them the "burnt-faces." The Greek word for burnt was *Ethios* and the word for face was *ops*. So *ethios* and *ops* became Ethiopian … The ancient Egyptians, as we have already noted, were considered by scholars of ancient Greece and Rome as Ethiopians.
>
> (J.G. Jackson 1970, 65 and 79)

Chancellor Williams did his undergraduate studies at Howard University and finished with a PhD from American University in 1949. His major work, *The Destruction of Black Civilization*, argues for a unitary understanding of African peoples:

> A Continent-wide study of the traditional customary laws of the Blacks, for example, enabled us to learn for the first time that a single constitutional system prevailed throughout all Black Africa, just as though the whole race, regardless of the countless differences in language and other locally determined cultural patterns, lived under a single government. A similar continent-wide study of African social and economic systems through the millenniums reveal the same overall pattern of unity and sameness of all fundamental institutions.
>
> (C. Williams 1987, 21)

On its face, this runs counter to most analyses of Africa, but it does express a great desire to find unity in the African experience and a basis for a common struggle against European and Arab domination.

James aims his book as a direct challenge to the argument that Greek philosophy is the beginning of rational reflective thought:

> This notion is based upon the notion of the Great Master Mind: Ye shall know the truth, and the truth shall make you free. Consequently, the book is an attempt to show that the true authors of Greek philosophy were not the

> Greeks; but the people of North Africa, commonly called the Egyptians; and the praise and honor falsely given to the Greeks for centuries belong to the people of North Africa, and therefore to the African continent. Consequently this theft of the African legacy by the Greeks led to the erroneous world opinion that the Africa Continent has made no contribution to civilization, and that its people are naturally backward. This is the misrepresentation that has become the basis of race prejudice, which has affected all people of color. (G.G.M. James 2016, 7)

He also makes an interesting point linking Socrates to the Egyptian Mysteries School. Socrates is known for teaching the idea that "The unexamined life is not worth living"—in other words, "Know thyself." James locates this idea as originating in the Egyptian Mysteries Schools:

> Self-knowledge is the basis of true knowledge. The Mysteries required as a first step, the mastery of the passions, which made room for the occupation of unlimited powers. Hence, as a second step, the Neophyte was required to search within himself for the new powers which had taken possession of him. The Egyptians consequently wrote on their temples 'Man, know thyself'" (G.G.M. James 2016, 88)

While Afrocentrism became a national theoretical tendency, two cities emerged as centers of this kind of theorizing: New York and Chicago. The foundational thinkers for the New York school were John Henrik Clarke (1915–1998) and Yosef Ben-Jochannan (1918–2015). Clarke was a product of a Harlem community education that included the mentorship of Arturo Schomburg (Clarke 1992, 1999, 2011). Ahati N.N. Toure sums up Clarke's contribution to Black Studies:

> One of the most brilliant scholars of Afrikan world history, Clarke possessed a prodigious, encyclopedic grasp of the global Afrikan experience, and was a fascinating and brilliant lecturer. During his 83 years he traveled Afrika and the world. A confidant and friend of Omowale Malcolm X; the author of the historic charter of Omowale's Organization of Afro-American Unity, an advisor to Osageyfo Kwame Nkrumah, editor of the legendary *Freedomways*, the journal of civil rights era activism, Clarke was an editor, writer, poet, journalist, and literary critic, a political activist and revolutionary, a Pan Afrikan nationalist, a formidable intellectual, historian, and scholar. He authored some 38 or more articles in academic, intellectual, political, and popular journals and magazines. He edited at least 17 books on subjects ranging from Marcus Garvey and Malcolm X to South African apartheid, slavery and the slave trade, and Pan Afrikanism and the liberation of southern Africa. He

> authored at least 11 books on topics ranging from poetry to Afrikan world history and Afrikan liberation struggle.
>
> (Toure, cited in J.L. Conyers and Thompson 2004, 7)

After an appointment at Cornell University (1967–1970), Clarke worked mainly in the Department of Africana and Puerto Rican/Latino Studies of Hunter College (1970–1985). The Africana Studies Library at Cornell University is named after him.

Yosef Ben-Jochannan, often referred to as Dr. Ben, was a close colleague of Clarke, sharing with him the position as the leading Afrocentric scholar of Harlem. He became a well-known community-based scholar activist, self-publishing many works that argued in favor of the main tenets of Afrocentrism, especially the historical contributions of Black people from the Nile Valley and Nubia, with a special focus on religion (Ben-Jochannan 1989, 1995, 2004).

The New York scene had other leading advocates of Afrocentrism, including Leonard Jeffries (1937–), Amos Wilson (1941–1995), and Marimba Ani. Jeffries earned a PhD at Columbia University and became head of Black Studies at City College of New York (CCNY). Wilson earned his PhD at Fordham University and also taught at CCNY. Ani, formerly known as the SNCC activist Donna Richards, earned her PhD at the New School for Social Research and taught in the Black Studies department at Hunter College (Ani 2014; A.N. Wilson 2011; "Leonard Jeffries Virtual Museum" 2007).

The Chicago school has been mainly based at the Center for Inner City Studies of Northeastern Illinois University. Key members include Jacob H. Carruthers (1930–2004), Bobby Wright (1934–1982), Frances Cress Welsing (1935–2016), Anderson Thompson (1932–2019), Harold Pates (1931–), and Conrad Worrill (1941–2020). Ife Carruthers describes their work, mainly their Kemetic Institute of Chicago:

> The Kemetic Institute, presently based in Chicago, Illinois, is a research organization concerned with the restoration and reconstruction of African civilization through scholarly research, African centered education, artistic creativity and spiritual development. The organization takes its name from ancient Egypt. The people who lived along the Nile River in Egypt over five thousand years ago called their country "Kemet," which means "the black city" or "the black community." These people who called themselves "Kemites," which means "the black people," developed the world's first civilization. The Kemetic Institute grew out of the organizational and scholarly efforts of what may be called the "Chicago Group," this being a group of African centered thinkers, which included Dr. Anderson Thompson, Dr. Harold Pates, Lorenzo Martin and Dr. Bobby Wright among others. Prior to the establishment of the Kemetic Institute, this group had launched the

> Communiversity, the Association of African Historians and the Association of Afro-American Educators. It had also published four issues of the *Afrocentric World Review*. The first discrete entity that led directly to the development of the Kemetic Institute was its research component, which was founded by Dr. Jacob Carruthers, Brother A. Josef Ben Levi, Dr. Anderson Thompson and Dr. Conrad Worrill in 1978. Shortly afterwards, Ms. Deidre Wimby, then a Ph.D. candidate in Egyptology at the University of Chicago, joined the group. Dr. Carruthers, a political scientist, historian and Egyptologist, became the founding director. He had long been concerned with the need for a scholarly research organization which would not only revitalize and reconstruct African history and culture but would serve as a reservoir for preserving and continuing the work begun by great black scholars during the 18th and 19th centuries.
>
> (I. Carruthers n.d.)

The current national leaders for Afrocentric theory are Maulana Karenga (1941–), based in Los Angeles, and Molefe Asante (1942–), based in Philadelphia.

Maulana Karenga (born Ron Everett, 1941) earned his BA and MA from UCLA, his first PhD from United States International University (1976), and his second from the University of Southern California (1994). While maintaining a controversial activist role in the Black Liberation Movement, he became the chair of the Department of Africana Studies at California State University at Long Beach, after teaching at several Black Studies programs. Karenga has been a major influence in promoting the Afrocentric framework within the NCBS and in Black Nationalist circles generally (M.K. Asante 2009).

Karenga's main contribution to Black thought is the creation of an ideological framework and associated cultural practices. More specifically, he has put forth three main innovations: Maat, Nguzo Saba, and Kwanzaa. To do this Karenga immersed himself in traditional African culture through the mastery of two African languages, in particular Kiswahili and Zulu. He contributed to the fundamental grounding of the Afrocentric paradigm by focusing in on the philosophical and ethical thinking of Ancient Egypt. His philosophical idealism is based on his interpretation of the ancient Egyptian concept of Maat. The content that drives this point of view is a prescriptive ethical system, more akin to religion than a scientific approach. Karenga posits a living meaning to this idea system developed in an ancient African society. In his study of Karenga, Asante makes the point that the teachings of an Egyptian King to his son provide ethical principles for the good life:

> Karenga, as a philosopher of ethics, advances an innovative approach to the study of ancient Egypt. He sees living documents as being important in a

> contemporary sense because they are vital, alive, and useful. He suggests in the end that we should emulate our ancestors and parents as instructed by the philosopher Kheti in his lessons to Merikare.
>
> (Asante 2009, 69)

Karenga formulated his approach to knowledge into his ethical system of the seven principles of the Nguzo Saba. Karenga expresses these seven principles in both Kiswahili and English:

1. Umoja: Unity
2. Kujichagulia: Self-Determination
3. Ujima: Collective Work and Responsibility
4. Ujamaa: Cooperative Economics
5. Nia: Purpose
6. Kuumba: Creativity
7. Imani: Faith

These prescriptive principles, formulated in 1965, were then used to invent the cultural practice of Kwanzaa in 1966. Kwanzaa is a cultural ritual that provides an alternative to the Christmas holiday anchored in Christianity and the capitalist marketplace. It spans seven days, with each day being devoted to one of the principles of the Nguzo Saba. This holiday has become very popular throughout the African Diaspora through the efforts of Black Studies programs and to a lesser extent the US government, which issued a Kwanzaa stamp in 1997 and then again in 2004.

The intellectual and cultural innovations of Karenga have become fixtures in Black Studies. He hosted a conference in 1984 that led to a new organization, the Association for the Study of Classical African Civilizations (ASCAC). This created a home base and regular meetings for Black Studies faculty and students grounded in the Afrocentric paradigm. Karenga has played a more general role by being one of the leading activists in NCBS. He has served as a member of the organization's national board, and has given more keynote plenary talks at NCBS meetings than anybody else.

His main academic contributions have been as a department chair working to formalize the organization of Black Studies and his authoring a textbook for the introductory course, *Introduction to Black Studies* (Karenga 2010). This popular text has chapters that cover history, religion, social organization, politics, economic, creative production, and psychology, and ends with challenges and possibilities. Each chapter has a different logic: the economics chapter, for example, lays out a series of problems and solutions, whereas the psychology chapter conceptualizes an approach to the intellectual history of the field. What it lacks in systematic analytic design it compensates for with insightful commentary.

Molefi Asante (born Arthur Smith) earned a PhD in Communications Studies from UCLA in 1968. He headed the Center for Afro-American Studies at UCLA from 1969 to 1973 and then chaired the Department of Communications at the University of Buffalo (1973–1980), before moving from Buffalo to Temple University to chair the Department of African American Studies in 1984. Having developed a relationship with the founders of Sage Publications, Asante helped found the *Journal of Black Studies* in 1969 and has edited this journal since then. It has been a major platform for Black Studies scholarship.

Asante is the most productive exponent of the school of Afrocentric thought. He anchors his thinking in intellectual influences:

> Three intellectual currents are directly linked to Afrocentricity: Negritude, Diopian historiography, and Kawaida. While each influenced the early work in Afrocentric theory, the development of Afrocentricity itself must be seen as linked to each one differently. Afrocentricity shares with Negritude its promotion of African agency, though Negritude was unable to deliver African centeredness. Afrocentricity and Diopian historiography share the same epistemology, but Afrocentricity is much broader in its reach in an effort to shape the discourse around the African world. Afrocentricity and Kawaida share the same epistemology but have emphasized different theoretical and philosophical methods. Kawaida is much more concerned with ethical aspects of actions than Afrocentricity which is more concerned with the structures that encourage moral decisions.
>
> (M.K. Asante 2013, 116)

He affirms his thinking about Africa by positing the origin of civilization in ancient Egypt. This is a fundamental attack on Eurocentrism:

> The first argument is that the ancient Greeks owed a great deal to ancient Africans. Indeed, Plato, Homer, Diodorus, Democritus, Anaxamander, Isocrates, Thales, Pythagoras, Anaxagoras, and many other Greeks studied and lived in Africa. (Asante and Mazama 2002). The other part of that argument is that the ancient Egyptians were black-skinned Africans. The proof had been given by Herodotus, Aristotle, Diodorus, and Strabo. They did not set out to make a case for the blackness of the ancient Egyptians to support modern arguments; yet their words are there to contradict the opinions of modern critics of Afrocentricity.
>
> (M.K. Asante 2013, 45)

Asante posits a three-stage historical development of academic study as movements: the Black Studies Movement, the Africana Studies Movement, and the Africological Movement. He sums up this last stage:

> The discipline of Africology is grounded in the principles of *Maat*. Those ancient African principles seem to hold for all African societies and most African people trans-generationally and transnationally. The principles of *Maat*, as recently clarified by Maulana Karenga, include harmony, balance, order, justice, righteousness, truth, and reciprocity.
>
> (M.K. Asante 2013, 102)

With several co-editors, Asante has produced three major reference works for Black Studies, grounded in Africology but of more general relevance. These include the following co-authored works: *Handbook of Black Studies*, edited by Molefi Kete Asante and Maulana Karenga (2006); *Encyclopedia of Black Studies*, edited by Molefi Kete Asante and Ama Mazama (2005); and *African Intellectual Heritage: A Book of Sources*, edited by Molefi Kete Asante and Abu Shardow Abarry (1996).

The headquarters of the Afrocentric school of thought is the Department of Africology and African American Studies at Temple University. Asante, as department head since 1984, has three particular academic achievements: publications that establish an academic literature for Afrocentrism; creating the first and largest PhD program in Black Studies; and organizing a conference of Africology called the Cheikh Anta Diop International Conference. This is from the call for papers for the 2018 Diop conference:

> At this historical juncture of our organization, we strive for the 2018 conference to be a critical reflection of not only the types of Afrocentric scholarship we produce, but an interrogation of how it is implemented in the world. We invite presentations that critically examine and reflect on what Africana Studies, Afrocentricity, and Diopian Thought will and should become, how they directly affect African people, and how they will continue to impact the future of African social development. We ask for scholars, educators, artists, and activists to highlight Diop's intellectual contributions that have shaped, expanded and enriched our various fields over the past 30 years, and to identify how Diop's scholarship can be extended to operate as a guiding force that will enhance the next 30 years of academic inquiry.
>
> (DISA 2018)

At least six additional scholars have made major contributions to Afrocentric theory: Wade Nobles, Asa Hilliard, Na'im Akbar, Ivan Van Sertima, Reiland Rabaka, and James Conyers. Ivan Van Sertima (2003) presented the argument that Africans were explorers of the Americas before Columbus, accounting for similarities in cultural development of the Olmec civilization and Africa. Asa Hilliard (1998) and Wade Nobles (1980) argued for a distinct African personality and educational styles of learning, anchored in their view linking the Black experience back to ancient African civilization. Reiland Rabaka (2006, 2011, 2016) and James Conyers (J.L. Conyers 1995, 2003; J.L. Conyers and Thompson 2004) have been the most prolific scholars, producing surveys and anthologies covering Black intellectual history from an Afrocentric perspective.

Followers of Afrocentricity began to unite. In February 1984, Carruthers and the Chicago school of Afrocentrism, along with John Henrik Clarke, Asa Grant Hilliard, Leonard Jeffries, Yosef Ben-Jochannan, and Maulana Karenga founded the ASCAC at the First Annual Ancient Egyptian Studies Conference in Los Angeles, California, at which Carruthers was elected the first president (J.H. Carruthers, Harris, and Association for the Study of Classical African Civilizations 2002).

There are three fundamental postulates for a general theory of Afrocentrism:

1. Egypt is the ancient origin for African and all of human civilization.
2. There is historical continuity to African identity throughout the African Diaspora based on this Egyptian origin.
3. Since then, fundamental differences continue to exist between Africans and Europeans.

In mainstream classical studies, Gerald Massey was an early defender of these theses, including that the Egyptians were Black. Martin Bernal (2006) has defended the basic theoretical propositions of Afrocentrism against their two main critics, Mary Lefkowitz and Stephen Howe (D.C. Moore 2009).

BLACK EXPERIENTIALISM

Afrocentrism begins by focusing on the Egyptian origin of the African experience, and from that perspective seeks to understand the Black experience across the entire African Diaspora from origin up to the present. The major alternative theoretical approach in Black Studies starts with the Black experience in the here and now, meaning at any specific point in African-American history, and then seeks to understand its relationship to all other human experiences. This was first named and elaborated in the 1960s as Black Experientialism through the work of the Organization of Black American Culture (OBAC) in Chicago (Alkalimat, Crawford, and Zorach 2017, 126–59).

There are two main uses of this theoretical approach regarding being and consciousness. One starts from consciousness to explain the Black experience, and the other starts from historical and social relations to explain consciousness. Some people have used both approaches, but for the most part Black Experientialist scholars have adopted one or the other exclusively. One way to compare these approaches is to categorize one as idealism and the other as materialism (Mao 2001).

The focus here has been on understanding the Black intellectual tradition. Henry Louis Gates Jr. begins his theoretical work in Black Studies with an argument based on an analogy between African and African-American folk wisdom, pointing to "how the vernacular informs and becomes the foundation for formal Black literature" (1988, xxii). He compares the Yoruba figure Esu-Elegbara with the Signifying Monkey of African-American folklore, and argues that Esu has been carried into the West by the Yoruba: in Brazil as "Exu," in Cuba as "Echu Elegua," in Haiti as "Papa Legba," and in the USA as "Papa La Bas." He argues that this is a pivotal African retention, "a sign of the disrupted wholeness of an African system of meaning ... recreated from memory, preserved by oral narration, improvised upon in ritual ... willed to their own subsequent generations as ... encoded charts of cultural descent" (Gates 1988, 5). Esu is the trickster, "the indigenous Black metaphor for the literary critic" (Gates 1988, 9). Gates matches him with the Signifying Monkey, "because of their functional equivalency as figures of rhetorical strategies and of interpretation" (1988, 53).

This is the beginning of several projects that emphasize the close reading of texts, a research strategy that seeks to establish a method for reading and valuing texts that can therefore constitute a canon of Black literature in general.

Gates became the pre-eminent entrepreneur in Black Studies via both television and publishing. He has led teams of scholars, technicians, and administrative staff in producing several nationally broadcast television documentaries on the global Black experience (Gates 2017). He has also monetized the use of DNA research for testing one's African ancestry (Nixon 2007). Gates has made a major contribution to the preservation of key texts by compiling many anthologies, including of slave narratives and of Black literature in general, as well as an encyclopedia with his close colleague Anthony Appiah (Gates and McKay 1996; Appiah and Gates 2005; C.T. Davis and Gates 1991).

In addition to literary studies that focus on culture and consciousness, there is a growing focus on Black religious belief systems and behavior. Major scholars in this area include James Cone (1969, 1970, 1975, 1991), Cornel West (1999), Cornel West and Eddie Glaude (2003), Dwight Hopkins (1999, 2005; Hopkins and Antonio 2012) and Cheryl Gilkes (2004).

The materialist tradition of Black Experientialism is rooted in social science. One of the early proponents of this was James Turner; as the long-time director of African Studies at Cornell, he made several summations of this position on Black Studies (Turner and Africana Studies and Research Center, Cornell University 1984):

> As a methodology, history in Black Studies constitutes the foundation for theoretical construction of an analysis of the fundamental relationship between the political economy of social developments and the racial divisions of labor and privilege, and the common patterns of life chances peculiar to the conditions of Black people … The theoreticians of Black studies use the basic social science concept of the sociology of knowledge to explain the legitimacy of the idea that the position of Black people in the social structure not only offers peculiar insights, but also represents a specific meaning about social truth. Furthermore, all knowledge is a perspective on shared experience.
>
> (S. Brown 2016, 171, 173–74)

The proponents of dialectical materialism represent the most explicit tendency of Black experientialism. They espouse an approach that links the particularity of the Black experience to the universality of class struggle and the national question, as developed in the tradition of Karl Marx. Examples of this tendency are Rod Bush, Clarence Munford, Barbara Ransby, Angela Davis, John McClendon, Stephen Ferguson, Manning Marable, Michael Dawson, Rose Brewer, Bill Sales, Sam Anderson, and Abdul Alkalimat. An important expression of this was under the leadership of Tom Porter, who led the Antioch Graduate School of Education and then Afro-American Studies at Ohio University. He recruited and worked with Jack O'Dell, Tony Monteiro, and Robert Rhodes, among others, during the 1970s and 1980s.

The most productive scholar in this Black Marxist tradition has been Gerald Horne. After earning academic degrees at Princeton, Columbia, and Berkeley, Horne became an activist lawyer and then went into academia as a historian. From 1986 to 2018, he published twenty-seven books. His work takes up five general themes, each listed here with a citation to one of his books on that theme: (1) biographical studies of Black radicals (Horne 2010); (2) the rethinking of critical moments of American history (Horne 2012); (3) communist activism's impact on American society (Horne 1988), (4) the fight for black liberation (Horne 1997); and (5) the connection of the African-American struggle to global social movements (Horne 2014).

Charisse Burden-Stelly insightfully summarizes what she calls the "Horne biographical method":

> What I am naming the "Horne biographical method" is a technique of interrogating, excavating, critiquing, and re-historicizing a crucial era of Black history, approximately bounded by the cases of Angelo Herndon (1932) and Angela Davis … On the one hand the Horne biographical method expounds the indelible contributions of Black radicals that have been largely excised from hegemonic narratives of the Black experience. On the other hand, it

> exposes the structures, processes, contexts, and conjunctures that have created the conditions for such epistemological and political exile.
>
> (Burden-Stelly 2017)

Horne has applied this method to the study of figures such as W.E.B. Du Bois, Shirley Graham Du Bois, Ben Davis, William Patterson, Claude Barnett, John Lawson, and Laurence Dennis.

Horne has called into question the usual narrative that the origin of the USA was in a revolution that charted a path for freedom by demonstrating that the US Constitution and the confrontation with the British was not going to liberate Black people. In fact, he has demonstrated that Black people were siding with the British, as they promised an end to slavery, while the USA was going to continue it (Horne 2012).

To counter the anti-communism anchored in the master narrative of US political discourse, Horne has taken up specific historical struggles exposing the contradictions and limitations of capitalist democracy. Two such examples are *Class Struggle in Hollywood 1930–1950* (Horne 1988) and *Communist Front? The Civil Rights Congress, 1946–1956* (Horne 2001). On the basis of such case studies, Horne has argued that the communist movement is a reflection of the organic historical aspirations of the US working class, especially Black workers. One of Horne's great strengths is that he is an internationalist and locates the Black freedom struggle in a global context.

BLACK WOMEN'S STUDIES

One of the greatest transformations in theory in Black Studies has been the development of Black Women's Studies. This body of theory in most cases corrects a gender bias in Afrocentrism and Black Experientialism. Black Women's Studies has seen a much needed end to two silences: on women's experience and of women's own voices. One, women participated equally in the fight against the institutional racism that led to Black Studies in the first place. Two, Black women had to battle the patriarchy that dominated Black Studies itself, as well as the marginalization of Black women in higher education generally.

Activism among Black women flourished alongside this as an expression of the Black Liberation Movement and as the academic discipline of Black Women's Studies. Black women began to form their own autonomous organizations. This became a battlefront led by Black women, usually in concert with other organizations fighting class struggles for Black liberation. Women fought against class exploitation and racist national oppression, but also against racism in the feminist movement and patriarchy in the Black Liberation Movement. Some of the organizations, the rise of which paralleled that of Black Studies as

Academic Profession, were the National Welfare Rights Organization (founded 1966), Black Women's Liberation Committee of SNCC (1968), Black Women's Alliance (1969), Third World Women's Alliance (1969), National Black Feminist Organization (1973), Black Women Organized for Action (1973), The Combahee River Collective (1974), and the National Association of Black Feminists (1976) (Springer 2005).

One of the important examples of the intellectual work done by these kinds of organizations is the newspaper published by the Third World Women's Alliance, *Triple Jeopardy*. This publication broke the taboo against openly educating Black and Puerto Rican women about health and domestic violence, as well as many other serious issues (Third World Women's Alliance n.d.).

Kimberly Springer sums up the impact of these organizations on what became academic-based Black Women's Studies theoretical work, and as such a major force in Black Studies in general:

> In general, I found that black feminist organizations as a social movement community did not succeed in achieving their main objectives: the eradication of racism and sexism. These persistent forms of discrimination, along with classism, heterosexism, and ableism, are still with us today. However, the black feminist movement was successful in initiating a process for thousands of black women who see the totality of their lives and resist white supremacy ills. Black feminist theory would not exist without the organizing of black women around their unique positions in U.S. society, and that theorizing has spread throughout the academy and into grassroots organizing.
>
> (Springer 2005, 169)

At a time of great Black feminist organizing, Black women were attacked as matriarchal authority figures in dysfunctional families. Social scientists were debunking such ideas, with the two leaders of this work being Joyce Ladner and Robert Hill, joined by Robert Staples, Carol Stack, Herbert Gutman, and Phyllis Wallace.

Robert Bernard Hill's case for the strength of the Black family (2003) summed up research and disputed the negative policy implications of the infamous Department of Labor report authored by Daniel Moynihan, "The Negro Family: The Case for National Action" (1965). Ladner sums up her study of Black girls and their families in the large Pruitt Igoe project in St. Louis:

> One of the major characteristics which define the Black woman is her stark realism as this relates to her resources. Instead of becoming resigned to her fate, she has always sought creative solutions to her problems. The ability to utilize her existing resources and yet maintain a forthright determination to struggle against the racist society in whatever overt and subtle ways neces-

> sary is one of her major attributes. Perhaps more than in any other way, the Black woman has suffered from the institutional racist impact upon her role in, and relationship to, her family. It has been within the family that much of her strength has developed because it is here that she was forced to accept obligations and responsibilities for not only the care and protection of her own life, but for that of her offspring as well. Still, under the most rugged conditions she has managed to survive and to offer substantial contributions to the society as well.
>
> (Ladner 1971, 282–83)

In this climate of the awakening of Black women's activism and related social-science-based activist research, the academic manifestation of Black Women's Studies began to take shape. Two foundational anthologies set the groundwork for Black Women's Studies: Toni Cade Bambara, *The Black Women* (1970) and Gerda Lerner, *Black Women in White America* (1972). These two works privileged the voices of Black women from the past, thus opening the door for legitimization for contemporary voices.

Ntozake Shange (1975) staged a dramatic presentation of the voices of seven Black women, poetry in motion, to make public the feelings and thoughts of Black women. Harley and Terborg-Penn (1978) issued the first anthology of original essays designed for curriculum adoption in Black Studies. Four years later, another important anthology, edited by Hull, Scott and Smith (1982), led to courses on Black women's studies. Two important works by Michele Wallace (1979) and Alice Walker (1982) directly confronted the patriarchy. Literary criticism remained a major focus in Black Women's Studies, notable examples being Carby (1987) and Christian (1985). Patricia Hill Collins (2000 [1990]) contributed one of the most comprehensive theoretical works (Shange 1982 [1975]; Harley and Terborg-Penn 1997 [1978]; Hull, Bell-Scott, and Smith 1982; M. Wallace 2015 [1979]; Carby 1987; B. Christian 1985; Hill Collins 2000 [1990]).

The three organizational initiatives that anchored Black Women's Studies during the founding years was the journal *Sage* appearing in 1984, published at Spelman, the Black women's college in Atlanta; a press, The Kitchen Table Press (founded in 1981); and an organization, the Association of Black Women Historians (founded in 1979). Spelman has been an anchor in this field, especially under the leadership of Beverly Guy-Sheftall (1992, 1995; Guy-Sheftall and Heath 1995). Also notable was a plenary session at the 1982 NCBS national conference, "Black Studies and Women's Studies: Search for a Long Overdue Partnership." The partnership between Women's Studies and Black Studies was clearly stated in the program notes:

> This is a difficult problem faced by two movements among activist intellectuals, the Black Studies movement and the Women Studies movement.

> Both of these movements are organized intellectual responses to oppression. However, both have been flawed. The Black Studies movement has been dominated by a male supremacist orientation in which the usual focus on women is on the Black family. Black history has been given a male bias. Women's Studies has a racist bias because it has mostly (or all too often solely) been "white" women's studies. This panel is designed to summarize and criticize these bad sources of sexism and racism. Further, as these times of crisis dictate, the search for unity between these two movements is our main concern.
>
> (National Council for Black Studies 1982, 4)

Participants in this NCBS plenary panel included Johnnella Butler from Smith College, Gloria Hull (University of Delaware), Florence Howe (The Feminist Press), Margaret Wilkerson (University of California Berkeley), and Victoria Spelman (Carleton College).

Two very prolific scholars have been key to Black Women's Studies. bell hooks has authored thirty-nine books, beginning in 1981, and Maya Angelou carried the autobiography genre to new heights as she authored hers in seven volumes beginning in 1969. Both of these women are consistently referenced on course syllabi.

BLACK QUEER STUDIES

On the heels of Afrocentrism, Black Experientialism, and Black Women's Studies, Black Queer Studies also launched into open discourse. Ready to be used in establishing this theoretical paradigm was the work of such artists and intellectuals as Alain Locke, Countee Cullen, Langston Hughes, Claude McKay, Wallace Thurman, Bessie Smith, Ma Rainey, Moms Mabley, Bayard Rustin, and James Baldwin. The leading scholar-activist who opened up Black Queer Studies was Audre Lorde. Her frankness became the new norm: "'I have always wanted to be both man and woman." Lorde declares in her Prologue to her novel *Zami*. "I want to enter a woman the way any man can, and to be entered—to leave and to be left—to be hot and hard and soft all at the same time in the cause of our loving" (De Veaux 2006, 54). Hers was a Black lesbian voice that inspired others to speak out about their thoughts and feelings, and their fears and sadness about omnipresent homophobia, including isolation and silencing, often in their very own families.

A major 2000 conference at the University of North Carolina, Black Queer Studies in the Millennium, was organized by Mae Henderson and E. Patrick Johnson (Alexander 2000; Brody 2000). It led to the anthology by the conference organizers titled *Black Queer Studies*, in which they state:

Despite its theoretical and political shortcomings, queer studies, like black studies, disrupts dominant and hegemonic discourses by consistently destabilizing fixed notions of identity by deconstructing binaries such as heterosexual/homosexual, gay/lesbian, and masculine/feminine as the concept of heteronormativity in general. Given its currency in the academic marketplace, then, queer studies has the potential to transform how we theorize sexuality in conjunction with other identity formations.

(E.P. Johnson and Henderson 2005, 5)

15
Norming Research

The foundational sustainability of an academic discipline is the productivity that performs its research agenda and feeds its curriculum. The research agenda for Black Studies has always had an anti-racist function: it combats the demeaning influence of mainstream scholarship and affirms the humanity of Black people. The key aspect of research in every field is a focus on methodology. Method in Black Studies has advanced a critique of mainstream scholarship. One starting point is an appendix to *Black Reconstruction* by Du Bois (1935): "The Propaganda of History." He confronts what he considers to be the main theses of a racist historiography concerning the Reconstruction period:

1. all Negroes were ignorant;
2. all Negroes were lazy, dishonest, and extravagant; and
3. Negroes were responsible for bad government during Reconstruction.

He then lays out the fundamental methodological perspective of a Black Studies critique of these kinds of racist beliefs that guide what passes itself off as legitimate scholarship:

> But are these reasons ... for denying Truth? If history is going to be scientific, if the record of human action is going to be set down with that accuracy and faithfulness of detail which will allow its use as a measuring rod and guidepost for the future of nations, there must be set some standards of ethics in research and interpretation.
>
> If, on the other hand, we are going to use history for our pleasure and amusement, for inflating our national ego, and giving us a false but pleasurable sense of accomplishment, then we must give up the idea of history either as a science or as an art using the results of science, and admit frankly that we are using a version of historic fact in order to influence and educate the new generation along the way we wish.
>
> (Du Bois 2007 [1935], 714)

For social science and sometimes beyond, the foundational data set is the decennial census that began in 1790. The history of how racism has been a factor in distorting and undercounting Black people in the US Census is a critical story that was thoroughly investigated by the Illinois Council for Black Studies in a conference titled "Black People and the 1980 Census" as explained in Chapter 13. These data are not only the baseline for social science scholarship, they are also used for all government appropriations and drawing the boundaries of voting districts. Undercounting people means less money, because government appropriations are based on census data, and less political representation, since political reapportionment of electoral districts is also based on census data (ICBS 1980; McWorter and Alkalimat 1980).

Another foundation stone for racist scholarship has been the use of IQ tests to argue fraudulently that Black people were mentally inferior as discussed in the introduction. A prime example of using IQ tests to allege Black inferiority is *The Bell Curve: Intelligence and Class Structure in American Life* by psychologist Richard J. Herrnstein and political scientist Charles Murray (1997 [1994]). This book was both highly praised and denounced as soon as it appeared. Much of the research it reports comes from South Africa and was designed and implemented to defend racist apartheid. The book's main errors involve mistakenly regarding intelligence as reducible to a quantitative metric and thinking of an IQ score as something one inherits, thus making the summation that Black and poor people are less intelligent. This is a form of biological racism that has been refuted many times over (Gould 1996; Kamin 1995; Graves 2008).

There were also sharp methodological critiques of two controversial award-winning books on the slave experience: *The Confessions of Nat Turner* by William Styron (2017 [1967]), for which he won the Pulitzer Prize, and *Time on the Cross: The Economics of American Negro Slavery* by Robert William Fogel and Stanley L. Engerman (1995 [1974]), for which they won the Bancroft Prize. These are two dramatic examples of how Black Studies scholars and their supportive colleagues have had to stand in opposition to badly flawed mainstream versions, fictional and non-fictional, of Black historical reality—versions that were honored! Both volumes were met with vigorous criticism. *William Styron's Nat Turner: Ten Black Writers Respond* (Clarke 1987) contends that Styron's novel about an iconic Black revolutionary goes beyond creative license in misrepresenting Turner's biography and historical context. Styron's book was a comment on Black people and the freedom struggle and was refuted as such by ten serious Black intellectuals. The Fogel and Engerman analysis uses quantitative data that leads them to minimize the impact of slavery on Black people. Critical works challenged this analysis, notably Gutman (2003).

In general, the methodological struggles that face all disciplines face Black Studies as well: quantitative versus qualitative, description versus causal explanation, gender bias, and storytelling versus analytical explanation. No one method ever completely dominates an academic discipline. The debate that sums up the diversity of research methods in a discipline is often the heartbeat of a discipline, forcing everyone to weigh the strengths and weaknesses of contrasting approaches. In fact, one can see this clearly in the work of such scholars as Du Bois, as he went beyond the social science alternatives of historical narrative and quantitative analysis of empirical data to include fiction and philosophical reflection (A.D. Morris 2015; Marable 2016; A.L. Reed 1997).

Another fundamental issue is whether to focus on the text, the person, or the event, and with or without the historical and social context. This points to the danger of creating a canonical set of texts, as these texts can take on a life of their own and elbow aside other works of value. In reality, these texts are historical artifacts of knowledge, and as such can only be understood in relation to their intertextuality—the texts on which they are based, the texts to which they are responding, and the texts that are subsequently based on them. This raises again the issue of whether the canonical tradition might be better thought of as the great debates that shaped the thinking of generations.

Now we must turn to the positive research strategies in Black Studies. A primary task has been to create a more accurate record of the Black experience, research that clarifies the very humanity of Black people. This has led to four major research activities:

1. Documenting the contributions of individuals
2. Creating major genre collections
3. Documenting major social institutions
4. Documenting major social movements

The publication of the collected works of key individuals has been a direct result of Black Studies. Table 34 lists some significant examples.

Table 34 Published Collected Works of Key African Americans

Scholar	*Editor*	*Institution*	*URL*
Frederick Douglass	John Blassingame	Yale	www.iupui.edu/~douglass/about%20fdp%20edition.html
Booker T. Washington	John Blassingame	Illinois	www.proquest.com/blog/pqblog/2014/Booker-T-Washington-Papers-Collection.html
W.E.B. Du Bois	Herbert Aptheker	U Mass	http://scua.library.umass.edu/ead/mums312
Marcus Garvey	Robert Hill	UCLA	www.international.ucla.edu/africa/mgpp/
Martin Luther King Jr.	Clayborn Carson	Stanford	https://kinginstitute.stanford.edu/

An equally comprehensive and overlapping activity is creating an archive of an individual's papers. Many institutions collect the papers of their faculty, and national institutions maintain special collections. Several major Black libraries/archives are noteworthy in this respect: the Schomburg Center for Research in Black Culture of the New York Public Library, the Vivian Harsh Research Collection of the Chicago Public Library, and the Moorland Spingarn Research Center at Howard University. There are also key websites that serve this function: Malcolm X (2020), Freedom Archives (2020), and the Marxists Internet Archive (2020).

On a smaller scale, usually in one or two volumes, there are anthologies that collect one person's key articles. In some cases, there can be many volumes, as in the case of C.L.R. James or Langston Hughes. On a related note, the main genre of Black intellectual production over the last century has been the autobiography and biography (Weixlmann 1990). Noted examples are Malcolm X (X and Haley 1992) and Maya Angelou (2019), who produced seven volumes beginning in 1969.

Another important act of scholarship in Black Studies is creating a genre collection. The first major such collection is Slave Voyages, or the Trans-Atlantic Slave Trade Database (Emory Center for Digital Scholarship, University of California at Irvine, and University of California at Santa Cruz 2018). This comprehensive data set has three parts: the Voyages Database, the Estimates database, and the Images database. One can access the data and carry out analyses. The next data set is the *Born in Slavery: Slave Narratives from the Federal Writers' Project 1936 to 1938* (Federal Writers' Project et al. 2001), which is now online at the Library of Congress. According to Library of Congress, it

> presents more than 2,300 first-person accounts of slavery and 500 black-and-white photographs of former slaves. Provides links from individual photographs to the corresponding narratives. Collected in the 1930s by the Federal Writers' Project of the Works Progress Administration (WPA), the narratives were assembled and microfilmed in 1941 as the seventeen-volume work entitled *Slave Narratives: A Folk History of Slavery in the United States, from Interviews with Former Slaves.*
>
> (Federal Writers' Project et al. 2001)

Examples of campus-based genre collections include the National Negro Convention Movement collection based at the University of Delaware, under the leadership of P. Gabrielle Foreman and Jim Casey (n.d.; see also Foreman, Casey, and Patterson 2021); The Project on the History of Black Writing under the leadership of Maryemma Graham (2013) at the University of Kansas; the Harvard Hiphop Archive & Research Institute under the leadership of Marcyliena Morgan (n.d.); the Black Press Research Collective at Purdue University under the direction of Kim Gallon (n.d.); and the African-American Religion:

A Documentary History Project, created by Albert Raboteau and David Wills, located at Amherst College (Raboteau and Wills n.d.).

Another key research focus is on social movements. A general source is the Freedom Archives, based in California (Freedom Archives 2020). The Civil Rights Movement is documented by organization, by location, and by campaign (www.crmvet.org/; http://mscivilrightsveterans.com/index.html). Movement veterans have done much of this archival work, with good examples being the archives of SNCC (https://snccdigital.org/; Chicago SNCC n.d.), the Black Panther Party (http://guides.osu.edu/blackpantherparty/archives), and the Marxist Internet Archive (https://web.stanford.edu/group/blackpanthers/index.shtml).

There continues to be an outpouring of excellent research on the role of Black women in the radical Black tradition. Bay et al. (2015) and Morris et al. (2017) are two anthologies that give a comprehensive overview. Blain (2018) and Taylor (2017) study the role of women in Black Nationalist movements, especially the UNIA and the Nation of Islam. Davies (2008), McDuffie (2011), and Gilyard (2017) focus on the Black women who played leading roles in the Communist Party USA. Women in the Civil Rights Movement, especially SNCC, are the subject of Crawford (2008), Lefever (2005), and Holsaert et al. (2010). Farmer (2017), Spencer (2016), and Phelps (2013) examine the role of women in various aspects of the Black Power Movement.

The material results of research begin with data and, as demonstrated, there is research that is fundamentally establishing a data foundation for Black Studies research. The key for sustaining this data production is method. Writing from an Afrocentric perspective, Serie McDougal produced a textbook titled *Research Methods in Africana Studies* (2014). This is an important book, because it makes a distinction between a paradigm and empirical research methodology. In other words, McDougal declares his affinity with Afrocentricity, but tries to avoid being ideologically biased in terms of research methods. He is clear that the assumptions of a paradigm are at a high level of abstraction. He refers to Thomas Kuhn for his definition of a paradigm: "A paradigm … in a practical sense is a systematic arrangement of explanations and ideas that guide policy and action" (McDougal 2014, 32). McDougal points to what he calls a basic assumption of the Afrocentric paradigm, including this critical point: "The fundamental substance of all reality is spirit, and not everything that is important is measurable" (2014, 37). Furthermore, he makes a distinction between methodology and method. His focus on method is about the techniques of collecting and analyzing data, while he considers methodology to be more broadly the link between paradigm and method as technique. Moving on to theory, McDougal defines it as the summation of patterns found in the concepts that define data. He attempts to be inclusive of what he considers the theoretical diversity in Africana Studies. He names fifteen paradigms and forty-two theories (McDougal 2014, 30–79). He surveys the key elements of research method, including research design and sampling, surveys and experiments, and quantitative and qualitative techniques. Another valuable work is Conyers (2016), which presents multiple views on the use of qualitative methods in Black Studies.

The use of digital technology has been an important innovation in method. Table 35 lays out the D-7 method, which incorporates digitization and difference into its model of Black Studies methodology.

Table 35 The D7 Method

D1. Definition	Defining the problem, summing up the relevant literature, formulating the research question and/or hypothesis
D2. Data	Operationalizing the variables, drawing a population sample, collecting data regarding the variables
D3. Digitization	Inputting, scanning, otherwise putting the data on a computer, organizing in a useful way
D4. Discovery	Analyzing the data to test the hypothesis or answer the research question
D5. Design	Laying out the data and analysis in text, tables, and figures to convey the findings to various audiences
D6. Dissemination	Sharing the findings with the various audiences as widely and effectively as possible
D7. Difference	Using the research to make a difference in your research community or the larger world

Black Studies has made major strides in all the disciplines covered in Chapter 1. This is not the place for a complete treatment of each discipline, but the mention of a few scholars makes the point. These are only examples of a much larger list than can be included here: Kehinde Andrews, Richard Benson, Keisha Blain, Charisse Burden-Stelly, Romi Crawford, Keona K. Ervin, Jonathan Fenderson, Eddie Glaude, Juliet Hooker, Ibram X. Kendi, Keisha Lindsay, Toussaint Losier, Tiya Miles, Russell Rickford, C. Riley Snorton, Robyn Spencer, Sandra Staton-Taiwo, Paul K. Taylor, Christopher M. Tinson, and Belinda Deneed Wallace.

SUMMARY

The most important historical development is that Black Studies is now a permanent part of the landscape of higher education. Part III has charted the process of its becoming an academic profession: the politics of origin, building a consensus, the processes of institutionalization and of professionalization, theorizing about and within the discipline, and norming research. This part of the book has summed up the institutionalization of Black Studies as academic profession by demonstrating its mastery of the norms of higher education. This includes meeting standards regarding faculty, leadership, curriculum, administrative structure, program and cultural activities, and funding for sustainability.

The full professionalization on a national level developed in journals, organizations, and institutions that granted the PhD in Black Studies. There is still work to do: Black Studies programs, especially the institutions granting the PhD degree, have not yet solidified the practice of hiring scholars with PhDs in Black Studies.

At the same time, on a general level, Black Studies is a leading path for hiring African-American faculty into many other disciplines. This establishes Black Studies as an affirmative action doorway into higher education. This inclusion into higher education has resulted in Black Studies having a hierarchal structure that includes an elite, at both the institutional and individual levels. Black women scholars are playing a powerful role, but gender disparity continues to be a significant challenge for Black Studies as an academic profession.

Conclusion

This book advances four important arguments in this history of Black Studies:

1. Black Studies is an anti-racist intellectual and cultural activity that affirms the importance of the Black experience for American society, as well as the universal human experience.
2. Black Studies has always been based on the intellectual agency of Black scholars, community institutions, and social movements as the foundation of the radical Black tradition, linking research and advocacy, study and struggle, theory and practice.
3. Black Studies has been developed by intellectuals representing the middle class and the working class, within the relative isolation of Black social institutions as well as mainstream institutions of higher education and culture.
4. The primary audience for Black Studies knowledge production and cultural affirmation is the Black community, and yet its importance is universal, enabling its particularity to serve as a pathway to the universal.

The importance of this work is not only that it establishes a framework for summing up the history of Black Studies, but that this very framework can be used to analyze and sum up subsequent future trends in Black Studies as well.

This history of Black Studies is a critical extension of many important studies. It is fitting to reconnect with this literature in summing up its main arguments and findings. The book is organized in three parts—intellectual history, social movement, academic profession—and so with this conclusion.

INTELLECTUAL HISTORY

Historical change should always be viewed against and linked with historical continuity. We are reminded of this with that old saying "the more things change, the more they stay the same." Black people have always dealt with key questions: Who are we? Where do we come from? What is our social experience and why are we exploited and oppressed? What are our cultural practices that constitute our unique experience? And, most of all, how can we get free? Black Studies is the diverse educational practice that has developed answers to these questions.

This book anchors the historical origin of Black Studies in the first two generations of Black PhD scholars and their struggles at HBCU institutions in which they were forced to work because of racist practices that segregated the mainstream elite institutions where they had obtained their degrees. Bond (1972) traces the social origin of these Black PhDs to high-achieving high schools in the Deep South. Harry Greene (1946) published a survey of Black PhD graduates that included information on field of study, institution, name of dissertation, and date degree conferred. This volume identifies key scholars who did the first major work in fifteen disciplines that anchor Black Studies scholarship in the present and will likely do so in the future.

Broad surveys of Black intellectual history validate this, for example, Bardolph (1959), Banks (1996), Meier and Rudwick (1986), and Norment (2007, 2019). The first three take a chronological approach, either to Black intellectuals in general (Bardolph and Banks) or the academic discipline of history (Meier and Rudwick). They argue that Black intellectuals in each generation responded to the social conditions facing Black people as a whole and the prevailing ideas of the mainstream. Norment provides an extensive encyclopedia of scholars who have historically contributed to African American Studies. Many of these scholars fall under the main argument of this book that Black Studies had its origin in Black intellectual history. The analysis of Black Studies in this book combines academic scholarship with the agency of Black people in working-class communities, even high schools and social movements.

SOCIAL MOVEMENTS

Every social movement emerging out of the Black community has had an educational component that constitutes a development of Black Studies. The basic need has been to arm Black people with knowledge of their history and their intellectual and cultural traditions. Hale (2017) presents an analysis of the freedom schools in Mississippi during the 1960s. Payne and Strickland (2008) broaden the scope to cover other educational programs of the Freedom Movement. Rickford (2016) presents a masterful treatment of the schools that emerged as manifestations of the Black Power Movement.

This history of Black Studies lays out a comprehensive discussion of the educational programs in six movements that were manifestations of Black Studies: the Freedom Movement, the Black Power Movement, the Black Arts Movement, The New Communist Movement, The Black Women's Movement, and the Black Student Movement. The general mission for the emergent institutions developed by these movements was to arm activists with the knowledge and ideological consciousness that would bolster their ability to fight against racist oppression. The Institute of the Black World was a major example of this, as discussed by Derrick White (2011). The Black Student Movement, fired up by Black Power, was the social force that entered mainstream institutions of higher education after the assassination of Martin Luther King Jr. and demanded and won formal Black Studies Programs.

Two important scholars focus on the development of the Black Student Movement. Ibram Rogers (2011, 2012) provides a comprehensive survey of the Black campus movement (1965–1972), while Bradley (2003, 2012, 2018) goes deep into case studies of the struggles at Columbia University, Barnard College, and the Ivy League institutions in general. Again, these studies confirm that Black Studies in the 1960s emerged out of the impact of the Black Power Movement.

This origin story of Black Studies in the 1960s is about Black Power. The two most important studies of Black Studies at the moment when it became part of the mainstream of higher education have been thoroughly analyzed by Martha Biondi (2012) and Rojas (2007). Biondi builds a story by focusing on regional case studies: San Francisco State in the West, Brooklyn College in the East, Northwestern in the Midwest, and the HBCUs in the South. She reviews developments off campus in one chapter. Fabio Rojas combines similar case studies with national survey data he collected from Black Studies faculty. The basic argument of both authors is that Black Studies is a case of a social movement initiative forcing its way into a formal organization and negotiating a permanent place within it. The surveys of institutions of higher education reviewed in Chapter 11 present new data and confirm this basic argument.

ACADEMIC PROFESSION

This volume presents a conceptual model for the process of Black Studies becoming an academic profession and organizationally a formal administrative unit. This is laid out in six parts: social disruption, collectivization of a definition of a discipline, institutionalization, professionalization, the theorizing of a discipline, and the norming of research and evaluation. This analysis is based on case studies and national surveys.

Discourse that struggled to define and theorize Black Studies began in earnest in 1969 with conferences at Yale University and Haverford College. The Yale discussion brought together some of the initial academic leaders of Black Studies with mainstream scholars from elite institutions. The Haverford discussion brought together Black scholars who had entered the mainstream before the emergence of Black Studies. In both instances, the Black scholars were skeptical and cautious, arguing that their form of Black Studies-oriented scholarship, without the sharp cutting edge of Black Power thinking, was more practical and likely to survive in what was a hostile environment for Black scholarship in general (A.L. Robinson et al. 1969; Lackey 2014).

Funding has been and remains a major issue for sustaining Black Studies as an academic profession. The Ford Foundation was the key early source of funding, leading some to argue that it had a significant impact on how Black Studies developed. McGeorge Bundy, the Ford Foundation president, funded and participated in the Yale conference and indicated his intention to support proposals to advance Black Studies scholarship and teaching. Both Rojas (2007, 130–66) and Rooks (2006, 93–121) argue that the foundation's funding was a decisive factor in determining the direction of Black Studies.

Marilyn Thomas-Houston, working with Irma McClaurin of the Ford Foundation, convened a gathering of academic leaders of Black Studies to discuss the topic "Sustaining Black Studies in the 21st Century." The papers of this gathering were published in a special issue of the *International Journal of Africana Studies* (Thomas-Houston 2008). This volume demonstrates that within the broad consensus of Black Studies scholars a vigorous discussion continues, including discussions of gender and technology.

The academic experience of Black Studies is documented in a series of autobiographical reflections. Charles Henry (2017) Perry and Hall (1999), both veteran academics with a background of leadership in the National Council of Black Studies, have described their move from a traditional discipline to Black Studies. Houston Baker describes his initial struggles at Yale in navigating between white professorial arrogance and the submission of Black tenured faculty. There is much more that needs to be done in this manner. Gordon and Gordon (2006a) is a major collection in this regard.

In sum, the main thrust of this literature confirms this history of Black Studies in granular detail. The study and celebration of the Black experience, in opposition to Eurocentrism and racist scholarship, mainly by Black scholars and cultural activists, has been a mainstay of the Black experience for well over one hundred years. Though it entered the mainstream institutions of US higher education in the late 1960s and took on the name Black Studies, it had been in existence under other names long before then.

This history of Black Studies is but a prologue to the future of Black Studies. Much of the practice of Black Studies will be continued into the future, especially within the collective practice that has become normal for each generation. On the other hand, each generation is also part of the historical changes in society and will adapt to become part of the new future that is coming into being. In the case of Black Studies, different kinds of institutions will evolve new norms for teaching, research, and community service. This institutional context becomes a commanding influence on new directions for each Black Studies program.

There are at least five major global and societal changes to consider when thinking about the future of Black Studies. Each one is transforming institutions of higher learning at the college level.

1. Globalization
2. Technological revolution
3. Gender equality and diversity

4. State (police) violence versus social justice
5. Historical periodization

Globalization consists of major worldwide changes that have restructured economic relations, political institutions, and cultural developments. This has led academic disciplines in the social sciences and humanities to theorize and conduct research on a global scale. This produces a conflict with the paradigmatic norm of American exceptionalism. Is the USA an almost magical exception in world history? Or is it merely another case of social development, with similarities and differences with other countries, with global influence that has a beginning and an end like every other empire? This is also a challenge for Black Studies: to end a US-centric focus.

Globalization pushes Black Studies in the direction of Africa and the African Diaspora for theorizing and research (Manning 2009; Gomez 2008). At the time of this work, the demographic influence of globalization is bringing people into the USA from all parts of Africa and the African Diaspora. Parents from the African Diaspora who relocate to the USA have children who grow up being African Americans. This also corresponds with a deeper understanding that racist systems of colonialism are not just in the history of other places in the African Diaspora but in the USA as well. This is particularly true with the racist colonial and neocolonial practices of England, France, and Spain as compared with the USA.

The African Diaspora is a framework for understanding the great global influence of Africa in all areas of social, cultural, and technological development. Black Studies will increasingly work with Caribbean Studies, African Studies, Brazilian Studies, and Afro-European Studies. New insights develop about the origin of cultural development when comparing different peoples before, within, and after being in different colonial systems. This includes music, language, religion, family practices, food culture, and aesthetics in general. This development also contributes to a political understanding of possible ways to change the international systems of racist oppression. Students of Black Studies can add a global dimension to their national identity. A well-known political maxim will then be realized: Think Global, Act Local.

This global identity builds on the technological tools of the information revolution. Black Studies is being transformed into eBlack Studies, an activity primarily based on using digital tools operating in cyberspace (Alkalimat 2000, 2003; Everett 2009). The first critical stage is moving information into a digital form. This involves three main digitization processes involving discourse, scholarship, and digital representation of experience in general. The main barriers to be overcome include time and space, the ability to act and archive simultaneously on a global level.

In this new technological age, there are new values that can be embraced in order to stabilize a new normal. This transformation of the new digital political culture should involve the following:

1. Cyberdemocracy: this requires universal digital literacy
2. Collective Intelligence: this requires inclusion of all voices as uploaders of information
3. Information freedom: this requires universal access to information

Of course, this is an optimistic view of the future. The opposite view is that of George Orwell's *1984*, in which technology is a tool for surveillance and total control over the thoughts and behavior of a population dominated by autocratic rule. These two alternatives are present in the current struggle over the dominance of social media corporations like Google, Facebook, Microsoft, and Twitter in the fight for privacy and social justice.

There is today a revolutionary transformation of sexuality and gender. All major narratives of our historical experience have the weakness of being patriarchal and gender binary. This requires a reconsideration of all history. This requires empowering people who represent communities that historically have been silenced. Black Studies is challenged to do this, as are all academic disciplines. The women's movement, the queer movement, including transgender folks, are all becoming frontline activists to transform knowledge about the human experience, including the Black experience.

Another great challenge is the fight for social justice in the confrontation with state violence. The police in the USA began as a force to controlling slaves. Today, the police are still in the role of violent control over Black people. Public and private police forces kill Black people at the rate of one every twenty-eight hours (Eisen 2012). This has given rise to the Black Lives Matter Movement. In global terms, this has produced the greatest anti-racist social movements since the anti-colonial wars in Africa.

This state violence has both racist and class aspects. The main debate on the USA has focused on whether there is systemic racism pervading the entire country, with the violent expression of police violence and subsequent injustice in the courts. The symbols of racism and slavery, expressed in monuments that glorify the Confederacy, have been attacked and taken down, both legally, as in the case of the Mississippi state flag, or illegally by popular protest movements. This debate takes a focus on the US Constitution, the slave-owning founding fathers, the genocide against the native population by the settler colonialists from Europe, and the general history of segregation and racist discrimination in all areas of social life.

All four of these new developments lead to thinking about the general future development of history. Each of these factors disrupts our understanding of modern history and forces us to begin thinking about the future. In Black Studies, this has taken the form of an intellectual tendency called Afro-Futurism (Zamalin 2019).

Taking all of this together suggests that we continue to reflect on the development of Black Studies. This reflection will have to focus on at least five key questions as the historical development of Black Studies continues to be written.

1. Who is in Black Studies—faculty and students?
2. What curriculum is taught?
3. What research is done?
4. What community engagement is involved?
5. What is the relation between academics and activism for Black Liberation?

The main development for the future of Black Studies will be anchored in the battle of ideas against racism. As in the past, the social movements will be important alongside academic activity on campuses.

Appendix

Degrees Awarded in African American Studies by US Colleges and Universities, 1987–2017

	Bachelor's degrees			*Master's degrees*			*Doctoral degrees*		
	Men	*Women*	*All*	*Men*	*Women*	*All*	*Men*	*Women*	*All*
1987–1988	61	95	156	12	13	25	1	2	3
1988–1989	74	111	185	15	20	35	0	0	0
1989–1990	88	147	235	19	18	37	1	0	1
1990–1991	92	182	274	22	26	48	2	2	4
1991–1992	148	262	410	28	34	62	2	3	5
1992–1993	159	274	433	21	47	68	4	4	8
1993–1994	175	317	492	36	43	79	3	3	6
1994–1995	191	325	516	28	43	71	4	6	10
1995–1996	213	393	606	23	45	68	4	7	11
1996–1997	206	352	558	21	45	66	3	6	9
1997–1998	202	413	615	26	42	68	9	5	14
1998–1999	186	444	630	34	50	84	3	7	10
1999–2000	203	401	604	29	41	70	5	2	7
2000–2001	188	411	599	18	36	54	4	10	14
2001–2002	228	440	668	19	51	70	9	13	22
2002–2003	217	428	645	29	46	75	1	7	8
2003–2004	228	454	682	31	54	85	6	9	15
2004–2005	247	491	738	34	65	99	5	8	13
2005–2006	265	541	806	25	58	83	7	14	21
2006–2007	256	498	757	34	68	102	13	4	27
2007–2008	252	535	787	29	58	87	9	15	24
2008–2009	240	485	725	28	59	87	13	11	24
2009–2010	256	454	710	35	60	95	8	6	14
2010–2011	329	668	997	49	66	115	5	13	18
2011–2012	255	526	781	33	61	94	7	10	17
2012–2013	194	457	651	34	64	98	12	13	25
2013–2014	205	434	639	23	52	75	10	15	25
2014–2015	182	442	624	24	54	78	9	10	19
2015–2016	214	439	653	23	47	70	12	12	24
2016–2017	215	456	671	26	40	66	7	25	32

Source: From the National Center for Educational Statistics.

Bibliography

"1967 Newark Riots." May 2, 2018. Wikipedia. https://en.wikipedia.org/w/index.php?title=1967_Newark_riots&oldid=839311712.

Abbott, Andrew. 2010. *The System of Professions: An Essay on the Division of Expert Labor*. Chicago, IL: University of Chicago Press.

"About the Harlem YMCA." n.d. New York City YMCA. Accessed May 8, 2018. www.ymcanyc.org/harlem/pages/about.

Abrahams, Roger D., Nick Spitzer, John F. Szwed, and Robert Farris Thompson. 2010. *Blues for New Orleans: Mardi Gras and America's Creole Soul*. Philadelphia, PA: University of Pennsylvania Press.

Abramson, Doris E. 1969. *Negro Playwrights in the American Theatre, 1925–1959*. New York: Columbia University Press.

Adams, Russell L. 1963. *Great Negroes Past and Present*. Chicago, IL: Afro-Am Publishing Co.

"African Free School." 2018. Wikipedia. https://en.wikipedia.org/w/index.php?title=African_Free_School&oldid=832634088.

Ailey, Alvin, and A. Peter Bailey. 1999. *Revelations: The Autobiography of Alvin Ailey*. Bridgewater, NJ: Replica Books.

"Albert Cleage." 2018. Wikipedia. https://en.wikipedia.org/w/index.php?title=Albert_Cleage&oldid=838730784.

Albright, Thomas, Judson L. Jeffries, and N. Michael Goecke. 2013. "A Ruckus on High Street: The Birth of Black Studies at The Ohio State University." *The Journal of Race & Policy* 9(a): 23–52.

Aldridge, Delores P. 2009. *Imagine a World: Pioneering Black Women Sociologists*. Lanham, MD: University Press of America.

Alexander, Bryant Keith. 2000. "Reflections, Riffs and Remembrances: The Black Queer Studies in the Millennium Conference (2000)." *Callaloo* 23(4): 1285–1305.

Alkalimat, Abdul. n.d. "Bibliographies." http://alkalimat.org/writings.html#11bibliographies.

Alkalimat, Abdul. n.d. "History of People's College: Some Notes." http://alkalimat.org/209%20history%20of%20peoples%20college%20some%20notes.pdf.

Alkalimat, Abdul. n.d. "Soulbook." *Black Liberation and Social Revolution*. Accessed June 8, 2018. http://theblm.net/saladin/organizations/#sb.

Alkalimat, Abdul. 1975. "Introduction to Afro-American Studies." Chicago, IL: People's College Press. http://alkalimat.org/091%201975%20intro%20to%20afro%20american%20studies.pdf.

Alkalimat, Abdul. 1977. *African Liberation Support Committee*. Unpublished.

Alkalimat, Abdul. 1980. "Search for a Vanguard: A Series of Anthologies Covering The Black Liberation Movement in the 1970s (Volume 5)." Unpublished.

Alkalimat, Abdul. 1982. "NCBS 1982 Conference Handbook." University of Illinois.

Alkalimat, Abdul. 1986. *Introduction to Afro-American Studies: A People's College Primer*. Chicago, IL: Twenty-First Century Books & Publications.

Alkalimat, Abdul. 2000. "eBlack Studies: A Twenty-First-Century Challenge." *Souls* (Summer): 69–76. http://alkalimat.org/319%20alkalimat%202000%20eBlack%20studies%20A%20twenty%20first%20century%20challenge%20-%20in%20Souls.pdf.

Alkalimat, Abdul. 2003. *The African American Experience in Cyberspace: A Resource Guide to the Best Web Sites on Black Culture and History*. London: Pluto Press.

Alkalimat, Abdul. 2006. *Africana Studies in New York State*. Toledo, OH: University of Toledo Africana Studies Program.

Alkalimat, Abdul. 2007. "Africana Studies in California." University of Toledo. http://alkalimat.org/353%20alkalimat%202007%20africana%20studies%20in%20calif.pdf.

Alkalimat, Abdul. 2008. "The Academic Journals of Black Studies: A Preliminary Report (Draft)." Abdul Alkalimat. http://alkalimat.org/384%20alkalimat%202008%20draft_report_black_studies_journals_dec_2008.pdf.

Alkalimat, Abdul. 2011. "St Clair Drake, 1911–1990." 2011. www.stclairdrake.net/.

Alkalimat, Abdul. 2012. "African American Bibliography: The Social Construction of a Literature of Record." http://alkalimat.org/346%20African%20American%20Bibliography%20oct%2027%202012.pdf.

Alkalimat, Abdul. 2015. *Rethinking Afro Cuba*. Urbana, IL: Twenty-First Century Books.

Alkalimat, Abdul, Ronald William Bailey, Sam Byndom, Desiree McMillion, LaTasha Nesbitt, Kate Williams, and Brian Zelip. 2013. *African American Studies 2013: A National Web-Based Survey*. Urbana, IL: University of Illinois Department of African American Studies.

Alkalimat, Abdul, Romi Crawford, and Rebecca Zorach. 2017. *The Wall of Respect Public Art and Black Liberation in 1960s Chicago*. Evanston, IL: Northwestern University Press.

Alkalimat, Abdul, and Kofi Wangara. 1969. "Two Continents of African Revolution." http://alkalimat.org/337%20wangara%20alkalimat%201968-69%20course%20two%20continents%20revolution%20ALSO.pdf.

Allen, Robert L. 1992. *Black Awakening in Capitalist America: An Analytic History*. Trenton, NJ: Africa World.

American Anthropological Association. 1998. "AAA Statement on Race." www.americananthro.org/ConnectWithAAA/Content.aspx?ItemNumber=2583.

American Negro Academy. 1969. *The American Negro Academy Occasional Papers, 1–22*. New York: Arno Press.

American Psychological Association. 2014. "Albert Sidney Beckham, PhD." Accessed May 8, 2018. www.apa.org/pi/oema/resources/ethnicity-health/psychologists/albert-sidney-beckham.aspx.

Amin, Samir, James Membrez, and Russell Moore. 2010. *Eurocentrism*. New York: Monthly Review Press.

Anderson, James D. 1988. *Education of Blacks in the South, 1860–1935*, new ed. Chapel Hill, NC: University of North Carolina Press.

Angelou, Maya. 2019 (1984). *I Know Why the Caged Bird Sings*. London: Virago.

Ani, Marimba. 2014. *Yurugu: An African-Centered Critique of European Cultural Thought and Behavior*. Baltimore, MD: Afrikan World Books.

Anthology of Negro Poets in the U.S.A.: 200 Years. 2006. Washington, DC: Smithsonian Folkways Recordings.

"Anton Wilhelm Amo." 2018. Wikipedia. https://en.wikipedia.org/w/index.php?title=Anton_Wilhelm_Amo&oldid=832730530.

Appiah, Kwame Anthony, and Henry Louis Gates. 2005. *Africana the Encyclopedia of the African and African American Experience*. Oxford: Oxford University Press.

Aptheker, Herbert. 1969. "The Negro College Student in the 1920s—Years of Preparation and Protest: An Introduction." *Science & Society* 33(2): 150–67.

Aptheker, Herbert. 1971. "Black Studies and United States History." *Negro History Bulletin*.

Aptheker, Herbert. 1973a. *Annotated Bibliography of the Published Writings of W.E.B. Du Bois*. Millwood, NY: Kraus-Thomson Organization.

Aptheker, Herbert. 1973b. *Collected Published Works of W.E.B. Du Bois Annotated Bibliography of the Published Writings of W.E.B. Du Bois*. Millwood, NY: Kraus-Thomson Organization.

Aptheker, Herbert. 1983. *American Negro Slave Revolts*. New York: International Publishers.

Aptheker, Herbert. 1990. *A Documentary History of the Negro People in the United States*. Secaucus, NJ: Carol Publishing Group.

Asante, Molefi Kete. n.d. "The Pursuit of Africology: On the Creation and Sustaining of Black Studies." Accessed August 28, 2018. www.asante.net/articles/59/afrocentricity/.

Asante, Molefi Kete. 2009. *Maulana Karenga: An Intellectual Portrait*. Cambridge: Polity.

Asante, Molefi Kete. 2013. *An Afrocentric Manifesto Toward an African Renaissance*. New York: John Wiley & Sons.

Asante, Molefi Kete. 2018. "The Creation of the Doctorate in African American Studies at Temple University: Knocking at the Door of Eurocentric Hegemony | Dr. Molefi Kete Asante." www.asante.net/articles/7/the-creation-of-the-doctorate-in-african-american-studies-at-temple-university-knocking-at-the-door-of-eurocentric-hegemony/.

Asante, Molefi Kete, and Abu Shardow Abarry, eds. 1996. *African Intellectual Heritage: A Book of Sources*. Philadelphia, PA: Temple University Press.

Asante, Molefi Kete, and Maulana Karenga, eds. 2006. *Handbook of Black Studies*. London: SAGE.

Asante, Molefi Kete, and Ama Mazama, eds. 2005. *Encyclopedia of Black Studies*. Thousand Oaks, CA: SAGE Publications.

Association for Black Culture Centers (ABCC). n.d. "Who We Are." Accessed August 12, 2018. www.abcc.net/who-we-are.

Association for the Study of African American Life and History. 2017. "ASALH—The Founders of Black History Month: Origins of Black History Month." *ASALH: The Founders of Black History Month (Est. 1915)* (blog). May 19, 2017. https://asalh.org/about-us/origins-of-black-history-month/.

Asukile, Thabiti. 2010. "Joel Augustus Rogers: Black International Journalism, Archival Research, and Black Print Culture." *The Journal of African American History* 95(3–4): 322–47. https://doi.org/10.5323/jafriamerhist.95.3-4.0322.

Backus, Rob. 1978. *Fire Music: A Political History of Jazz*. Chicago, IL: Vanguard Books.

Bacote, Clarence A. 1969. *The Story of Atlanta University: A Century of Service, 1865–1965*. Atlanta, GA: Atlanta University.

Baker, Houston. 2006. "Black Studies: A Yale Story." In *A Companion to African American Studies*, edited by Lewis R. Gordon and Jane Anna Gordon. Malden, MA: Blackwell.

Baker, Lee D. 1998. *From Savage to Negro Anthropology and the Construction of Race, 1896–1954*. Berkeley, CA: University of California Press.

Baldwin, James. 1962. *Another Country*. New York: Dial Press.

Baldwin, James. 1964 (1961). *More Notes of a Native Son*. London: Michael Joseph.

Baldwin, James. 1995a. *Go Tell It on the Mountain*. New York: Modern Library.

Baldwin, James. 1995b. *Going to Meet the Man*. New York: Vintage Books.

Baldwin, James. 1998. *Baldwin*. New York: Library of America.

Baldwin, James. 2014 (1955). *Notes of a Native Son*. Boston, MA: Beacon Press.

Baldwin, James E., Steve Schapiro, John Robert Lewis, and John Karefa-Smart. 2017 (1963). *The Fire Next Time*. Cologne: Taschen.

Ballard, Allen B. 2004. *The Education of Black Folk: The Afro-American Struggle for Knowledge in White America*. Lincoln, NE: iUniverse.

Bambara, Toni Cade. 1970. *The Black Woman; an Anthology*. New York: New American Library.

Banks, William M. 1996. *Black Intellectuals: Race and Responsibility in American Life*. New York: W.W. Norton.

Baraka, Amiri. 1965. "The Revolutionary Theater." *Liberator*, July, 4–6.

Baraka, Amiri. 1966. *Home: Social Essays*. New York: William Morrow and Co.

Baraka, Amiri (LeRoi Jones). 1969. *Four Black Revolutionary Plays*. New York: Bobbs-Merrill and Co.

Baraka, Amiri (LeRoi Jones). 1978. *The Motion of History and Other Plays*. New York: William Morrow and Co.

Baraka, Amiri. 1984. *The Autobiography of LeRoi Jones*. New York: Freundlich Books.

Baraka, Amiri. 2016. *S O S: Poems, 1961–2013*.

Baraka, Amiri, and Larry Neal. 1968. *Black Fire: An Anthology of African-Americans Writing*. New York: Morrow.

Bardolph, Richard. 1959. *The Negro Vanguard*. New York: Rinehart.

Barnes, S. Brandi. 1996. "On Stage: Kuumba Theater's Comeback." *Chicago Reader*, October 31. www.chicagoreader.com/chicago/on-stage-kuumba-theaters-comeback/Content?oid=891932.

Baron, Harold M. 1971. *The Demand for Black Labor: Historical Notes on the Political Economy of Racism*. Somerville, MA: New England Free Press.

Basie, Count, Albert Murray, and Dan Morgenstern. 2016. *Good Morning Blues: The Autobiography of Count Basie*. Minneapolis, MN: University of Minnesota Press.

Bass, George Houston, and Rhett S. Jones. 2004. "Rites and Reason: A Theatre that Lets the People Speak." *The Langston Hughes Review* 19: 3–26.

Bass, Jack. 1978. *Widening the Mainstream of American Culture: A Ford Foundation Report n Ethnic Studies*. New York: Ford Foundation.

Bay, Mia, Farah Jasmine Griffin, Martha S. Jones, and Barbara Dianne Savage, eds. 2015. *Toward an Intellectual History of Black Women*. Chapel Hill, NC: University of North Carolina Press.

Bearden, Romare, and Harry Henderson. 1993. *A History of African-American Artists: From 1792 to the Present*. New York: Pantheon Books.

Beckles, Colin. 1996. "Black Bookstores, Black Power, and the F.B.I.: The Case of Drum and Spear." *The Western Journal of Black Studies* 20(2): 63–71.

Belgrave, Faye Z., and Kevin W. Allison. 2006. *African American Psychology: From Africa to America*. Thousand Oaks, CA: Sage Publications.

Bell, Bernard W. 2012. "Passing on the Radical Legacy of Black Studies at the University of Massachusetts: The W.E.B. Du Bois Department of Afro-American Studies, 1968–1971." *Journal of African American Studies* 16(1): 89–110.

Benjamin, Michael. 2010. "Sadie Tanner Mossell Alexander." In *The African American Experience: An American Mosaic*, edited by Spencer R. Crew, Vicki Ruiz, Joe E. Watkins, and Marian Perales. Santa Barbara, CA: ABC-CLIO.

Ben-Jochannan, Yosef. 1989. *Black Man of the Nile and His Family*. Baltimore, MD: Black Classic Press.

Ben-Jochannan, Yosef. 1995. *African Origins of the Major Western Religions*. Baltimore, MD: Black Classic Press.

Ben-Jochannan, Yosef. 2004. *Cultural Genocide in the Black and African Studies Curriculum*. Baltimore, MD: Black Classic Press.

"Bennett Johnson." n.d. The HistoryMakers. Accessed May 8, 2018. www.thehistorymakers.org/biography/bennett-johnson.

Bennett, Jr., Lerone. 1964. *What Manner of Man: A Biography of Martin Luther King, Jr.* Chicago, IL: Johnson Publishing Company.

Bennett, Jr., Lerone. 1965. *Black Power*. Vol. 21. Chicago, IL: Johnson Publishing Co.

Bennett, Jr., Lerone. 1969. *Before the Mayflower: A History of Black America*. Chicago, IL: Johnson Publishing Co.

Bennett, Jr., Lerone, IL. 2000. *Forced into Glory: Abraham Lincoln's White Dream*. Chicago: Johnson Publishing Co.

Benson, Richard D. 2014. *Fighting for Our Place in the Sun: Malcolm X and the Radicalization of the Black Student Movement 1960–1973*, new ed. New York: Peter Lang Publishing.

Benson, Richard D. 2017a. "Black Student-Worker Revolution and Reparations: The National Association of Black Students, 1969–1972." *Phylon (1960–)* 54(1): 57–78.

Benson, Richard D. 2017b. "Black Power, Education, and the History of the Peoples College – AAIHS." May 17. www.aaihs.org/black-power-education-and-the-history-of-the-peoples-college/.

Bernal, Martin. 2006. *Black Athena: The Afroasiatic Roots of Classical Civilization, The Linguistic Evidence*. Piscataway, NJ: Rutgers University Press.

"Biography of Ruth Winifred Howard." n.d. American Psychological Association Division 35: Society for the Psychology of Women. Accessed May 8, 2018. www.apadivisions.org/division-35/about/heritage/ruth-howard-biography.aspx.

Biondi, Martha. 2012. *The Black Revolution on Campus*. Berkeley, CA: University of California Press.

Biondi, Martha. 2014. *The Black Revolution on Campus*. Berkeley, CA: University of California.

Black Cultural Center. n.d. "Our Center: Black Cultural Center: Purdue University." Accessed August 12, 2018. www.purdue.edu/bcc/facility/our_center.php.

The Black Scholar. n.d. *The Black Scholar: Journal of Black Studies and Research*. Accessed June 8, 2018. www.theblackscholar.org/.

Blackwell, James Edward, Morris Janowitz, and National Conference on Black Sociologists. 1974. *Black Sociologists: Historical and Contemporary Perspectives*. Chicago, IL: University of Chicago Press.

Blain, Keisha N. 2018. *Set the World on Fire: Black Nationalist Women and the Global Struggle for Freedom*. Philadelphia, PA: University of Pennsylvania Press.

Blassingame, John W. 1973. *New Perspectives on Black Studies*. Urbana, IL: University of Illinois Press.

Blaut, James M. 1993. *The Colonizer's Model of the World: Geographical Diffusionism and Eurocentric History*. New York: Guilford Press.

Blaut, James M. 2000. *Eight Eurocentric Historians*. New York: Guilford Press.

"Blaxploitation." 2018. Wikipedia. https://en.wikipedia.org/w/index.php?title=Blaxploitation&oldid=842813947.

Bloom, Joshua, and Waldo E. Martin. 2013. *Black Against Empire: The History and Politics of the Black Panther Party*. Berkeley, CA: University of California Press.

Boas, Franz. 1899. "The Cephalic Index." *American Anthropologist* 1(3): 448–61.

Boggs, James. 1967. "Black Power: A Scientific Concept." *Liberator* 7(4): 4–7.

Boggs, James. 1968a. "The Final Confrontation." *Liberator* 8(10): 4–8.

Boggs, James. 1968b. "The American Revolution." *Liberator* 8(3): 4–9.

Boggs, James, and Stephen M. Ward. 2011. *Pages from a Black Radical's Notebook a James Boggs Reader*. Detroit, MI: Wayne State University Press.

Bond, Horace Mann. 1966 (1934). *The Education of the Negro in the American Social Order*. New York: Octagon Books.

Bond, Horace Mann. 1969 (1939). *Negro Education in Alabama: A Study in Cotton and Steel.* New York: Octagon Books.

Bond, Horace Mann. 1972. *Black American Scholars: A Study of Their Beginnings.* Detroit: Balamp Publishing.

Bond, Horace Mann. 1976. *Education for Freedom: A History of Lincoln University, Pennsylvania*. Lincoln, PA: Lincoln University.

Bond, Julian, and Sondra K. Wilson. 2000. *Lift Every Voice and Sing: A Celebration of the Negro National Anthem: 100 Years, 100 Voices*. New York: Random House.

Bone, Robert. 1986. "Richard Wright and the Chicago Renaissance." *Callaloo* 28: 446–68. https://doi.org/10.2307/2930839.

Bontemps, Arna. 1969. *Hold Fast to Dreams: Poems Old and New Selected*. Chicago, IL: Follett Pub. Co.

Bontemps, Arna. 1971. *Free at Last: The Life of Frederick Douglass*. New York: Dodd, Mead & Company.

Bontemps, Arna. 2003. *Black Thunder*. Boston, MA: Beacon Press.

Bontemps, Arna, and Jack Conroy. 1997. *Anyplace but Here*. Columbia, MO: University of Missouri Press.

"Books by Harper, Frances Ellen Watkins." n.d. Project Gutenberg. Accessed May 8, 2018. www.gutenberg.org/ebooks/author/345.

Boston, Thomas D. 1997. *African American Economic Thought*. London: Routledge.

Boston, Thomas D. 2005. *A Different Vision. Vol. 2. Race and Public Policy*. London: Taylor & Francis e-Library.

Boston, Thomas D. 2018. *Leading Issues in Black Political Economy*. London: Routledge.

Boykin, A. Wade, Anderson J. Franklin, J. Frank Yates, and Conference on Empirical Research in Black Psychology, and Conference on Empirical Research in Black Psychology. 1979. *Research Directions of Black Psychologists*. New York: Russell Sage Foundation.

Bracey, John. 1971. "The Graduate School Experience: A Black Student Viewpoint." *The Graduate Journal* 8(2): 445–51.

Bracey, John H., August Meier, and Elliott M. Rudwick. 1971. *The Black Sociologists: The First Half Century.* Belmont, CA: Wadsworth Pub. Co.

Bradley, Stefan M. 2003. "'Gym Crow Must Go!' Black Student Activism at Columbia University, 1967–1968." *Journal of African American History* 88(2): 163–98.

Bradley, Stefan M. 2012. *Harlem vs. Columbia University: Black Student Power in the Late 1960s*. Urbana, IL: University of Illinois Press.

Bradley, Stefan M. 2018. *Upending the Ivory Tower: Civil Rights, Black Power, and the Ivy League*. New York: New York University Press.

Brawley, Benjamin. 1937. *Negro Builders and Heroes.* New York: Van Rees Press.

Brawley, Benjamin. 1939 (1913). *A Short History of the American Negro*. New York: The Macmillan Company.

Brawley, Benjamin. 1967 (1936). *Paul Laurence Dunbar, Poet of His People*. Port Washington, NY: Kennikat Press.

Brawley, Benjamin. 1968. *Early Negro American Writers; Selections with Biographical and Critical Introductions*. Freeport, NY: Books for Libraries Press.

Brawley, Benjamin. 1970. *History of Morehouse College, Written on the Authority of the Board of Trustees*. College Park, MD: McGrath Pub. Co.

Brawley, Benjamin. 1971 (1918). *The Negro in Literature and Art in the United States*. New York: AMS Press.

Brawley, Benjamin, University of Virginia, Library, and Electronic Text Center. 1998. *The Negro in American Fiction*. Charlottesville, VA: University of Virginia Library.

Briggs, Cyril. 1966a. "American Neo-Colonialism #1." *Liberator* 6(10): 14–17.

Briggs, Cyril. 1966b. "American Neo-Colonialism #2." *Liberator* 6(11): 14–16.

Briggs, Cyril. 1966c. "American Neo-Colonialism #3." *Liberator* 6(12): 14–15.

Briggs, Cyril. 1967. "American Neo-Colonialism #4." *Liberator* 7(1).

Brody, Jennifer DeVere. 2000. "Theory in Motion: A Review of the Black Queer Studies in the Millennium Conference." *Callaloo* 23(4): 1274–77.

Brown, Jr., Oscar. 2005. *What It Is: Poems and Opinions of Oscar Brown, Jr.* Chicago, IL: Oyster Knife Publishing.

Brown, Jr., Oscar, Julieanna L. Richardson, and Paul Bieschke. 2016. *The HistoryMakers Video Oral History with Oscar Brown, Jr.* Chicago, IL: HistoryMakers.

Brown, Scot. 2016. *Discourse on Africana Studies: James Turner and Paradigms of Knowledge*. Brooklyn, NY: Diasporic Africa Press.

Brown, Sterling A. 1969 (1937). *Negro Poetry and Drama, and the Negro in American Fiction*. New York: Atheneum.

Brown, Sterling A., Arthur Paul Davis, and Ulysses Lee. 1941. *The Negro Caravan: Writings by American Negroes*. New York: Dryden Press.

Brown, Sterling A., and Michael S. Harper. 1980. *The Collected Poems of Sterling A. Brown*. New York: Harper & Row.

Brown, Sterling A., and Mark A. Sanders. 1996. *A Son's Return: Selected Essays of Sterling A. Brown*. Boston, MA: Northeastern University Press.

Bullins, Ed, ed. 1968. Black Theatre: Special Issue. *The Drama Review* 12(4).

Bullock, Henry Allen. 1967. *A History of Negro Education in the South: From 1619 to the Present*. Cambridge, MA: Harvard University Press.

Bunche, Ralph J., and Charles P. Henry. 1995. *Ralph J. Bunche: Selected Speeches and Writings*. Ann Arbor, MI: University of Michigan Press.

Burden-Stelly, Charisse. 2018. "Black Radicalism, Repression, and the 'Horne Biographical Method.'" *Black Perspectives*, August 22. www.aaihs.org/black-radicalism-repression-and-the-horne-biographical-method-2/.

Bureau of Labor Statistics. 2018. "Union Members 2017." US Department of Labor. www.bls.gov/news.release/pdf/union2.pdf.

Burley, Dan. 1944. *Dan Burley's Original Handbook of Harlem Jive*. New York: D. Burley.

Burroughs, Margaret T.G. 2003. *Life with Margaret: The Official Autobiography*. Chicago, IL: In Time Pub. and Media Group.

Bush, Rod. 2000. *We Are Not What We Seem: Black Nationalism and Class Struggle in the American Century*. New York: New York University Press.

"*California Eagle*." 2018. Wikipedia. https://en.wikipedia.org/w/index.php?title=California_Eagle&oldid=825461302.

Callahan, Mike, and David Edwards. n.d. "The Chess Story." The Chess Records Main Page. Accessed May 8, 2018. www.bsnpubs.com/chess/chesscheck.html.

Calloway, Cab. 1944. *The New Cab Calloway's Hepster's Dictionary: Language of Jive.* [New York]: Cab Calloway, Inc.

Calverton, V.F. 1929. *Anthology of American Negro Literature.* New York: The Modern Library.

Carby, Hazel V. 1987. *Reconstructing Womanhood: The Emergence of the Afro-American Woman Novelist.* New York: Oxford University Press.

Carmichael, Stokely, and Charles V. Hamilton. 1992. *Black Power: The Politics of Liberation in America.* New York: Vintage Books.

Carmichael, Stokely, and Michael Thelwell. 2003. *Ready for Revolution: The Life and Struggles of Stokely Carmichael (Kwame Ture).* New York: Scribner.

"Carruthers Center for Inner City Studies." n.d. Northeastern Illinois University. Accessed May 8, 2018. www.neiu.edu/academics/carruthers-center/.

Carruthers, Ife. n.d. "About Us: The Kemetic Institute of Chicago." Kemetic Institute Chicago. Accessed September 3, 2018. www.ki-chicago.org/about_us.htm.

Carruthers, Jacob H., Leon C. Harris, and Association for the Study of Classical African Civilizations. 2002. *African World History Project: The Preliminary Challenge.* Los Angeles, CA: The Association.

Cederholm, Theresa Dickason. 1973. *Afro-American Artists: A Bio-Bibliographical Directory.* Boston, MA: Trustees of the Boston Public Library.

Chicago SNCC. n.d. "Chicago SNCC (Student Nonviolent Coordinating Committee) History Project Archives." Chicago Public Library. www.chipublib.org/fa-chicago-sncc-student-nonviolent-coordinating-committee-history-project-archives/.

Chicago State University. 1990. "Gwendolyn Brooks Center." www.csu.edu/gwendolynbrooks/.

Chin, Elizabeth. 2014. *Katherine Dunham: Recovering an Anthropological Legacy, Choreographing Ethnographic Futures.* Santa Fe, NM: School for Advanced Research Press.

Chrisman, Robert. n.d. "Robert Chrisman: Poet, Author, Scholar." Accessed June 8, 2018. http://robertchrismanpoetauthorscholar.weebly.com/.

Christian, Barbara. 1985. *Black Feminist Criticism: Perspectives on Black Women Writers.* New York: Pergamon Press.

Christian, Mark. 2007. "Notes on Black Studies: Its Continuing Necessity in the Academy and Beyond." *Journal of Black Studies* 37(3): 348–64.

Christie Gonzalez, Mollie E. 2015. "Katherine Dunham Technique and Philosophy: A Holistic Dance Pedagogy." Dance Master's thesis, SUNY Brockport. https://digitalcommons.brockport.edu/dns_theses/4.

Chronicle of Higher Education. 2005. "Whither Black Studies?" *Chronicle Forums* (blog). May 12.

Clarida, Matthew Q., and Nicholas P. Fandos. 2013. "$15 Million Gift To Launch Center for African and African-American Research." *Harvard Crimson*, September 19. www.thecrimson.com/article/2013/9/19/hutchins-center-gift-launch/.

Clark, Jawanza Eric. 2016. *Albert Cleage Jr. and the Black Madonna and Child.* New York: Palgrave Macmillan.

Clark, Kenneth Bancroft. 1965. *Dark Ghetto: Dilemmas of Social Power.* New York: Harper & Row.

Clark, Kenneth Bancroft. 1988. *Prejudice and Your Child*. Middletown, CT: Wesleyan University Press.

Clark, Kenneth Bancroft. 1989. *Dark Ghetto: Dilemmas of Social Power*. Hanover, NH: Wesleyan University Press.

Clarke, John Henrik. 1976. "The African Heritage Studies Association (AHSA): Some Notes on the Conflict with the African Studies Association (ASA) and the Fight to Reclaim African History." *Issue: A Journal of Opinion* 6(2/3): 5–11. https://doi.org/10.2307/1166439.

Clarke, John Henrik. 1977. "The University of Sankore at Timbuctoo: A Neglected Achievement in Black Intellectual History." *The Western Journal of Black Studies* 1(2): 142–46.

Clarke, John Henrik, ed. 1987. *William Styron's Nat Turner: Ten Black Writers Respond*. Westport, CT: Greenwood Press.

Clarke, John Henrik. 1992. "The Influence of Arthur A. Schomburg on My Concept of Africana Studies." *Phylon (1960–)* 49(1/2): 4–9. https://doi.org/10.2307/3132612.

Clarke, John Henrik. 1998. *Harlem, USA*. Brooklyn, NY: A & B Publishers Group.

Clarke, John Henrik. 1999. *My Life in Search of Africa*. Chicago, IL: Third World Press.

Clarke, John Henrik. 2011. *Christopher Columbus and the Afrikan Holocaust: Slavery and the Rise of European Capitalism*. Buffalo, NY: Eworld Inc.

Cohen, Harvey G. 2004. "Duke Ellington and Black, Brown, and Beige: The Composer as Historian at Carnegie Hall." *American Quarterly* 56(4): 1003–34. https://doi.org/10.1353/aq.2004.0051.

Cole, Johnnetta B. 1999. "John Langston Gwaltney (1928–1998)." *American Anthropologist* 101(3): 614–16. https://doi.org/10.1525/aa.1999.101.3.614.

"The Combahee River Collective Statement." n.d. Accessed June 22, 2013. http://circuitous.org/scraps/combahee.html.

Cone, James H. 1969. *Black Theology and Black Power*. New York: Seabury Press.

Cone, James H. 1970. *A Black Theology of Liberation*. Philadelphia, PA: J.B. Lippincott Co.

Cone, James H. 1975. *God of the Oppressed*. New York: Seabury Press.

Cone, James H. 1991. Cone, Martin & Malcolm & America: A Dream or a Nightmare. Maryknoll, NY: Orbis Books.

Cone, James H. 1999. *Risks of Faith the Emergence of a Black Theology of Liberation, 1968–1998*. Boston, MA: Beacon Press.

Congressional Quarterly. 1968. *Revolution in Civil Rights*. Washington, DC: Quarterly Service.

Conot, Robert E. 1968. *Rivers of Blood, Years of Darkness: The Unforgettable Classic Account of the Watts Riot*. New York: Morrow.

Constant, Isabelle, and Kahiudi C. Mabana. 2009. *Negritude: Legacy and Present Relevance*. Newcastle-upon-Tyne: Cambridge Scholars Publishing.

Conyers, James E. 1968. "Negro Doctorates in Sociology: A Social Portrait." *Phylon (1960–)* 29(3): 209–23. https://doi.org/10.2307/273485.

Conyers, James E. 1986a. "Black American Doctorates in Sociology: A Follow-Up Study of Their Social and Educational Origins." *Phylon (1960–)* 47(4): 303–17. https://doi.org/10.2307/274626.

Conyers, James E. 1986b. "Who's Who Among Black Doctorates in Sociology." *Sociological Focus* 19(1): 77–93.

Conyers, James L. 1995. *The Evolution of African American Studies: A Descriptive and Evaluative Analysis of Selected African American Studies Departments and Programs.* Lanham, MD: University Press of America.

Conyers, James L. 2003. *Afrocentricity and the Academy: Essays on Theory and Practice.* Jefferson, NC: McFarland.

Conyers, Jr., James L., ed. 2016. *Qualitative Methods in Africana Studies An Interdisciplinary Approach to Examining Africana Phenomena.* Lanham, MD: University Press of America.

Conyers, James L., and Julius Eric Thompson. 2004. *Pan African Nationalism in the Americas: The Life and Times of John Henrik Clarke.* Trenton, NJ: Africa World Press.

Cook, Will Mercer, and Stephen Evangelist Henderson. 1969. *The Militant Black Writer in Africa and the United States.* Madison, WI: University of Wisconsin Press.

Cooper, Anna J. 2000. *Voice of Anna Julia Cooper: Including a Voice from the South and Other Important Essays, Papers, and Letters.* Lanham, MD: Rowman & Littlefield Publishers.

Cooper, Anna Julia. 1925. *L'attitude de la France à l'égard de l'esclavage pendant la Révolution. Thèse pour le doctorat.* Paris: Impr. de la Cour d'Appel.

Cortada, Rafael L. 1974. *Black Studies: An Urban and Comparative Curriculum.* Lexington, MA: Xerox College Publishers.

"Council of Independent Black Institutions." n.d. Accessed June 20, 2018. www.cibi.org/.

Cox, Oliver C. 1938. "Factors Affecting the Marital Status of Negroes in the United States." PhD diss., University of Chicago.

Cox, Oliver C. 1970. *Caste, Class, & Race: A Study in Social Dynamics.* New York: Monthly Review Press.

Cox, Oliver C. 1990. *Race Relations: Elements and Social Dynamics.* Detroit, MI: Wayne State University Press.

Cox, Oliver C. 2006a. *Capitalism and American Leadership.* New Smyrna Beach, FL: Oliver Cromwell Cox Online Institute.

Cox, Oliver C. 2006b. *Capitalism as a System.* New Smyrna Beach, FL: Oliver Cromwell Cox Online Institute.

Cox, Oliver C., and Harry Elmer Barnes. 2006. *The Foundations of Capitalism.* New Smyrna Beach, FL: Oliver Cromwell Cox Institute.

Crawford, Vicki L. 2008. *Women in the Civil Rights Movement: Trailblazers and Torchbearers, 1941–1965.* Bloomington, IN: Indiana University Press.

Cromwell, Adelaide. 1995. *The Other Brahmins: Boston's Black Upper Class, 1750–1950.* Fayetteville, AR: University of Arkansas Press.

Cruse, Harold. 1964a. "The Economics of Black Nationalism: Part One of Three." *Liberator* 4(7): 8–11.

Cruse, Harold. 1964b. "The Economics of Black Nationalism: Part Two of Three." *Liberator* 4(8): 8–9.

Cruse, Harold. 1964c. "The Economics of Black Nationalism: Part Three of Three." *Liberator* 4(9).

Cruse, Harold. 1967a. *The Crisis of the Negro Intellectual.* New York: Morrow.

Cruse, Harold. 1967b. *The Crisis of the Negro Intellectual: [From Its Origins to the Present].* New York: Morrow & Comp.

Cruse, Harold, and William Jelani Cobb. 2002. *The Essential Harold Cruse: A Reader.* New York: Palgrave.

Cunard, Nancy, and Hugh Ford, eds. 1970. *Negro: An Anthology. Collected and Edited by Nancy Cunard*. Abridged with an Introduction by Hugh Ford. New York: F. Ungar Publishing Co.

Dagbovie, Pero Gaglo. 2007. *The Early Black History Movement, Carter G. Woodson, and Lorenzo Johnston Greene*. Urbana, IL: University of Illinois Press.

Dallas Museum of Art. 1989. *Black Art Ancestral Legacy: The African Impulse in African-American Art*. Dallas, TX: Dallas Museum of Art.

Dalton, Karen, ed. 2000. *Department of Afro-American Studies, Harvard University: Thirtieth Anniversary Celebration*. Cambridge, MA: Harvard University.

Dance, Stanley. 2000. *The World of Duke Ellington*. New York: Da Capo Press.

"Katherine Dunham: Dance Technique." n.d. Missouri Historical Society. Accessed May 8, 2018. http://mohistory.org/exhibitsLegacy/KatherineDunham/dance_technique.htm.

Danns, Dionne. 2018. "High School Student Activism: Past and Present." *American Historical Association* (blog). March 14. http://blog.historians.org/2018/03/high-school-student-activism-past-and-present/.

Davidson, Douglas. 1970. "The Furious Passage of the Black Graduate Student." *Berkeley Journal of Sociology* 15: 192–211.

Davies, Carole Boyce. 2008. *Left of Karl Marx: The Political Life of Black Communist Claudia Jones*. Durham, NC: Duke University Press.

Davies, Carol Boyce. 2018. "The Persistence of Institutional Sexism in Africana Studies." *Black Perspectives: African American Intellectual History Society* (blog). September 12. www.aaihs.org/the-persistence-of-institutional-sexism-in-africana-studies/.

Davis, Allison. 1948. *Social-Class Influences upon Learning*. Cambridge, MA: Harvard University Press.

Davis, Allison. 1983. *Leadership, Love, and Aggression*. San Diego, CA: Harcourt Brace Jovanovich.

Davis, Allison, John Dollard, American Council on Education, and American Youth Commission. 1940. *Children of Bondage: The Personality Development of Negro Youth in the Urban South*. Washington, DC: American Council on Education.

Davis, Allison, Burleigh B. Gardner, Mary R. Gardner, and W. Lloyd Warner. 1941. *Deep South: A Social Anthropological Study of Caste and Class*. Chicago, IL: University of Chicago Press.

Davis, Arthur P., Jay Saunders Redding, and Joyce Ann Joyce. 1992. *The New Cavalcade African American Writing from 1760 to the Present*. Washington, DC: Howard University Press.

Davis, Benjamin J. 1969. *Communist Councilman from Harlem: Autobiographical Notes Written in a Federal Penitentiary*. New York: International Publishers.

Davis, Charles T., and Henry L. Gates. 1991. *The Slave's Narrative*. Oxford: Oxford University Press.

Davis, John Preston. 1966. *The American Negro Reference Book*. Yonkers, NY: Educational Heritage.

Dawson, Michael C. 1994. *Behind the Mule: Race and Class in African-American Politics*. Princeton, NJ: Princeton University Press.

DC Cultural Tourism. n.d. "Drum and Spear Bookstore Site, African American Heritage Trail." Accessed June 20, 2018. www.culturaltourismdc.org/portal/drum-and-spear-bookstore-site-african-american-heritage-trail.

, Lawrence B. 1970. "The City of Black Angels: Emergence of the Los Angeles ,tto, 1890–1930." *Pacific Historical Review* 39(3): 323–52. https://doi. .g/10.2307/3637655.

: Lerma, Dominique-René, ed. 1973. *Reflections on Afro-American Music.* Kent, OH: Kent State University Press.

De Lerma, Dominique-René. 1981–1984. *Bibliography of Black Music*, 4 vols: Vol. 1: Reference Materials; Vol. 2 Afro-American Idioms; Vol. 3 Geographical Studies, Vol. 4: Theory, Education, and Related Studies. Westport, CT: Greenwood Press.

De Lerma, Dominique-René, and Marsha J. Reisser. 1989. *Black Music and Musicians in the New Grove Dictionary of American Music and the New Harvard Dictionary of Music.* Chicago, IL: Columbia College, Center for Black Music Research.

De Veaux, Alexis. 2006. *Warrior Poet a Biography of Audre Lorde.* New York: Norton.

Dean, Terry. 2011. "'School for Children' Founder Dies." *Austin Weekly News*, July 6. www.austinweeklynews.com/News/Articles/7-6-2011/%27School-for-children%27-founder-dies/.

DeCarava, Roy, and Langston Hughes. 1991 (1955). *The Sweet Flypaper of Life.* Washington, DC: Howard University Press.

Department of African and African American Studies. n.d. "Department Chairs." Accessed August 18, 2018. https://aaas.fas.harvard.edu/department-chairs.

"Detroit Public Television's American Black Journal." n.d. Accessed June 22, 2018. http://abj.matrix.msu.edu/index.php.

Dhondy, Farrukh. 2001. *C.L.R. James.* London: Weidenfeld & Nicolson.

Dillard, Joey Lee. 1972. *Black English: Its History and Usage in the United States.* New York: Random House.

Dillard, Joey Lee. 1975. *Perspectives on Black English.* The Hague: Mouton.

"Dillard University." 2018. Wikipedia. https://en.wikipedia.org/w/index.php?title=Dillard_University&oldid=834456685.

DISA (Diopian Institute for Scholarly Advancement). 2018. "30th Years of Afrocentric Scholarship and Praxis." The Cheikh Anta Diop International Conference, October 12–13. www.diopianinstitute.org/index.php/conference/past-conferences.

Dodson, Howard. 1988. "The Schomburg Center for Research in Black Culture, New York Public Library." *The Library Quarterly* 58(1): 74–82.

Dodson, Owen. 1970. *Powerful Long Ladder.* New York: Farrar, Straus and Giroux.

Dodson, Owen. 1980. *Boy at the Window: A Novel.* New York: Farrar, Straus & Giroux.

Douglas, Emory, and Sam Durant. 2014. *Black Panther: The Revolutionary Art of Emory Douglas.* New York: Rizzoli International Publications.

Douglas, Emory, and Shaun Roberts. 2011. *Emory Douglas: The Visual History of the Black Panther Party.* San Francisco, CA: High Speed Productions.

Dover, Cedric. 1960. *American Negro Art.* Greenwich, CT: New York Graphic Society.

Dowd, Douglas Fitzgerald. 1997. *Blues for America: A Critique, a Lament, and Some Memories.* New York: Monthly Review Press.

Doyle, Bertram Wilbur. 1944. *A Study of Business and Employment Among Negroes in Louisville.* Louisville, KY: Louisville Municipal College, University of Louisville, Louisville Urban League, Central Colored High School.

Doyle, Bertram Wilbur. 1971. *The Etiquette of Race Relations in the South: A Study in Social Control.* New York: Schocken Books.

Drake, St. Clair. 1959. "Pan Africanism: What Is It?" *Africa Today* 6(1): 6–10.

Drake, St. Clair. 1965. "The Social and Economic Status of the Negro in the United States." *Daedalus* 94(4): 771–814.

Drake, St. Clair. 1975. "The Black Diaspora in Pan-African Perspective." *The Black Scholar* 7(1): 2–13. https://doi.org/10.1080/00064246.1975.11413763.

Drake, St. Clair. 1978. "Reflections on Anthropology and the Black Experience." *Anthropology & Education Quarterly* 9(2): 85–109. https://doi.org/10.1525/aeq.1978.9.2.04x0741m.

Drake, St. Clair. 1980. "Anthropology and the Black Experience." *The Black Scholar* 11(7): 2–31. https://doi.org/10.1080/00064246.1980.11414141.

Drake, St. Clair. 1987. *Black Folk Here and There: An Essay in History and Anthropology*. Los Angeles, CA: Center for Afro-American Studies, University of California.

Drake, St. Clair, and Horace R. Cayton. 1945. *Black Metropolis: A Study of Negro Life in a Northern City*. New York: Harcourt Brace & World.

Driskell, David C. 1985. *Hidden Heritage: Afro-American Art, 1800–1950. Exhibit Organized by Bellevue Art Museum (Wash.) and Art Museum Association of America*. San Francisco, CA: The Association.

Driskell, David C., and Leonard Simon. 1976. *Two Centuries of Black American Art: [Exhibition], Los Angeles County Museum of Art, the High Museum of Art, Atlanta, Museum of Fine Arts, Dallas, the Brooklyn Museum*. Los Angeles, CA: Los Angeles County Museum of Art; New York: Knopf.

Du Bois, W.E.B. 1899. *The Philadelphia Negro: A Social Study*. Philadelphia, PA: University of Pennsylvania Press.

Du Bois, W.E.B. 1903. *The Soul of Black Folk: Essays and Sketches*. Chicago, IL: A.C. McClurg and Co.

Du Bois, W.E.B. 1915. "The African Roots of War." *Atlantic Monthly*, May.

Du Bois, W.E.B. 1944. "My Evolving Program for Negro Freedom." In *What the Negro Wants*, edited by Rayford W. Logan, 31–70. Chapel Hill, NC: University of North Carolina Press.

Du Bois, W.E.B. 1968. *The Autobiography of W.E.B. Du Bois: A Soliloquy on Viewing My Life from the Last Decade of Its First Century*. New York: International Publishers.

Du Bois, W.E.B. 2007 (1935). *Black Reconstruction in America: An Essay Toward a History of the Part Which Black Folk Played in the Attempt to Reconstruct Democracy in America, 1860–1880*. Edited by Henry Louis Gates and David Levering Lewis. Oxford: Oxford University Press.

Dunbar, Paul Laurence. 1922. *The Complete Poems of Paul Laurence Dunbar*. New York: Dodd, Mead & Company. www.gutenberg.org/files/18338/18338-h/18338-h.htm.

Dunbar, Paul Laurence. 2014. *Lyrics of Lowly Life*. New York: BiblioLife.

Dunbar-Nelson, Alice. 1988. *The Works of Alice Dunbar-Nelson Vol. 3*. New York: Oxford University Press.

Dunbar-Nelson, Alice, and Akasha Gloria T. Hull. 1988. *The Works of Alice Dunbar-Nelson*. New York: Oxford University Press.

Dunbar-Nelson, Alice Moore, and Akasha Gloria T. Hull. 1984. *Give Us Each Day: The Diary of Alice Dunbar-Nelson*. New York: W.W. Norton.

Dunham, Katherine. 1983. *Dances of Haiti*. Los Angeles, CA: Center for Afro-American Studies, University of California, Los Angeles.

Dunham, Katherine. 2012. *Island Possessed*. New York: Doubleday & Co.

Easter, Makeda. 2019. "Ernie Barnes' 'Sugar Shack': Why Museum-Goers Line Up to See Ex-NFL Player's Painting." *LA Times*, August 28. www.latimes.com/entertainment-arts/story/2019-08-27/ernie-barnes-sugar-shack-painting-at-caam.

"Edmund Barry Gaither." n.d. *The Museum of the NCAAA* (blog). Accessed June 7, 2018. http://ncaaa.org/about-the-museum/edmund-barry-gaither/.

…ual Opportunity Program (EOP). n.d. "Guidelines for the Operation Of." …ssed June 7, 2018. www.suny.edu/sunypp/documents.cfm?doc_id=557.

…ards, Linda McMurry. 1985. *Recorder of the Black Experience : A Biography of Monroe Nathan Work*. Baton Rouge, LA: Louisiana State University Press.

…isen, Arlene. 2012. "Operation Ghetto Storm: 2012 Annual Report on the Extrajudicial Killing of 313 Black People by Police, Security Guards and Vigilantes." www.operationghettostorm.org/.

Elbaum, Max. 2002. *Revolution in the Air: Sixties Radicals Turn to Lenin, Mao and Che*. London: Verso.

Elfman, Lois. 2017. "UMass Amherst African-American Studies Program Comes of Age." *Diverse Issues in Higher Education* (blog). March 17. https://diverseeducation.com/article/94346/.

Ellington, Duke. 1990. *Music Is My Mistress*. New York: Da Capo Press.

Ellison, Ralph. 1964. *Shadow and Act*. New York: Random House.

Ellison, Ralph. 2015 (1952). *Invisible Man*. Bronx, NY: Ishi Press International.

Ellison, Ralph, and John F. Callahan. 1995. *The Collected Essays of Ralph Ellison*. New York: Modern Library.

"Elma Lewis." n.d. *The Museum of the NCAAA* (blog). Accessed June 7, 2018. http://ncaaa.org/about-the-museum/elma-ina-lewis-1921-2004/.

Emery, Lynne Fauley, Brenda Dixon-Stowell, and Lynne Fauley Emery. 1988. *Black Dance: From 1619 to Today*. London: Dance Books.

Emory Center for Digital Scholarship, University of California at Irvine, and University of California at Santa Cruz. 2018. "Slave Voyages." www.slavevoyages.org/.

Epperson, Lia B. 1998. *Knocking down Doors: The Trailblazing Life of Sadie Tanner Mossell Alexander, Pennsylvania's First Black Woman Lawyer*. Stanford, CA: Women's Legal History Biography Project, Stanford University Law School. http://wlh-static.law.stanford.edu/papers/Alexander-epperson98.pdf.

Essien-Udom, Essien Udosen. 1962. *Black Nationalism; a Search for an Identity in America*. Chicago, IL: University of Chicago Press.

ETA. n.d. "ETA Creative Arts Foundation." Accessed June 20, 2018. www.etacreativearts.org/.

Evans, Stephanie. 2006. "The State and Future of the PhD in Black Studies: Assessing the Role of the Comprehensive Examination." *The Griot: The Journal of African American Studies* 25(1): 1–16.

Evanzz, Karl. 1998. *The Judas Factor: The Plot to Kill Malcolm X*. New York: Thunder's Mouth Press.

Evanzz, Karl. 2001. *The Messenger the Rise and Fall of Elijah Muhammad*. New York: Vintage Books.

Everett, Anna. 2009. *Digital Diaspora: A Race for Cyberspace*. New York: State University of New York Press.

Exum, William H. 1985. *Paradoxes of Protest: Black Student Activism in a White University*. Philadelphia, PA: Temple University Press.

Farmer, Ashley D. 2017. *Remaking Black Power How Black Women Transformed an Era*. Chapel Hill, NC: University of North Carolina Press.

Fauset, Arthur Huff. 1981. *For Freedom: A Biographical Story of the American Negro*. Philadelphia, PA: Franklin Pub. and Supply Co.

Fauset, Arthur Huff. 2002. *Black Gods of the Metropolis: Negro Religious Cults of the Urban North*. Philadelphia, PA: University of Pennsylvania Press.

Feather, Leonard G., and Ira Gitler. 2007. *The Biographical Encyclopedia of Jazz*. New York: Oxford University Press.

Federal Writers' Project. 2001. *Born in Slavery: Slave Narratives from the Federal Writers' Project, 1936–1938*. Library of Congress Collection. Washington, DC: Library of Congress. http://hdl.loc.gov/loc.mss/collmss.ms000008.

Fenderson, Jonathan Bryan. 2011. *"Journey Toward a Black Aesthetic" Hoyt Fuller, the Black Arts Movement & the Black Intellectual Community*. Amherst, MA: University of Massachusetts Amherst.

Fergus, Charles. 2003. "Boas, Bones, and Race." *Penn State News*, May 1. https://news.psu.edu/story/140739/2003/05/01/research/boas-bones-and-race.

Ferris, William Henry. 1969. *Alexander Crummell, an Apostle of Negro Culture*. New York: Arno Press.

Fischer, Claude S. 1996. *Inequality by Design: Cracking the Bell Curve Myth*. Princeton, NJ: Princeton University Press.

Fishel, Leslie H., and Benjamin Quarles. 1968. *The Negro American: A Documentary History*. New York: Morrow.

Fisher, Maisha T. 2006. "Earning 'Dual Degrees': Black Bookstores as Alternative Knowledge Spaces." *Anthropology & Education Quarterly* 37(1): 83–99.

"Fisk University Program of African Studies." 1943. Department of Social Science, Fisk University. Pamphlet in possession of the author, 16 pages.

Floyd, Samuel A. 1995. *The Power of Black Music: Interpreting Its History from Africa to the United States*. New York: Oxford University Press.

Floyd, Samuel A., ed. 1999. *International Dictionary of Black Composers*, 2 vols. Chicago, IL: Fitzroy Dearborn.

Fogel, Robert William, and Stanley L. Engerman. 1995 (1974). *Time on the Cross: Economics of American Negro Slavery*. New York: W.W. Norton.

Foner, Philip S., ed. 1983. *Black Socialist Preacher: The Teachings of Reverend George Washington Woodbey and His Disciple, Reverend G.W. Slater, Jr.* San Francisco, CA: Synthesis Publications.

Ford, Nick Aaron. 1973. *Black Studies: Threat or Challenge?* Port Washington, NY: Kennikat Press.

Foreman, P. Gabrielle, and Jim Casey n.d. Colored Conventions. https://coloredconventions.org/about/team/.

Foreman, P. Gabrielle, Jim Casey, and Sarah Lyn Patterson, eds. 2021. *Colored Conventions Movement: Black Organizing in the Nineteenth Century*. Chapel Hill, NC: University of North Carolina Press.

Forman, James. 1968. *Sammy Younge, Jr.: The First Black College Student to Die in the Black Liberation Movement*. New York: Grove Press.

Forman, James. 1970. *The Political Thought of James Forman*. Detroit, MI: Black Star Publishing.

Foster, William Zebulon. 1947. *The Communist Position on the Negro Question*. New York: New Century Pub.

Foster, William Zebulon. 1982. *The Negro People in American History*. New York: International Publishers.

Franklin, John Hope. 1967. *From Slavery to Freedom: A History of Negro Americans*. New York: Knopf.

Franklin, John Hope. 1985. *George Washington Williams: A Biography*. Chicago, IL: University of Chicago Press.

Vincent P. 1992 (1984). *Black Self-Determination: A Cultural History of ...an-American Resistance*. Brooklyn, NY: Lawrence Hill Books.

..lin, Vincent P., and James D. Anderson. 1978. *New Perspectives on Black ...ducational History*. Boston, MA: G.K. Hall.

ranklin, Vincent P., and Carter Julian Savage. 2004. *Cultural Capital and Black Education African American Communities and the Funding of Black Schooling, 1865 to the Present*. Greenwich, CT: Information Age Pub.

Fraser, Nancy, and Linda Gordon. 1994. "A Genealogy of Dependency: Tracing a Keyword of the U.S. Welfare State." *Signs: Journal of Women in Culture and Society* 19(2): 309–36. https://doi.org/10.1086/494886.

Frazier, E. Franklin. 1957. *The Negro in the United States*. New York: Macmillan.

Frazier, E. Franklin. 1962. "The Failure of the Negro Intellectual." *Negro Digest*, February.

Frazier, E. Franklin. 1966. *The Negro Family in the United States*. Chicago, IL: University of Chicago Press.

Frazier, E. Franklin. 1968. *The Free Negro Family*. New York: Arno Press.

Frazier, E. Franklin. 1997. *Black Bourgeoisie*. New York: Free Press Paperbacks.

Frazier, E. Franklin, American Council on Education, and American Youth Commission. 1967. *Negro Youth at the Crossways, Their Personality Development in the Middle States*. New York: Schocken Books.

Frazier, E. Franklin, and G. Franklin Edwards. 1968. *On Race Relations; Selected Writings*. Chicago, IL: University of Chicago Press.

Frazier, E. Franklin, and Kenneth Thompson. 2005. *The Negro Family in Chicago*. London: Routledge.

Freedom Archives. 2020. https://freedomarchives.org/

"Freedom School Curriculum." n.d. Accessed June 7, 2018. www.educationanddemocracy.org/ED_FSC.html.

Fuller, Howard. 1972. "Proposal for Malcolm X Liberation University 1972–1973." In the archive of Abdul Alkalimat.

Fuller, Howard, and Lisa Frazier Page. 2014. *No Struggle, No Progress: A Warrior's Life from Black Power to Education Reform*. Milwaukee, WI: Marquette University Press.

Fuller, Hoyt. 1971. *Journey to Africa*. Chicago, IL: Third World Press.

Fuller, Hoyt, and Dudley Randall. 1984. *Homage to Hoyt Fuller*. Detroit, MI: Broadside Press.

Fulop, Timothy E., and Albert J. Raboteau. 1997. *African-American Religion: Interpretive Essays in History and Culture*. New York: Routledge.

Gaither, Edmund Barry. 1975. *Jubilee: Afro-American Artists in Afro-America*. Boston, MA: Boston Museum of Fine Arts.

Gallon, Kim. n.d. "Black Press Research Collective." http://blackpressresearchcollective.org/.

Gates, Henry Louis. 1988. *The Signifying Monkey: A Theory of African-American Literary Criticism*. New York: Oxford University Press.

Gates, Henry Louis. 2017. "Africa's Great Civilizations." PBS. www.pbs.org/show/africas-great-civilizations/.

Gates, Henry Louis, and Nellie Y. McKay. 1996. *The Norton Anthology of African American Literature*. New York: W.W. Norton & Co.

Gayle, Addison, ed. 1971. *The Black Aesthetic*. Garden City, NY: Doubleday.

Gellman, Erik S. 2012. *Death Blow to Jim Crow: The National Negro Congress and the Rise of Militant Civil Rights*. Chapel Hill, NC: University of North Carolina Press.

Gilkes, Cheryl Townsend. 2004. *"If It Wasn't for the Women...": Black Women's Experience and Womanist Culture in Church and Community*. New York: Palgrave Macmillan.

Gilpin, Patrick J., Marybeth Gasman, and David Levering Lewis. 2014. *Charles S. Johnson: Leadership Beyond the Veil in the Age of Jim Crow*. Albany, NY: State University of New York Press.

Gilyard, Keith. 2017. *Louise Thompson Patterson: A Life of Struggle for Justice*. Durham, NC: Duke University Press.

Glasker, Wayne. 2002. *Black Students in the Ivory Tower: African American Student Activism at the University of Pennsylvania, 1967–1990*. Amherst, MA: University of Massachusetts Press.

Gloster, Hugh M. 1965. *Negro Voices in American Fiction*. New York: Russell & Russell.

Goggin, Jacqueline Anne. 1993. *Carter G. Woodson: A Life in Black History*. Baton Rouge, LA: Louisiana State University Press.

Gomez, Michael A. 2008. *Reversing Sail: A History of the African Diaspora*. Cambridge: Cambridge University Press.

Gordon, Ann D., and Bettye Collier-Thomas. 1997. *African American Women and the Vote, 1837–1965*. Amherst, MA: University of Massachusetts Press.

Gordon, Lewis R. 1997. *Existence in Black: An Anthology of Black Existential Philosophy*. New York: Routledge.

Gordon, Lewis R. 2008. *An Introduction to Africana Philosophy*. Cambridge: Cambridge University Press.

Gordon, Lewis R., and Jane Anna Gordon. 2006a. *A Companion to African-American Studies*. Malden, MA: Blackwell Pub.

Gordon, Lewis R., and Jane Anna Gordon. 2006b. *Not Only the Master's Tools: African-American Studies in Theory and Practice*. Boulder, CO: Paradigm.

Gordon, Milton M. 1963. "Recent Trends in the Study of Minority and Race Relations." *The Annals of the American Academy of Political and Social Science* 350: 148–56.

Gordy, Berry. 2013. *To Be Loved: The Music, the Magic, the Memories of Motown*. Boston, MA: Rosetta Books.

Gould, Stephen Jay. 1996. *The Mismeasure of Man*. New York: W.W. Norton & Co.

Gourse, Leslie. 2003. *Art Blakey: Jazz Messenger*. New York: Schirmer.

Graham, Maryemma. 1986. *Richard Wright: A Special Issue*. Baltimore, MD: Johns Hopkins University Press.

Graham, Maryemma. 2013. "The Project on the History of Black Writing." University of Kansas. https://hbw.ku.edu/dr-maryemma-graham.

Graves, Joseph L. 2005. *The Race Myth: Why We Pretend Race Exists in America*. New York: Plume.

Graves, Joseph L. 2008. *The Emperor's New Clothes: Biological Theories of Race at the Millennium*. New Brunswick, NJ: Rutgers University Press.

Greene, Harry W. 1946. *Holders of Doctorates among American Negroes: An Educational and Social Study of Negroes Who Have Earned Doctoral Degrees in Course, 1876–1943*. Boston, MA: Meador Pub. Co.

Greene, Lorenzo J. 1974. *The Negro in Colonial New England*. New York: Atheneum.

Greene, Lorenzo J., and Arvarh E. Strickland. 1989. *Working with Carter G. Woodson, the Father of Black History: A Diary, 1928–1930*. Baton Rouge, LA: Louisiana State University Press.

Greene, Lorenzo J., and Carter Godwin Woodson. 1930. *The Negro Wage Earner*. Washington, DC: Association for the Study of Negro Life and History.

ˏh Jasmine. 2007. *Inclusive Scholarship: Developing Black Studies in the United A 25th Anniversary Retrospective of Ford Foundation Grant Making, 1982–2007.* York: Ford Foundation.

ˏsman, James R. 1989. *Land of Hope Chicago, Black Southerners, and the Great Migration.* Chicago, IL: University of Chicago Press.

Guinier, Ewart. 1975. "Black Studies: Training for Leadership." *Freedomways* 15(3): 2–11.

Guthrie, Robert V. 2003. *Even the Rat Was White: A Historical View of Psychology.* 2nd ed. Boston, MA: Pearson.

Gutman, Herbert George. 2003. *Slavery and the Numbers Game: A Critique of Time on the Cross.* Urbana, IL: University of Illinois Press.

Guy-Sheftall, Beverly. 1992. "Black Women's Studies: The Interface of Women's Studies and Black Studies." *Phylon (1960–)* 49(1/2): 33–41. https://doi.org/10.2307/3132615.

Guy-Sheftall, Beverly. 1995. *Daughters of Sorrow: Attitudes Toward Black Women, 1880–1920.* Brooklyn, NY: Carlson.

Guy-Sheftall, Beverly, and Susan Heath. 1995. *Women's Studies: A Retrospective: A Report to the Ford Foundation.* New York: Ford Foundation.

Hale, Jon N. 2017. *The Freedom Schools: Student Activists in the Mississippi Civil Rights Movement.* Columbia Scholarship Online. http://dx.doi.org/10.7312/columbia/9780231175685.001.0001.

Hall, Perry A., ed. 1981. *Black Studies Core Curriculum.* Bloomington, IN: National Council for Black Studies.

Hall, Perry A. 1999. *In the Vineyard: Working in African American Studies.* Knoxville, TN: University of Tennessee Press.

Harding, Vincent. 1970. "Black Students and the Impossible Revolution." *Journal of Black Studies* 1(1): 75–100.

Harding, Vincent. 1980. *The Other American Revolution.* Los Angeles, CA: Center for Afro-American Studies, University of California.

Harding, Vincent. 1981. *There Is a River: The Black Struggle for Freedom in America.* New York: Harcourt Brace Jovanovich.

Harley, Sharon, and Rosalyn Terborg-Penn. 1997 (1978). *The Afro-American Woman: Struggles and Images.* Baltimore, MD: Black Classic Press.

Harper, Frances Ellen Watkins. 2018. "Learning to Read." Poetry Foundation. May 8. www.poetryfoundation.org/poems/52448/learning-to-read-56d230edofdco.

Harris, Abram Lincoln. 1968 (1938). *The Negro as Capitalist: A Study of Banking and Business among American Negroes.* College Park, MD: McGrath Pub. Co.

Harris, Abram Lincoln, and William A. Darity. 1989. *Race, Radicalism, and Reform: Selected Papers.* New Brunswick, NJ: Transaction Publishers.

Harris, Leonard. 1983. *Philosophy Born of Struggle: Anthology of Afro-American Philosophy from 1917.* Dubuque, IA: Kendall/Hunt Pub. Co.

Harris, Leonard, and Charles Molesworth. 2010. *Alain L. Locke: The Biography of a Philosopher.* Chicago, IL: University of Chicago Press.

Harris, Marvin. 2001. *The Rise of Anthropological Theory: A History of Theories of Culture.* Updated ed. Walnut Creek, CA: AltaMira Press.

Harris, Michael W. 1994. *The Rise of Gospel Blues: The Music of Thomas Andrew Dorsey in the Urban Church.* New York: Oxford University Press.

Harris, Robert, Carlos A. Cooks, Nyota Harris, and Grandassa Harris. 1992. *Carlos Cooks and Black Nationalism from Garvey to Malcolm.* Dover, MA: Majority Press.

Harris, Robert L. 1982. "Coming of Age: The Transformation of Afro-American Historiography." *The Journal of Negro History* 67(2): 107–21. https://doi.org/10.2307/2717569.

Harris, Robert L., and Rosalyn Terborg-Penn. 2008. *The Columbia Guide to African American History Since 1939*. New York: Columbia University Press.

Harris, Sheldon. 1979. *Blues Who's Who: A Biographical Dictionary of Blues Singers*. New Rochelle, NY: Arlington House

Harrison, Faye Venetia, Association of Black Anthropologists, and American Anthropological Association. 1991. *Decolonizing Anthropology: Moving Further Toward an Anthropology for Liberation*. Washington, DC: Association of Black Anthropologists; American Anthropological Association.

Harrison, Hubert H., and Jeffrey Babcock Perry. 2001. *A Hubert Harrison Reader*. Middletown, CT: Wesleyan University Press.

Hartford, Bruce. n.d. "Civil Rights Movement History & Timeline, 1960." Veterans of the Civil Rights Movement. Accessed May 8, 2018. www.crmvet.org/tim/timhis60.htm.

Haynes, George Edmund. 1945. *The Work of the Department of Race Relations of the Federal Council of Churches*. New York: n.p.

Haynes, George Edmund. 2008. *The Negro at Work in New York City A Study in Economic Progress*. Project Gutenberg. www.gutenberg.org/etext/24712.

Haywood, Harry. 1948. *Negro Liberation*. New York: International Publishers.

Haywood, Harry. 1978. *Black Bolshevik: Autobiography of an Afro-American Communist*. Chicago, IL: Liberator Press.

Heller, Michael C. 2017. *Loft Jazz: Improvising New York in the 1970s*. Oakland, CA: University of California Press.

Helmreich, Stefan. 2004. "Race and Science." MIT OpenCourseWare. https://ocw.mit.edu/courses/anthropology/21a-240-race-and-science-spring-2004/.

Henderson, George, Sterlin N. Adams, Sandra D. Rouce, and Ida Elizabeth Mack Wilson. 2010. *Race and the University: A Memoir*. Norman, OK: University of Oklahoma Press.

Henderson, Stephen Evangelist. 1980. *Understanding the New Black Poetry: Black Speech and Black Music as Poetic References*. New York: Morrow Quill Paperbacks.

Henry, Charles P. 2004. *Ralph Bunche: Model Negro or American Other?* New York: New York University Press.

Henry, Charles P. 2017. *Black Studies and the Democratization of American Higher Education*. Cham: Springer International Publishing.

Herrnstein, Richard J., and Charles A. Murray. 1997 (1994). *The Bell Curve: Intelligence and Class Structure in American Life*. New York: Free Press.

Hill, Anthony D., and Douglas Q. Barnett. 2009. *Historical Dictionary of African American Theater*. Lanham, MD: Scarecrow Press.

Hill Collins, Patricia. 2000 (1990). *Black Feminist Thought Knowledge, Consciousness, and the Politics of Empowerment*. New York: Routledge.

Hill, Errol. 1980. *The Theater of Black Americans: A Collection of Critical Essays*. Englewood Cliffs, NJ: Prentice-Hall.

Hill, Errol, and James V. Hatch. 2003. *A History of African American Theatre*. Cambridge: Cambridge University Press.

Hill, Robert. 2005. *The Marcus Garvey Reader*. Oxford: Blackwell.

Hill, Robert A., and Barbara Bair. 1987. *Marcus Garvey: Life and Lessons: A Centennial Companion to the Marcus Garvey and Universal Negro Improvement Association Papers*. Berkeley, CA: University of California Press.

Bernard. 2003. *The Strengths of Black Families*. Lanham, MD: University . America.

.h Edmonds, Patricia Miller King, and Arthur and Elizabeth Schlesinger Library the History of Women in America. 1989. *The Black Women Oral History Project: A Guide to the Transcripts*. Cambridge, MA: Radcliffe College.

ıilliard, Asa G. 1998. *SBA: The Reawakening of the African Mind*. Gainesville, FL: Makare Publishing Co.

Hine, Darlene Clark, and American Historical Association, eds. 1986. *The State of Afro-American History: Past, Present, and Future*. Baton Rouge, LA: Louisiana State University Press.

Hine, Darlene Clark, Elsa Barkley Brown, and Rosalyn Terborg-Penn. 1993. *Black Women in America: An Historical Encyclopedia*. Brooklyn, NY: Carlson Pub.

Hine, Darlene Clark, and Kathleen Thompson. 1998. *A Shining Thread of Hope: The History of Black Women in America*. New York: Broadway Books.

History. 2021 (2017). "1967 Detroit Riots." *History*, September 27, 2017, updated March 23. Accessed June 7, 2018. www.history.com/topics/1967-detroit-riots.

The History Makers. n.d. "Kalamu Ya Salaam: Interview" November 14, 2002. Accessed June 20, 2018. www.thehistorymakers.org/biography/kalamu-ya-salaam-39.

Holloway, Jonathan Scott. 2002. *Confronting the Veil: Abram Harris, Jr., E. Franklin Frazier, and Ralph Bunche, 1919–1941*. Chapel Hill, NC: University of North Carolina Press.

Holmes, Eugene C. 1959. "Alain Leroy Locke: A Sketch." *The Phylon Quarterly* 20(1): 82–89. https://doi.org/10.2307/273159.

Holmes, Eugene C. 1963. "The Legacy of Alain Locke." *Freedomways* 3(3): 293–306.

Holmes, Eugene C. 1969. "A Philosophical Approach to the Study of Minority Problems." *The Journal of Negro Education* 38(3): 196–203. https://doi.org/10.2307/2294002.

Holmes, Eugene C., and Rayford Whittingham Logan. 1956. *The New Negro Thirty Years Afterward: Papers Contributed to the Sixteenth Annual Spring Conference of the Division of the Social Sciences April 20, 21, and 22, 1955*. Washington, DC: Howard University Press.

Holsaert, Faith S. et al. eds. 2010. *Hands on the Freedom Plow: Personal Accounts by Women in SNCC*. Urbana, IL: University of Illinois Press.

Hopkins, Dwight N. 1999 (1993). *Shoes That Fit Our Feet: Sources for a Constructive Black Theology*. Maryknoll, NY: Orbis Books.

Hopkins, Dwight N. 2005 (1989). *Black Theology USA and South Africa: Politics, Culture, and Liberation*. Maryknoll, NY: Orbis Books.

Hopkins, Dwight N., and Edward P. Antonio, eds. 2012. *The Cambridge Companion to Black Theology*. Cambridge: Cambridge University Press.

Horne, Gerald. 1988. *Communist Front? The Civil Rights Congress, 1946–1956*. Rutherford, NJ: Associated University Presses.

Horne, Gerald. 1997. *Fire This Time: The Watts Uprising and the 1960s*. New York: Da Capo Press.

Horne, Gerald. 2001. *Class Struggle in Hollywood 1930–1950: Moguls, Mobsters, Stars, Reds, and Trade Unionists*. Austin, TX: University of Texas Press.

Horne, Gerald. 2010. *W.E.B. Du Bois: A Biography*. Santa Barbara, CA: Greenwood Press.

Horne, Gerald. 2012. *Negro Comrades of the Crown: African Americans and the British Empire Fight the U.S. before Emancipation*. New York: New York University Press.

Horne, Gerald. 2014. *Race to Revolution the United States and Cuba during Slavery and Jim Crow*. New York: Monthly Review Press.

Hountondji, Paulin J. 2007. *African Philosophy: Myth and Reality*. Bloomington, IN: Indiana University Press.

Houston, Charles Hamilton, and James L. Conyers. 2012. *Charles H. Houston: An Interdisciplinary Study of Civil Rights Leadership*. Lanham, MD: Lexington Books.

Huggins, Nathan Irvin, and Ford Foundation. 1985. *Afro-American Studies: A Report to the Ford Foundation*. New York: Ford Foundation.

Huggins, Nathan Irvin, Martin Kilson, and Daniel M. Fox. 1971a. *Key Issues in the Afro-American Experience*. Vol. 1. New York: Harcourt Brace Jovanovich.

Huggins, Nathan Irvin, Martin Kilson, and Daniel M. Fox. 1971b. *Key Issues in the Afro-American Experience*. Vol. 2. New York: Harcourt Brace Jovanovich.

Hughes, Langston. 2004 (1926). "The Negro Artist and the Racial Mountain." In *The Norton Anthology of African American Literature*, edited by Henry Louis Gates and Nellie Y. McKay, 1311–14. New York: Norton.

Hughes, Langston, and Dianne Johnson. 2003. *The Collected Works of Langston Hughes*. Vol. 11. Columbia, MI: University of Missouri Press.

Hughes, Langston, Milton Meltzer, Hugh H. Smythe, and Mabel M. Smythe. 1956. *A Pictorial History of the Negro in America*. New York: Crown.

Hughes, Langston, R. Baxter Miller, and Arnold Rampersad. 2002. *The Collected Works of Langston Hughes. Vol. 9*. Columbia, MO: University of Missouri Press.

Hughes, Langston, and Arnold Rampersad. 2002. *The Collected Works of Langston Hughes*. Vol. 2. Columbia, MO: University of Missouri Press.

Hughes, Langston, Arnold Rampersad, Dolan Hubbard, Leslie Catherine Sanders, Donna Sullivan Harper, Christopher C. De Santis, Dianne Johnson, Steven C. Tracy, Joseph McLaren, and Dellita Martin-Ogunsola. 2001. *The Collected Works of Langston Hughes*. 18 Volumes. Columbia, MO: University of Missouri Press.

Hull, Akasha Gloria T., Patricia Bell-Scott, and Barbara Smith. 1982. *All the Women Are White, All the Blacks Are Men, but Some of Us Are Brave: Black Women's Studies*. Old Westbury, NY: Feminist Press.

HumanitiesDC. 2011. *Under the Radar: The New School of Afro-American Thought*. YouTube video, www.youtube.com/watch?v=KPD9KmvOM7g.

Hunt, Darnell M., and Ana-Christina Ramón. 2010. *Black Los Angeles: American Dreams and Racial Realities*. New York: New York University Press.

Hunter, Herbert M. 2008. *The Sociology of Oliver C. Cox: New Perspectives*. London: JAI Press.

Hunter, Herbert M., and Sameer Y. Abraham. 1987. *Race, Class, and the World System: The Sociology of Oliver C. Cox*. New York: Monthly Review Press.

ICBS (Illinois Council for Black Studies), ed. 1980. *Black People and the 1980 Census: Proceedings from a Conference on the Population Undercount*. Chicago, IL: Published and distributed for the Illinois Council for Black Studies by the Chicago Center for Afro American Studies and Research.

ICBS, ed. 1982. "The Crisis of Consolidation Facing Black Studies in the 1980s: The Case of Ethnic Studies at Illinois State University." Chicago, IL: Illinois Council for Black Studies.

ICBS, ed. 1984. "Proceedings of the ICBS Conference: A Search for a Partnership." Chicago, IL: Illinois Council for Black Studies.

"In Memoriam: Julian Richardson." 2000. *The Black Scholar* 30(3–4): 66.

Institute of African Studies. n.d. "About Us." Accessed June 7, 2018. https://ias.ug.edu.gh/about-us.

Institute for Dunham Technique Certification. n.d. "Institute for Dunham Technique Certification." Accessed June 22, 2018. http://dunhamcertification.org/Home.html.

Institute of Positive Education. n.d. "Community Organization, Pre-School, Cultural Programs, Pre-School: Chicago, IL." Accessed June 20, 2018. www.ipeclc.org/index.html.

Invisible Bison. n.d. *Eyes on The Prize—Howard University—Muhammad Ali*. YouTube video. Accessed July 21, 2018. www.youtube.com/watch?v=5boSGJudTUk.

"*Invisible Man*." 2018. Wikipedia. https://en.wikipedia.org/w/index.php?title=Invisible_Man&oldid=840244355.

"Ishmael Flory." n.d. Wikipedia. Accessed May 8, 2018. https://en.wikipedia.org/wiki/Ishmael_Flory.

Jackson, Esther Cooper. 1953. *This Is My Husband: Fighter for His People, Political Refugee*. Brooklyn, NY: National Committee to Defend Negro Leadership.

Jackson, George, and Jonathan Jackson. 2006. *Soledad Brother: The Prison Letters of George Jackson*. Chicago, IL: Lawrence Hill Books.

Jackson, James E. 1963. *The View from Here*. New York: Publishers New Press.

Jackson, John G. 1970. *Introduction to African Civilizations*. New York: University Books.

Jackson, Luther Porter. 1971. *Free Negro Labor and Property Holding in Virginia, 1830–1860*. New York: Russell & Russell.

Jackson, Luther Porter. 2003. *Negro Office-Holders in Virginia, 1865–1895*. Norfolk, VA: Guide Quality Press.

Jacoby, Russell, and Naomi Glauberman. 1998. *The Bell Curve Debate: History, Documents, Opinions*. New York: Times Books.

Jones-Hogu, Barbara. 2012. "The History, Philosophy and Aesthetics of AFRICOBRA." *Area Chicago*. January 8. www.areachicago.org/the-history-philosophy-and-aesthetics-of-africobra/.

James, C.L.R. 1953. *Mariners, Renegades, and Castaways: The Story of Herman Melville and the World We Live In*. New York: C.L.R. James.

James, C.L.R. 1969. *Black Studies and the Contemporary Student*. Detroit, MI: Friends of Facing Reality.

James, C.L.R. 2001 (1953). *The Black Jacobins: Toussaint L'ouverture and the San Domingo Revolution*. London: Penguin Books.

James, C.L.R. 2013. *Modern Politics*. Oakland, CA: PM Press.

James, C.L.R. 2018. *C.L.R. James and Revolutionary Marxism: Selected Writings of C.L.R. James, 1939–1949*. Edited by Scott McLemee and Paul Le Blanc. Chicago, IL: Haymarket Books.

James, C.L.R., Raya Dunayevskaya, and Grace Lee Boggs. 2013. *State Capitalism and World Revolution*. Oakland, CA: PM Press.

James, George G.M. 2016. *Stolen Legacy: The Egyptian Origins of Western Philosophy*. Brattleboro, VT: Echo Point Books & Media.

"James Porter's Biography." 2013. *James A. Porter Colloquium on African American Art* (blog). www.art.howard.edu/portercolloquium/james-porter-bio/.

"Jazz Messengers Alumni." n.d. *Art Blakey* (blog). Accessed May 8, 2018. http://artblakey.com/jazz-messengers-alumni/.

Johnson, Charles Spurgeon. 1923. *The Negro in Chicago*. Chicago, IL: University of Chicago Press.

Johnson, Charles Spurgeon. 1934. *Shadow of the Plantation*. Chicago, IL: University of Chicago Press.

Johnson, Charles Spurgeon. 1969. *Negro College Graduate*. New York: Negro Universities Press.

Johnson, Charles Spurgeon. 1970. *The Negro in American Civilization: A Study of Negro Life and Race Relations in the Light of Social Research*. New York: Johnson Reprint Corp.

Johnson, Charles Spurgeon, American Council on Education, and American Youth Commission. 1941. *Growing up in the Black Belt; Negro Youth in the Rural South*. Washington, DC: American Council on Education.

Johnson, E. Patrick, and Mae Henderson. 2005. *Black Queer Studies: A Critical Anthology*. Durham, NC: Duke University Press.

Johnson, Howard Eugene, and Wendy Johnson. 2014. *A Dancer in the Revolution: Stretch Johnson, Harlem Communist at the Cotton Club*. Bronx, NY: Fordham.

Johnson, James Weldon. 1931. *The Book of American Negro Poetry*. New York: Harcourt, Brace and Co.

Johnson, James Weldon, John Rosamond Johnson, and Lawrence Brown. 1925. *The Book of American Negro Spirituals*. New York: Viking Press.

Johnson, Nelson. 1971. "Black Studies and Revolution." *SOBU Newsletter*, February, 4.

Jones, LeRoi (Amiri Baraka) 1964. *Dutchman and the Slave*. New York: William Morrow and Co.

Jones, LeRoi (Amiri Baraka) 1967. *The Baptism and the Toilet*. New York: Grove Press.

Jones, Reginald L. 1972. *Black Psychology*. New York: Harper & Row.

Jones, Reginald L. 1999. *Advances in African American Psychology*. Hampton, VA: Cobb & Henry.

Joseph, Peniel E. 2006. *Waiting 'til the Midnight Hour: A Narrative History of Black Power in America*. New York: Henry Holt and Co.

Joseph, Peniel E. 2009. "The Black Power Movement: A State of the Field." *The Journal of American History* 96(3): 751–76.

Joyce, Donald Franklin. 1988. "Vivian G. Harsh Collection of Afro-American History and Literature, Chicago Public Library." *The Library Quarterly* 58(1): 67–74.

Joyce, Donald Franklin. 1991. *Black Book Publishers in the United States: A Historical Dictionary of the Presses, 1817–1990*. New York: Greenwood Press.

"Julie Dash." 2018. Wikipedia. https://en.wikipedia.org/w/index.php?title=Julie_Dash&oldid=841177329.

Kahn, Jeffery. 2004. "Ronald Reagan Launched Political Career Using the Berkeley Campus as a Political Target." *UC Berkeley News*, June 8. www.berkeley.edu/news/media/releases/2004/06/08_reagan.shtml.

Kaiser, Ernest. 1985. *Freedomways* 25(3): 204.

Kamin, Leon J. 1995. "Lies, Damned Lies, and Statistics." In *The Bell Curve Debate: History, Documents, Opinions*, edited by Russell Jacoby and Naomi Glauberman, 81–105. New York: Times Books.

Kardiner, Abram, and Lionel Ovesey. 1962. *The Mark of Oppression: Explorations in the Personality of the American Negro*. Cleveland, OH: World Pub. Co.

Karenga, Maulana. 2010 (1982). *Introduction to Black Studies*. Los Angeles, CA: University of Sankore Press.

Karenga, Maulana. 2015. "Knowing and Honoring Nathan Hare: Thinking and Thundering Black." *Los Angeles Sentinel* (blog). April 30. https://lasentinel.net/knowing-and-honoring-nathan-hare-thinking-and-thundering-black.html.

Kennedy, Al. 2006. *Chord Changes on the Chalkboard: How Public School Teachers Shaped Jazz and the Music of New Orleans*. Lanham, MD: Scarecrow Press.

Kennedy, Gary W. 2003. "Dyett, Capt. Walter [Henri Walter]." In *Grove Music Online*. Oxford University Press. https://doi.org/10.1093/gmo/9781561592630.article.J791000.

Khair, Zulkifli. n.d. "The University of Sankore, Timbuktu." *Muslim Heritage*. Accessed May 22, 2017. www.muslimheritage.com/article/university-sankore-timbuktu.

Kilson, Martin, Bayard Rustin, and A. Philip Randolph Educational Fund. 1969. *Black Studies: Myths and Realities*. [New York]: A. Philip Randolph Educational Fund.

King Jr., Martin Luther. 1967. "The Role of the Behavioral Scientist in the Civil Rights Movement." American Psychological Association. www.apa.org/monitor/features/king-challenge.aspx.

King Jr., Martin Luther, Malcolm X, James Baldwin, Kenneth Bancroft Clark, and Kenneth Bancroft Clark. 1985. *King, Malcolm, Baldwin: Three Interviews*. Middletown, CT: Wesleyan University Press.

Kirschke, Amy Helene. 1999. *Aaron Douglas: Art, Race, and the Harlem Renaissance*. Jackson, MS: University Press of Mississippi.

Koestler, Arthur, and R.H.S Crossman. 1949. *The God That Failed*. New York: Harper.

Konadu, Kwasi. 2005. *Truth Crushed to the Earth Will Rise Again! The East Organization and the Principles and Practice of Black Nationalist Development*. Trenton, NJ: Africa World Press.

Kornberg, Allan, and Joel Smith. 1969. "'It Ain't Over Yet': Activism in a Southern University." In *Black Power and Student Rebellion: Conflict on the American Campus*, edited by James McEvoy and Abraham Miller, 100–121. Belmont, CA: Wadsworth Publishing Company.

Kornweibel, Theodore. 1998. *"Seeing Red": Federal Campaigns Against Black Militancy, 1919–1925*. Bloomington, IN: Indiana University Press.

Kruk, Matthew. 2010. "Curtis Ellis Sr., 82, Pioneering Black Bookstore Owner." *Sun Times*, April 20. https://groups.google.com/forum/#!topic/alt.obituaries/ZwhgK57RnYY.

Kuhn, Thomas S. 1996. *The Structure of Scientific Revolutions*. Chicago, IL: University of Chicago Press.

Lackey, Michael, ed. 2014. *Haverford Discussions: A Black Integrationist Manifesto for Racial Justice*. Charlottesville, VA: University of Virginia Press.

Ladner, Joyce A. 1971. *Tomorrow's Tomorrow: The Black Woman*. Garden City, NY: Doubleday.

Ladner, Joyce A. 1973. *The Death of White Sociology*. New York: Random House.

Land, Roderick, and M. Christopher Brown. n.d. "African-American Studies: The Foundations of African-American Studies, The Emergence of African-American Studies Departments." http://education.stateuniversity.com/pages/1742/African-American-Studies.html#ixzz5JIQpO4e5.

Landry, Bart. 1988. *The New Black Middle Class*. Berkeley, CA: University of California Press.

"L.A. Rebellion." 2018. Wikipedia. https://en.wikipedia.org/w/index.php?title=L.A._Rebellion&oldid=843203588.

Larsen, Julia. 2008. "David Ruggles (1810–1849)." *The Black Past*, June 29, 2008. Accessed June 8, 2018. www.blackpast.org/aah/ruggles-david-1810-1849.

Lefever, Harry G. 2005. *Undaunted by the Fight: Spelman College and the Civil Rights Movement, 1957/1967*. Macon, GA: Mercer University Press.

Lenin, Vladimir Ilyich. 1901. "Where to Begin?" www.marxists.org/archive/lenin/works/1901/may/04.htm.

Lenin, Vladimir Ilyich. 1901–1902. "What is to Be Done?" www.marxists.org/archive/lenin/works/1901/witbd/.

Lenin, Vladimir Ilyich. 1913. "Russians and Negroes." Accessed June 7, 2018. www.marxists.org/archive/lenin/works/1913/feb/00b.htm.

LeNoble, Marie-Edith. 2010. "Black Studies @ Northwestern University." www.ideals.illinois.edu/handle/2142/15175.

"Leonard Jeffries Virtual Museum." 2007, July 22. https://web.archive.org/web/20070722042838/http://www.nbufront.org/html/MastersMuseums/LenJeffries/LenJeffriesVMuseum.html.

Lerner, Gerder. 1972. *Black Women in White America: A Documentary History.* New York: Random House.

Levin, Matt, and Jackie Botts. 2019. "California's Homelessness Crisis—and Possible Solutions—Explained." *CalMatters*, December 31. https://calmatters.org/explainers/californias-homelessness-crisis-explained/.

Lewis, George E. 2009. *A Power Stronger than Itself: The AACM and American Experimental Music.* Chicago, IL: University of Chicago Press.

Lewis, Rupert. 1988. *Marcus Garvey: Anti-Colonial Champion.* Trenton, NJ: Africa World Press.

Lewis, Samella S. 1973. *The Street Art of Black America.* Houston, TX: Exxon USA.

Lewis, Samella S. 1990. *Art: African American.* 2nd ed. Los Angeles, CA: Hancraft Studios.

Lewis, Samella S. 2003. *African American Art and Artists.* Berkeley, CA: University of California Press.

Lewis, Samella S., and Ruth G. Waddy. 1969. *Black Artists on Art.* Los Angeles, CA: Contemporary Crafts Publishers.

Lewis, W. Arthur. 1954. "Economic Development with Unlimited Supplies of Labour." *The Manchester School* 22(2): 139–91. https://doi.org/10.1111/j.1467-9957.1954.tb00021.x.

Lewis, W. Arthur. 1969. "Black Power and the American University." *Princeton Alumni Weekly.* March 18. www.princeton.edu/paw/web_exclusives/plus/plus_032206blackp.html.

Lewis, W. Arthur. 2013. *Theory of Economic Growth.* London: Routledge.

Lewis, W. Arthur, and Mark Gersovitz. 1983. *Selected Economic Writings of W. Arthur Lewis.* New York: New York University Press.

Lewontin, Richard C., Steven P.R. Rose, and Leon J. Kamin. 1984. *Not in Our Genes: Biology, Ideology, and Human Nature.* New York: Pantheon Books.

Lightfoot, Claude M. 1969. *Ghetto Rebellion to Black Liberation.* New York: International Publishers.

Lincoln, C. Eric, and Lawrence H. Mamiya. 1990. *The Black Church in the African-American Experience.* Durham, NC: Duke University Press.

Lindfors, Bernth. 2011. *Ira Aldridge.* Rochester, NY: University of Rochester Press.

"List of Museums Focused on African Americans." 2018. Wikipedia. https://en.wikipedia.org/w/index.php?title=List_of_museums_focused_on_African_Americans&oldid=840228494.

Little, William A., Edward Crosby, and Carolyn M. Leonard, eds. 1981. *National Council of Black Studies: Proposed Afrocentric Core Curriculum.* Prepared by the National Council of Black Studies.

Lloyd, Judith Burson, and Florence Hamlish Levinsohn. 1993. *The Flowering African-American Artists and Friends in 1940s Chicago: A Look at the South Side Community Art Center*. Chicago, IL: Illinois Art Gallery.

Locke, Alain. 1969 (1936). *The Negro and His Music. Negro Art: Past and Present*. New York: Arno Press.

Locke, Alain. 1971. *The Negro in Art; a Pictorial Record of the Negro Artist and of the Negro Theme in Art*. New York: Hacker Art Books.

Locke, Alain, and Leonard Harris. 1989. *The Philosophy of Alain Locke: Harlem Renaissance and Beyond*. Philadelphia, PA: Temple University Press.

Locke, Alain LeRoy. 2015 (1925). *The New Negro*. Eastford, CT: Martino Fine Books.

Locke, Alain, Bernhard Joseph Stern, Progressive Education Association (U.S.), and Committee on Workshops. 1942. *When Peoples Meet, a Study in Race and Culture Contacts*. New York: Committee on Workshops, Progressive Education Association.

Logan, Rayford Whittingham. 1954. *The Negro in American Life and Thought, the Nadir, 1877–1901*. New York: Dial Press.

Logan, Rayford Whittingham. 1969. *Howard University: The First Hundred Years, 1867–1967*. New York: New York University Press.

Logan, Rayford Whittingham. 2011. *The Diplomatic Relations of the United States with Haiti, 1776–1891*. Chapel Hill, NC: University of North Carolina Press.

Lombardi, John. 1971. *Black Studies in the Community College*. Los Angeles, CA: ERIC Clearinghouse for Junior Colleges.

Lomotey, Kofi. 2010. *Encyclopedia of African American Education*. Los Angeles, CA: SAGE.

Looker, Benjamin. 2004. *Point from Which Creation Begins: The Black Artists' Group of St. Louis*. St. Louis, MO: Missouri Historical Society Press.

Lovett, Bobby L. 1999. *The African-American History of Nashville, Tennessee, 1780–1930: Elites and Dilemmas*. Fayetteville, AR: University of Arkansas Press.

Luna, Claire. 2002. "Alfred Ligon, 96; Started Oldest Black Bookstore." *Los Angeles Times*, August 16. http://articles.latimes.com/2002/aug/16/local/me-ligon16.

Lupalo, Lawrence E.K. 2016. *Three African Visionaries: Nkrumah, Nyerere and Senghor*. Scotts Valley, CA: CreateSpace.

McAdam, Doug. 1990. *Freedom Summer*. New York: Oxford University Press.

McAllister, Marvin Edward. 1997. "'White People Do Not Know How to Behave at Entertainments Designed for Ladies and Gentlemen of Colour': A History of New York's African Grove/African Theatre." PhD diss., Northwestern University, Evanston, IL.

McClaurin, Irma. 2001. *Black Feminist Anthropology: Theory, Politics, Praxis, and Poetics*. East Brunswick, NJ: Rutgers University Press.

McClendon, John. 2009. "Freedomways." In *Encyclopedia of African American History, 1896 to the Present: From the Age of Segregation to the Twenty-First Century*, edited by Paul Finkelman. Oxford: Oxford University Press.

McClendon, John H. 1980. *Afro-American Philosophers and Philosophy: A Selected Bibliography*. Urbana, IL: Afro-American Studies and Research Program, University of Illinois at Urbana-Champaign.

McCormick, Richard Patrick. 1989. *The Black Student Protest Movement at Rutgers, the State University*. New Brunswick, NJ: Rutgers University Press.

McDougal, Serie. 2014. *Research Methods in Africana Studies*. New York: Peter Lang.

McDuffie, Erik S. 2011. *Sojourning for Freedom: Black Women, American Communism, and the Making of Black Left Feminism*. 1st ed. Durham, NC: Duke University Press.

McGee, Julie L., and David C. Driskell. 2006. *David C. Driskell: Artist and Scholar*. San Francisco, CA: Pomegranate.

McGowan, Todd. 2017. *Spike Lee*. Champaign, IL: University of Illinois Press.

McIntyre, Niamh. 2017. "Harvard University Will Hold First Ever Black Only Graduation Ceremony." *The Independent*, May 11. www.independent.co.uk/news/world/americas/harvard-university-black-only-graduation-ceremony-graduates-may-2017-ivy-league-a7730686.html.

McKay, Claude. 1919. "If We Must Die." *The Liberator*, July 1919.

McLaughlin, Malcolm. 2014. "Storefront Revolutionary: Martin Sostre's Afro-Asian Bookshop, Black Liberation Culture, and the New Left, 1964–75." *The Sixties* 7(1): 1–27. https://doi.org/10.1080/17541328.2014.930265.

McLellan, Dennis. 2007. "Documentary Maker Focused on Black Issues." *Los Angeles Times*, December 19. www.latimes.com/archives/la-xpm-2007-dec-19-me-bourne19-story.html.

McNeil, Genna Rae. 1983. *Groundwork: Charles Hamilton Houston and the Struggle for Civil Rights*. Philadelphia, PA: University of Pennsylvania Press.

McPherson, James M. 1971. *Blacks in America: Bibliographical Essays*. Garden City, NY: Doubleday.

McWorter, Gerald A. 1967. *The Political Sociology of the Negro: A Selective Review of the Literature*. New York: Anti-Defamation League of B'nai B'rith.

McWorter, Gerald A., ed. 1968. *Negro Digest Black University Part 1* 17(5). Chicago, IL: Johnson Publications. http://freedomarchives.org/Documents/Finder/DOC513_scans/Negro_Digest/513.NegroDigest.NegroDigest.March.1968.pdf.

McWorter, Gerald A., ed. 1969. *Negro Digest Black University Part II* 18(5). Chicago, IL: Johnson Publications. http://freedomarchives.org/Documents/Finder/DOC513_scans/Negro_Digest/513.NegroDigest.NegroDigest.March.1969.pdf.

McWorter, Gerald A., ed. 1970. *Negro Digest Black University Part III* 19(5). Chicago, IL: Johnson Publications. www.freedomarchives.org/Documents/Finder/DOC513_scans/Negro_Digest/513.NegroDigest.NegroDigest.March.1970.pdf.

McWorter, Gerald A. 1981. *Guide to Scholarly Journals in Black Studies*. Chicago, IL: Chicago Center for Afro American Studies and Research.

McWorter, Gerald A. 1986. "The Professionalization of Achievement in Black Studies: A Report on Ranking Black Studies in Universities: A Reply to. Brossard." *Journal of Negro Education* 55(2): 229–35.

McWorter, Gerald A., and Abdul Alkalimat. 1980. "Racism and the Numbers Game: Black People and the 1980 Census." *The Black Scholar* 11(4): 61–71.

McWorter, Gerald A., and Ronald Bailey. 1984a. "An Addendum to Black Studies Curriculum Development in the 1980s: Its Patterns and History." *The Black Scholar* 15(6): 56–58.

McWorter, Gerald A., and Ronald Bailey. 1984b. "Black Studies Curriculum in the 1980s." *Black Scholar* 15(2): 18–31.

Magee, Jeffrey. 2005. *The Uncrowned King of Swing: Fletcher Henderson and Big Band Jazz*. Oxford: Oxford University Press.

Malcolm X. 2020 "A Research Site." www.brothermalcolm.net/

Makalani, Minkah. 2014. *In the Cause of Freedom: Radical Black Internationalism from Harlem to London, 1917–1939*. Chapel Hill, NC: University of North Carolina Press.

Manning, Patrick. 2009. *The African Diaspora: A History Through Culture*. New York: Columbia University Press.

Mao, Tse-tung. 1966. Statement Supporting the American Negroes in Their Just Struggle Against Racial Discrimination by U.S. Imperialism." Accessed June 7, 2018. www.marxists.org/subject/china/peking-review/1966/PR1966-33h.htm.

Mao, Zedong. 2001. *Four Essays on Philosophy*. Honolulu, HI: University Press of the Pacific.

Marable, Manning. 2005. *New Black Renaissance: The Souls Anthology of Critical African-American Studies*. Boulder, CO: Routledge.

Marable, Manning. 2016. *W.E.B. Du Bois: Black Radical Democrat*. London: Routledge.

Marable, Manning, and Leith Mullings. 2000. *Let Nobody Turn Us Around: Voices of Resistance, Reform, and Renewal: An African American Anthology*. Lanham, MD: Rowman & Littlefield.

Marano, Carla. 2014. "'We All Used to Meet at the Hall': Assessing the Significance of the Universal Negro Improvement Association in Toronto, 1900–1950." *Journal of the Canadian Historical Association / Revue de La Société Historique Du Canada* 25(1): 143–75. https://doi.org/10.7202/1032801ar.

Marsh, Carole. 2002. *John Harold Johnson: Creator of Ebony Magazine*. Peachtree City, GA: Gallopade International.

Marshall, Herbert, and Mildred Stock. 1993. *Ira Aldridge: The Negro Tragedian*. Washington, DC: Howard University Press.

Martin, Courtney J. 2011. "From the Center: The Spiral Group 1963–1966." *Nka: Journal of Contemporary African Art* 29(1): 86–98.

Martin, Douglas. 2012. "Una Mulzac, Harlem Bookseller With a Passion for Black Politics, Dies at 88." *New York Times*, February 4. www.nytimes.com/2012/02/05/nyregion/una-mulzac-harlem-bookseller-with-a-passion-for-black-politics-dies-at-88.html.

Martin, Waldo E. n.d. "'A Dream Deferred': The Southern Negro Youth Congress, the Student Nonviolent Coordinating Committee, and the Politics of Historical Memory." Accessed March 9, 2020. www.scribd.com/document/385725479/Waldo-Martin-a-Dream-Deferred-SNYC-SNCC-and-the-Politics-of-Historical-Memory-1.

Marx, Karl. 1864. "Chapter Thirty-One: Genesis of the Industrial Capitalist." *Capital, Volume I*. Accessed June 7, 2018. www.marxists.org/archive/marx/works/1867-c1/ch31.htm.

Marxists Internet Archive. 2020. www.marxists.org/

May, Vivian M. 2012. *Anna Julia Cooper, Visionary Black Feminist: A Critical Introduction*. New York: Routledge.

Mays, Benjamin E. 1968 (1938). *The Negro's God, as Reflected in His Literature*. New York: Russell & Russell.

Mays, Benjamin E., and Freddie C. Colston. 2002. *Dr. Benjamin E. Mays Speaks: Representative Speeches of a Great American Orator*. Lanham, MD: University Press of America.

Mays, Benjamin E., and Theodore Jones. 1971. *Born to Rebel: An Autobiography*. New York: Charles Scribner's Sons.

Mays, Benjamin E., and Joseph William Nicholson. 1969 (1934). *The Negro's Church*. New York: Arno Press.

Mealy, Rosemari. 1993. *Fidel & Malcolm X: Memories of a Meeting*. Melbourne, VIC: Ocean Press.

Meier, August. 1992a. *A White Scholar and the Black Community, 1945–1965: Essays and Reflections*. Amherst, MA: University of Massachusetts Press.

Meier, August. 1992b. *Negro Thought in America 1880–1915: Racial Ideologies in the Age of Booker T. Washington*. Ann Arbor, MI: University of Michigan Press.

Meier, August, and Elliott M. Rudwick. 1986. *Black History and the Historical Profession, 1915–1980*. Urbana, IL: University of Illinois Press.

Meier, August, and Elliott M. Rudwick. 1993. *From Plantation to Ghetto*. New York: Hill and Wang.

Merton, Robert K. 1968. *Social Theory and Social Structure*. Enlarged ed. New York: Free Press.

Middleton, Lorenzo. 1981. "Black Studies Professors Say Hard Times Will Undermine Struggle For Legitimacy." *The Chronicle of Higher Education* (March), 1, 6–7.

Miller, Karen. 2014. "Memories of Old School Black Book Stores." *The Philadelphia Sunday Sun* (blog). November 29. www.philasun.com/local/memories-of-old-school-black-book-stores/.

Mitchell, Arthur, Julieanna L. Richardson, Scott Stearns, and HistoryMakers. 2016. *The HistoryMakers Video Oral History with Arthur Mitchell*. http://marc.thehistorymakers.org/A2016.034.htm.

Mitchell, Loften. 1967. *Black Drama: The Story of the American Negro in the Theatre*. New York: Hawthorn Books.

Mitchell, Loften. 1976. *Voices of the Black Theatre*. Clifton, NJ: White.

Molzahn, Laura. 1993. "Chi Lives: Darlene Blackburn, Ambassador of Dance." *Chicago Reader*, June 24. www.chicagoreader.com/chicago/chi-lives-darlene-blackburn-ambassador-of-dance/Content?oid=882210.

Moon, Henry Lee. 1948. *Balance of Power: The Negro Vote*. Garden City, NY: Doubleday.

Moore, David Chioni. 2009. *Black Athena Writes Back: Martin Bernal Responds to His Critics*. Durham, NC: Duke University Press.

Moore, Richard B. 1992 (1960). *The Name "Negro": Its Origin and Evil Use*. Baltimore, MD: Black Classic Press.

Moore, Richard B., W. Burghardt Turner, and Joyce Moore Turner. 1988. *Richard B. Moore, Caribbean Militant in Harlem: Collected Writings, 1920–1972*. Bloomington, IN: Indiana University Press.

Morgan, Marcyliena. n.d. "Hiphop Archive and Research Institute." Hutchins Center for African and African American Research, Harvard University. http://hiphoparchive.org/.

Morris, Aldon D. 2015. *The Scholar Denied: W.E.B. Du Bois and the Birth of Modern Sociology*. Berkeley, CA: University of California Press.

Morris, Catherine, Rujeko Hockley, Connie H. Choi, Carmen Hermo, Stephanie Weissberg, Brooklyn Museum, and 1965–85 at the Brooklyn Museum Brooklyn Exhibition We Wanted a Revolution: Black Radical Women. 2017. *We Wanted a Revolution Black Radical Women, 1965–85: A Sourcebook : Published on the Exhibition We Wanted a Revolution: Black Radical Women, 1965–85 at the Brooklyn Museum, April 21–September 17, 2017*. Brooklyn, NY: Brooklyn Museum.

Morris, Vivien, and Freedom Road Socialist Organization. 1991. *Ain't Gonna Let Nobody Turn Us Around: The Birth and Development of the Black Student Movement, 1960–1990*. Boston, MA: Freedom Road Socialist Organization.

Morse, David. 1972. *Motown and the Arrival of Black Music*. New York: Collier Books.

Moynihan, Daniel P. 1965. "The Negro Family: The Case for National Action." Washington, DC: US Department of Labor Office of Policy, Planning, and Research.

Muhammad, Ahmad. 1978. "On the Black Student Movement: 1960–70." *The Black Scholar* 9(8/9): 2–11.

Mullen, Bill. 2015. *Popular Fronts: Chicago and African-American Cultural Politics, 1935–46*. Champaign, IL: University of Illinois Press.

Munford, Clarence J. 1978. *Production Relations, Class and Black Liberation: A Marxist Perspective in Afro-American Studies*. Amsterdam: B.R. Grüner Publishing Co.

Murrell, Gary, and Bettina Aptheker. 2015. *The Most Dangerous Communist in the United States A Biography of Herbert Aptheker*. Amherst, MA: University of Massachusetts Press.

National Black Theater. 1968. "Mission and History." www.nationalblacktheatre.org/mission.

National Council for Black Studies. 1976. "Constitution of the National Council for Black Studies." National Council for Black Studies.

National Council for Black Studies. 1982. "1982 Conference Program, 6th Annual National Conference."

NCBS (National Council for Black Studies). 2018. "Africana Studies Graduate Programs." July 29. www.ncbsonline.org/africana_studies_graduate_programs.

Neal, Larry. 1968. "The Black Arts Movement." *The Drama Review: TDR*: 29–39.

Nelson, Vaunda Micheaux. 2018. *No Crystal Stair: A Documentary Novel of the Life and Work of Lewis Michaux, Harlem Bookseller*. S.l.: Carolrhoda Lab.

Nelson, Vaunda Micheaux, and R. Gregory Christie. 2012. *No Crystal Stair: A Documentary Novel of the Life and Work of Lewis Michaux, Harlem Bookseller*. Minneapolis, MN: Carolrhoda Lab.

Nelson, Vaunda Micheaux, and R. Gregory Christie. 2015. *The Book Itch: Freedom, Truth, and Harlem's Greatest Bookstore*. Minneapolis, MN: Carolrhoda Books.

Nelson, William Stuart. 1945. *Religion and Racial Tension in America Today*. Washington, DC: Journal of Religious Thought.

Nelson, William Stuart. 1949. *Bases of World Understanding: An Inquiry into the Means of Resolving Racial, Religious, Class, and National Misapprehensions and Conflicts*. Calcutta: Calcutta University.

Nelson, William Stuart, Howard University, and Institute of Religion. 1948. *The Christian Way in Race Relations*. New York: Harper.

New Federal Theatre. n.d. "New Federal Theatre History and Mission." Accessed June 20, 2018. www.newfederaltheatre.com/about1.

"New Orleans." 2018. Wikipedia. https://en.wikipedia.org/w/index.php?title=New_Orleans&oldid=840081427.

Nixon, Ron. 2007. "DNA Tests Find Branches but few Roots." *New York Times*, November 25. www.nytimes.com/2007/11/25/business/25dna.html.

Nkrumah, Kwame. 1965. *Neo-Colonialism: The Last Stage of Imperialism*. London: Thomas Nelson & Sons.

Nkrumah, Kwame. 1968. *Handbook of Revolutionary Warfare: A Guide to the Armed Phase of the African Revolution*. London: Panaf Books.

Nkrumah, Kwame. 1970. *Class Struggle in Africa*. London: Zed Books.

Noble, Gil. 2011. "Like It Is." ABC7 New York. http://abc7ny.com/archive/6650885/.

Nobles, Wade W. 1980. *Voodoo or IQ: An Introduction to African Psychology*. Chicago, IL: Third World Press.

Norment, Nathaniel. 2007. *The African American Studies Reader*. 2nd ed. Durham, NC: Carolina Academic Press.

Norment, Nathaniel. 2019. *African American Studies: The Discipline and Its Dimensions*. New York: Peter Lang.

Northwestern University. n.d. "About the Department." Department of African American Studies. www.afam.northwestern.edu/about/.

Okafor, Victor Oguejiofor. 2007. "Shortcomings in Wilson's 'Chronicle of Higher Education' Article on the State of Black Studies Programs." *Journal of Black Studies* 37(3): 335–47.

O'Neal Parker, Lonnae. 2002. "Cosby Collection Curator Puts Passion on Display." *Chicago Tribune*, April 3. www.chicagotribune.com/news/ct-xpm-2002-04-03-0204030029-story.html.

O'Neill, Rosary. 2014. *New Orleans Carnival Krewes: The History, Spirit and Secrets of Mardi Gras*. Charleston, SC: The History Press.

Osofsky, Gilbert. 1996. *Harlem, the Making of a Ghetto: Negro New York, 1890–1930*. Chicago, IL: Ivan R. Dee.

Ottley, Roi. 1955. *The Lonely Warrior the Life and Times of Robert S. Abbott*. Chicago, IL: H. Regnery Co.

"Our Publisher." n.d. *Third World Press Foundation & Bookstore* (blog). Accessed May 8, 2018. https://thirdworldpressfoundation.org/our-publisher/.

Page, Yolanda Williams. 2007. *Encyclopedia of African American Women Writers*. Westport, CT: Greenwood Press.

Painter, Nell Irvin. 1979. *The Narrative of Hosea Hudson: His Life as a Negro Communist in the South*. Cambridge, MA: Harvard University Press.

Park, Robert E., and Ernest W. Hughes. 2009. *Introduction to the Science of Sociology*. www.gutenberg.org/ebooks/28496.

Patton, Gwendolyn. 1981. *My Race to Freedom: A Life in the Civil Rights Movement*. Montgomery, AL: NewSouth Books.

Payne, Charles M., and Carol Sills Strickland. 2008. *Teach Freedom: Education for Liberation in the African-American Tradition*. New York: Teachers College Press.

People's College. 1974. "Imperialism and Black Liberation: A Study Program." *The Black Scholar* 6(1): 38–42.

Perlo, Victor. *Economics of Racism*. New York: International Publishers.

Perry, Jeffrey Babcock. 2011. *Hubert Harrison: The Voice of Harlem Radicalism, 1883–1918*. New York: Columbia University Press.

Person-Lynn, Kwaku. 1996. *First Word: Black Scholars, Thinkers, Warriors: Knowledge, Wisdom, Mental Liberation*. New York: Harlem River Press.

Phelps, Carmen L. 2013. *Visionary Women Writers of Chicago's Black Arts Movement*. Jackson, MS: University Press of Mississippi.

Pittman, John P. 1997. *African-American Perspectives and Philosophical Traditions*. New York: Routledge.

Platt, Tony. 1991. *E. Franklin Frazier Reconsidered*. New Brunswick, NJ: Rutgers University Press.

Plumpp, Sterling. 1976. *Clinton*. Detroit, MI: Broadside Press.

Plumpp, Sterling. 1982. *Somehow We Survive: An Anthology of South African Writing*. New York: Thunder's Mouth Press.

Plumpp, Sterling. 1991. *Black Rituals*. Chicago, IL: Third World Press.

Pohlmann, Marcus D. 2003. *African American Political Thought*. New York: Routledge.

"Political Culture." 2019. Wikipedia. https://en.wikipedia.org/w/index.php?title=Political_culture&oldid=886249715.

Pollard, Sam. 1989. "Interview with Ed Vaughn." *Eyes on the Prize II Interview*. June 6. http://digital.wustl.edu/e/eii/eiiweb/vau5427.0309.166edvaughn.html.

Porter, Dorothy B. 1936. "The Organized Educational Activities of Negro Literary Societies, 1828–1846." *The Journal of Negro Education* 5(4): 555–76. https://doi.org/10.2307/2292029.

Porter, Dorothy B. 1959. "The African Collection at Howard University." *African Studies Bulletin* 2(1): 17–21. https://doi.org/10.2307/522962.

Porter, James A. 1937. "The Negro Artist and Racial Bias." *Department of Art Faculty Publications*, June. http://dh.howard.edu/art_fac/3.

Porter, James A. 1942. "Four Problems in the History of Negro Art." *The Journal of Negro History* 27(1): 9–36. https://doi.org/10.2307/2715087.

Porter, James A. 1969 (1941). *Modern Negro Art*. New York: Arno Press.

Porter, James A., Starmanda Bullock Featherstone, and Constance Porter Uzelac. 1992. *James A. Porter, Artist and Art Historian: The Memory of the Legacy: Howard University Gallery of Art, College of Fine Arts, October 15, 1992–January 8, 1993*. Washington, DC: Howard University Gallery of Art.

Powell, Adam Clayton. 1938. *Against the Tide: An Autobiography*. New York: R.R. Smith (Reprinted 1992 by Salem, NH: Ayer Co).

Powell Jr., Adam Clayton. 1945. *Marching Blacks: An Interpretative History of the Rise of the Black Common Man*. New York: Dial Press.

Powell Jr., Adam Clayton. 1971. *Adam by Adam: The Autobiography of Adam Clayton Powell, Jr.* New York: Dial Press.

Preston, Michael B., Lenneal J. Henderson, and Paul Lionel Puryear. 1982. *The New Black Politics: The Search for Political Power*. New York: Longman.

Prewitt, Kenneth. 2013. *What Is Your Race? The Census and Our Flawed Efforts to Classify Americans*. Princeton, NJ: Princeton University Press.

Price, Gregory N., and Maxton Allen. 2014. "The Scholarly Status of Blacks in the Economics Profession: Have the National Economic Association and the Review of Black Political Economy Mattered?" *The Review of Black Political Economy* 41(1): 1–11.

Prigoff, James, and Robin J. Dunitz. 2000. *Walls of Heritage, Walls of Pride: African American Murals*. San Francisco, CA: Pomegranate.

Proctor, Roscoe. 1973. *Black Workers and the Class Struggle*. New York: New Outlook Publishers.

Project 500. n.d. "Record Breaking Arrest." Accessed June 7, 2018. http://project500.omeka.net/exhibits/show/bpi/unrest/recordbreakingarrest.

Pruter, Robert. 2008. *Doowop: The Chicago Scene*. Urbana, IL: University of Illinois Press.

Quarles, Benjamin. 1989. *The Negro in the Civil War*. New York: Da Capo Press.

Quartey, Kojo A. 2003. *A Critical Analysis of the Contributions of Notable Black Economists*. Aldershot: Ashgate.

Rabaka, Reiland. 2006. "The Souls of Black Radical Folk W.E.B. Du Bois, Critical Social Theory, and the State of Africana Studies." *Journal of Black Studies* 36(5): 732–63. https://doi.org/10.1177/0021934705285941.

Rabaka, Reiland. 2011. *Forms of Fanonism: Frantz Fanon's Critical Theory and the Dialectics of Decolonization*. Lanham, MD: Lexington Books.

Rabaka, Reiland. 2016. *The Negritude Movement: W.E.B. Du Bois, Leon Damas, Aime Cesaire, Leopold Senghor, Frantz Fanon, and the Evolution of an Insurgent Idea*. New York: Lexington Books.

Raboteau, Albert, and David Wills. n.d. "African-American Religion: A Documentary History Project." Amherst College. https://aardoc.sites.amherst.edu/.

Rampersad, Arnold. 2008. *Ralph Ellison: A Biography*. New York: Knopf.

Randall, Dudley. 2014. *Roses and Revolutions: The Selected Writings of Dudley Randall*, edited by Melba Joyce Boyd. Detroit, MI: Wayne State University Press.

Randall, Dudley, and Margaret Taylor Burroughs, eds. 1969. *For Malcolm: Poems on the Life and Death of Malcolm X*. Detroit, MI: Broadside Press.

Ransby, Barbara. 2003. *Ella Baker and the Black Freedom Movement a Radical Democratic Vision*. Chapel Hill, NC: University of North Carolina Press.

Raushenbush, Winifred, and Everett Cherrington Hughes. 1992. *Robert E. Park: Biography of a Sociologist*. Ann Arbor, MI: University Microfilms International.

Ray, LeRoi R. 1976. "Black Studies: A Discussion of Evaluation." *The Journal of Negro Education* 45(4): 383–96. https://doi.org/10.2307/2966852.

Reddick, Lawrence Dunbar. 1944. *The Negro in the North during Wartime*. New York: Payne Educational Sociology Foundations.

Reddick, Lawrence Dunbar. 1978. *Crusader without Violence: A Biography of Martin Luther King*. New York: Harper.

Redding, J. Saunders. 1939. *To Make a Poet Black*. Chapel Hill, NC: University of North Carolina Press.

Redding, J. Saunders. 1942. *No Day of Triumph*. New York: Harper and Bros.

Redding, J. Saunders. 1950. *Stranger and Alone*. New York: Harcourt, Brace and Co.

Redding, J. Saunders. 1950. *They Came in Chains*. Philadelphia, PA: J.B. Lippincott Co.

Redding, J. Saunders. 1954. *An American in India: A Personal Report on the Indian Dilemma and the Nature of Her Conflicts*. Indianapolis, IN: Bobbs-Merrill Co.

Redding, J. Saunders. 1969. *On Being Negro in America*. New York: Harper and Row.

Redding, J. Saunders, and Faith Berry. 1992. *A Scholar's Conscience: Selected Writings of J. Saunders Redding, 1942–1977*. Lexington, KY: University Press of Kentucky.

Redding, Jay Saunders. 1958. *The Lonesome Road: The Story of the Negro's Part in America*. Garden City, NY: Doubleday.

Redmond, Eugene. 1976. *Drumvoices: The Mission of Afro-American Poetry: A Critical History*. Garden City, NY: Anchor Press.

Reed, Adolph L. 1997. *W.E.B. Du Bois and American Political Thought: Fabanism and the Color Line*. New York: Oxford University Press.

Reed, Christopher Robert. 2014. *Knock at the Door of Opportunity: Black Migration to Chicago, 1900–1919*. Carbondale, IL: Southern Illinois University Press.

Reid, Calvin. 2017. "Third World Press's 50 Years of Black Literature and Politics." *Publishers Weekly*, September 29. www.publishersweekly.com/pw/by-topic/industry-news/publisher-news/article/74931-third-world-press-s-50-years-of-black-literature-and-politics.html.

Reid, Ira De Augustine, dir. 1930. *Negro Membership in American Labor Unions*. New York: Alexander Press. http://catalog.hathitrust.org/api/volumes/oclc/1547079.html.

Reid, Ira De Augustine. 1970. *The Negro Immigrant: His Background, Characteristics, and Social Adjustment, 1899–1937*. New York: AMS Press.

Reid, Ira De Augustine, American Council on Education, and American Youth Commission. 1940. *In a Minor Key: Negro Youth in Story and Fact*. Washington, DC: American Council on Education.

Reid, John P. 1990. *J. Saunders Redding, 1906–1988*. Stanton, DE: John P. Reid.

Revolutionary Union. 1972. *Red Papers #5: National Liberation and Proletarian Revolution in the U.S.* www.marxists.org/history/erol/periodicals/red-papers/red-papers-5/index.htm,

Rhodes, Jane. 2017. *Framing the Black Panthers: The Spectacular Rise of a Black Power Icon*. Champaign, IL: University of Illinois Press.

Rich, Wilbur C. 2007. *African American Perspectives on Political Science*. Philadelphia, PA: Temple University Press.

Richardson, Joe Martin. 1980. *A History of Fisk University, 1865–1946*. Tuscaloosa, AL: University of Alabama Press.

Rickford, John Russell, and Russell J. Rickford, 2000. *Spoken Soul: The Story of Black English*. New York: Wiley.

Rickford, Russell John. 2016. *We are an African People: Independent Education, Black Power, and the Radical Imagination*. Oxford: Oxford University Press.

Rise Up Newark. n.d. "The Black Power Conference | Newark." *Rise Up Newark: North* (blog). Accessed June 7, 2018. http://riseupnewark.com/chapters/chapter-3/part-3/the-black-power-conference/.

Robb, F.H. Hammurabi. 1951. *The Chicago Round-Up, 1779–1951: A Vest Pocket Encyclopedia*. Chicago, IL: House of Knowledge.

Robinson, Armstead L., Craig C. Foster, Donald H. Ogilvie, and Black Student Alliance at Yale, eds. 1969. *Black Studies in the University: A Symposium*. New Haven, CT: Yale University Press.

Robinson, Cedric J. 1983. *Black Marxism: The Making of the Black Radical Tradition*. London: Zed Books.

Robinson, Lisa Clayton. 2005. *Harlem Writers Guild*. Oxford: Oxford University Press.

Rogers, Ibram H. 2011. "The Black Campus Movement: The Case for a New Historiography." *The Sixties: A Journal of History, Politics and Culture* 4(2): 171–86.

Rogers, Ibram H. 2012. *The Black Campus Movement: Black Students and the Racial Reconstitution of Higher Education, 1965–1972*. New York: Palgrave Macmillan.

Rojas, Fabio. 2004. "Faculty Development Issues In a Department of Black Studies." In *Unleashing Suppressed Voices on College Campuses: Diversity Issues in Higher Education*, edited by Kandace G. Hinton, Valerie Grim, Mary F. Howard-Hamilton, O. Gilbert Brown, and Mona Y. Davenport, 181–89. New York: Peter Lang.

Rojas, Fabio. 2007. *From Black Power to Black Studies: How a Radical Social Movement Became an Academic Discipline*. Baltimore, MD: Johns Hopkins University Press.

Rojas, Fabio. 2010. *From Black Power to Black Studies: How a Radical Social Movement Became an Academic Discipline*. Baltimore, MD: Johns Hopkins University Press.

Rooks, Noliwe M. 2006. *White Money/Black Power: The Surprising History of African American Studies and the Crisis of Race in Higher Education*. Boston, MA: Beacon Press.

Roper, Robert. 2006. "Glorious Dust." *The American Scholar*, December.

Rose, Peter Isaac. 1968. *The Subject Is Race: Traditional Ideologies and the Teaching of Race Relations*. New York: Oxford University Press.

Rowe, Cyprian Lamar. 1970. "Crisis in African Studies: The Birth of the African Heritage Studies Association." *Black Academy Press* 1(3): 3–10.

Rowley, Hazel. 2008. *Richard Wright: The Life and Times*. Chicago, IL: University of Chicago Press.

"Roy Wilkins Facts." n.d. Accessed June 7, 2018. http://biography.yourdictionary.com/roy-wilkins.

St. Cloud State University. n.d. "Ethnic and Women's Studies Working Papers." https://repository.stcloudstate.edu/ews_wps/.

Sanders, Kimberly. 2016. "Black Culture Centers: A Review of Pertinent Literature." *Urban Education Research & Policy Annuals* 4(1). https://journals.uncc.edu/urbaned/article/view/443.

Sanders-Cassell, Katrina M. 2005. *Intelligent and Effective Direction: The Fisk University Race Relations Institute and the Struggle for Civil Rights, 1944–1969*. New York: Peter Lang.

Sankofa. n.d. "Sankofa Video Books & Cafe: Books, DVD's & Events about People of African Descent + Cafe." Accessed June 8, 2018. www.sankofa.com/bookstorecafe/.

Saunders, Frances Stonor. 2013. *The Cultural Cold War: The CIA and the World of Arts and Letters*. New York: The New Press.

Savchuk, Katia. 2015. "California has More Billionaires Than Every Country Except the U.S. and China." *Forbes*, March 4. www.forbes.com/sites/katiasavchuk/2015/03/04/california-has-more-billionaires-than-every-country-except-the-u-s-and-china/?sh=7ebb3ea3637c.

Scally, M. Anthony. 1985. *Carter G. Woodson: A Bio-Bibliography*. Westport, CT: Greenwood Press.

Scott-Heron, Gil. 2017. *The Last Holiday: A Memoir*. Edinburgh: Canongate.

Seale, Bobby. 1991. *Seize the Time: The Story of the Black Panther Party and Huey P. Newton*. Baltimore, MD: Black Classic Press.

Selby, Mike. 2019. *Freedom Libraries: The Untold Story of Libraries for African Americans in the South*. Lanham, MD: Rowman and Littlefield.

Semmes, Clovis E. 1998. *Roots of Afrocentric Thought: A Reference Guide to Negro Digest/Black World, 1961–1976*. Westport, CT: Greenwood Press.

Shange, Ntozake. 1982 (1972). *For Colored Girls Who have Considered Suicide*. New York: Bantam Books.

Shell-Weiss, Melanie. 2007. "Immigration, Race, and Nation: Baltimore's Immigrant Recruitment and Response, 1880–1910." Center for Africana Studies Working Paper Series, Johns Hopkins University. https://jscholarship.library.jhu.edu/bitstream/handle/1774.2/32741/WP005.pdf.

Sherwood, Marika. 1995. *Manchester and the 1945 Pan-African Congress*. London: Savannah Press.

Shockley, Ann Allen. 1988. *Afro-American Women Writers, 1746–1933: An Anthology and Critical Guide*. Boston, MA: G.K. Hall.

Sides, Josh. 2003. *L.A. City Limits: African American Los Angeles from the Great Depression to the Present*. Berkeley, CA: University of California Press.

Siegel, Jeanne. 2011. "Why Spiral?" *Nka: Journal of Contemporary African Art* 29(1): 78–84.

"Sigerist Circle Bibliography on Race and Medicine." n.d. RaceSci: History of Race in Science. Accessed May 8, 2018. http://web.mit.edu/racescience/bibliographies/current_scholarship/sigerist.html.

Skinner, Elliott P. 1976. "African Studies, 1955–1975: An Afro-American Perspective." *Issue: A Journal of Opinion* 6(2–3): 57–67. https://doi.org/10.2307/1166446.

Skocpol, Theda, Ariane Liazos, and Marshall Ganz. 2008. *What a Mighty Power We Can Be: African American Fraternal Groups and the Struggle for Racial Equality*. Princeton, NJ: Princeton University Press.

Slater, Robert Bruce. 1993. "Rating the Leading Black Studies Departments." *The Journal of Blacks in Higher Education* 1: 38–46. https://doi.org/10.2307/2962511.

Slaughter, Diana T., and Abdul Alkalimat. 1985. "Social Origins and Early Features of the Scientific Study of Black American Families and Children." In *Beginnings: The*

Social and Affective Development of Black Children, edited by Margaret Beale Spencer, Geraldine Kearse Brookins, and Walter Recharde Allen, 5–19. Hillsdale, NJ: L. Erlbaum.

Smethurst, James Edward. 2005. *The Black Arts Movement: Literary Nationalism in the 1960s and 1970s*. Chapel Hill, NC: University of North Carolina Press.

Smethurst, James Edward. 2021. *Behold the Land: The Black Arts Movement in the South*. Chapel Hill, NC: University of North Carolina Press.

Smith, Arthur L. 1972. Review of *The American Negro: His History and Literature; The Antislavery Crusade*, edited by William Loren Katz. *Journal of Black Studies* 3(1): 117–19.

Smith, Barbara. 1989. "A Press of Our Own Kitchen Table: Women of Color Press." *Frontiers: A Journal of Women Studies* 10(3): 11. https://doi.org/10.2307/3346433.

Smith, Jessie Carney. 1977. *Black Academic Libraries and Research Collections: A Historical Survey*. Westport, CT: Greenwood Press.

Smith, Jessie Carney, and Shirelle Phelps. 1992. *Notable Black American Women*. Detroit, MI: Gale Research.

Smith, Justin E.H. 2013. "The Enlightenment's 'Race' Problem, and Ours." *Opinionator* (blog). February 10. https://opinionator.blogs.nytimes.com/2013/02/10/why-has-race-survived/.

Smith, Klytus, Abiola Sinclair, and Hannibal Ahmed. 1995. *The Harlem Cultural/Political Movements, 1960–1970: From Malcolm X to "Black Is Beautiful."* New York: Gumbs & Thomas Publishers.

Smith, Robert C., Cedric Johnson, and Robert G. Newby. 2014. *What Has This Got to Do with the Liberation of Black People? The Impact of Ronald W. Walters on African American Thought and Leadership*. Albany, NY: State University of New York Press.

Smitherman, Geneva. 1977. *Talkin' and Testifyin': Language of Black America*. Detroit, MI: Wayne State University Press.

Smitherman, Geneva. 2000. *Talkin That Talk: Language, Culture and Education in African America*. New York: Routledge.

Smythe, Mabel M., John Preston Davis, and Phelps-Stokes Fund. 1976. *The Black American Reference Book*. Englewood Cliffs, NJ: Prentice-Hall.

"Sounds of Blackness." n.d. Wikipedia. Accessed August 12, 2018. https://en.wikipedia.org/wiki/Sounds_of_Blackness.

Southern, Eileen. 1972. *Readings in Black American Music*. New York: W.W. Norton.

Southern, Eileen. 1982. *Biographical Dictionary of Afro-American and African Musicians*. Westport, CT: Greenwood Press.

Southern, Eileen. 1983. *The Music of Black Americans: A History*. New York: W.W. Norton.

Sowell, Thomas. n.d. "Thomas Sowell: Curriculum Vita." Accessed June 22, 2018. www.tsowell.com/cv.html.

Sowell, Thomas. 1974. "The Plight of Black Students in the United States." *Daedalus* 103(2): 179–96.

Sowell, Thomas. 1999. "The Day Cornell Died." *Hoover Digest*, October 30. www.hoover.org/research/day-cornell-died.

Spencer, Robyn C. 2016. *The Revolution Has Come: Black Power, Gender, and the Black Panther Party in Oakland*. Durham, NC: Duke University Press.

Spero, Sterling D., and Abram Lincoln Harris. 1968. *The Black Worker: The Negro and the Labor Movement*. New York: Atheneum.

Springer, Kimberly. 2005. *Living for the Revolution: Black Feminist Organizations, 1968–1980*. Durham, NC: Duke University Press.

Stampp, Kenneth Milton. 1972. *The Peculiar Institution: Negro Slavery in the American South*. New York: Knopf.

Stewart, Jeffrey C. 2018. *The New Negro: The Life of Alain Locke*. New York: Oxford University Press.

"The Studio Museum in Harlem." n.d. Accessed June 7, 2018. www.studiomuseum.org/.

Styron, William. 2017 (1967). *The Confessions of Nat Turner*. La Vergne, TN: Dreamscape Media.

Szwed, John F. 2012. *Space Is the Place: The Lives and Times of Sun Ra*. New York: Pantheon Books.

Tapscott, Horace, and Steven Louis Isoardi. 2001. *Songs of the Unsung: The Musical and Social Journey of Horace Tapscott*. Durham, NC: Duke University Press.

Taylor, Alrutheus Ambush. 1973. *The Negro in the Reconstruction of Virginia*. Washington, DC: Association for the Study of Negro Life and History.

Taylor, Alrutheus Ambush. 1974. *The Negro in Tennessee: 1865–1880*. Spartanburg, SC: Reprint Co.

Taylor, Nikki M. 2013. *America's First Black Socialist: The Radical Life of Peter H. Clark*. Lexington, KY: University Press of Kentucky.

Taylor, Ula Yvette. 2017. *The Promise of Patriarchy: Women and the Nation of Islam*. Chapel Hill, NC: The University of North Carolina Press.

Third World Women's Alliance. n.d. *Triple Jeopardy*, archive, *flickr*. www.flickr.com/photos/27628370@N08/sets/72157605547626040/.

"Thomas Theorem." 2018. Wikipedia. https://en.wikipedia.org/w/index.php?title=Thomas_theorem&oldid=823986852.

Thomas-Houston, Marilyn. 2008. *Sustaining Black Studies in the 21st Century* (14)1. National Council for Black Studies.

Thompson, Charles Henry. 1928. "The Educational Achievements of Negro Children." *Annals of the American Academy of Political and Social Science* 140: 193–208.

Thompson, Charles Henry. 1946. "The Control and Administration of the Negro College." *Journal of Educational Sociology* 19(8): 484–95. https://doi.org/10.2307/2263571.

Thompson, Charles Henry. 1948. "Separate but Not Equal; the Sweatt Case." *Southwest Review* 33(2): 105–12.

Thompson, Charles Henry. 1959. "The Prospect of Negro Higher Education." *Journal of Educational Sociology* 32(6): 309–16. https://doi.org/10.2307/2264794.

Thompson, Charles Henry. 1961. *African Education South of the Sahara*. Washington, DC: Published for the Bureau of Educational Research, Howard University by Howard University Press.

Thompson, Ernest, and Mindy Thompson. 1976. *Homeboy Came to Orange: A Story of People's Power/ by Ernest Thompson and Mindy Thompson*, with an Introduction by Mayor Coleman A. Young. Newark, NJ: Bridgebuilder Press.

Thompson, Julius Eric. 2005. *Dudley Randall, Broadside Press, and the Black Arts Movement in Detroit, 1960–1995*. Jefferson, NC: McFarland.

Thonvis, Gregory. 1971. "Historical Survey of Black Education as a Means of Black Liberation 1875–1969." PhD diss., Ohio State University.

Thorpe, Earl E. 1971. *Black Historians: A Critique*. New York: Morrow.

Thurman, Howard. 1981. *With Head and Heart: The Autobiography of Howard Thurman*. San Diego, CA: Harcourt Brace Jovanovich.

Thurman, Howard. 1996. *Jesus and the Disinherited*. Boston, MA: Beacon Press.

Thurman, Howard, and Luther E. Smith. 2006. *Howard Thurman: Essential Writings*. Maryknoll, NY: Orbis Books.

Tidwell, John Edgar. 2013. "Sterling Brown. A Bibliography." *Oxford Bibliographies*. http://dx.doi.org/10.1093/OBO/9780199827251-0046.

Tidwell, John Edgar, and Steven C. Tracy. 2009. *After Winter: The Art and Life of Sterling A. Brown*. Oxford: Oxford University Press.

Tillmon, Johnnie. 1972. "Welfare Is a Women's Issue." *Ms*. www.msmagazine.com/spring2002/tillmon.asp.

Tinson, Christopher M. 2017. *Radical Intellect: Liberator Magazine and Black Activism in the 1960s*. Chapel Hill, NC: University of North Carolina Press.

Tolbert, Emory J. 1980. *The UNIA and Black Los Angeles: Ideology and Community in the American Garvey Movement*. Los Angeles, CA: Center for Afro-American Studies, University of California.

Tracy, Jan. 2017. "The Biggest Beneficiaries of the Government Safety Net: Working-Class Whites." *Washington Post*, February 16. www.washingtonpost.com/news/wonk/wp/2017/02/16/the-biggest-beneficiaries-of-the-government-safety-net-working-class-whites/?noredirect=on&utm_term=.e443a288907e.

Trescott, Jacqueline. 1996. "Harvard's Dream Team." *Washington Post*, February 26. www.washingtonpost.com/archive/lifestyle/1996/02/26/harvards-dream-team/62f2c97d-e97a-456e-b86e-43bc13b27a80/.

T'Shaka, Oba. 2012. "Africana Studies Department History: San Francisco State University." *Journal of Pan African Studies* 5(7): 13–32.

Turner, James E., and Africana Studies and Research Center (Cornell University), eds. 1984. *The Next Decade: Theoretical and Research Issues in Africana Studies*. Ithaca, NY: Africana Studies and Research Center, Cornell University.

Turner, Lorenzo Dow. 1949. *Africanisms in the Gullah Dialect*. Chicago, IL: Chicago University Press.

Turner, W. Burghardt. 1975. "J.A. Rogers: Portrait of an Afro-American Historian." *The Black Scholar* 6(5): 32–39.

United States Congress, House Committee on House Administration, and Office of History and Preservation House. 2008. *Black Americans in Congress, 1870–2007*. Washington, DC: U.S. G.P.O.

University of Chicago Arts. n.d. "Artists-in-Residence." https://arts.uchicago.edu/artsandpubliclife/artists-programs/residencies.

University of Massachusetts Amherst. n.d. "Alumni." W.E.B. Du Bois Department of Afro-American Studies. www.umass.edu/afroam/alumni-afroam.

Urban, Wayne J. 1992. *Black Scholar: Horace Mann Bond, 1904–1972*. Athens, GA: University of Georgia Press.

Valdés, Vanessa Kimberly. 2018. *Diasporic Blackness: The Life and Times of Arturo Alfonso Schomburg*. Albany, NY: State University of New York Press.

Van Deburg, William L. 1992. *New Day in Babylon: The Black Power Movement and American Culture, 1965–1975*. Chicago, IL: University of Chicago Press.

Van Der Zee, James, Owen Dodson, and Camille Billops. 1978. *The Harlem Book of the Dead*. Dobbs Ferry, NY: Morgan & Morgan.

Van Sertima, Ivan. 2003. *They Came before Columbus: The African Presence in Ancient America*. New York: Random House.

Vincent, Charles. 1981. Review of *The UNIA and Black Los Angeles: Ideology and Community in the American Garvey Movement*, by Emory J. Tolbert. *The Journal of Negro History* 66(1): 56–58. https://doi.org/10.2307/2716885.

Wade-Lewis, Margaret 1988. *Lorenzo Dow Turner: First African-American Linguist.* Philadelphia, PA: Temple University, Institute of African and African Affairs.

Wade-Lewis, Margaret. 2005. "Mark Hanna Watkins: African American Linguistic Anthropologist." *Histories of Anthropology Annual* 1(1): 181–218. https://doi.org/10.1353/HAA.0.0001.

Wade-Lewis, Margaret. 2007. *Lorenzo Dow Turner: Father of Gullah Studies*. Columbia, SC: University of South Carolina Press.

Walker, Alice. 1982. *The Color Purple*. New York: Harcourt Brace Jovanovich.

Walker, Dara. 2018. "Black Power and the Detroit High School Organizing Tradition—AAIHS." *African American Intellectual History* (blog). January 11. www.aaihs.org/black-power-and-the-detroit-high-school-organizing-tradition/.

Walker, Margaret. 1989. *This Is My Century: New and Collected Poems*. Athens, GA: University of Georgia Press.

Walker, Margaret. 2016. *Jubilee*. Boston, MA: Houghton Mifflin.

Walker, Margaret. 2018. "For My People." Text/html. Poetry Foundation. May 8. www.poetryfoundation.org/poetrymagazine/poems/21850/for-my-people.

Walker, Margaret, and Maryemma Graham. 2002. *Conversations with Margaret Walker*. Jackson, MS: University Press of Mississippi.

Wallace, Michele. 2015 [1979]. *Black Macho and the Myth of the Superwoman*. London: Verso.

Wallace, Phyllis Ann, Linda Datcher, and Julianne Malveaux. 1982. *Black Women in the Labor Force*. Cambridge, MA: MIT Press.

Walters, Ronald W. 1988. *Black Presidential Politics in America: A Strategic Approach*. Albany, NY: State University of New York Press.

Walton, Sid. 1969. *The Black Curriculum: Developing a Program in Afro-American Studies*. East Palo Alto, CA: Black Liberation Publishers.

Ward, Jerry Washington, and Robert Butler. 2008. *The Richard Wright Encyclopedia*. Westport, CT: Greenwood Press.

Ward, Stephen. 2016. "The Third World Women's Alliance." *The Black Power Movement: Rethinking the Civil Rights–Black Power Era*, edited by Peniel E. Joseph, 119–144. New York: Routledge.

Ward, Theodore. 2007. *Big White Fog*. London: Nick Hern Books.

Warren, Robert Penn, and David W. Blight. 2014. *Who Speaks for the Negro?* New Haven, CT: Yale University Press.

Watkins, Mark Hanna. 1943. "The West African 'Bush' School." *American Journal of Sociology* 48(6): 666–75.

Watkins, Mark Hanna. 1956. "The Study of Culture." *The Journal of Negro Education* 25(2): 143–45.

Watkins, Mark Hanna. 1973. *A Grammar of Chichewa, a Bantu Language of British Central Africa*. New York: Kraus Reprint.

Watkins, Sylvestre C. 1944. *Anthology of American Negro Literature*. New York: Modern Library.

Watkins, William H. 2001. *The White Architects of Black Education: Ideology and Power in America, 1865–1954*. New York: Teachers College Press.

Watson, Jamal. 2013. "Gates Criticized for Securing $15 Million Gift from Wealthy Alumnus." *Diverse Issues in Higher Education*, September.

Weaver, Robert C. 1967 (1948). *The Negro Ghetto.* New York: Russell & Russell.

Weaver, Robert C. 1969 (1946). *Negro Labor: A National Problem.* Port Washington, NY: Kennikat Press.

Weissinger, Thomas. 2010. "The Core Journal Concept in Black Studies." *The Journal of Academic Librarianship* 36(2): 119–24. https://doi.org/10.1016/j.acalib.2010.01.001.

Weissinger, Thomas. 2017. "Black Studies Scholarly Journals." African American Research Center, University of Illinois Library. www.library.illinois.edu/afx/aajournals/.

Weixlmann, Joe. 1990. "African American Autobiography in the Twentieth Century: A Bibliographical Essay." *Black American Literature Forum* 24(2): 375–415. https://doi.org/10.2307/3041713.

Wells-Barnett, Ida B., and Jacqueline Jones Royster. 2016. *Southern Horrors and Other Writings: The Anti-Lynching Campaign of Ida B. Wells, 1892–1900.* 2nd ed. Boston, MA: Bedford/St. Martins, Macmillan Learning.

Wells-Barnett, Ida B., Dorothy Sterling, Miriam DeCosta-Willis, and Mary Helen Washington. 1995. *The Memphis Diary of Ida B. Wells.* Boston, MA: Beacon Press.

Wesley, Charles H. 1967. *Negro Labor in the United States, 1850–1925: A Study in American Economic History.* New York: Russell and Russell.

Wesley, Charles H., and James L. Conyers. 1997. *Charles H. Wesley: The Intellectual Tradition of a Black Historian.* New York: Garland Publishing.

Wesley, Dorothy Porter. 1969. *A Working Bibliography on the Negro in the United States.* Ann Arbor, MI: University Microfilms International.

West, Cornel. 1999. *The Cornel West Reader.* New York: Basic Books.

West, Cornel, and Eddie S. Glaude. 2003. *African American Religious Thought: An Anthology.* Louisville, KY: Westminster John Knox Press.

West, James. 2016. "Power Is 100 Years Old: Lerone Bennett Jr., Ebony Magazine and the Roots of Black Power." *The Sixties* 9(2): 165–88. https://doi.org/10.1080/17541328.2016.1241601.

White, Derrick E. 2011. *The Challenge of Blackness the Institute of the Black World and Political Activism in the 1970s.* Gainesville, FL: University Press of Florida.

White, Joseph L. 1984. *The Psychology of Blacks: An Afro-American Perspective.* Englewood Cliffs, NJ: Prentice-Hall.

Whitehead, Alfred North. 1985 (1925). *Science and the Modern World.* London: Free Association Books.

Widener, Daniel. 2009. *Black Arts West.* Durham, NC: Duke University Press Books.

Wiegand, Wayne A. 2015. *Part of Our Lives: A People's History of the American Public Library.* New York: Oxford University Press.

Wikipedia. 2010. "University of North Carolina Academic-Athletic Scandal." https://en.wikipedia.org/wiki/University_of_North_Carolina_academic-athletic_scandal.

Wikipedia. 2017. "Theodore Ward." https://en.wikipedia.org/w/index.php?title=Theodore_Ward&oldid=816774027.

Wikipedia. 2018a. "Spiral (Arts Alliance)." https://en.wikipedia.org/w/index.php?title=Spiral_(arts_alliance)&oldid=828654425.

Wikipedia. 2018b. "Katherine Dunham." https://en.wikipedia.org/w/index.php?title=Katherine_Dunham&oldid=839278468.

Wilder, Craig Steven. 2013. *Ebony & Ivy: Race, Slavery, and the Troubled History of America's Universities.* New York: Bloomsbury Press.

Williams, Alma René. 1978. *Robert C. Weaver: From the Black Cabinet to the President's Cabinet.* St. Louis, MO: Washington University.

Williams, Chancellor. 1987. *The Destruction of Black Civilization: Great Issues of a Race from 4500 B.C. to 2000 A.D.* Chicago, IL: Third World Press.

Williams, George Washington. 1883a. *History of the Negro Race in America from 1619 to 1880. Volume 1. Negroes as Slaves, as Soldiers, and as Citizens.* New York: G.P. Putnam's Sons. www.gutenberg.org/ebooks/15735.

Williams, George Washington 1883b. *History of the Negro Race in America from 1619 to 1880. Volume 2. Negroes as Slaves, as Soldiers, and as Citizens.* New York: G.P. Putnam's Sons. www.gutenberg.org/ebooks/21851.

Williams, Jasmin K. 2008. "Dr. Barbara Ann Teer: A Life Lived 'Free, Open and Black.'" *New York Post*, September 15. http://nypost.com/2008/09/15/dr-barbara-ann-teer-a-life-lived-free-open-and-black/.

Williams, Juan. 2011. *Thurgood Marshall: American Revolutionary.* New York: Three Rivers Press.

Williams, Sonja D. 2017. *Word Warrior: Richard Durham, Radio, and Freedom.* Urbana, IL: University of Illinois Press.

Williamson-Lott, Joy Ann. 2003. *Black Power on Campus: The University of Illinois, 1965–75.* Urbana, IL: University of Illinois Press.

Willis, Deborah. 2000. *Reflections in Black: A History of Black Photographers, 1840 to the Present.* New York: W.W. Norton.

Wilmore, Gayraud S. 1972. *Black Religion and Black Radicalism.* Garden City, NY: Doubleday.

Wilmore, Gayraud S., and James H. Cone. 1979. *Black Theology: A Documentary History.* Maryknoll, NY: Orbis Books.

Wilson, Amos N. 2011. *Black-on-Black Violence: The Psychodynamics of Black Self-Annihilation in Service of White Domination.* New York: Afrikan World InfoSystems.

Wilson, James Q. 1980. *Negro Politics: The Search for Leadership.* New York: Octagon Books.

Wilson, Robin. 2005. "Are Black Studies Programs Obsolete?" *The Chronicle of Higher Education*, April 18.

Winston, Henry. 1977. *Class, Race and Black Liberation.* New York: International Publishers.

Winston, Michael R. 1973. *Howard University Department of History, 1913–1973.* Washington, DC: Department of History, Howard University.

Wiredu, Kwasi. 2004. *A Companion to African Philosophy.* Malden, MA: Blackwell Pub.

Wispé, L., P. Ash, J. Awkard, L.H. Hicks, M. Hoffman, and J. Porter. 1969. "The Negro Psychologist in America." *The American Psychologist* 24(2): 142–50. https://doi.org/10.1037/h0027107.

Witham, Barry. 2009. *The Federal Theatre Project: A Case Study.* Cambridge: Cambridge University Press.

Wolseley, Roland Edgar. 1990. *The Black Press, U.S.A.* Ames, IA: Iowa State University Press.

Woodard, Komozi. 1999. *A Nation Within a Nation.* Chapel Hill, NC: University of North Carolina Press.

Woodford, John. 1991. "Testing America's Promise of Free Speech: Muhammad Speaks in the 1960s, A Memoir." *Voices of the African Diaspora, Center for Afro-American and African Studies, University of Michigan* 7(3): 3–16.

Woodrow Wilson National Fellowship Foundation. n.d. "Past Programs." Accessed July 12, 2018. https://woodrow.org/about/past-programs/#MLK.

Woodruff, Hale, and Robert Blackburn. n.d. *Hale Woodruff: Selections from the Atlanta Period, 1931–1946. A Portfolio of Eight Prints.* New York: Printmaking Workshop.

Woodruff, Hale, and Studio Museum in Harlem. 1979. *Hale Woodruff: 50 Years of His Art, April 29 Thru June 24, 1979, the Studio Museum in Harlem*. New York: Studio Museum in Harlem.

Woodson, Carter Godwin. 1918. *A Century of Negro Migration*. Washington, DC: The Association for the Study of Negro Life and History.

Woodson, Carter Godwin. 1921. *The History of the Negro Church*. Washington, DC: Associated Publishers.

Woodson, Carter Godwin. 1936. *The African Background Outlined, or Handbook for the Study of the Negro*. Washington, DC: Association for the Study of Negro Life and History.

Woodson, Carter Godwin. 1968. *The Education of the Negro Prior to 1861*. New York: Arno Press.

Woodson, Carter Godwin, and Association for the Study of Negro Life and History. 1930. *The Rural Negro*. Washington, DC: Association for the Study of Negro Life and History.

Woodson, Carter Godwin, Frederick Douglass, and Association for the Study of Afro-American Life and History. 1926. *The Mind of the Negro as Reflected in Letters Written during the Crisis, 1800–1860*. Washington, DC: Association for the Study of Negro Life and History.

Woodson, Carter Godwin, and Charles H. Wesley. 1962. *The Negro in Our History*. Washington, DC: Associated Publishers.

Woodward, C. Vann. 2006. *The Strange Career of Jim Crow*. New York: Oxford University Press.

Woodward, C. Vann. 2013. *Origins of the New South, 1877–1913*. Baton Rouge, LA: Louisiana State University Press.

Work, John Wesley. 1969. *Folk Songs of the American Negro*. New York: Negro Universities Press.

Work, Monroe Nathan. 1912. *Negro Year Book: An Annual Encyclopedia of the Negro. 1912*. Nashville, TN: Sunday School Union Print.

Work, Monroe Nathan. 1913. *Negro Year Book: An Annual Encyclopedia of the Negro. 1913*. Tuskegee, AL: Negro Year Book Publishing Co.

Work, Monroe Nathan. 1914. *Negro Year Book: An Annual Encyclopedia of the Negro. 1914–1915*. Tuskegee, AL: Negro Year Book Publishing Co.

Work, Monroe Nathan. 1916. *Negro Year Book: An Annual Encyclopedia of the Negro. 1916–1917*. Tuskegee, AL: Negro Year Book Publishing Co.

Work, Monroe Nathan. 1918. *Negro Year Book: An Annual Encyclopedia of the Negro. 1918–1919*. Tuskegee, AL: Negro Year Book Publishing Co.

Work, Monroe Nathan. 1921. *Negro Year Book: An Annual Encyclopedia of the Negro. 1921–1922*. Tuskegee, AL: Negro Year Book Publishing Co.

Work, Monroe Nathan. 1925. *Negro Year Book: An Annual Encyclopedia of the Negro. 1925–1926*. Tuskegee, AL: Negro Year Book Publishing Co.

Work, Monroe Nathan. 1931. *Negro Year Book: An Annual Encyclopedia of the Negro. 1931–1932*. Tuskegee, AL: Negro Year Book Publishing Co.

Work, Monroe Nathan. 1937. *Negro Year Book, 1937–1938*. Tuskegee, AL: Negro Year Book Publishing Co.

Work, Monroe Nathan. 1965 (1928). *A Bibliography of the Negro in Africa and America*. New York: Octagon Books.

Wright, Earl. 2005. "W.E.B. Du Bois and the Atlanta Sociological Laboratory." *Sociation Today* 3(1). www.ncsociology.org/sociationtoday/v31/wright.htm.

Wright, Earl. 2015. *The First American School of Sociology: W.E.B. Du Bois and the Atlanta Sociological Laboratory*. New ed. Burlington, VT: Ashgate Publishing.
Wright, Richard. 1937. "Blueprint for Negro Writing by Richard Wright." First published in *New Challenge: A Literary Quarterly* 2(1) (Fall). https://thirtiesculture.files.wordpress.com/2011/10/wright-blueprint.pdf.
Wright, Richard. 1938. *Uncle Tom's Children*. New York: Harper & Bros.
Wright, Richard. 1940. *Native Son*. New York: Harper & Bros.
Wright, Richard. 1941. *12 Million Black Voices: A Folk History of the Negro in the United States*. New York: Viking Press.
Wright, Richard. 1945. *Black Boy*. New York: Harper & Bros.
Wright, Richard. 1995 (1954). *Black Power*. New York: Harper.
Wright, Richard, Ellen Wright, and Michel Fabre. 1997. *Richard Wright Reader*. New York: Da Capo Press.
Malcolm X. 1964. "The Ballot or the Bullet by Malcolm X, April 3, 1964." *Cleveland, Ohio Social Justice Speeches*, www.edchange.org/multicultural/speeches/malcolm_x_ballot.html.
Malcolm X. 1965a. "The Last Message." February 14, *Malcolm X*, www.malcolm-x.org/speeches/spc_021465.htm.
X, Malcolm. 1965b. *Malcolm X Talks to Young People*. New York: Young Socialist.
X, Malcolm. 2010 (1963). "Message to the Grassroots." *Black Past*, August 16. www.blackpast.org/african-american-history/speeches-african-american-history/1963-malcolm-x-message-grassroots/.
X, Malcolm, and George Breitman. 1990. *Malcolm X Speaks: Selected Speeches and Statements*. New York: Grove Weidenfeld.
X, Malcolm, and Alex Haley. 1992. *The Autobiography of Malcolm X*. New York: Ballantine Books.
Ya Salaam, Kalamu. 2016. *The Magic of Juju: An Appreciation of the Black Arts Movement*. Chicago, IL: Third World Press.
Yates, James. 1989. *Mississippi to Madrid: Memoir of a Black American in the Abraham Lincoln Brigade*. Seattle, WA: Open Hand.
Yelvington, Kevin A. 2018. "'A Conference That Didn't': African Diaspora Studies and an Episode in Anthropology's Identity Politics of Representation." *Critique of Anthropology* 38(4): 407–32. https://doi.org/10.1177/0308275X18806574.
Young, Ann Venture. 1992. "Nick Aaron Ford: Teacher, Critic, Scholar, Writer 'Seeking a Newer World.'" *CLA Journal* 35(4): 467–87.
Young, Harvey. 2013. *The Cambridge Companion to African American Theatre*. Cambridge: Cambridge University Press.
Young, Harvey, and Queen Meccasia Zabriskie. 2014. *Black Theater is Black Life: An Oral History of Chicago Theater and Dance, 1970–2010*. Evanston, IL: Northwestern University Press.
Zamalin, Alex. 2019. *Black Utopia: The History of an Idea from Black Nationalism to Afrofuturism*. New York: Columbia University Press.
Zheng, John. ed. 2016. *Conversations with Sterling Plumpp*. Jackson, MS: University Press of Mississippi.
"Zora Neale Hurston." n.d. Association for Feminist Anthropology. Accessed May 8, 2018. http://afa.americananthro.org/zora-neale-hurston/.
Zulu, Itibari M. 2017. "Scholarly Journals in Africology: An Introductory Descriptive Review." *Africology: The Journal of Pan African Studies* 10(3): 8–61.
Zumoff, Jacob A. 2015. *The Communist International and US Communism: 1919–1929*. Chicago, IL: Haymarket Books.

Index

The letters *t* and *f* following a page number denote a table and a figure, respectively.

Thanks to our Patreon Subscribers:

Lia Lilith de Oliveira
Andrew Perry

Who have shown generosity and comradeship in support of our publishing.

Check out the other perks you get by subscribing to our Patreon – visit patreon.com/plutopress.

Subscriptions start from £3 a month.

PGIL2021USA